THE LAUGH'S ON ME

BENNETT CERF

BENNETT CERF'S

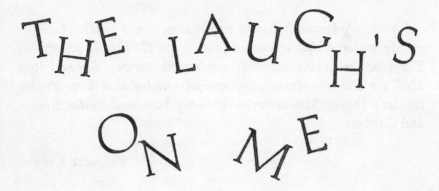

THE LAUGH'S ON ME

2000 Stories, Anecdotes, and Amiable Observations,
conveniently arranged for retelling in 100 categories.

★ ★ ★

A brand-new collection by
America's number-one raconteur

WITH ILLUSTRATIONS BY DOUG ANDERSON

1959
DOUBLEDAY & COMPANY, INC.
Garden City, New York

I acknowledge with thanks permission to use in The Laugh's on Me *material that appeared first in my Cerfboard column in* This Week *magazine; my daily syndicated feature, "Try and Stop Me," for King Features; and special articles that I wrote for* Reader's Digest, The Saturday Evening Post, *and* Better Homes and Gardens.

BENNETT CERF

LIBRARY OF CONGRESS CATALOG CARD NUMBER 59–12621

CONTENTS

CONTENTS 7

8 CONTENTS

FOREWORD

THE STORYTELLERS

There now are more than 175 million people, census takers tell us, in this blessed land of ours, and as I write this probably fifty million of them are telling a story. Just how well they are telling it is another matter.

Nobody is a "born" storyteller. The art of squeezing the ultimate drop of laughter from a droll tale must—and can—be learned. Dreary, pompous stuffed shirts aspiring to high political offices have been transformed into charming, accomplished raconteurs by knowing tutors. On the stage, Jack Benny made his debut in Waukegan as a violinist, billed as "the fiddlin' kid." Sam Levenson was a Brooklyn schoolteacher. Fred Allen stacked books in the Boston Public Library. The boy George Jessel warbled sad ballads in a Gus Edwards vaudeville revue. Myron Cohen was a traveling salesman who switched in desperation to professional raconteurritory when prospects scorned his samples and demanded more rib ticklers.

When Will Rogers, probably the best American storyteller of them all, first braved the pitfalls of the New York stage, he didn't intend even to open his mouth. He was billed as a lariat thrower, and ambled to the center of the stage dressed as a cowboy, chewing gum and twirling a couple of ropes. The house manager was dubious from the start, and the behavior of the tough Monday matinee audience did nothing to allay his fears. Rogers and his rope tricks—most of them, because he was nervous, didn't work—

was laying an egg all Wall Street couldn't duplicate until 1929. To cover his chagrin, Rogers started to talk, saying anything that came into his head. And, to the amazement of both himself and the house manager, the audience responded with laughter—tentative at first, then whole-souled and ungrudging. They loved Will's drawling Oklahoma twang, and they loved even better his uninhibited comments on the passing scene. By the time he walked off that stage, he was a lariat twirler no longer, but a monologist.

It is sad to reflect, incidentally, that Will Rogers' freewheeling barbs at the greats and would-be greats in high places received with such universal acclaim forty years ago probably would horrify audiences today, and brand him as a subversive and worse in the eyes of oversensitive public officials. "Slowly but surely," warns Corey Ford, "the wellsprings of humor are drying up today. Derision is taken for disloyalty. Political satire is extinct, personal caricature is libel, parody is illegal, dialect jokes are strictly taboo." "You can't even kid about the man-eating shark these days," adds Franklin P. Adams, "or the sharkskin-suit manufacturers will land on you like a ton of bricks."

Will Rogers instinctively adopted a technique of storytelling that today stands Bob Hope in good stead. Quips and witty observations follow one another with the speed of machine-gun bullets. The audience soon surrenders, and laughs at the clinkers as well as the highlights.

Contrast this calculated rapid-fire delivery with Jack Benny's equally effective "slow take." Benny's innocent bewilderment delights the audience because they get the point so long before he does. He recalls that one of the biggest laughs he ever earned on television came the evening a robber plunked a gun into his ribs and snarled, "Your money or your life!" Benny turned to the audience for one of his famous "slow takes." The longer he weighed the possibilities, the harder they laughed. By the time he assured the impatient robber, "I'm trying to make up my mind," the studio audience was in convulsions.

Groucho Marx's lecherous leer, emphasized by adroit maneuvering of his inevitable cigar, takes the sting out of his "insult" brand of humor, and makes hilarious thrusts like "I never forget a face, but I'm willing to make an exception in your case," or (to his memorable foil, Mrs. Rittenhouse), "Your eyes shine like the seat of my blue serge pants."

Sam Levenson achieves maximum results for his stories by the "cheerleader" technique: his own merry peals of laughter invite the customers to join in, which they invariably do. Levenson gets his best results from stories that bear the ring of truth—authentic, if justifiably exaggerated, reminiscences of his old days in pedagoguery.

In addition to telling you jokes so rapidly that you laugh before you have time to decide whether they're funny or not, Bob Hope insures the acclaim of every on-the-spot audience by peppering his introductory remarks with sure-fire local allusions. You can't go wrong at an army encampment, for instance, if you aim a few broadsides at the commanding officer, shoot holes in some deeply resented local restrictions, and kid the techniques of the beautiful nurses, WAC's, and local belles in the background.

The storyteller, in other words, who identifies himself with his audience at the start has them on his side from then on. Nor need he hesitate to tell a story that isn't new, so long as it's opportune—and funny. Experts insist there's no such thing as a new story, anyhow. There are possibly fifty basically humorous stories in the world, and most of them date back to Homer and Aristophanes. Accomplished technicians through the ages equip these basic tales with a revised cast of characters, a new background, and a novel catch ending—and presto!—a brand "new" story is born! A tale of Achilles before the walls of Troy becomes an exploit of President Eisenhower on the golf links at Augusta. "If Adam came to earth again," reflected Rev. Sydney Smith, "I dare say the only thing he would recognize would be the current jokes."

The political arena abounds with superb storytellers. In the forefront was ex-Mayor Bill O'Dwyer of New York, whose Irish brogue, virtually imperceptible at first, grew broader and broader as the evening progressed. O'Dwyer indignantly denied he was laying it on on purpose, but the twinkle in his eyes belied his words.

The late Al Smith was another canny politico who knew how to embellish a story with appropriate dialect. When he chose, he could speak impeccable English, but when the occasion warranted, he slipped effortlessly into a "dese and dose" East Side vernacular that made so many thousands of underprivileged supporters chortle, "He's from our side of the tracks." ("In the part of Manhattan where I was brought up," Governor Smith liked to recall, "*both* sides of the tracks were the wrong side!")

Adlai Stevenson's ready wit and propensity for recalling apropos stories have actually been cited as character flaws by critics who believe that in a presidential candidate, at least, a little sense of humor is a dangerous thing.

When it suited his purpose, Franklin D. Roosevelt could rank with the best of raconteurs. Often he assumed this role when a visitor was anxious to tell F.D.R. something he didn't want to hear. During World War II, I remember, a couple of English economists came to Washington specifically to urge a course of action the President distrusted. "I had to invite them to dine with me here at the White House," he told me, "but I have a sneaking idea that the subject they insist upon hashing over with me never is going to come up."

Sure enough, when these two Englishmen paused at New York on their way home, one complained bitterly, "Your President is a charming host, and he certainly tells wonderful stories—but he doesn't know when to stop. You know, we flew all the way from London to discuss a very important matter with him, but he babbled on so all evening, we were ushered out before we had a chance to do so much as bring it up!"

Greatest natural wit of twentieth-century statesmen is, of course, Winston Churchill. He has an added advantage. He is so wonderful a speaker that he could enrapture an audience by reading a page of the New York telephone directory. Like Jack Benny, Mr. Churchill relies upon perfect timing to insure maximum effect.

Robert Sherwood dubbed him "the master of the pregnant pause." His gar-rumphs and resonant throat clearings come at precisely the right moments.

Two of the great storytellers I've met in private life are playwrights Moss Hart and Sam Behrman. Both of them are the kind of party guests a hostess dreams of having: they act as though they realize it's up to them to keep things moving, and have learned to put such gusto and color into their stories that most of the guests are sitting, figuratively and literally, at their feet. Both are careful not to suffocate their anecdotes with endless and unnecessary details. Both stop short while the audience is clamoring for more— and gracefully turn the spotlight over to somebody else. Moss Hart, incidentally, tells the story of his early days in his beguiling autobiography, *Act One*. Behrman has already detailed his in *Worcester Account*.

Whatever technique he chooses to achieve his purpose, the man who can bring the spirit of laughter into a room with him is indeed blessed. There are too many pontificators around these days, "beatniks" and prophets of doom; not enough wits and pretense-shatterers like the renowned "Algonquin set" of the twenties: George S. Kaufman, Robert Sherwood, Heywood Broun, Marc Connelly, Dorothy Parker, Robert Benchley! When will we encounter an assembly like that again? Critic Carl Van Doren singled out Robert Benchley for the highest praise of all. "Bob," he said, "can make everybody else at a party seem a little jollier and more attractive than he really is!"

In a book called *Applied Imagination*, Alex Osborn calls attention to a Swiss gentleman of eighty who meticulously calculated that he had spent twenty-six of his years asleep and twenty-one working. Eating consumed another six. So did being angry. He frittered away five more waiting for tardy people. Shaving took up 228 days, and lighting his pipe twelve days. He concluded mournfully, "I figure that I have laughed for only forty-six hours in my entire life."

Hopefully, I plan to send this misguided gentleman a copy of

The Laugh's on Me. Granted a favorable break or two, this conceivably could mark the beginning of an entirely new Swiss movement!

BENNETT CERF

Random House, New York
August, 1959

1. ACROSS THE U.S.A.

Within the next four months, regardless of season, twenty million vacation-minded citizens will roll their partially paid-for automobiles out of their garages and set out to "see America first." If you are one of these intrepid explorers, here's a little test to take before you depart. Answer four of the five questions—three will pass in a pinch—and you're entitled to strap down your wife, offspring, and baggage securely, and hit the road.

QUESTION: Just where in the U.S.A. will you be if a request for directions elicits the following responses:

1. Yes, this is the right building. The room you want is three flights up, but don't try to ring the bell. It's cracked.

2. The railroad station? Well, mister, just go to the end of Pennsylvania and through New York till you hit Massachusetts; then go back till you come to Maryland.

3. Sorry, suh, but I can't give you the directions to Fort Worth. Nobody, suh, in this town has ever *been* to Fort Worth.

4. Yup, that's the highest mountain in the state. Bet it would take you all of five minutes to climb to the top.

5. It's quite a show, all right. Goes on once an hour, but if you want to sit way down front, you'll get soaked plenty.

ANSWERS: 1. The tourist is in Philadelphia, near Independence Hall, which houses the Liberty Bell. 2. The tourist is in Washington, D.C., quite near the White House. Avenues in the capital are named after states. 3. The tourist is in Dallas, which for many years has carried on (or, at least, pretended to carry on) a feud with Fort Worth. 4. The tourist is in Florida, near the hill that is called Iron Mountain. 5. The tourist is in Yellowstone Park, near Old Faithful Geyser, which spouts hot water about once an hour.

★ ★ ★

"A city," declares Ted Breton, "is remembered for its food, not its architecture. I remember the French market in New Orleans for the best cup of coffee I ever drank, and Truro, Nova Scotia, for the worst. The finest raisin pie was in Mansfield, Ohio, and the grandest bread at the Army Cooks and Bakers School at Spartanburg, South Carolina. Any town in Massachusetts will give you as good gingerbread as you ever ate. I'll take Boston for codfish, Kansas City for steaks, Baltimore for oysters, San Diego for chili, Seattle for loganberries, and Biloxi for stewed chicken. San Francisco has a biscuit called 'snails' and Portland, Maine, a stew called 'smother,' neither to be found elsewhere." To this list Jack Kofoed adds stone crab in Miami, and I nominate the spaghetti at Joe Consolino's Stamford, Connecticut, mansion. Any readers care to add to this list? (The late Morton Thompson once described a horrendous repast that gave him "gastric gymnastics, jejunal jerks, duodenal dribblings, hepatic heaves, and sigmoid sighs.")

★ ★ ★

In a lifetime of tracking down elusive manuscripts, humorous anecdotes, patient lecture audiences—and, more recently, the occupations of sundry whale counters, poodle manicurists, and billiard-table-pocket knitters—I've prowled happily through all fifty states. One of my favorite ports of call, however, always has been and always will be the city of Boston.

"Boston," observes author Cleveland Amory, "is not only a city; it is a state of mind."

No place in the world can top the relaxation and feeling of security proffered by a room in a fine Boston hotel, facing the historic Common and Public Gardens.

★ ★ ★

A carefully attired banker, Boston to his fingertips, hailed author John Marquand at the Harvard Club one evening and announced, "I've read all your books, Marquand, and let me tell you this. You never wrote anything better than *Sorrel and Son*."

"Thank you," nodded Mr. Marquand with a trace of a smile, "but that wasn't mine. *Sorrel and Son* was written by Warwick Deeping."

"Nonsense," snapped the Bostonian, and stalked off to the washroom.

★ ★ ★

A couple of television producers, relates comic Morton Sahl, concluded their labors about nine one evening in a Boston sector where the sidewalks apparently were rolled up at sundown. They finally unearthed a taxi driver and implored, "How's for steering us to a place where there's a little action?"

"How do I know you fellows aren't cops?" asked the driver suspiciously. Ultimately reassured by their credentials, however, he ordered, "Get in. I know a place you fellows will love."

He thereupon drove them twenty miles to a secluded spot on the Massachusetts coast—where they could fish without a license!

★ ★ ★

A helpful little lady in Revere Beach sends me this inspiring poem:

> Marilyn of Boston, Mass.
> Was in water up to her ankles.
> It doesn't rhyme now,
> But wait till the tide rolls in!

★ ★ ★

Think of Indiana, the Hoosier state, and it's very likely you'll start humming its nostalgic official state song, "On the Banks of the Wabash." Composer Paul Dresser, older brother of novelist Theodore Dreiser, wrote the song in 1899, ironically enough, on a portable organ in Chicago's Auditorium Hotel, and his "gleaming candlelights" were reflected not by the Wabash River but by the waters of Lake Michigan.

Indiana has turned out in its time not only political powerhouses and basketball phenoms, but a prize collection of nationally loved humorists, including George Ade, Booth Tarkington, James Whitcomb Riley, Ernie Pyle, Emily Kimbrough, and Kim Hubbard. More serious literary luminaries born in Indiana numbered, besides Dreiser, George Jean Nathan, Elmer Davis, Lloyd Douglas, Lew Wallace, Joseph Hayes, Meredith Nicholson, and Gene Stratton Porter. Alfred Kinsey wrote his eye-opening reports at Indiana University (one of the country's best), Ross Lockridge, Jr., completed *Raintree County* not many miles away, and Wendell Willkie wrote his first political speech for a class election at the elementary school in Elwood, Indiana.

★ ★ ★

James Whitcomb Riley became a poet and homespun philosopher via the unlikely route of purveyor of a cure-all patent medicine. In his early twenties he traveled all over the country with a quack doctor, and wrote poems on the backs of envelopes while the doctor was hornswoggling ruralites into buying bottles of his worthless elixir.

Jim Farmer, of the Indianapolis *Star*, tells about a buggy ride shared by Riley and the late Indiana journalist, William R. Herschell. Herschell asked how far Riley had gone in school. "Fourth grade," admitted Riley. "And you?" "Seventh grade," boasted Herschell. Riley slapped him on the leg and roared, "Why, you overeducated son-of-a-gun!"

★ ★ ★

Just about the time Minnesota was becoming a state in 1858, Cyrus Eaton completed the laying of the first transatlantic cable, Boston introduced the first street-corner mailboxes, Oliver Wendell Holmes published his *The Autocrat of the Breakfast Table*, and George M. Pullman got the very first sleeping car onto the track. I think I rode on it the last time I traveled to Duluth by train.

For Minnesota's Centennial in 1958, Mox Lindquist compiled a booklet of *Manasota Foklore* that sold like St. Paul's celebrated hotcakes. Typical tale concerns a stubborn Swede named Gus who quit a fine job on a farm near Anoka. "Ay get along yust yim dandy with my boss Gundeson," explained Gus, "but ay yust couldn't stand his old voman, the old tightvad. You know how ay lak flapjacks. Vel, one morning that tightvad Yennie yells out before all the mens, 'Gus, dees flapjacks you now have in your mouth is the twenty-sax you have et dis morning.' Val, ven she show me up lak that it make me so dam mad ay get right up from the table and quit—WITHOUT MY BREAKFAST!"

★ ★ ★

Life in a northern Minnesota logging camp took on new zest when a pair of powerful but unbelievably gullible giants named Olaf and Yon joined the crew. One evening they were told that a Chicago pet shop was offering sixty dollars apiece for Angora cats. "These woods are full of cats like that. Why not cash in while the going is good?" urged the foreman.

Olaf and Yon decided to go into the Angora cat business then and there. Of course the first cat they cornered was a wildcat. We'll let Olaf take it from there.

"Dis big cat take a gude look at us, go op a tree, and out on de end of a big limb. Ay tell Yon to go stand under dis branch and ay vill climb tree and shake dis cat off so Yon could catch him. Dis bane some easy vay to make $60!

"Ven Yon say he's ready ay shake de branch and down comes de cat—right in Yon's arms. And den, yumpin himminie, vat a fight! The big cat scratch so it's terrible and ay yell to Yon, 'Skol ay com down and help yu hold him?'

"Yon yells back, 'Yudas Priest, Olaf, NO. Come down and help me let him go!'"

★ ★ ★

There's an outraged bear in the Yellowstone Park area who's taken to writing letters of complaint to the country's syndicated columnists. Washington, he says, has paid no attention to his demands for simple justice. Virtually every day, protests this bear, some confounded little girl with long golden hair breaks into his little home, eats his porridge, and takes a nap in his freshly made bed!

★ ★ ★

In the Yellowstone area, Joseph Wood Krutch saw a lady tourist re-enter her hotel laden down with useless souvenirs and knick-knacks, heard her husband's oft-echoed observation: "Isn't it amazing how many things there are that women would rather have than money!"

★ ★ ★

There is just one spot in the U.S.A. where it's possible for a person to stand in four states at the same time. Look at a map and you'll see that it's at the southwestern tip of Colorado, with New Mexico to the south, Utah to the west, and Arizona to the southwest.

★ ★ ★

Once it was gold and silver that lured prospectors and fortune hunters to the wide-open spaces out West. Today, of course, it's uranium. One old-timer was mighty mystified by the new invaders. "Dunno what this excitement is all about," he confided to a reporter. "Fust thing I knew was when some feller come on the place with a contraption called a Goober counter and seemed hell-bent on huntin' for geraniums."

★ ★ ★

A town on the edge of the Mojave Desert boasts four gas stations. Three of them plan to sue the owner of the first station on the line. He's put up a big sign proclaiming, "This is your last chance to fill up before you hit the desert. The three other stations you think you see are mirages!"

★ ★ ★

Ernie Kovacs, California bound on a jet 707, was told he could smoke one of those formidable cigars of his—if he didn't annoy the lady passengers. "So I decided not to smoke," concludes Ernie. "It was more fun to annoy the lady passengers."

★ ★ ★

In the wild and woolly West of today, where the roaming buffalo has been replaced by herds of Jaguars and Thunderbirds, and lo, every poor Indian has installed air conditioning in his tepee, you don't hardly never see a real, honest-to-goodness desert rat no more.

Yet Southern California boasts one in the person of Harry Oliver, the genuine article right down to his dust-specked sombrero, grizzled beard, boots, and houn' dog. He's so genuine, in fact, that I began to smell a desert rat in the presentation. Sure enough, next to Harry's sun-bronzed skin I found Sulka undies of purest rayon serene! Harry first panned gold as an art director at the Fox Film Studios!

All that is behind him, however. In 1941, Harry packed his family and gear into his station wagon and, bidding a fond farewell to "smog eaters and smudge pot feeders," lit out for Thousand Palms, just a "hop and a holler up U.S. 60 and 70 from Palm Springs." Here he is monarch of all he surveys in a mission-type adobe called Old Fort Oliver, built by his own hands, and in a strategic spot to relocate the fabulous old Peg Leg Mine, lost so long that skeptics maintain nobody every found it in the first place.

Here, too, Oliver publishes his flourishing *Desert Rat Scrap Book*, which appears quarterly, or "whenever he's good and ready," and has achieved a world-wide circulation of over twenty-five thousand copies. It's printed on light tagboard, so folded that it contains five pages, and is "the only newspaper you can open in the wind." The contents are a wonderful melange of authentic Americana, typographical errors, unabashed corn as high as a buckin' bronc's eye, and the editor's own excellent woodcuts.

"My paper is not entered as second-class mail," boasts Oliver, "because it is first class in every respect." "I like new subscribers best," he adds, "because I can use old jokes on them again." Contributors get to see the editor of the *Scrap Book* by throwing a rock through the window or firing a couple of shots in the air.

At the moment, Harry Oliver is off on a praiseworthy kick to clean up the desert. Whenever he sees a pile of trash left behind by heedless tourists along the roadside, he posts a sign reading "SHAME! Look what YOU did! Beauty was here until you came!" His one-man campaign is achieving results, too. Last spring there actually were more desert wildflowers than discarded beer cans.

Here are a few typical items from recent issues of Oliver's *Desert Rat Scrap Book*:

"The prospectors over near Quartzside ain't mining much gold, but their television reception is excellent.

"'Liminatin' Lem says, The worst part of doin' nothing is you never can take any time off.

"Seems like us Americans are spending more these days for guvverment than for food. Getting more bellyaches out of it, too.

"Anatomy's something everybody's got—but it sure looks better on a girl.

"There's a big bargain waiting for a lucky customer out Garnet way—6o acres, and if snatched up before the next windstorm, a 3-room shack will be included."

★ ★ ★

When a Princeton graduate inherited a cattle ranch out West, he soon discovered that the ornery galoot on an adjoining ranch was rustling his stock. "Be careful," he was warned. "That old crook is as liable as not to drill a coupla holes in your hide." So this is the warning note that the Princeton grad typed out: "Dear sir: I'd appreciate it if you'd stop leaving your hot branding irons out where my fool cattle can sit down on them."

★ ★ ★

A Los Angeles soft-drink magnate initiated a prize contest for undergraduates. First prize went to the youngster who submitted three box tops and a short piece beginning, "I like Los Angeles because . . ." limited strictly to twenty-five thousand words.

"Two mysteries hinder all efforts to end smog in Los Angeles," writes Ray Duncan. "Nobody knows exactly what smog is, and nobody knows exactly what Los Angeles is."

A tourist patronized a gypsy fortuneteller in Venice, California, and got something of a surprise. "Hey!" he exclaimed. "Do you realize your crystal ball has two holes in it?" "Sure," beamed the gypsy. "I put 'em there myself. I also give bowling lessons."

A horrified cop collared a cute young thing at Malibu Beach dressed in the scantiest of bikinis and demanded reproachfully, "What would your ma say if she saw you in this suit?" "She'd say plenty," admitted the cute young thing. "It's her suit."

Nobody begrudges a man an initial success, but if he dominates his field too long, and wins too many honors, a fickle public sometimes gets a bit bored with him, and clamors for new gods to adulate.

Walt Disney is a case in point. He has collected Academy

Awards and other tributes with such monotonous regularity, been accorded such reams of publicity, that doubting Thomases have sprung up to whisper, "How much of the talent is Disney's, how much that of the unsung people around him?"

One creation of Walt Disney's, however, that nobody can belittle, or credit to anybody but himself, is Disneyland, the wonderful 160-acre play park he opened some miles south of Los Angeles on July 18, 1955. Here is a Coney Island of the atomic age—a continuous carnival made magical with infinite care, soaring imagination, and, last but not least, over twenty-eight million dollars in cash. It is Disney's wildest, most improbable dream come true. "This time," said one of his assistants, "the boss hasn't expanded; he's exploded!"

Characteristically, Disney brushes aside attractions already in existence, and spreads out on his desk plans for wonders to come. "Here's a model for a giant monorail system," he enthuses, "that will whisk you from one end of Disneyland to the other. And here's where we're going to build a replica of the Matterhorn 146 feet high. That's equal to a fourteen-story building!"

Of Disneyland's myriad distractions, what delighted me most was a replica of the Main Streets both Walt and I knew in our boyhood. Horsecars and surreys with a fringe on top meandered from the railroad depot past the oprey house. Here was a grocery store with potbellied stove, coffee grinder, and cracker barrel; there an ice-cream parlor with penny jawbreakers and licorice shoelaces—just as I remembered them! "This script," I whispered to my wife, Phyllis, "must have been written by Horatio Nostalger, Jr.!"

★ ★ ★

One thing courtin' couples will seek in vain at Disneyland is an old-fashioned Tunnel of Love. Maybe Walt Disney heard about the gangly Dakotan who took his gal to Coney Island, and came home enthusiastic about everything *but* that Tunnel of Love.

"A bum deal," he scoffed. "It was dark, damp, lonesome, and worse still we got soaking wet."

"Wet!" echoed his paw. "Did the boat leak?"

The Dakotan looked surprised, and asked, "There's a *boat?*"

★ ★ ★

Traveling with teen-agers across the continent provides unexpected dividends. Take the souvenir boodle collected between Buffalo and Beverly Hills by my younger son (thirteen) Jonathan. It included 118 timetables, nine airline "sick bags," thirty-one pop bottle tops, two redwood burls (promptly named "Milton" and "Ives"), and a shrunken head bagged at Disneyland. Despite the acquisition of these treasures, our baggage grew miraculously lighter as we advanced on our way. Possibly this was due to the fact that our boys succeeded in leaving behind one pair of shoes in Banff, a pajama top in Vancouver, a camera in San Francisco, and a complete toilet kit at the Grand Canyon.

★ ★ ★

Another puzzling facet of the teen-ager's behavior today is his passion for peppering his dialogue with disconcertingly irrelevant remarks called, justifiably, "conversation stoppers." Our first glimpse of the awe-inspiring glacier at Lake Louise, for instance, evoked a gasp of wonder, followed by a pensive, "Green lights will never burn on Balch Hill." And Jonathan's response to the giant redwood trees was, "The goat is a much maligned animal." Our prize "conversation stopper," however, was supplied by a lady sitting just ahead of us on the plane from L.A. to Phoenix, who visibly upset her companion by remarking suddenly, "Poor Otto burst in the swimming pool yesterday." We're still trying to figure that one out!

★ ★ ★

"Don't fuss with the boys," counseled my all-knowing wife when it struck me that insufficient attention was being paid to my travelogues. "They're picking up a lot more than you think."

How right she was! Our older son, Chris (eighteen), picked up the addresses and phone numbers of eleven new girls from coast to coast. And when a teacher from Friends School asked Jonathan, "Did you learn anything on your trip?" he answered stoutly, "I certainly did! That left-field fence at the Los Angeles Coliseum makes games played there a travesty on baseball!"

2. ACTORS AND ACTRESSES

A very competent actor experienced a run of such bad luck that he had to take a temporary job in a cafeteria to make ends meet.

Then one day he got a break. His agent told him, "Kazan wants you for the role of Abraham Lincoln in a historical play."

"Elia Kazan?" cried the actor. "How wonderful."

"Your date's for next Tuesday," the agent said. "Steep yourself in Lincolniana meanwhile, and make up very carefully before you go. Everything may depend on the way you look."

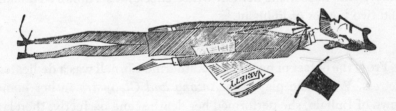

The elated thespian faithfully buried himself in a set of Carl Sandburg's *Lincoln,* and set about acquiring the proper wardrobe. When he left the house on Tuesday, he was attired in just the right suit, a shawl, and a stovepipe hat, and, with the proper set of whiskers and a mole on his cheek, was a perfect double for Abraham Lincoln.

He had gone only half a block, however, when misfortune overtook him again. One might say that it was an occupational hazard. He was assassinated.

★ ★ ★

Another great performer, Miss Gypsy Rose Lee, told me of some trouble *she* ran into last Christmas season. Determined to learn how to ski, she enrolled for a course in a Manhattan department store, and let a suave salesman talk her into six hundred dollars' worth of equipment.

All dolled up in same, she arrived for lesson number one, but lost her nerve. Caught up in a welter of screaming kids, she was hustled to the top of the ski run nevertheless. There she attempted to anchor herself—but the kids pushed her again. Miss Rose came hurtling down, hugging a papier-mâché Santa Claus in one arm and two pine trees in the other. She wound up in a jumble of merchandise in the adjoining haberdashery department.

"I want my money back," screamed Gypsy. "Impossible," said the clerk. "It's against the house policy." "You hand me that money," threatened Gypsy, "or I'll put on my standard act right here and now."

The management knew that Gypsy was the girl who could do it, too. The house policy was changed faster than Gimbel could tell Macy. Miss Rose made her exit with a check for six hundred dollars and two bottles of liniment.

★ ★ ★

From the outset of her career, Katharine Cornell was a dedicated actress. When she played in *Antony and Cleopatra* in her home town of Buffalo, she performed her death scene perfectly, then lay motionless on the stage for several minutes while other members of the cast delivered their final lines.

Later, in Miss Cornell's dressing room, a friend of the family commented, "Kit was superb in her last scene. And did you notice that after she was supposed to be dead she never moved a muscle. You could only tell by the slight tremor of her chest that she was alive at all."

Miss Cornell's father cautioned, "Please, please! Don't let Kit hear you—or tomorrow night she'll stop breathing!"

★ ★ ★

An actor turned up at a cocktail party tanned a deep bronze. "What a wonderful sunburn," enthused a blond girl. "How did you acquire it?" The actor explained sourly, "I have a terrible agent."

★ ★ ★

Betty Hutton knows an actress who got rid of 215 pounds of excessive, flabby fat in ninety days. She divorced him.

★ ★ ★

Time magazine advances a theory to explain the glamour and perfection that actor Rex Harrison exudes from every pore in his portrayal of Professor 'Iggins in the triumphant musical, *My Fair Lady*. "It's his subtle changes of pitch and his timing—the envy of the profession," says *Time*.

My Fair Lady was Harrison's first musical, which is understandable, since he really cannot sing a note. But how he socks a song across by merely talking the lines! "I had a terrible time memorizing the lyrics," he confesses. "There's just no means of finding your way back when you blow a line; you have to keep on because the damned orchestra won't stop!"

Harrison has an equally hard time keeping track of the fat salary he earns. Once he decided to keep a written record of every cent he spent—a system which he pursued faithfully for exactly one day. His entry for that day read: "Taxi, $1.50; tip, 50 cents; miscellaneous items, $83."

★ ★ ★

Sir Alec Guinness, the brilliant but self-effacing British star, was a captain in World War II, much of which he spent ferrying provisions aboard a small craft to Yugoslav Partisans. On convoy duty, he found it next to impossible to keep his ship in line, finally received a cryptic blinker message from the admiral's flagship that read: "Hebrew, 13-8." Guinness' crew thought at first this was a soccer score, then a divinity student decoded it by referring to the ship's Bible: "Jesus Christ the same yesterday, and today, and forever."

Captain Guinness squared accounts with his admiral by contriving somehow to get ashore first in the invasion of Sicily. When the surprised admiral strode across the beach, Guinness remarked softly, "Such a tardy entrance would never be tolerated in the theater!"

★ ★ ★

George Jessel, who counts that day lost when he doesn't deliver two eulogies, had just concluded one of his most eloquent orations. Then his glance fell accidentally on the deceased in the coffin, and he turned three shades of green. "Good heavens," gasped Jessel weakly. "I *know* this man!"

★ ★ ★

Dear to the heart of everybody interested in show business is the good old legend of the overnight star: the humble, overlooked chorus girl who substitutes for the lead at a moment's notice and brings down the house, not to mention Sam Goldwyn, who happens to be sitting in the second row with a seven-year contract in his pocket.

Only slightly less shopworn is the tale of the unknown who inherits a specialty song just before a show opens, and vaults to fame on its wings. Remember how Ethel Merman wowed them with "I Got Rhythm" in *Girl Crazy?* And how Mary Martin stopped the show with "My Heart Belongs to Daddy" in *Leave It to Me?* And how Beatrice Lillie won the keys to New York with "March with Me to the Sound of the Drum" in Charlot's *Revue?*

Yet virtually every "overnight sensation" in show business has slaved for years in order to be ready for the big chance. Relentless drudgery in tank-town carnivals and dreary one-night stands gave them the experience and the equipment that made their triumph possible.

Danny Kaye, one of the great clowns of all time, is a case in point. By the time Broadway discovered him in *Lady in the Dark*

Kaye had spent twelve long years perfecting his technique in grubby vaudeville houses and nightclubs all over the world.

Most recent overnight sensation on Broadway is twenty-six-year-old Anne Bancroft, whose bewitching portrayal of the role of Gittel Mosca in *Two for the Seesaw* made sedate critics stand up and cheer on opening night. An added fillip came with the discovery that (1) this daughter of a phone operator in Macy's department store lived in a cold-water flat in Greenwich Village, and (2) this was her very first appearance on Broadway. She had walked in unheralded to read the part for director Arthur Penn some months previous, and he, unable to contain his excitement, had phoned his wife to report, "I met Gittel this afternoon!"

Investigation proved, however, that in the preceding six years, Anne Bancroft had served the usual exacting apprenticeship, appearing in fifteen motion pictures and almost a hundred TV shows. At first she used her real name, Anna Italiano, then Anna Marno. She chose "Bancroft" from a list drawn up by Darryl Zanuck.

"Bancroft was the only name," she explains, "that didn't make me sound like a bubble dancer."

★ ★ ★

Roberta Sherwood, by virtue of her own abundant talents plus the all-out endorsement of Walter Winchell, is a ranking star in the nightclub firmament today, earning thousands of dollars for a single week's engagement. When Winchell discovered her, however, just a few short years ago, she was singing her heart out for peanuts in obscure Miami retreats.

"How much could those one-horse outfits afford to pay you?" Walter asked after he had helped to make her a star.

"Sometimes," she told him, "I did three full shows for as little as ten dollars a night."

Winchell was shocked. "What kind of people," he demanded, "would dream of performing for ten dollars for a whole night?"

"Hungry people," answered Miss Sherwood.

★ ★ ★

A very famous actress and an equally famous leading man undertook a road tour with a well-tried vehicle one winter. In every city they were wined and dined to a fare-thee-well.

One evening the wining definitely was overdone, and, as a result, neither could remember the lines when the curtain went up. Finally, the frantic prompter, hoarse from overwork, repeated a key speech of the actress's in vain six times, each time a little louder. The audience did not explode with laughter, however, until she strode toward the wings and announced imperiously, "We can hear the lines perfectly, young man. *But which one of us says them?*"

★ ★ ★

Whenever he had occasion to enter the ladies' dressing room backstage at a Toronto theater, electrician Lyle Alton fell into the habit of singing out, "Close your eyes, girls! I'm coming through!"

Variety reports that one of the girls who'd been appearing in that theater for ten solid weeks suddenly gasped with the realization that she'd been falling for the gag from the first performance on!

★ ★ ★

"So you want to marry my daughter?" boomed a millionaire. "May I inquire into the nature of your profession?" "I am an actor," said the suitor proudly. "Raus!" ordered the millionaire, "before my foot lights."

★ ★ ★

Speaking of footlights, an aspiring actor gave a reading for the late George M. Cohan one day. After a few moments, Cohan called out from Row M in the empty orchestra, "Step back a little. "You're too close to those footlights." A bit later, Cohan ordered, "Go back farther still."

"But, Mr. Cohan," protested the actor, "if I go back any farther I'll be off the stage entirely." Cohan admitted, "You get the idea perfectly."

★ ★ ★

Ad in a theatrical weekly: "Not-very-good actor desires engagements. Particularly experienced as dead body or offstage shouts."

★ ★ ★

Recalls Gracie Allen: "The first time I ever met George Burns he gave me a pass to the theater in Union Hills, New Jersey, where he was doing a vaudeville act. I went to the matinee the next day and was I surprised! George was being costarred with a movie called *The Birth of a Nation* and ten other acts, but he was so modest he hadn't even mentioned them. I felt very proud. There must have been eight or nine people in that audience and I was the only one with a pass."

Gracie had a fine vacation in Honolulu recently, and was telling a reporter all about it. "Did you go by boat or plane?" asked the reporter. "I don't really know," admitted Gracie. "George bought the tickets."

★ ★ ★

George Oppenheimer, member of the Players' Club, found a letter in his box one evening, and tore it open and read it before he discovered it was not addressed to him at all. As a matter of fact, it was meant for one of his actor friends—and it came from a tailor pleading for payment of a bill now almost a year overdue.

Oppenheimer scarcely had had time to deposit the letter in the proper box when his friend bustled in, radiating his usual charm and air of opulence. He glanced hastily at the note, tore it into shreds, and remarked in a stage whisper, "Poor, deluded little girl!"

★ ★ ★

At a school of dramatic art, the late Louis Calhern urged, "Don't be discouraged if you make mistakes. The best of us have blundered. In my first chance on Broadway, my one line came when the big star made his entrance. I was supposed to say, 'He looks like a Greek god.' Opening night, it came out like this: 'He looks like a Greek. *God!*'"

3. ADVERTISING

Thanks to the success of novels like *The Hucksters* and *The Man in the Gray Flannel Suit*, the popular conception of a big-time advertising man is an equal compound of Madison Avenue, ulcers, padded expense accounts, commuter trains to Westport, and bizarre conferences where some joker invariably suggests, "Let's send it uptown as a local and see if it comes back as an express" or "Let's smear it on the cat and see if she licks it off."

As a matter of fact, some of my best friends are advertising men, and there are only two things that make them any more tense and frenetic than other business executives of the times. One is opinionated clients who insist upon butting into carefully planned campaigns at the last moment. The other is sneaky account executives who waltz off with half of the total billings at the drop of a competitor's certified check.

Advertising is the invaluable oil that lubricates American industry. Maybe you think there should be more "soft sell," and less shrill repetition and overclaims? Hearken to these words from a fellow sympathizer: "The trade of advertising is now so near perfection, that it is not easy to propose any improvement. But as every art ought to be exercised in due subordination to the public good, I cannot but propose it as a moral question to these masters of the public ear, whether they do not sometimes play too wantonly with our passions." No, these words were not penned by some jaded TV critic in 1959, but over 250 years ago—in the year 1700. The author: Dr. Samuel Johnson!

★ ★ ★

Overexposure on the television commercials necessitates frequent changes of advertising slogans today. When I was a boy, campaigns lasted much longer. How well I remember Sapolio's Spotless Town, Force's Sunny Jim, the Gold Dust Twins, Victor's attentive fox terrier, and the Uneeda Biscuit Boy in his yellow raincoat! Ivory Soap floated; when better cars were built, Buick built them; Ingersoll was the watch that made the dollar famous; children cried for Castoria; and Phoebe Snow wheeled direct from Thirty-Third to Buffalo upon the Road of Anthracite. Eventually, as Mr. Pillsbury insisted, we were bound to switch to these well-exploited brands: why not now?

"Advertise," warned showman P. T. Barnum, "or the chances are that the sheriff will do it for you." To illustrate his thesis, he pointed out that there are twenty-six mountains in Colorado higher than Pike's Peak—but how many people can recall the name of any one of them?

★ ★ ★

Frantic copywriters, wallowing in a maze of secret formulas, astounding discoveries, giant economy sizes, and non-irritating filters, spend their days—and nights—seeking new keys to the public's pocketbooks. One ingenious soul came up recently with the notion of printing ads backward on the reverse sides of postage stamps, so that when you licked one, you would involuntarily carry the slogan around on your tongue for the rest of the day. Unfeeling post-office authorities gave him the heave-ho.

★ ★ ★

Another genius extolled the merits of a new club soda with a "wonderful new formula so secret that only the executives and bottling master knew it." At least, that's how his send-off blurb was worded, with a postscript to the effect that the magic formula was safely locked in a bank vault on Fifth Avenue.

Only a few mean and nasty critics pointed out that, in order to conform with the Pure Food and Drug Act, the top-guarded secret "magic formula" is also printed on every bottle cap, open to the gaze of anybody who can read English!

★ ★ ★

Joke current in Madison Avenue advertising agencies: An account executive was told to provide an exhaustive study about fleas. He laboriously trained a medium-sized flea to jump over his finger every time he said "Hup." Then he pulled off two of the flea's six legs. "Hup," he grunted. The flea jumped over his finger. Off came two more legs. "Hup," repeated the executive. Again the flea jumped. Then he pulled off the flea's last two legs. Alas, the flea no longer moved. The executive nodded sagely, and wrote in his report: "When a flea loses all six of its legs, it becomes deaf."

★ ★ ★

More last-minute jargon from the advertising lads:
"Let's take it to the lab and see if it's a mushroom or a toadstool."
"We've got the motor running, but the mixture is a little rich." ("Cut out those full-color pages and go back to one-column stuff in black and white.")
"Let's drive this into a parking lot and see if we dent any fenders."
"We still insist that this campaign adhered to every principle of sound advertising." ("So it flopped. Fire us!")
"Let's run it up the flagpole and see who salutes."

"Let's get down on all fours and have a look at the problem from the client's point of view."

★ ★ ★

Cowboys, Indians, stagecoach robbers, and two-gun sheriffs are riding so far, wide, and handsome on the television ranges nowadays that Alan Wilson figures their lingo is bound to be adopted before long *in toto* by the advertising fraternity. Here's the sort of talk Wilson thinks you'll soon be hearing around the agencies:

WRITER (about another writer). "That script rustler stole my original and put his own brand on it."

AGENT (to sponsor). "Just got a smoke signal from my buckeroo. He refuses to be hogtied to your outfit unless you pony up more wampum pronto."

ACTOR (to reviewer). "I see you're diggin' your spurs into my hide again, you yellow-livered varmint. So what? I got me a three-hundred-room bunkhouse in Beverly nevertheless and five Eldorado stagecoaches in my corral!"

SECRETARY (to amorous director). "No last roundup with you, pardner, till you shed yourself of that squaw and three papooses!"

★ ★ ★

What price those glowing testimonials you read in the ad pages? An old-time West Point gridiron star, notes William Freeman in *The Big Name,* once said in a paid ad that a certain typewriter "was the greatest thing he knew for keeping his grades high." The next week it was revealed that in a class of 266 men, the star stood 232nd in math, 207th in English, and 237th in French. But he sure could score touchdowns!

Norma Talmadge once endorsed four hundred products in a single day. Another famous stage beauty wrote the owner of a "strength-reviving" tonic, "Your product is the best ever! I have taken three bottles so far, and I feel like a new man!"

★ ★ ★

Advertising wizard Bernice Fitz-Gibbon describes the teen-age period as "perhaps the most important in a lifetime—the bridge between adolescence and adulthood, between Maltex and Miltown, between Buster Brown and Balenciaga, between mudpies and mudpacks, between spinning the bottle and heating it at 2 A.M."

"Cast your bread upon the *daughters*," Miss Fitz-Gibbon advises prospective advertisers. "Teen-age business is almost recession-proof. Mom may let out her old yellow, Dad may pull in his belt, but you can just bet Sister's going to get a new dress for that Saturday night prom! Americans are that way."

★ ★ ★

The head of a big advertising agency was lunching with a group of his top executives—all of whom had unlimited expense accounts. When the check appeared, everybody made a grab for it, but the boss won out. "I'll take care of this, boys," he said firmly. "That's the one way I can be sure I'll only pay for it once."

★ ★ ★

John Wanamaker, credited by many with revolutionizing department store advertising in America, was aware that much of his effort went for naught. "Fully half the money I spend on advertising is wasted," he admitted, "but I can never find out which half."

★ ★ ★

A very sincere copywriter—in fact, he was wearing a sincere-sucker suit—summed up his pitch like this:

> The constant drop of water wears away the
>   hardest stone;
> The constant gnaw of Towser masticates
>   the toughest bone;
> The constant wooing lover carries off the
>   blushing maid;
> And the CONSTANT ADVERTISER is the one who
>   gets the trade.

4. ANIMALS

Things are rather topsy-turvy in the animal world these days. For one thing, there aren't enough kings left for a cat to look at, and, for another, since some sleep-loving chemist has discovered a drug that will keep canines from barking at night, not even every dog has his bay.

Even pink elephants aren't pink elephants any more. They're beasts of bourbon.

There *are* a few cats who have been making news of a sort, however:

1. The puss—in Meowmi, Florida, who ate cheeses so he could peer down ratholes with baited breath.

2. The pathetic cat—several degrees below purr—who was always getting in the way at Sam Levenson's house. Sam's mother stepped on its paws one night and the cat screamed bloody murder. Its felines were hurt. "Serves her right," commented Mrs. Levenson grimly. "Who tells her to walk around barefoot?"

3. The all-American cat. He made forty-eight yards in one night!

4. This story doesn't really belong in this cat-egory because it's about a dog, but—well, judge for yourself. It was a dog with such a high I.Q. that his owner sent him to college. Home for Christmas, the dog admitted he had learned neither history nor economics, but added proudly, "I *did* make rather a good start in foreign languages. "O.K.," conceded the owner, "say something in a foreign language." The dog said, "Meow."

★ ★ ★

From Ivan Sanderson's *Living Mammals of the World* you will learn that (1) there are more brown rats in North America than there are people ("the result of the greater stamina and, frankly, common sense of the rats"); (2) you couldn't have a more docile and trustworthy pet than a hyena; (3) vampire bats do not suck blood. They take a little nip with their very sharp teeth, then lap up the blood as it flows; (4) lions are terrified of small children and flapping laundry strung up to dry.

★ ★ ★

Biggest gross for an animal act at a Midwestern carnival was rung up by a novelty: a tiger and a sheep performing tricks in the same cage.

"Amazing," commented a visitor. "Do those oddly assorted creatures always get along so amiably together?"

"They do have a bit of a dust-up every now and then," admitted the trainer, "but we don't let that bother us. We just buy a new sheep."

★ ★ ★

A lady in a sleeping car climbed to her upper berth—and let out a bloodcurdling screech. "Porter," she cried, "I do declare there's a live zebra here in this upper. Isn't that amazing?"

"Sure is," agreed the porter. "When he got on at Louisville, his ticket called for a drawing room."

★ ★ ★

A stalwart lad learned to dive into a big tank and wrestle with a shark. "How's business?" he was asked one day. "Can't complain," he answered cheerfully. "I'm managing to keep my head below water."

★ ★ ★

Paul Bruun has come up with a foolproof labor-saving mousetrap. You buy it with the mice already in it.

★ ★ ★

A tourist wandered into a flea circus and watched spellbound while the head flea did his tricks. "Did you educate that flea yourself?" he asked the owner of the show. "I did," was the proud reply. "I raised him from a pup."

★ ★ ★

In Wisconsin, Dick Jones tells about a dog who loved country sausages. When he begged hard enough, his mistress wrote out an order for a few, and the dog grasped it between his jaws and trotted off to the butcher's with it.

In time the butcher took the dog's appearance as a matter of course, and counted off a half-dozen sausages without even consulting the order the dog dropped at his feet. When the dog arrived one day for the fourth time, however, the butcher made an interesting discovery. The paper was absolutely blank. Wise old Towser, whenever a craving for sausage overtook him, simply snatched up any piece of paper in sight and waltzed off to the butcher's with it.

★ ★ ★

In a verdant pasture in Montana, four young bulls indulged, naturally enough, in a bull session.

"I," said the first, "shall go to Rome and become a papal bull."

"I," said the second, "shall get a job in a brokerage office and become a Wall Street bull."

"I," said the third, "am determined to become a bull in a china shop."

"Okay," nodded the fourth bull cheerfully. "Go out into the world if you will. But I love it right in this pasture and intend to stay here for heifer and heifer and heifer."

★ ★ ★

Nature class is now called to order. What's the heaviest flying bird in North America? Answer: the trumpeter swan which has a maximum weight of over forty pounds. What is the only bird in the Western Hemisphere whose upper bill is movable? Answer: the woodcock. Addenda: the ostrich cannot fly, but its twelve-foot stride carries it over the terrain at forty miles an hour. The wild goose, on the other hand—or wing—can fly at sixty miles an hour and holds the bird altitude record of nearly five and a half miles. Class is dismissed while the goose hangs high!

★ ★ ★

A wise old man in a small town passed a pet shop, and was astonished to note that the price tag on a mean-looking parrot in the window was one hundred dollars. Arrived home, he shooed a turkey into a cage and marched it down to the pet shop. "This gobbler," he announced, "is yours for two hundred dollars."

The pet shop owner laughed. "You must be joking," he said. "Not at all," the wise man told him. "If that mangy parrot is worth a hundred, this fat, succulent turkey ought to be priced at three hundred."

"But," protested the owner, "my parrot talks. What can your fool turkey do?"

"My turkey," said the wise man proudly, "is a philosopher. He *thinks!*"

★ ★ ★

All heck broke loose in the little town of Winder, Georgia, one day this spring when Lucy, a great big elephant, broke loose from a traveling circus. With the help of most of the local population, Lucy finally was cornered in a barn and chained up. Lucy fell in love with her captor, however. Every time he walked away, she broke the chain and stomped after him.

Police and zoo officials from Atlanta then arrived to take charge. A truck was backed up to Lucy with the rear door wide open, and a patrol car drove behind her to urge her into the truck. The siren's shrill sound brought prompt results. Lucy flapped her huge ears, and, instead of lumbering into the truck, she went into reverse, knocking the patrol car into a pine tree.

She finally walked into the truck of her own accord. The patrol car, however, will never be the same.

The biggest elephant in the Berlin Zoo expired of old age, and his trainer was inconsolable. Finally the Zoo superintendent told him, "It's ridiculous to carry on that way about the loss of one elephant. We expect to replace him, you know."

"Easy enough for you to talk," wailed the trainer. "Just remember who has to dig the grave!"

★ ★ ★

Dr. Thomas Snyder, consultant to the Smithsonian Institution, estimates that termites do a hundred million dollars' damage to United States buildings every year. To make matters worse, South American and Hawaiian termites are establishing a beachhead here, and they're even more destructive than the native breed. Possibly it was a Hawaiian termite who boasted to a pal, "Waikikeep your eyes on me, toots! This'll bring down the house," and an interloper from Brazil who invaded a saloon to inquire, "Is this bar tender?" Could be, too, that it was the owner of this very saloon who discovered that some choice liquor he had imported from Russia was way below par. He just poured ale on the troubled vodka.

★ ★ ★

A hunt club in Long Island promoted a pet show for the children of its members, and one proud six-year-old entered the family basset hound. That night the father inquired, "Well, son, how did that old dog of ours make out?" "He had best of breed all sewed up," boasted the youngster, "but at the last minute another basset hound showed up!"

★ ★ ★

Most famous and sweet-dispositioned basset in the world is undoubtedly Cleo, star of countless TV shows. Cleo gives her trainer only one big headache, in fact: she positively refuses to snarl. For a while, when a script called for Cleo to give a show of bad temper, the trainer tried rubber bands to curl Cleo's lips up into a sneer, but the basset soon was smilin' through again. In desperation, a bad-tempered double has been provided for emergencies, and showed he meant business by giving the trainer the old ankle number his very first morning on the job. Cleo didn't say a word: just beamed and played a tune on the piano. (Her Bach is worse than her bite.)

Another famous Hollywood dog, Rin-Tin-Tin, received a long and worshipful letter from a youthful admirer recently. The letter began, "Dear Mr. Tin."

★ ★ ★

A New England manufacturer was in the market for bullfrog skins, and a Texan promptly wrote that he could supply any quantity up to 100,000. "Send them all," invited the manufacturer.

A few days later one forlorn frogskin arrived with this attached to the box: "Turned out this is all the frogskins there was. The noise sure fooled me!"

★ ★ ★

An intrepid naturalist in Omaha has just succeeded in crossing a bulldog with a Plymouth Rock hen. The hen promptly laid six pooched eggs.

This put the nose of comic Joe E. Lewis slightly out of joint. Last season Joe crossed one rooster with another rooster, and all he got for his pains was one mighty cross rooster.

★ ★ ★

"Contrary to public opinion," insists Ernie Kovacs, in a magazine appropriately named *Mad*, "waving a red flag at a bull does not irritate him at all. Actually cows are the ones who get irritated when a red flag is waved at them. The reason a bull gets mad when a red flag is waved at him is because he dislikes being mistaken for a cow." So now you know!

★ ★ ★

Things were zoo-ming in Bronx Park one day not long ago. In one sector, "Adorable" Arlene Francis and her son Peter were inspecting one of the outdoor pens. "Mom," inquired Peter, "what's the peculiar object on the ground underneath that funny-looking animal?" Arlene looked intently, then assured Peter, "There's nothing, son, under the gnu."

Nearby, a hatchet-faced lady tapped the keeper of the monkey house indignantly on the shoulder. "Those wretched animals of yours appear to be engaged in shooting dice. I demand that you break up the game at once." "Shucks," shrugged the keeper, "they're keeping strictly within the law, ma'am. They're only playing for peanuts."

Finally, the headwaiter of a very expensive midtown restaurant and his son were exploring the lion house at feeding time. The keeper casually threw a huge slab of raw meat into the biggest lion's cage and proceeded on his way.

"That wasn't very polite," noted the son. "Why doesn't he serve with style the way you do to your patrons?"

The father made sure the animal was beyond hearing distance, then whispered to his son, "Confidentially, lions are lousy tippers."

5. THE ARMY

Straight from President Eisenhower comes the story of a time when he was heading the Allied forces in Europe near the climax of World War II. He and a member of his staff were on an inspection tour, forward, when they were caught in a sudden downpour. The two generals managed to find a couple of tarpaulins to throw over their shoulders, but their feet were soaked.

Happily, they spotted a supply depot, where General Ike asked a corporal, "Could we have some fresh boots?" "Sure," said the corporal. "How big's your feet?" "Nine and a half," said the general. "You'll take eights," decided the corporal.

As General Ike struggled to get the small boots on his wet feet, the tarpaulin slipped off his shoulders, and revealed the cluster of five stars on each one.

"Holy Moses!" gasped the corporal. "It's the Milky Way!"

★ ★ ★

A veteran parachute jumper submitted to a TV interview by a lady gabber. "When did you get your greatest kick?" asked the lady. "That's easy, ma'am," answered the jumper. "Once I hesitated too long in the plane door."

★ ★ ★

In a depressed area in the Southwest, GI's out on maneuvers have perfected a new technique. They give the local belles one lovely stocking, then wait to see how much they want the other one.

★ ★ ★

An uptown draft board is still wondering what to do with this letter: "We beg you to exempt our employee Joe Sneagle. He is the only man left in our plant, and at the moment is carrying on with fourteen inexperienced girls."

★ ★ ★

Alan Dunn overheard a 1960-model army induction officer telling a group of new draftees, "First I must warn you that army life may be something of a letdown after those modern war novels."

★ ★ ★

Indiana University Press has published a *Draftee's Confidential Guide* that contains numerous invaluable, offbeat tips for gawky youth who find themselves in the Army for the first time. Examples: "On the range, try to get on the 'Ammo' detail. A little work carrying boxes may get you a ride back to the company on the ammunition truck"; "Carry a couple of candy bars along every day. You get mighty hungry out in the field after an hour or two of training"; "Don't stay in the barracks during off-duty hours or you may be picked for a detail. *The library is one place they'll never find you!*"

★ ★ ★

In Officers' Training School, a lieutenant was questioning a candidate. "Say you're on duty on a pitch-black night," he proposed. "Suddenly somebody sneaks up behind you and wraps two arms around you so tightly you just can't use your rifle. What would you say?" The candidate answered hopefully, "Let go, honey!"

★ ★ ★

A new draftee was assigned to a bumptious captain as his new filing clerk. Some hours after he reported for the job the captain wanted some important papers and called for the recruit to bring them on the double.

Five minutes later the captain roared, "You dummy, where are those papers?" The recruit called back cheerfully, "Keep your shirt on, Cap. So far I haven't even located the filing cabinet."

★ ★ ★

John Straley tells about a GI who was having such a ball while on leave that he put in a long-distance call to his sergeant. "Look, Sarge," he begged, "lemme stay over a coupla days. I've got a beautiful party going on. Sixteen of us. If I leave, it'll break up the whole affair."

"Whaddya mean," snorted the sergeant. "One person out of sixteen leaves and it breaks up the party? Who are you that you got so important?"

"You see, Sarge," explained the GI, "the other fifteen are girls."

★ ★ ★

Michael Connolly dedicates this stirring new ballad to the Armed Forces. "She Was Swell to the Division, but Rotten to the Corps."

★ ★ ★

In their book, *Rascals in Paradise,* James Michener and Grove Day tell about a learned gentleman in the thirties who clearly foresaw that a great war was about to engulf the world. After consultation with several top military men he decided that his only secure refuge from the world's insanity lay on some tropical isle, far from civilization.

So in 1939, one week before Germany invaded Poland, this wise man fled to his chosen idyllic, almost unknown South Pacific refuge. It was an island called Guadalcanal.

★ ★ ★

"Some people," observes Jack Herbert ruefully, "treat our war heroes like Christmas trees. First they decorate them, later they want to throw them away."

★ ★ ★

Roger Angell tells about an unfortunate second lieutenant and his wife who lived during World War II at a post where the C.O.

was a pretty tough hombre. The lieutenant had a playful young puppy who was at the stage where he chewed up slippers, pillows, and anything else in which he could sink his teeth. The lieutenant and his wife developed a little family joke about this: she pretended to blame her *husband* for all the puppy's depredations.

One Sunday morning the grumpy C.O. and his wife made a surprise call, and the flustered lieutenant had just gotten them seated when his bride, unaware that there were callers in the house, yelled down cheerfully from above, "John! Have you been chewing the seat out of my pajamas?"

There was a sudden silence. The lieutenant realized bitterly that the true explanation would sound too utterly fantastic, so he said nothing. The C.O. and his wife looked grim, and left shortly thereafter.

The lieutenant's transfer to another post came through within the week.

6. ART

Posing for artists in the altogether is a lucrative and entirely respectable occupation for a young lady who knows how to take care of herself. It also presents some odd problems not visible, so to speak, to the naked eye.

Al Baldwin tells of one model who sent a group of artists a bill that called for ten dollars more than had been stipulated in the original agreement. Her reason? "I was about to pose," she declared, "when my fine young artists discovered that the garter marks on my legs would show. So they shoved a chair at me and waited twenty minutes for the marks to disappear. O.K.; that was my fault. But then it was another half-hour before we got down to work, and for that I think they should pay." "How come?" prompted Baldwin. "The chair they plopped me into," said the model indignantly, "had a cane bottom."

★ ★ ★

A young couple at an art gallery lingered so long in front of a picture of Adam and Eve that the guard grew suspicious and strolled over to investigate. "This picture has a special meaning for us," explained the man hurriedly. "We happen to know the anecdote behind it."

★ ★ ★

An amateur painter submitted one of his better efforts to be exhibited at his home-town art exhibition. He was asked over the phone to identify the spot he had painted. "Wiesbaden, Germany," he replied. The caption he found affixed to his masterpiece when the exhibition opened was "A wee spot in Germany."

★ ★ ★

Mr. Mothcroft paused before a painting called "Spring," which depicted a ravishing young nymph clad only in a couple of strategically distributed leaves. Mr. Mothcroft, in fact, seemed rooted to the spot.

"Come on, Henry," urged his wife. "What are you waiting for?"

"Autumn," sighed Mr. Mothcroft.

★ ★ ★

In England, a distinguished portrait painter, the late Sir John Lavery, stared fixedly at a lady attending a tea party, then strode to her side and confessed, "I don't recall your name, but your features certainly are familiar to me." "They ought to be," she told him sharply. "I paid you five thousand pounds to paint them!"

★ ★ ★

The owner of a sprawling chain of grocery stores sat for his portrait by another English painter recently, and was so delighted with the result that he ordered six hundred copies! "You're jesting," gasped the artist. "I'm doing nothing of the sort," the owner assured him. "I propose to hang one copy in each of my branches."

It was a great windfall for the artist, but it had one unfortunate result. Now he won't accept any commission unless the sitter agrees to purchase a minimum of two hundred copies. He's finding that market definitely limited.

★ ★ ★

A newly rich patroness of the arts asked a dealer, "Do these artists whose pictures cost so much learn to paint when they grow up, or do they inherit their talent?"

"My dear lady," the dealer replied patiently, "this heredity business is nonsense. Did you ever hear of the mothers and fathers of Renoir and Rouault?"

"No, I didn't," admitted the patroness, "and, to tell you the truth, I never heard of Renoir and Rouault, either."

★ ★ ★

The daughter of a famous American artist had a passion for flitting about barefoot, but her mother frowned on the practice. "You're getting to be a grown-up young lady now," she pointed out, "and I insist that you wear shoes."

One morning the daughter ignored the "Keep Out" sign on the door of her father's studio, and came upon him painting a model in the nude. She raced right to her mother, and announced triumphantly, "You see, Mamma? *She's* allowed to go barefoot!"

★ ★ ★

On the Riviera, a couple of wealthy American expatriates were told their new villa would not be complete without an original mural by Picasso. Impressed by the idea, they summoned the great Spanish painter, who named a staggering fee, and got it without argument.

Came the day when the Picasso mural was to be unveiled. Invited big shots pressed forward as the obscuring curtain was removed. What met their eyes was an absolutely blank white wall —with just a tiny gray circle in the lower left-hand corner. "What daring!" enthused the husband. "He sensed exactly what we wanted," gushed the wife.

Two months later, the couple were convinced a Picasso mural on the opposite wall was another "must." Again Picasso took up his brush—for an even steeper fee. Again the unveiling revealed a bare white wall—but this time there was a little blue square in the corner, surmounted by a red triangle.

"I like it," declared the husband promptly.

"So do I," agreed the wife, who had been reading up on modern art at a furious clip, "but don't you think it's a bit BUSY?"

★ ★ ★

A tourist bought an old canvas in Rome, and lugged it to a Fifty-seventh Street dealer to ascertain its true worth. "At first sight," opined the dealer, "I'd say it's either a Titian or a repetition."

★ ★ ★

Cover artist Jon Whitcomb has gotten a lot of mileage out of his story of a painter whose model complained one wintry morning that the studio was too darn cold for posing in the raw.

"You're right," agreed the painter. "I don't feel like working today anyhow. Sit down and have a cup of coffee with me." Some minutes later he heard a determined pounding on the door. "Quick!" he commanded the model. "Get your clothes off! It's my wife!"

★ ★ ★

One model agency in town believes in giving its spectacularly handsome young ladies spectacularly unusual names. Its last list of available lasses included Miss September Maughan, Miss Eyeful Tower, and Miss Berthe Daye Sute.

7. AUTHOR, AUTHOR!

William Faulkner, Nobel and Pulitzer prize-winning author, wrote his first novel, *Soldier's Pay*, in New Orleans in 1926. "Sherwood Anderson was a successful writer there," recalls Mr. Faulkner, "and the life he was leading struck me as downright appealing, so I figured I'd be a writer too. When I finished my novel, Anderson said, 'I'll make a trade with you. If you'll let me off reading your manuscript, I'll make my publisher accept it.' 'Done,' said I—and that's how I became a writer."

In an engrossing interview with Miss Jean Stein for the *Paris Review*, William Faulkner told about his first movie job. It consisted of going to parties and sailing on yachts with a director named Browning for three solid weeks, trying in vain to discover for just what purpose he had been hired. "When you've written your dialogue," Browning would tell him, "I'll let you see the story!"

The picnic ended with a wire from the studio that read: "Faulkner is fired. MGM." "Don't worry," counseled Browning. "I'll make those so-and-sos not only put you back on the payroll, but send you a written apology as well." Five minutes later, another telegram arrived. This one said: "Browning is also fired. MGM."

When William Faulkner visited Japan on behalf of the State Department, he spoke to a conclave of several thousand students. Few of them understood what he was saying, but all were deeply respectful.

Faulkner spun out one amusing anecdote for fifteen minutes, at the end of which the official interpreter thought it wise to repeat the story in Japanese. This he somehow managed to accomplish in less than twenty words—yet the audience burst out into tumultuous laughter.

"How could you tell my story in so few words?" marveled Faulkner.

"I didn't tell it at all," admitted the interpreter. "I simply said, 'Mr. Faulkner has just told a very funny story. Everybody will kindly laugh.'"

★ ★ ★

John O'Hara and Quentin Reynolds are two of the most successful and popular authors in America today, but Reynolds remembers when neither of them had it quite so good. It was in the early thirties, when neither writer had a book to his name—or his name to a book. Pooling their resources (two battered typewriters), they rented a grubby two-room-and-kitchenette basement apartment in the East Fifties and settled down to work so earnestly they rarely saw each other.

One morning Reynolds was bowled over when his breakfast was brought in to him—on a tray, no less!—by an elegant stranger. He proved to be an out-of-work ship's steward with whom O'Hara had struck up an acquaintance the previous night and lured home to serve as general factotum.

It soon developed that the sailor took a very dim view of two hulking gents who did nothing all day but write, and he was even more scornful of their solicitude for each other's privacy when the muse was upon them. One morning Reynolds asked, "Is O'Hara busy?" "Busy!" snorted the sailor. "Nah. He's just sprawled out in there beatin' the hell out of that typewritin' machine."

Reynolds didn't bother O'Hara that morning. His friend was indeed busy—writing the last pages of the novel that was to catapult him to fame: *Appointment in Samarra.*

★ ★ ★

A customer bought a copy of John O'Hara's most recent novel, *From the Terrace*, but when he got home he found that by some mechanical error it was the pages of *The Memoirs of Casanova* that were bound into the O'Hara cover. The bookseller readily exchanged the defective copy for a perfect one, and assured his customer, "This isn't the first time Casanova's been found under the wrong covers!"

★ ★ ★

Harvey Breit's *The Writer Observed* contains some revealing comments by the authors interviewed. Truman Capote, for instance, confessed, "I'm about as high as a shotgun—and just as noisy. I think I have rather heated eyes." Evelyn Waugh declared that no writer should be caught dead with a message. "A writer," he said, "has no right to be like Lawrence or Hemingway, thinking they're prophets." Hemingway himself said, "As a Nobel prize winner I cannot but regret that the award never was given to Mark Twain or Henry James." Carl Sandburg reserved his barbs for TV. "I am disgusted," he fulminated, "with people who just watch indiscriminately for hours and hours. These machines are thieves of time, with not even a mechanical conscience about the hours they will waste in a day."

★ ★ ★

Ernest Hemingway, world traveler, received a letter in Cuba recently addressed simply, "To Ernest Hemingway. God Knows Where." The sender got a reply very promptly. "You were so right," scribbled Hemingway. "God knew!"

★ ★ ★

One contemporary American author genuinely appreciated in Italy is John Steinbeck. A baker in Rome actually reproduced a half-dozen covers of Steinbeck novels in pastry form. John Fuller called the window display to the attention of Steinbeck, who dutifully bought *The Wayward Bus*, and had it for dessert that evening.

"This is the first time," notes Fuller, "that I ever saw an author eat his own words."

★ ★ ★

A reasonably distinguished author dropped in to visit his publisher but was stopped by a too-honest receptionist. "You can't see the boss now," she told him. "He's taking a nap."

★ ★ ★

Daniel George has written this "Epitaph of a Dead Author":

I suffered so much from printers' errors
That death for me can hold no terrors
No doubt this stone has been misdated
Oh, how I wish I'd been cremated!

★ ★ ★

Maybe ghostwriting is being overdone a bit these days. Cleveland Amory tells about one well-known journalist who was hired to write the "autobiography" of a big political wheel. Later, a prominent lawyer was tapped to write a review of the book for a New York newspaper, and hired the same journalist to do the job for him.

"Possibly," surmises Cleveland Amory, "this was the first time a ghost-written book was ghost-reviewed by the ghost who wrote it in the first place!"

P.S. The review was a very favorable one.

★ ★ ★

The real names of some very famous authors may surprise you. Recognize Timothy Sparks Cecily Isabel Fairfield Andrews? That formidable mouthful, my friends, was the real name of Charles Dickens!

Josef Teodor Konrad Korzeniowcki was not a Notre Dame fullback, but the Joseph Conrad who gave us *Lord Jim* and *Victory*.

Edward Everett Tanner attempted to break into the light-fiction best-seller lists with a novel called *House Party*, submitted under the pseudonym of Virginia Rowan. He did much better the second time out, when he used the name of Patrick Dennis for *Auntie Mame*.

The "John Sedges" who wrote *The Townsman*, was, in private

life, Pearl Buck. The "Tom Graham" who wrote one of the first boys' books about flying machines later won the Nobel prize as Sinclair Lewis. John Galsworthy's first four books bore the author's name of John Sinjohn. "Nancy Boyd" was Edna St. Vincent Millay. The real name of the author of "Nineteen Eighty-Four" was Eric Arthur Blair—not George Orwell.

The reasons for writers attempting to disguise their identities vary widely. In some cases, two authors pretend to be one—or, contrariwise, insinuate they are three. Men pretend to be women —and women, men. One writer had a very practical reason for dissembling: he was married to two women at the same time—and both of them were trying to track him down! Often authors with a very high literary reputation are trying to make a real killing and, at the same time, to protect their lofty standing from the taint of "rank" commercialism.

★ ★ ★

An ironic observation on the literary life is contributed by a cartoonist in *Look,* who shows a couple of scientists toying with the dials of a huge mechanical brain. Something definitely has gone haywire with the darn thing. One scientist suddenly discovers what's wrong. "We've left this brain idle too long," he decides. "It's trying to write a novel."

RING LARDNER

Don Elder is an ex-editor of Doubleday's who quit publishing because his heart was set on writing a book about the late Ring Lardner. And a fine job he made of it. Like Lardner, Elder grew up in Niles, Michigan. He has long known the Lardner family and has the background to convey the best picture yet of one of the strangest, most complex figures in American literature.

One of the great sports writers and short-story masters of our time, Lardner has been variously hailed, and with some justice, as "a supreme humorist," "a wonderful friend," "a slave of the bottle," "a puritanical pessimist," and "the bitterest satirist of his day."

His hilarious stories about a baseball busher, *You Know Me, Al*, which brought him fame in 1916, reduced to the ridiculous the sycophantic slop that had dominated the sports pages before his emergence. So many readers asked Lardner to name the man on whom his caricature was based that he added this footnote to subsequent editions: "The original of Jack Keefe is not a ballplayer at all, but Jane Addams of Hull House, a former Follies girl."

Succeeding stories like "Haircut," "Champion," and "A Day with Conrad Green" showed that Lardner's humor was tinged with cynical despair and contempt for false values.

I met Ring Lardner just once. He was sitting with George Kaufman, Scott Fitzgerald, and Heywood Broun at the Algonquin Hotel. I didn't say a word because I was awed. Lardner didn't say a word because he was in a black mood. He just drank steadily and stared into space. Don Elder writes that he frequently behaved this way. He broke one protracted silence just long enough to stop an actor with a mop of wild, unruly hair and a Svengali-like beard and demand, "How do you look when I'm sober?"

On one occasion, he arrived at the Friars Club after the theater in evening clothes and sat there for two days and nights. Finally somebody drove him away with "Have you heard the one about the——" Lardner liked to tell funny stories but couldn't stand listening to them. A few minutes later an actor looked over and exclaimed, "Hey, the statue's gone!"

Another time, a fellow member insisted that Lardner read aloud a poem written by the member's brother, now twenty years dead. When he finished, Lardner asked, "Did he write it before or after he died?" A second poet Lardner frequently recalled was an ex-coroner of St. Paul who wrote an ode to his mother that contained this priceless line: "If by perchance the inevitable should come."

One day President Warren Harding invited Ring Lardner to play golf with him, and enjoyed the round so thoroughly he was in a very expansive mood when they returned to the clubhouse.

"Is there anything I can do for you?" asked Harding.

"Yes," said Ring. "I want to be ambassador to Greece."

"Why would you like to go there?" Harding wanted to know.

"Because," explained Ring, "my wife has grown tired of Great Neck."

Auto-racing was among Lardner's many hates. One of his news stories began "The Del Ray Motordrome at Los Angeles burned to the ground with a great saving of life." He once met Coolidge and reported that he had told the President a humorous anecdote, adding, "He laughed until you could hear a pin drop."

Lardner visited Paducah one day to interview Irvin Cobb. "Mr. Cobb took me into his library," reported Lardner, "and showed me his books, of which he has a complete set."

A bit of Lardner dialogue that I remember with particular delight went: BUSINESSMAN: Been having any luck with your hogs this year? FARMER: Oh, we don't play for money!

★ ★ ★

There never has been an author quite like Gerard Lambert, whose memoirs, *All Out of Step*, were published recently.

Back in the days when big corporations' ad budgets were as minuscule as those of book publishers, Mr. Lambert launched a block-busting five-million-dollar campaign for a new mouthwash called "Listerine" that featured "Fifteen Times a Bridesmaid—but Never a Bride" and turned halitosis into a household word. Then he "retired" at forty-two to devote himself to yachting, architecture, and the mysteries of government. He came out of "retirement" to head Gillette and invent the Blue Blade, mentioned more frequently during the last World Series than Mantle, Turley, Burdette, and Spahn combined.

Perhaps Lambert's sharpest non-Gillette accomplishment came when he agreed to buy a full page in every issue of the Mencken-edited *American Mercury* for one year—with the proviso that he might run any copy he wished short of libel and licentiousness.

For twelve months Lambert lambasted Mencken's conduct of the magazine, his point of view, and his language. By that time, recalls Lambert, the sage of Baltimore was so all-fired mad no attempt was made to renew the contract.

★ ★ ★

Rumer Godden, talented English authoress, received a telephone call in her London home from an American lady who declared she was a great admirer, and had read every one of Miss Godden's books. "I'd love to drop round and pay my respects in person," she trilled. "Come by all means," agreed the courteous Miss Godden. The lady thereupon turned up for tea with SIXTEEN other ladies! It developed that the American admirer ran a tour of Europe in which the customers were promised they would meet famous authors and be entertained by them in their homes!

Miss Godden told Roger Smith, of *Publishers' Weekly*, about another "fan" who wrote to ask for her autograph. Miss Godden mailed it, and in due course received another note from the fan which read: "I have analyzed your handwriting. You are deceitful, selfish, and mean."

★ ★ ★

George Bernard Shaw's cellophane-wrapped romance with the actress, Ellen Terry, has been the subject of infinite anecdotes and conjectures. When she requested permission to publish some of the voluminous correspondence he had addressed to her in the course of a lifetime, he refused indignantly, declaring, "I will not play the horse to your Lady Godiva." "Ours was an ideal love affair," he explained to the press, "because it was conducted principally by post. Ellen got tired of five husbands, but she never got tired of me."

★　★　★

Archibald Henderson, biographer of George Bernard Shaw, tells about the time GBS received a fan letter addressed to George Bernard Shawm. "The idiot can't even spell my name," roared Shaw. "Furthermore, there's no such word as 'shawm.'" His wife begged to disagree, quietly showed him this definition in the dictionary: "SHAWM: An old-fashioned wind instrument long since passed out of common use."

★　★　★

One of the masterpieces of literature is Gibbon's formidable three-volume *Decline and Fall of the Roman Empire.* And what did England's Duke of Gloucester (brother of King George III) say when, in 1781, author Gibbon presented him with the just-published work? Here, according to Gibbon's diary, were the good Duke's words. "What? More of those damned, fat, square, thick books? Always scribble, scribble, scribble, eh, Mr. Gibbon?"

★　★　★

In a dream one night, the British author Maurice Baring made the inevitable journey across the River Styx, and was asked by a "customs house" inspector on the far side, "Have you anything to declare?" But the printed form that was handed to Baring listed no such items as jewels, silks, or laces. No, he was being asked to declare what *literary* baggage he had traveled with in his lifetime —the enduring classics and gems of philosophy that had been his as free gifts at all times by the mere reaching for a book! Baring awoke with a fresh resolve to read more and better literature for the balance of his days!

"MIGHTY OAKS FROM LITTLE ACORNS . . ."

In the year 1855, a new lecturer in mathematics made his appearance at Christ Church College in England. His name was Charles Lutwidge Dodgson. He was a brilliant scholar, and, though he could not help stammering when he warmed to his subject, students soon came flocking to his lectures.

Charles Dodgson had another hobby besides solving difficult equations. He loved to gather children around him and spin wondrous, fanciful tales for them—and when children composed his audience, his stammer miraculously disappeared.

On July 4, 1862, Charles Dodgson went on a boating expedition with the three young daughters of Dean Liddell of Christ Church College. The second daughter's name was Alice. In a casual last line to his diary for that day, Dodgson noted: "I told them a fairy tale about a little girl's adventures underground, which I have promised to write out for Alice."

Mr. Dodgson kept his promise. Furthermore, his story was published in book form in 1865. Would people think it too frivolous an exercise for a learned mathematician? He took the precaution of publishing under the pen name of Lewis Carroll. And he called his book *Alice in Wonderland.*

Another tale that will delight boys and girls for generations to come had its inception in an equally casual and unpremeditated way.

In 1882, Robert Louis Stevenson, convalescing in Scotland from a serious illness, found himself alone one morning with his young stepson, Lloyd Osbourne. Seeking to amuse the boy, he idly sketched a map on a scrap of paper, and scrawled across it the name, "Treasure Island." "Pirates!" he whispered darkly. "Tell me about them," pleaded the boy, clapping his hands.

Then and there that wonderful, bloodthirsty, one-legged scoundrel, Long John Silver, came into being, and one new chapter a day was added until the tale was concluded. At the last moment,

Stevenson could not bring himself to allow Long John to be hung from a yardarm—the fate he so richly deserved. "To this day," Stevenson wrote shortly before his death, "I rather admire that smooth and formidable adventurer!"

* * *

It happened over a hundred years ago, but in the town of Newport, in western New Hampshire, they still tell the story of a lady named Sarah Josepha Hale, who never lost interest in the little red schoolhouse where she had mastered the three "R's," and was loved alike by the teachers and the pupils there.

She was just leaving a classroom one morning when she distinctly heard a muffled "Ba-a-a." The teacher heard it, too—and promptly discovered that one little girl was trying desperately to hide a woolly, white, and very lively lamb under her desk.

"I found it in a field yesterday—all alone," explained the little girl tearfully, while the rest of the class exploded with laughter. "I fed it, took it home—and now it won't let me out of its sight."

Classmates were still poking fun at the little girl the next morning when Sarah Hale reappeared. Sweeping the youngster into her arms, Miss Hale told her, "I liked what you did yesterday so much I wrote a little poem about it. I want to read it to you boys and girls."

Miss Hale's poem has not been forgotten. It began, "Mary had a little lamb. Its fleece was white as snow . . ."

* * *

Herr Brockhaus, publisher of Schopenhauer's works in Germany, once sent the philosopher a gold watch for Christmas. Schopenhauer said, "Thank you—but the watch doesn't go." Brockhaus replied, "I guess it takes after your last book. That's not going either."

* * *

A lovely lady from the Social Register married a successful writer some years ago, but finally had to divorce him. Writers evidently were too temperamental and unpredictable, she complained, and she no longer could put up with this one's quirks and peccadillos.

What did she do then, however, but fall in love with another famous man of letters! The ex-husband read the wedding announcement in a European paper, and sent his former bride this cable: "Heartiest congratulations and best wishes. [Signed] Frying Pan."

8. AUTOMOBILES

When the next automobile show opens—bigger and better than ever, of course—there will still be a few misty-eyed graybeards in the crowd recalling the days when America's mighty automobile industry was in its infancy, and the very first auto show was held at the old Madison Square Garden on Twenty-seventh Street.

That first show opened on Saturday evening, November 3, 1900, with competition from a drizzling rain and a presidential campaign parade past Madison Square. "Vote for Bryan! Down with McKinley!" chanted the Tammany cohorts outside. Bluebloods within the Garden preferred such slogans as "Ride with the wind in a Duryea," "One ride in a Winton will convince you," and "No cranking with a Riker Electric!"

A wooden track, one-eighth of a mile long, was erected in the Garden for demonstration purposes, and a special ramp on the roof was built to prove to skeptics the hill-climbing ability and sturdy brakes of the Mobile Steamer. For risking her famous limbs in a single drive up the ramp, Lillian Russell, Marilyn Monroe of her day, was awarded a Mobile as a gift. She took one look at a photograph of herself in her second-act costume for Weber and Fields's *Fiddle-dee-dee*, another in the elaborate camouflage duster, bonnet, goggles, veil—without which no motorist would dare venture forth on the muddy roads of the era—and prudently decided to give the new auto away and stick to her victoria, liveried flunkeys, and spanking bays.

★ ★ ★

The 11 P.M. closing time of the show in those days was signaled each night by the simultaneous blasting of every automobile horn and bell in the Garden—possibly the very first, and most melodious, rendition of rock-and-roll music in America.

Although Inventor Thomas Edison confidently announced "The horse is doomed!" most other Americans were harder to convince. When P. T. Barnum bought one of the newfangled contrivances for his circus, a waspish editorialist wrote: "As it bumbles along, spasmodically coughing and belching noxious smoke, just ahead of the other freaks and wild animals, it is obvious that the automobile has found its appropriate place."

It was the idle rich who had the curiosity—and funds—to keep the early builders of automobiles in business. Mrs. Belmont and Colonel John Jacob Astor drove their horseless chariots up and down Bellevue Avenue in Newport. Mrs. Hamilton Fish steered her electric down Third Avenue in Manhattan—or at least she did until she encountered a hapless male pedestrian and ran over him. Then she backed up, and ran over him again. Resuming her forward direction, she clipped him a third time. This was enough for both Mrs. Fish and her victim. Both abandoned the electric on foot, she for the Waldorf, he for Bellevue Hospital.

Everybody knew that automobiles were here to stay by the time William K. Vanderbilt donated a huge silver cup for the first of a dozen annual races in 1904. Thousands of thrill-seeking spectators watched the daredevil drivers burn up the roads of Nassau County, Long Island, with George Heath the winner in his Panhard "Ninety" at an average speed of fifty-two miles an hour.

But the Panhard, like winners of most other early races, was a European car. It remained for Henry Martin Leland to prove that American mass-production methods could produce machines that were not only cheaper but more dependable.

He shipped three Cadillac cars to England in 1906. Officials of the Royal Automobile Club ripped them to pieces and scattered parts, bolts, and wires in reckless confusion on the dock. Then Cadillac mechanics, using only commonplace tools like wrenches and screwdrivers, put the three cars together again. British officials then drove them five hundred miles without a single mishap!

Leading the applause were men like Henry Ford, James Ward Packard, David Dunbar Buick, and Ransom E. Olds. American automobile manufacture was truly "on the move" at last. It hasn't stopped ever since!

* * *

"There were just as many foolhardy drivers fifty years ago," the San Francisco *Chronicle* reminds us, "but in those days they drove something that had more sense than they did."

* * *

An experienced motorist named Harold Coffin gives his own interpretation of highway phenomena:

1. Lots of trucks parked at a drive-in restaurant: the food is terrible, the coffee worse, but there's a beautiful waitress.

2. Car off the road with two punctured tires: the driver canceled his auto club membership yesterday.

3. Car persistently straddling two lanes on a crowded thruway: the driver's wife can't make up her mind.

4. Beautiful scenery unmarred by billboards: you're on the wrong road!

* * *

Bob Sylvester has been entertaining an author who is making his first visit to the Big Stem in ten years. "Note any significant changes?" asked Bob. "Yes," answered the author. "The cabs are smaller and the tabs are bigger."

* * *

Asked for a slogan to encourage safe driving over a big holiday weekend, George Gobel suggested: "Ladies and gentlemen, this is a holiday weekend. The National Safety Council estimates that 354 people will be killed. So far only 172 have been killed. Some of you folks aren't trying!"

* * *

Advice from a used-car dealer in Woodstock: "If your headlights are out of order, don't stop to have them fixed that night. Just turn on your radio real loud: this will help drown out the noise of the crash."

★ ★ ★

This is the way the boys at Duke University think Gray might have written his *Elegy*, had he lived today:

> The curfew tolls the knell of parting day;
> The line of cars winds slowly o'er the lea.
> Our friend jay-walked his absent-minded way—
> And left the world most unexpectedly.

★ ★ ★

An indignant citizen of Montreal writes that he saw the driver of a car with a Florida license cut into line so sharply ahead of the driver of a car with a Michigan license that the latter's left fender was crumpled. The Michigan driver promptly alighted from his car, took a quick look at the damage, and punched the Florida driver solidly on the jaw. The Florida driver reeled against a wall, and complained to onlookers, "Some idea of hospitality you guys have up here in Canada!"

★ ★ ★

Deep in the Canadian Rockies, a motorist was having his gas tank filled at an isolated service station. "You're the last one through here to get a tankful at the old price," the attendant told him cheerfully. The motorist felt pretty good about it till the attendant added, "Yup, five minutes from now the price of gas goes down three cents a gallon."

★ ★ ★

AUTO SUGGESTIONS:

Poor Lung Fin, the Chinese laundryman, was flattened by an automobile as he attempted to cross Mott Street—but he went down with flying collars.

Jean Sheppard reports the perfection of a new tinted windshield for automobiles. No more red traffic lights with this innovation! It makes red light look bright green. The windshield sells for sixty-five dollars—including funeral expenses.

Army Archerd reports that the gown a blond starlet wore to a prevue was "a new convertible with the top down." And veteran comic Julius Tannen told him that the reason so many people buy new automobiles is because they have to pay cash when riding on a bus.

Walter Slezak looked wistfully out of the picture window of his West Coast hacienda and remarked, "I always can tell when my wife has taken out the car—by the tracks across the lawn."

At a recent auto show, a dealer saw a man consult the price tag on a new model, smile happily, and call over his wife. The dealer hastily explained, "That price tag, you must realize, covers only the federal, state, county, and city taxes. The price of the car is additional."

The nimblest character in Hollywood, avers Terry Moore, is the man who can shift gears in a Volkswagen without getting his face slapped.

A very, very ancient jalopy wheezed up to the tollgate of a new superhighway.

"Eighty cents," said the attendant.

"Sold!" cried the driver.

★ ★ ★

One of Cornelia Otis Skinner's most nerve-wracking experiences came when she saw a little boy stroll unconcernedly directly into the path of an oncoming convertible. She screamed, snatched him up under her arm, and jumped with him to the safety of the curbstone. He turned out to be a midget of forty, smoking a pipe, with a quaint and extensive vocabulary.

★ ★ ★

It was raining cats and dogs, but a gallant driver saw a woman alone in the mud trying to change a flat tire, and couldn't bear passing her by. He completed the job for her, and, soaked to the skin, exclaimed jovially, "There, little lady, that's done!" "Quiet," she ordered him. "You'll wake up my husband. He's taking a nap in the back seat."

★ ★ ★

A lady had just taken over her car from a parking attendant, but paused at the gate to call out a last query to him. "Tell me," she urged, "just what do you fellows use to clean the grease off your hands when you run out of steering wheels?"

★ ★ ★

Sam Himmell tells about a character in Holyoke, Massachusetts, who finally has achieved an ambition he's nourished since 1936. He just bought a 1936 Cadillac.

★ ★ ★

A city man had a tough time persuading his wife to journey to the seashore for a Sunday on the beach. The traffic on the roads, the crowds on the beach, the humidity and dust all were even worse than she had bargained for. Back home at last, she sank gratefully into the easy chair in her air-conditioned room and sighed, "Ed, I'm so happy to be home again, I'm glad I went!"

★ ★ ★

A collection of candidates for a juvenile delinquency home were tearing down a road in a rickety hotrod at about a hundred miles an hour. One young goon in the rear seat noticed that the door on his side wasn't properly closed. Hastily he opened it and slammed it shut. The driver, without turning his head, snarled, "WHO just got in there?"

★ ★ ★

John D. Rockefeller, Jr., was hurrying to a directors' meeting in New Jersey one day when he was arrested for speeding. "Let's see your license," demanded the cop. When he saw the name on same he gave a low whistle. "Zowie!" he exclaimed. "Looks like this time we've really hit the jackpot."

★ ★ ★

Bill Kennedy says he bought a new "magic" carburetor "guaranteed" to save 30 per cent on gas, a timer that saves 50 per cent on gas, and spark plugs that save 30 per cent on gas. He put them all on his jalopy, drove ten miles—and the gas tank overflowed.

★ ★ ★

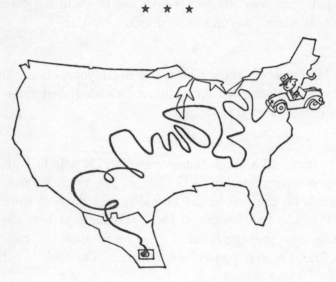

A grimly determined inventor, undaunted by a series of grisly failures, kept working away on a long-range automobile powered by electricity instead of gasoline. He dashed triumphantly into the Explorers' Club in New York one evening and cried, "I've done it! All the way here from Mexico City without a single mishap!" Pressed for a report on the cost of the trip, the inventor replied, "Exactly $3955.88—three dollars for electricity and $3952.88 for the extension cord."

★ ★ ★

A long string of drivers was waiting patiently for the green light at an important intersection when suddenly a snazzy little foreign runabout started hippety-hopping all over the place. A cop ran up to holler, "What the blank blank do you think you're doing there?" "Nothing, officer," the embarrassed occupant assured him. "I've just got the hiccups."

★ ★ ★

The long-suffering husband of an erratic—to put it mildly—lady driver handed her two loaded bags—one large, one small—just before she set out for a hundred-mile journey. "The big bag," he told her, "contains a sledge hammer. Every time you run into something or somebody, I want you to promise me you'll pull out the hammer and hit yourself on the head."

"What's in the little bag?" demanded the wife.

The husband said, "Aspirin."

★ ★ ★

You've heard lots of mean stories about agents for finance companies swooping down on delinquents and repossessing autos, TV sets, pianos, and what not. Here's a nice story for a change.

An agent had to remind a nice old farmer that he hadn't paid the last two of fifty installments on a new car. "It's in the barn," said the farmer sadly—and in a low voice so his wife couldn't hear. "Sickness cost us too much this year. I'm afraid you'll have to take that car of yours back."

The agent reluctantly walked to the barn. There he was amazed to find the automobile shiny and new, up on blocks, carefully covered with a tarpaulin, with the speedometer showing only twelve miles—the distance from the auto sales room to the farmer's barn.

"But you've never driven this car!" exclaimed the agent.

"Didn't feel I should," explained the farmer. "I figured she's not mine till she's fully paid for."

The agent slammed shut his collection book, put the tarpaulin back over the car, and said, "Pop, I guess we'll just let you have this car till your crops come in."

9. AVIATION

Remember the airlift to Berlin in 1948 that thwarted the Russian attempt to freeze the Americans out of the Western Zone and prevented the Soviet from gobbling up the whole of Germany? It was one of America's greatest "peacetime" victories. The airlift operated for eleven months—until the Russians cried "Uncle" and called off their blockade. At the height of the operation, U.S. planes, loaded with food and other supplies, were landing in Berlin at the rate of more than one a minute!

Berlin would have frozen without the coal we flew in—up to seventy-five hundred tons a day, almost a million and a half tons in all. American officials in Berlin doubted that coal could be delivered by air at all, but the U.S. Air Force chief in Europe, General Curtis LeMay, insisted without hesitation, "Our Air Force can *deliver* anything!"—and he proved his point.

★ ★ ★

It was Mr. Snodgrass' first trip by airplane, and he was scared stiff. When the motors began to roar, he gripped the arms of his seat, closed his eyes tightly, and determinedly counted to one hundred.

Then he opened his eyes and looked down out of the window. "Look at those tiny people below," he marveled to his seat partner. "They look just like ants."

"They *are* ants," said the man in the other seat gently. "We haven't left the ground yet."

★ ★ ★

A timid little lady refused to board a plane headed for Denver unless the pilot promised her personally not to fly above an altitude of four thousand feet. "Higher than that," she explained, "my doctor says would be more than my heart could stand."

"But, my dear lady," blustered the pilot, "Denver itself is one mile high." "Then I just won't go there," decided the little lady. "I always thought Denver was on the ground."

★ ★ ★

Couple of sweet girl graduates were discussing their future careers. "It's me for the life of an airline hostess," caroled one. "That's the way to meet a well-heeled man-of-the-world." "There must be a less wearing way of meeting men," pondered the other. "Could be," said the first, "but you won't meet them strapped in!"

★ ★ ★

The stewardess on a plane coming down at Salt Lake City, writes Gene Sherman, clicked on the intercom and went through the usual routine about keeping seated until all motors had stopped and what a pleasure it had been to serve the passengers. "And if anybody finds a green button," she added hopefully, "it's mine."

★ ★ ★

Broker drove his wife to Idlewild Airport and put her aboard a non-stop plane for Denver, Colorado. Driving back to town, he hit the peak of the morning traffic jams, arrived at his office in a state of exhaustion and aggravation. Propped up on his desk was a telegram from his wife: "Arrived safely in Denver. Perfect trip. Love and kisses."

★ ★ ★

Authorities at the London airport think that a zany sense of humor does not become a licensed pilot of a passenger stratocruiser. They suspended one pilot for thirty days for walking up and down a queue of ticket buyers, in full uniform, ostentatiously reading a book called *How to Fly in Ten Easy Lessons*.

★ ★ ★

A streamlined flying saucer, maintains Sam Levenson, deposited a dozen Martians on Broadway, the electric bulbs atop their metal heads flashing with excitement. Their leader strode unhesitatingly to a fire hydrant and demanded, "Are you the boss around here?" The leader's aide, however, pulled him back. "What do you want to bother with him for?" he grumbled. "Can't you see he's only a kid?"

★ ★ ★

If you can stand one more of those stories of outer-space robots landing on earth and demanding audience with kings, queens, hydrants, pinball machines, and what not, there's the Martian who caught his first glance of a blinker light at an intersection. A crafty look came into his metallic eyes. "Oh no, you don't," he chuckled. "My mother warned me in advance about dames like you."

★ ★ ★

Caskie Stinnett, bound by plane from Philadelphia to New Orleans, heard one pretty airline hostess whisper to her assistant, "Careful, Toots, if you have to carry anything up front. They've got the automatic pilot on."

★ ★ ★

An international film star fell ill suddenly, and the two leading specialists on the coast were hastened to her bedside. They agreed on an emergency operation, but decided to fly her to a hospital in New York, where special equipment would facilitate their task.

The star was bundled up in her sables and driven to the airport just in time to make the last scheduled non-stop flight of the day. But for one solid hour, while studio executives fumed—and photographers photographed—she was not allowed to board the plane.

"Every minute counts," stormed one of the specialists. "What's causing the delay?"

"It's the wind," explained an attendant. "It's blowing so hard we can't lay down the red carpet."

10. BABIES

"From the day your baby is born," counseled a famous scholar, "you must teach him to do without things. Children today love luxury too much. They have execrable manners, flaunt authority, have no respect for their elders. They no longer rise when their parents or teachers enter the room. What kind of awful creatures will they be when they grow up?"

The scholar who wrote these words, incidentally, was Socrates, shortly before his death in 399 B.C.

★ ★ ★

Seven-year-old Wilbur already had a younger brother and an even younger sister, so when his parents revealed that still another addition to the family was on its way, Wilbur was understandably wary. "Which would you prefer?" twitted his father. "Another brother or another sister?" "Everything else being equal," decided Wilbur, "and if it won't put Ma out too much, I'd rather have a pony."

★ ★ ★

In Superior, Wisconsin, reports Dale Wilson, the Gundersons, a fine Swedish-American couple, had trouble naming their new baby. "We loved the name 'Wirwinia,'" explained Mrs. Gunderson, "but we couldn't pronounce Wirwinia so we named her 'Yenaweave.'"

★ ★ ★

A harassed father-to-be paced the corridor of the hospital where his wife was producing their first-born. The nurse finally appeared

—beaming. "What did you want?" she inquired. "A boy or a girl?" "A boy," said the father. "Well, this time you got a girl," the nurse told him. "That's O.K., too," philosophized the father. "A girl was my second choice."

★ ★ ★

A gracious nurse in a maternity ward tapped a gentleman at the bedside of a brand-new mother and said, "Would you like to see the baby?" The man nodded and was taken to the nursery. The baby was shown to him through the window. "It looks exactly like you," enthused the nurse. The man thanked her for the compliment.

Later the nurse told the mother, "Your husband seemed simply delighted with the baby." The mother corrected her, "That man wasn't my husband. He was here to collect two overdue installments on my TV set."

★ ★ ★

A nurse in the maternity ward of a local hospital discovered suddenly last week that a distant relative had left her a hundred thousand dollars.

"How does it feel to be an heiress?" she was asked.

"I was so nervous and excited," admitted the nurse, "I had to ask two expectant fathers to calm me down."

★ ★ ★

A little poem I like is called "Infant Prodigy." It's by Margaret Fishback (I like her, too). It goes:

> At six weeks Baby grinned a grin
> That spread from mouth to eyes to chin,
> And Doc, the smartie, had the brass
> To tell me it was only gas!

★ ★ ★

A German couple had fourteen daughters, all of whose names began with a "B" except the very newest. They named her Alice.

"Run out of names beginning with 'B'?" smiled the census taker. "*Ach,* no," sighed the mother, "but when they told Pop it was still another girl he cried, *'Das ist alles.'* "

★ ★ ★

Jean Kerr, author of *Please Don't Eat the Daisies,* isn't fooled by the charms of her seventeen-month-old son Gilbert, since his three older brothers have taught her what to expect. "It's too early to tell yet about Gilbert," she notes. "As a matter of fact, we can tell, all right, but we're not ready to face it. Once upon a time we might have been taken in by smiles and gurgles and round blue eyes, but no more. We know he is just biding his time. Today he can't do much more than eat his shoelaces and suck off an occasional button. Tomorrow the world. . . ."

★ ★ ★

"The first lesson," notes Emily Kimbrough, "that a babe learns at his mother's knee nowadays is to be very careful of her stockings."

★ ★ ★

Little Janet had never been on a farm before. Left to her own devices for a spell, she came tumbling into the house in great excitement and cried, "Come quick, Mamma! There's a wonderful big pig lying on the ground and seven little pigs are blowing her up!"

★ ★ ★

Mother dashed into the nursery when she heard her five-year-old howling. His baby sister, it developed, was pulling his hair.

"Never mind," she counseled the lad. "Your baby sister doesn't know that it hurts you."

A couple of minutes later Mother had to come back to the nursery. This time the baby was bawling.

"What's the matter with the baby?" she demanded.

"Nothing much," replied the five-year-old calmly. "Only now she knows."

★ ★ ★

A visitor to a Beverly Hills mansion found himself alone with the four-year-old son of the house, kindergarten student in a progressive school. "What are you studying now?" asked the visitor. The answer was, "I'm majoring in sandpile."

★ ★ ★

A Wisconsin furniture emporium inserted this plaintive ad in a local gazette: "Will the mother whose little boy laid his half-sucked lollipop on a mahogany end table please come in again? She can have the end table for exactly one dollar, with the lollipop still intact."

★ ★ ★

Five-year-old Peter came home from his first day at kindergarten to face a quiz from his father. "Do you like the other boys in the class?" "You bet." "And the girls?" Peter registered disgust. "Come now," pleaded Papa. "You like Judy just a little, don't you?"

Peter registered astonishment. "Don't tell me," he pleaded, "that Judy is a GIRL!"

11. BANQUETS AND DINNER PARTIES

It's a funny thing about dinner parties.

One evening, when you've decided to pay off obligations to a collection of clunks, and moan beforehand to your wife, "I'd give my right arm to have this party over and done with," something ignites a spark, and everybody, including yourself, has a rousing good time.

Another evening, when you've assembled a star-spangled cast and everybody is expecting one of the galas of the season, the party never gets off the ground. Almost immediately after the last guest has swept grandly—and forty minutes late—into the drawing room, you know you're about to go under for the third time.

There *are* ways, however, to plug those dismal gaps, when, as though by prearrangement, all conversation at a dinner table suddenly comes to a halt.

Broadcaster Paul Gibson turns to the grumpiest-looking gent at the table and asks loudly, "How's that big project of yours coming along?" If the party addressed hasn't *got* a big project under way, chances are ten to one he'll invent one on the spot—and first thing you know all the other VIP's present are clamoring for attention.

Editor Albert Erskine has a more subtle approach. He gazes soulfully at a new dinner partner and announces, "I can tell by the look in your eyes that you've had a soul-shattering experience in the past six months." This gambit has never failed.

A socialite friend of mine stirred one dinner party out of its lethargy by proposing, "Let's all take turns telling how our parents met." This game progressed splendidly until one guest refused to participate. Too late, everybody remembered that his birth had set off a front-page scandal, some thirty years earlier.

Playwright Ruth Goetz inspired a theatrically minded group by demanding opening lines of a play that would be bad enough to send seatholders screaming into the streets. Examples:

1. A plantation in Malaya. Man in soiled whites slumps over brandy bottle. Wife cocks head and asks slowly, "DO THOSE DRUMS MEAN ANYTHING TO YOU?"

2. Woman in flowing robe, hair down, leans far back against pillar of a temple and announces, "ZEUS IS ANGRY!"

3. Woman at table in a saloon indicates old bum teetering at bar and whispers, "HE USED TO BE A GREAT SURGEON."

4. Man in colonial costume enters empty set and calls up into the wings, "HURRY DOWN, MY DEAR. BENJAMIN FRANKLIN AND ALEXANDER HAMILTON ARE COMING FOR DINNER."

John O'Hara added another line that makes him reach automatically for his hat. It's the dogged detective demanding, "BUT HOW DID YOU KNOW SHE WAS STABBED? THERE HAD BEEN NO MENTION OF THE MANNER IN WHICH SHE MET HER DEATH!"

★ ★ ★

Winston Churchill offers this advice to banquet speakers (and I fervently hope that a lot of them will heed it!): "Say what you have to say and the first time you come to a sentence with a grammatical ending, sit down!"

Judge Jacob Braude adds this reminder: "All work and no plagiarism usually makes a mighty dull speech."

George Jessel, toastmaster at so many banquets he's thinking of calling his autobiography *Dais without End*, concludes this advisory paragraph with, "If you haven't struck oil in your first three minutes, *stop boring!*"

★ ★ ★

Jessel, officiating at one banquet, announced proudly, "And now, that hero of heroes, Admiral Nimitz, master of all our great ships at sea. Just two words, please, Admiral Nimitz."

The admiral confined his answer to the exact two words requested. They were: "Name's King."

★ ★ ★

A London dinner table conversation relayed by Frederico Babcock: "Being a publisher must be a very pleasant job." "Yes." "You must meet such interesting people." "Yes." "And what thrills you must get!" "Yes." "I mean, when you discover a brand-new writer." "Yes." "A few, I guess, turn out to be failures." "Yes." "But there's always a chance of spotting another *Gone with the Wind*." "Yes." "That must be terribly exciting." "Yes." "I suppose it's largely a matter of luck, but flair comes into it, too, doesn't it?" "Yes." "I daresay you have to read plenty of rubbish." "Yes." "Boring for you." "Yes." "But you wouldn't change your job, would you?" "Yes." "Well, I mustn't waste any more of your time, must I?" "No."

★ ★ ★

What do you write when a hostess suddenly thrusts a guest book and a leaky pen into your hand? Joan Crawford solved just such a problem at a Hollywood dinner party recently. She wrote in a bold, flowing hand: "The drapes in your bedroom need cleaning. Sincerely, J.C."

★ ★ ★

George De Witt explains the difference between an after-dinner speaker and a toastmaster. "An after-dinner speaker," he says, "makes a speech when there's a half of a grapefruit on the table, whereas a toastmaster won't make a speech unless the half of grapefruit has a maraschino cherry in the center."

★ ★ ★

The new ghost writer for a Hollywood tycoon received this anguished appeal: "Please don't use such long words for my next banquet speech. I like to know what the hell I'm talking about!"

"Propaganda," ventured Walter Lippmann at a banquet in Washington, "is that branch of lying which often deceives your friends without ever deceiving your enemies."

At the same affair, a bitter author confided, "My publisher is so crooked that every time I shake hands with him I count my fingers." And another well-known man-about-town mourned, "My wife lost her head and ran out of the house Tuesday night—but then I lost mine and let her back in."

The things a man hears at a big banquet! I only miss them when I can think up an acceptable excuse!

★ ★ ★

"This here town has been mighty good to me," boomed the guest of honor at a reception signalizing his fifty years of service to the community. "When I first arrived here, I was an inexperienced tenderfoot with only one suit on my back and all my worldly possessions wrapped in a red bandanna over my shoulder. Today I own the bank, the newspaper, the two hotels, nine oil wells, and the TV station!"

Later an impressed visitor asked, "Would you tell us just what was in that red bandanna when you arrived here fifty years ago?"

"Let's see now," mused the guest of honor. "If I recall rightly, I was carrying about $400,000 in cash, and $750,000 in negotiable securities."

★ ★ ★

They were honoring Lord Macauley in London for fifty years of distinguished service to the crown. Macauley began his speech of acknowledgment with these sad words: "Gentlemen, I understand that Man inherited three basic vices. I must report to you that I quit one, and one quit me—but I still smoke."

★ ★ ★

A United States senator was regaling a banquet audience one evening when a heckler disturbed the smooth flow of his oratory.

The senator frowned, and spoke as follows: "When I was a lad back on the farm, my dad once gave me for my birthday a wonderful little donkey. 'This is a mighty fine animal,' he told me, 'and I expect you to treat it accordingly. See that he's properly fed, curried down, and bedded. And always end up by locking the barn door.'

"Well, gentlemen, there came an evening, unfortunately, when I forgot to lock the barn door. The donkey walked out and got himself run over by a truck. My dad looked sadly at the carcass and said, 'Son, that animal's going to haunt you for the rest of your life.' And my dad sure hit the nail on the head."

The senator pointed to the heckler and concluded, "There sits that jackass now!"

★ ★ ★

When prominent bookstores feature in their windows more manuals on dieting than cookbooks, it's a sure sign that people's troubles are spreading—especially in the midsection! Folks no longer worry about what they're going to eat for dinner, but what they're NOT going to eat for dinner. This makes for better figures but worse farm surpluses. You can't even call it a pretty kettle of fish. Too many calories!

Jackie Gleason says it's come to a point where somebody is constantly taking the starch out of him, teaching him to say "No more, thank you," and reminding him that it isn't the minutes that pile up the poundage, but the *seconds*. Gleason found the Rockefeller Diet the most trying of all. He kept choking on all those shiny new dimes. Now he's found a solution to his weighty problem, however: He eats as much as he pleases and he drinks as much as he pleases. He just doesn't swallow.

★ ★ ★

A visitor from *la belle France* informs us that our food is not only too abundant but too *clean*. "Those spotless, antiseptic kitchens of yours," he exclaims, wrinkling his nose with distaste. "We

French have learned that it is a little bit of dirt that gives our roasts and sauces their special tang and *je-ne-sais-quoi!*"

★ ★ ★

Attending a dinner party while he was on vacation, a stoutish gentleman suffered a sudden attack of indigestion, and sought help from the one and only village doctor. "Eat nothing but meat for the next week," was the doctor's surprising suggestion. "Go down to Joe's butcher shop and load up on chops, steaks, fillets— stuff like that." "Will this cure me?" asked the vacationist anxiously. "Darned if I know," admitted the doctor, "but it sure will make my brother Joe happy."

★ ★ ★

Another doctor had to cope with a formidable lady and her hen- pecked husband. "The minute he gets out of my sight at a dinner party," she complained, "he eats starches he isn't supposed to. They make him whistle through his teeth all night in his sleep."

"Are you certain it's he who's doing the whistling?" asked the doctor. "Am I certain?" echoed the lady angrily. "This morning when he woke up there were eleven dogs sitting on his stomach."

12. BARBERS

Are you one of those unfortunate males who have to shave off a tough beard every morning? You'll notice Shakespeare never bothered with nonsense like that. That's why they called him the Beard of Avon.

Poughkeepsie's Smith Brothers had no time for shaving, either. They were too busy swelling their coughers. And how they had to shout! It was difficult to hear when they spoke above a whisker.

Remington Rand, whose interest in beards coincided with their introduction of an electric razor, have opened a Shaver Museum in Bridgeport, Connecticut. It's a formidable collection of blades, pincers, gouges, bones, sharks' teeth, and clam shells. Whisker removing obviously was one of the greatest punishments our ancestors ever inflicted on themselves. The little shaver of 1960 doesn't know how good he has it!

When even peaches and clothes brushes are shaved daily (on TV), face foliage is an unusual sight. Back in the days of Babylon, however, men held their beards in such high esteem that no oath was considered binding unless sworn on the chin whiskers. And the Pharaohs, when too busy pyramiding their prophets to grow beards, strapped on false ones, made of gold and silver wire, to insure the respect of the populace.

Soap never was a problem to the ancients. The Gauls concocted soap from tallow and wood ashes. A soap factory over two thousand years old was discovered in the excavations of Pompeii.

Alexander the Great was the first leader to order his legions into battle clean-shaven—lest the enemy grab their beards, tilt their heads back, and make further shaving quite unnecessary.

Beards achieved a genuine comeback—a final "hay-day," as it were—in Victorian England, where gallants were so afraid of disarranging their precious whiskers, they encased them in jeweled "protective" sheaths before vaulting into their four-posters for a night's sleep.

The doom of the beard can be laid to adequate razors. Best of the early ones were made by the Chinese, presumably searching for something deadlier than gunpowder. One mandarin slit the throats of three offspring with his newly perfected razor—a plain case of heir removal. A single Korean fob in the Shaver Museum contains five delicately wrought shaving pieces, including a razor, a tweezer, and a gouge.

Forerunner of the electric razor of 1959 was a contraption patented in London in 1790. It looks like an overgrown Swiss cheese. The shaver ventured into a circular room which was surrounded by a moatlike corridor. In this corridor, by putting his face to any one of sixty portholes, he would be shaved—and how!—by razors attached to a big wheel which was activated by a melancholy donkey. With this elaborate setup, in other words, there was an ass at each end. The game finally was called on account of blood.

★ ★ ★

"One more increase in the price of haircuts," threatens Perry Como, "and television may lose me forever."

★ ★ ★

McKeever's Corners, Maine, boasts a hard-working citizen who tends a wealthy New Yorker's estate in the daytime and serves as town barber after dark. What's more, one sign serves him for both jobs. It reads, "Otis Elroy, Head Gardener."

★ ★ ★

And a Times Square tonsorial parlor advertises:

"SIX BARBERS

CONTINUOUS DISCUSSION"

★ ★ ★

A story calculated to razor eyebrows a notch or two concerns a wife who poked her head into the bathroom where her husband was shaving, and announced, "I want to try out the new color film in my camera. CUT YOURSELF!"

★ ★ ★

Walter Pidgeon has a baffling answer for those eager-beaver barbers who hold up a mirror behind him after a haircut and ask, "Is this just the way you want it, sir?" Pidgeon takes a long, hard look, then says, "Not quite. A little longer in the back, please."

★ ★ ★

CBS's tonsorial expert, Dr. Kayser, is absorbed in his laboratory perfecting a fluid which he expects to produce under the name of "Tame Root Hair Oil." It's for pipsqueaks with tame hair roots who long to have locks as wild and unruly as some of the new movie he-men and TV sheriffs and desperadoes. Tame Root, promises Dr. Kayser, will come in four grades: Regular, Strong, Stronger, and Leopold Stokowski.

★ ★ ★

Young Glenmore had completed his course in the barber college and as part of his final exam was shaving the principal. Suddenly he stopped to ask, "I say, Dr. Schlitz, was your necktie red when you sat down?" "No, my boy," said Dr. Schlitz. "It was green." Glenmore threw down his razor and said, "I resign."

13. BASEBALL

Ex-pitching great, Dizzy Dean, thinks that the big-league ball-player of today is too soft and peaceable. "The Cards had one pitcher," he claims, "who won fourteen straight games in a period of twenty-four days. Then when he lost his fifteenth game, 1–0, the manager fined him fifty bucks!"

"What baseball needs," Diz told reporter John Lardner, "is wild men like we used to have on the old St. Louis Cards—the gashouse gang—such as me, Rip Collins, Pepper Martin, Frank Frisch, and them." "What was the salary scale in those days?" asked Lardner. "That," explained Dizzy Dean, "is what drove us wild."

★ ★ ★

Dean tells this story on himself. When he was pitching for an Arkansas hillbilly nine in his salad days, a rival outfit, determined to undo him, sprinkled broken glass around the mound. Diz, barefoot, hurled six shutout innings without a squawk, but then he stalked over to the rival manager and grumbled, "Joe, you just gotta get this broken glass away from here. It's cuttin' up the ball!"

★ ★ ★

Rube Waddell was not only one of the greatest southpaws in the history of big-league baseball, but one of its most eccentric and unpredictable characters. Fined a hundred dollars by a thoroughly exasperated manager, Waddell, the picture of injured innocence, demanded, "What did I do now?" "The fine," explained the manager, "is for that disgraceful hotel episode in Detroit."

"You're a liar," shouted Waddell. "There *ain't* no Hotel Episode in Detroit."

★ ★ ★

"I know they're hanging up new baseball records every season," admits Lefty Gomez, one-time pitching great of the New York Yankees, "but they don't seem able to break my record for the longest home run ever hit in the Stadium. Jimmy Foxx hit it off me!"

★ ★ ★

A few facts from the latest edition of the Official Encyclopedia of Baseball:

Commonest name of big-league ballplayers: Smith. There have been eighty-two of them to date.

Among the cities that at one time or another have held big-league franchises are, believe it or not, Altoona, Elizabeth, Keokuk, and Middletown.

The first professional ball team was the Cincinnati Red Stockings. It made money the first year out, too—the stupendous sum of $1.39 net.

Up to the season of 1959, there were 147 no-hit games pitched in the big leagues—and six of them were lost! Biggest heartbreaker was the double no-hitter that Jim Vaughn of the Cubs lost to Fred Toney of the Redlegs in the tenth inning on May 2, 1917.

★ ★ ★

The most conceited rookie who ever went South with the New York Yankees got his chance in a game against the Cardinals at St. Petersburg, and promptly walked the first five men who faced him. Manager Casey Stengel motioned him to the showers and brought in another pitcher.

The rookie slammed his glove to the mound and demanded, "How do you like that? The big jerk takes me out while I got a no-hitter going!"

★ ★ ★

Frank Boyden, headmaster of the Deerfield School, tells about the day a Southern rookie was called up by the Philadelphia Nationals, and reported at the Polo Grounds. The manager said, "Sit next to me on the bench, and I'll point out the fine points of the way baseball is played in the majors."

In the second inning, the Phils had a fleet runner on first, when the next batter slashed a single to right field. The Giants had the great Mel Ott patrolling that sector at the time. Noting that the runner was trying to go from first to third on the hit, Master Mel threw a bullet shot smack into the third baseman's mitt, and the runner was out sliding in.

The Philly manager told the rookie, "He was right to try for third. You won't see a play like that again in a hundred years."

In the eighth inning the same runner was on first, the same batter behind him singled to right, and the same phenomenal Mel Ott threw out the runner trying to take third on the hit.

The Southern rookie shook his head in disbelief and murmured reverently, "Time sure does fly up heah in the North!"

★ ★ ★

A baseball manager sought out his regular third baseman in the locker room. "Joe," he said, putting his arm around the player's shoulder, "it's perfectly O.K. for you to forget all those batting tips I've given you. We just traded you to Kansas City."

★ ★ ★

A new girl in the typists' pool at a big office was cute as a button, but painfully thin. One of the younger V.P.'s decided to take her out to a ball game and then for a big Italian dinner. "The kid looks half starved," he explained.

He never got her past the Yankee Stadium, however. She was wearing an all-beige outfit, and every time the V.P. turned his head, the bat boy handed her to Mickey Mantle.

★ ★ ★

One of the darnedest baseball yarns I ever heard was told by my Mount Kisco neighbor, H. Allen Smith.

In June, 1911, a man sat in the death house of the Nevada State Penitentiary awaiting execution for murder. His name was Pat Casey, and in better days he had been a professional baseball umpire.

His last request? He had one, all right. He wanted to umpire one more ball game.

So the game was arranged. It was played the afternoon before Pat Casey marched forth to his death. Casey called balls and strikes for nine innings—and not once did a convict player dispute a decision.

★ ★ ★

A couple of Yogi Berra's waggish teammates on the New York Yankee ball club swear that one night the stocky catcher was horrified to see a baby toppling off the roof of a cottage across the way from him. He dashed over and made a miraculous catch—but then force of habit proved too much for him. He straightened up and threw the baby to second base.

14. BATTLE OF THE SEXES

Just because James Thurber seemingly has lost interest in "The Battle of the Sexes," a few ludicrous optimists have concluded that that particular cold war is waning. They're wrong.

Indeed, Philosopher Russell Lynes believes that American husbands have become so punch-drunk their shameful status today is that of "part-time wives"—reduced to washing dishes, changing diapers, or flourishing the strings of their barbecue aprons. Nor does Lynes see many prospects for improvement. The poor boobs "have made their bed," he concludes, "and now they must not only lie in them—but make them every morning!"

I do not mean to imply that wives cannot whip up a pretty good case for themselves, too. One disillusioned bride now defines a gentleman as "a man who, when his wife drops something, kicks it over to where she can pick it up easily." A second, who lives on East River Drive, complains that when her husband begins to snore in his real midseason form, all the tugboats start answering. A third greeted her homecoming husband in a new dress she absolutely "adored," only to have him grumble (he was a real surly bird), "Better take off that sailor's blouse. You haven't got the right coast-line for it."

Here are a few other skirmishes and resorts to skulduggery in the unceasing—if stimulating—war between male and female:

1. One back-seat driver is bad enough, but poor Mr. Gruber had to motor all the way from the Bronx to Buffalo with two constant advisers behind him: his wife and his mother-in-law. Along about

Syracuse, the worm finally turned. "Once and for all," he demanded of his wife, "who's driving this hack? You or your mother?"

2. The owner of a small business was saddled with his wife's lazy, fat brother. "He loafs half the time," complained the husband. "So what?" countered the wife. "Half a loafer is better than none."

3. Congratulated on his tenth wedding anniversary, a man sighed to his partner, "You're right: my wife has absolutely everything a man can desire—including muscles and a mustache."

4. A habitual man-about-town (on his fifty-ninth birthday he finally admitted he was on "the threshold of middle age") suddenly turned up at Palm Beach with a bride—young, well rounded, and peroxide blond. "Hooray," cheered a friend. "Where did you dig her up?" "I'm not exactly sure," admitted the M.A.T. "I opened my wallet and there she was."

5. "I can't figure you out," a housewife told her husband angrily. "Monday night you liked beans, Tuesday night you liked beans, Wednesday night you liked beans, and now, all of a sudden, on Thursday night, you DON'T like beans!"

6. "I don't know how it happened," reported the stewardess on a San Francisco-bound plane, "but we seem to have left your wife behind in Chicago." "Thank heaven," exclaimed the husband. "I thought I had gone deaf."

7. A man born in Karachi (that's in Henpakistan) had been seeing too many science-fiction dramas on TV, and he dreamed one night that he and his overbearing wife were suddenly confronted by a huge dragon, breathing fire. The wife, furthermore, propelled him toward the awesome beast. "Don't just stand there," she told him. "SLAY something."

8. One couple have evolved a plan that seems to work. One night a week he goes out with the boys. The other six, she does.

9. A wife complained bitterly, "The fool I married can't drink and he can't play cards." "Are those faults?" chided her pastor. "I wish that none of our young men could drink or play cards." "You don't understand," continued the wife. "My husband *can't*, but he *does*."

10. A formidable lady complained to a cemetery superintendent that she had been unable to locate the grave of her departed husband, Eustace Filbrink. The superintendent consulted his records, and reported, "The only Filbrink we seem to have buried here is Amanda Filbrink." "That's him," she nodded. "Everything's in my name."

*   *   *

A lonely little widow in Los Angeles has one pleasure left in life: every morning a gentleman leaves a rose for her. "It's from his garden," she explained to a visitor. "Here he comes now." Sure enough, the gentleman handed her a beauty. "I grew this one just for you," he said with a gallant bow.

The visitor left with the donor of the rose. "I've never been in a garden in my life," he explained sheepishly. "I buy her a rose in the florist shop across the street every morning. It gives her such a happy look for a few moments!"

*   *   *

A lawyer wired one of his clients: "Your mother-in-law passed away in her sleep last night. Shall we order burial, embalming, or cremation?" The client wired back: "Take no chances, order all three."

*   *   *

Advice to wives from that sage old philosopher, Peter Lind Hayes: "Remember, girls, your hubby still gets a bang out of golf, hunting trips, and all-night poker. Show him you're thinking of him! Speak of them occasionally!"

*   *   *

A dress manufacturer had been henpecked by a shrewish wife for years, and finally mustered sufficient courage to walk out on her. He changed his name, had his nose fixed, dyed his hair, and began life all over again in a city a thousand miles away.

The wife never gave up her search for him, however, and twelve years later tracked him down. He saw her coming and took refuge in the washroom—but she battered down the door, and collared him.

"What's the matter?" he protested weakly. "Can't a man even go to the washroom in peace any more?"

★ ★ ★

WIVES BY THE SCORE:

1. The wife who announced, "I'm leaving my husband. He upsets me so I'm losing weight. The minute I'm down to 112, out I march!"

2. The wife who conceded, "I know I am outspoken." "I can't believe it," gasped her husband. "By whom?"

3. The wife who has something that will knock your eye out: a jealous husband.

4. The deceitful wife whose husband appeared unexpectedly while she was entertaining his best friend. The friend sought shelter in the shower, but the enraged husband spotted him and tore back the shower curtain. Game to the end, the friend commanded, "Close the curtain of this booth! How dare you interfere with my voting?"

5. The wife who told her bridge cronies, "This is my husband's birthday." A friend asked, "What are you getting for him?" The wife answered, "Make me an offer."

6. The wife whose better half didn't forget her while making a "business trip" abroad. "Run around to some smart shops," he wrote her, "and pick out a few nice things for yourself. But don't get caught."

7. The wife who tried a new diet: nothing but coconuts. "Has it made her lose weight?" her husband was asked. "Not a pound," he declared. "But you should see her shinny up a tree!"

8. The wife who came out of the ocean at Palm Beach and announced ecstatically, "The water is divine this morning. Full of men."

9. The wife who shot her husband twelve times. "Why so often?" asked the judge. Her lawyer explained, "She's hard of hearing."

10. The wife who refused the gift of a broadtail coat. "Take it away," she implored. "My husband rather fancies himself as a comedian."

11. The wife who silenced her husband with, "O.K., so I like to spend money. Name one *other* extravagance."

12. The wife who told her husband's secretary, "You look like a million—and I mean every year of it."

13. The wife who believed a modern woman's place is in the home—working out slogans for soaps, soups, and coffee contests.

14. The wife at a brassy nightclub who upbraided her mate, "Why can't you be like other husbands and never take me any place?"

15. The wife who always beats her husband to the withdraw.

16. The wife who sought the help of an analyst. "My husband," she sighed, "goes around telling everybody he's Henry VIII. Is that bad?" "I wouldn't really worry," counseled the analyst, "till he starts calling you Anne Boleyn."

17. The wife whose exhausted spouse told a judge, "I can't go on feeding eight small mouths—and listening to one big one."

18. The wife who sued her husband for bigamy. "I'll teach the rat," she promised, "that he can't have his Kate and Edith, too."

19. The Soviet wife who was shot by her commissar spouse. He nabbed her talking on the telephone ten days before he invented it.

20. The frugal wife who discovered a foolproof way to hold bills down. She switched to a heavier paperweight.

★ ★ ★

As Richard Armour notes in his excellent collection of verse, *Light Armour:*

> Some hoist the windows, gasp for air,
> While others find it chilly.
> Some turn up thermostats a hair,
> While others think them silly.
> Some like it cold, some like it hot,

Some freeze while others smother.
And by some fiendish, fatal plot,
They marry one another.

★ ★ ★

New York's most sadistic wife tantalizer was sunning himself on the stoop of his private brownstone when he called to his wife, "Come quick if you want to see the woman Frank Collins is mad about." His wife dropped everything and rushed out to "get the goods" on her old neighbor. "Where?" she demanded. "That lady there in the beaver coat," said her husband.

"You must be out of your head," cried she. "That's Frank Collins' wife."

"Of course," he nodded, with a fiendish chuckle.

★ ★ ★

A grumpy deacon was complaining about the short dresses being worn by young girls in his town. "What would people say," he asked the leading banker, "if it was your wife who was gallivantin' around in shorts?" "I imagine they'd say," sighed the banker, "that I must have married her for her money."

★ ★ ★

"Of course I trust my husband," maintained the wife of a celebrated matinee idol stoutly, "and would you like to know why? Because I never let the so-and-so out of my sight!"

★ ★ ★

To end this section on a more upbeat, romantic note, there's a story about a very lovely young lady, wise beyond her years, who was conducting a course in short story writing in a Southern university.

In the middle of a lecture on technique, a man—all-American fullback type—burst unannounced into the room, swept her into his arms, kissed her, and walked out without uttering a word. The teacher straightened her hair and said, "Well, boys, there's the last paragraph of a story for you. Now you write the beginning."

15. BOOKS

Dave Randall, now librarian at Indiana University in Blooming-ton, was once the head of Scribner's rare book department. Item one on his agenda was persuading the persnickety owner of one of the thirteen original copies of the Declaration of Independence to part with same.

The owner capitulated suddenly one Friday, and the next morn-ing Randall motored triumphantly to Greenwich, Connecticut, where the old gentleman handed him a beautiful morocco slipcase in exchange for a check.

"But, Mr. Randall," demurred the old gentleman, "this check is not certified."

"It's not my check," declared Randall, "it's Mr. Scribner's."

"Can't help that," snapped the old gentleman. "No way to do business. And what were you intending to do with my irreplacea-ble document until Monday?"

"I was going to take it back to my house."

"Might easily burn down."

"Well, it hasn't for 150 years," snapped Randall, growing im-patient.

"Young man, that won't stop it from burning down tomorrow. I will bring the document in to Scribner's by train on Monday—in-sured all the way—and then you will hand me a certified check."

"How cautious can you get?" muttered Randall to himself as he drove off empty-handed.

But it was an amply vindicated, satisfied old man who handed over the precious document on Monday morning and collected his certified check. For just twelve hours earlier, Mr. Randall's 150-year-old house had burned to the ground.

★ ★ ★

A clerk in a Fifth Avenue bookstore had a disquieting brush with a well-dressed lady in the rare book department recently. "How is this volume bound?" she inquired. "Genuine calf," said the clerk. "How was that again?" "Calf—genuine calf." "WHAT did you say?" she persisted. The clerk threw back his head, closed his eyes, and roared, "MOO." The lady settled for a first edition of *Sanctuary*.

★ ★ ★

"What the book industry needs," a wise Forty-second Street retailer wrote to a publisher last week, "is a good five-cent illustrated sex manual."

★ ★ ★

Mort Sahl swears he saw a lurid paperback in a drugstore rack that pictured a scantily clad siren on the jacket and bore the title *Take My Flesh*. In much, much smaller type the publisher admitted, "This book was published in its hardbound edition under the name of *Principles of Accounting*."

★ ★ ★

In a Stamford bookshop a couple came upon twenty-five copies of Homer's *Odyssey*. "I wonder why they stock that book so heavily?" observed the wife. The husband surmised, "Probably a local author."

★ ★ ★

There's a bookseller in Chicago, says Irv Kupcinet, who's a genuine, fourteen-carat pessimist. He's always building dungeons in the air.

★ ★ ★

Edward Streeter, author of the memorable *Father of the Bride*, has a new winner called *Mr. Robbins Rides Again*, the dedicatory page of which reads, "To Judy . . . stubborn ingrate that she is . . . I love her still." Judy, in case you are puzzled, is a horse—possibly the first nag in history to whom a best-seller ever has been dedicated.

★ ★ ★

Peter DeVries' novel, *Mackerel Plaza*, received consistent huzzahs from the critics, but one of them voiced a serious objection. "DeVries' sense of humor," he maintained, "deserted him when he named his hero. What's so funny about the name Mackerel?" The name of the critic who raised this point, incidentally, is Pickerell.

★ ★ ★

The newly published Thirteenth—and Centennial—Edition of *Bartlett's Familiar Quotations* is the best and biggest yet: 1,068 pages, to be exact, with over 110,000 entries. Among the authors included for the first time are Douglas MacArthur, J. Frank Dobie, William Faulkner, Adlai Stevenson, and Dylan Thomas.

John Bartlett didn't know what he was starting when, in 1855, he allowed himself to be persuaded to bring out in a 295-page book the collection of noteworthy quotations he had been amassing privately over the years. Cautiously, he limited the first edition to a thousand copies, and sold most of them himself at his bookstore opposite the Harvard yard. Returned from a hitch in the Navy during the Civil War, Bartlett joined the publishing house of Little, Brown. By the time he died in 1905—at the age of eighty-five—his compendium had made not only his own fortune but those of Little and Brown as well.

★ ★ ★

When a new book on cats hit the bookstalls, one enthusiastic bibliophile sold his entire stock in two hours and reordered a hundred copies more. The publisher wired: "100 more cats on the way. Are your customers mice or men?"

★ ★ ★

A publisher in Indianapolis received an unsolicited manuscript entitled, "How to Make Your Own Mink Coat." Opening line: "First catch sixty-two minks."

★ ★ ★

A publisher's favorite of the year's top cartoons shows an obviously delighted surgeon standing over a patient on the operating table and telling the other doctors, "Gentlemen, this is Mr. Hellman, author of that best-selling exposé, *All Doctors Are Quacks.*"

★ ★ ★

In the reference library of the large and prosperous publishing house of Doubleday and Company, there is a copy of a special edition of Edwin Markham's *The Man with the Hoe,* with illustrations by Howard Pyle, published way back in 1900. Written on the flyleaf is this inscription, by the then boss man of the firm, F. N. Doubleday: "This edition was made to please the author and get his next book. It did neither."

★ ★ ★

Harry Hershfield had a disillusioning visit with a pompous old publisher recently. The publisher interrupted Harry in the middle of one of his best anecdotes to upbraid his butler. "How many times," he yelled, "have I told you how to take one of my books out of the bookcase? *Always blow the dust off first.*"

★ ★ ★

A lady tentatively tapped a librarian in Pittsburgh recently and said she wanted to pay for a book she had borrowed three weeks previous and could not return. "No need to do that," counseled the librarian. "Even if you keep it another month the charges won't equal the cost of the book." "I'm afraid it's gone for good," sighed the lady. "You see, when Grandpa died, we put the book under his beard to prop up his chin, and forgot to get it out before he was buried."

★ ★ ★

The dignified representative of an old Boston publishing house was exhibiting his spring line to a West Coast bookseller when a clerk, climbing a rickety ladder to fetch a rarely requested volume, upset a pyramided display on top of the shelving. Books cascaded down upon the poor representative's noggin, sending him, dazed and bloody, to the floor. "Be careful, you fool," shouted the bookseller to the clerk. "Suppose that had been a customer!"

★ ★ ★

The Princeton University Store sold so many books about birds last year that they decided to add a sideline: an Audubon Birdcaller, which retails at $1.25. It has delighted the customers, too— all but one, that is, who reported bitterly, "I have used your birdcaller faithfully now for three days—and the only answers I get back are from squirrels."

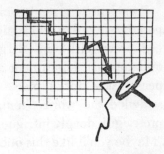

16. BUSINESS

Working nineteen hours a day or marrying the boss's daughter are not the only ways to get rich quick. A clever tobacconist in Tel Aviv, for instance, has amassed a fortune in less than a year. He invented a gefüllte-tipped cigarette. A Michigan confectioner also hit the jackpot with a new candy bar diet-conscious fatties can eat with impunity. Its deceptive chocolate covering conceals a center of solid lettuce. And a TV producer in Ireland has just come up with a quiz program that's captured the entire Irish nation. It's called "Dublin or Nothing."

They had to put a Madison Avenue billing clerk away for mental care last week. He kept hearing strange invoices.

The advertising manager of a big shirt company spent seven weeks selecting the right secretary for himself. He knows it pays to have a good head on your shoulder.

A mighty tycoon came stamping out of his private office in a fine rage the other afternoon. "They're going to have to do something about those eight phones on my desk," he thundered. "I've just been speaking to myself for nearly five minutes!"

The head of a big corporation handed out cigars to everybody one morning. "My son," he exulted, "made his first dollar yesterday since he got out of college six months ago. He sold the watch we gave him for graduation."

Complaint from the head of the research department of a billion-dollar pharmaceutical corporation: "If only we could invent things in our laboratories one-tenth as quickly as they do in our publicity department!"

President of a steel combine to his board of directors: "All opposed to my plan will signify by saying 'I resign.'"

A pretty girl is in charge of the fountain-pen department in a Philadelphia department store. A prospect picked up one of the pens, asked for a piece of scratch paper, and experimentally scrawled the words *"tempus fugit"* several times thereon. The pretty girl, deeply intrigued, handed him another pen, suggesting, "Maybe you'll like this one better, Mr. Fugit."

★ ★ ★

The sales manager of a fast-growing outfit sticks pins in a big relief map behind his desk to show where every one of his salesmen is at a given moment. Ragsdale, of the New England sector, was not, in the opinion of the manager, living up to his early promise, and was summoned to the home office for a pep talk and reindoctrination. "I'm not saying you're in imminent danger yet of being fired," was the stern finale of the sales manager's warning, "but if you'll look carefully at my map, Ragsdale, you'll note I've loosened your pin!"

★ ★ ★

A mighty magnesium magnate summoned a timid, long-time employee to his inner sanctum and bellowed, "What's this I hear about your praying in church for a raise? Don't you know I never stand for anybody going over my head?"

★ ★ ★

BUSINESS AS USUAL:

A harassed manufacturer phoned his wife at 5:30 P.M. to report, "Four important customers simply won't leave, and I guess I'll just have to ask them for dinner. Go out and get the biggest damn squab you can find!"

A new secretary ended her first day on the job by inquiring of the bookkeeper, "Doesn't that sourpuss boss of yours ever laugh out loud?" "Only," sighed the bookkeeper, "if we ask him for a raise."

An office manager shot his newest wage slave a scathing look, and rasped, "I don't know how you managed it, Wimpfheimer, but you've only been here four weeks and already you're six months behind in your work!"

A big-shot magnate was on the verge of committing suicide until he discovered that the cleaning woman had hung the graph behind his desk upside down.

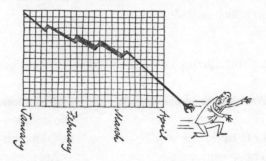

A cautious garment manufacturer was asked if he intended to invest any money in his son-in-law's new business. "Confidentially," he replied, "I'd rather trust a rabbit to deliver a head of lettuce."

Employees of a big sardine plant struck for higher pay recently. Pickets' signs proclaimed angrily, "We've been canned too!"

A little shop featuring materials used in ladies' dresses has opened in Tulsa, Oklahoma. It's called "The Tulle Shed."

A department head looked really apologetic. "Honest, Wilkins," he said soothingly, "I wouldn't wake you if it wasn't important. You're fired."

★ ★ ★

A pompous lady stamped into an elevator and declared, "I'm in a great hurry, young man. Take me right up to the ninth floor."

"Whom do you wish to see on that floor?" asked the operator.

"What business is that of yours?" countered the lady.

"None, madam," admitted the operator, "but there are only eight floors in this building."

"I know one way to get a raise out of that stingy boss of yours," insisted a nagging wife to her spouse. "Play on his sympathies. Tell him about your nine children, the sick mother you have to sit up with two nights a week, and how you have to wash all the dishes because we can't afford a maid."

The husband promised to try. That night the wife demanded, "Did you get that raise?"

"On the contrary," sighed the husband. "The boss fired me. He said I had too many outside activities."

★ ★ ★

Frightening statistical chart circulated at a recent convention of realtors:

"Population of the U.S.A.	175,000,000
Those over 65	60,000,000
Left to do the work	115,000,000
Those under 21	57,000,000
Left to do the work	58,000,000
Government employed	26,000,000
L.T.D.T.W.	32,000,000
In the armed forces	4,000,000
L.T.D.T.W.	28,000,000
In state or city jobs	24,000,000
L.T.D.T.W.	4,000,000
In hospitals or asylums	3,700,000
L.T.D.T.W.	300,000
Bums who *won't* work	299,998

"That leaves two to do the work—you and me—and I'm getting tired!"

★ ★ ★

"I'm reading here," a schoolboy told his father, "about a boy who started as a bootblack and wound up with ten million dollars."

"Ten million dollars!" echoed the father. "He couldn't have used much polish."

★ ★ ★

Sears, Roebuck has reproduced on microfilm its annual mail-order catalogues, the first of which bears an 1888 dateline. The 140,000 pages thus assembled give a graphic picture of the changing tastes of the American public—not to mention the diminishing value of the American dollar. A five-piece parlor set in an early Sears catalogue bore a price tag of $22.90; a man's fine Sunday suit was listed at $11.00. Whole pages were devoted to celluloid collars, portable bathtubs, and fancy mustache cups. Kitchen stoves and porch furniture showed a distinct trace of the Spanish Inquisition. Men's pajamas were introduced tentatively in 1899, but, in the parlance of *Variety*, they laid an egg, and did not reappear until 1908.

★ ★ ★

It's a far cry from the "mechanical marvels" described in early Sears catalogues to the electric computing machines now coming off the line in a big Dayton factory. One new model, boasted an official, can duplicate the exact workings of a man's mind. "Prove it," demanded a skeptical prospect.

Out of the wings there undulated a ravishing blonde. The machine stopped clicking, and emitted a long, appreciative whistle. "I'm convinced," said the skeptic. "Ship me two dozen!"

★ ★ ★

Employers he meets nowadays, grumbles Stubby Kaye, are the kind who are looking only for alert young men between the ages of twenty-five and thirty-five—with forty years of experience.

★ ★ ★

If a man really is made of the right stuff, insists paper magnate Sam Himmell, a certain amount of disappointment and failure serve only to toughen his hide and spur him on to fresh endeavor. "The best baseball team in the world," he points out, "loses fifty to sixty games a season. Babe Ruth struck out more than anybody. Three of F. W. Woolworth's first five chain stores failed and Cyrus H. K. Curtis lost $800,000 on *The Saturday Evening Post* before he could turn a single penny of profit. Abraham Lincoln suffered successive failures and was beaten badly in five different elections before becoming one of our greatest Presidents."

★ ★ ★

Somebody in the upper echelon of a California aircraft plant had sufficient sense of humor to post this notice on the bulletin board:

"To all Employees: Due to increased competition and a keen desire to avoid bankruptcy, we find it necessary to institute a new policy. Effective immediately, we are asking that somewhere between starting and quitting time and without infringing too much on the time devoted to lunch period, coffee breaks, rest period, storytelling, ticket selling, golfing, auto racing, vacation planning, and rehashing of yesterday's TV programs that each employee try to find some time that can be set aside and be known as *The Work Break.*

"To some, this may seem to be a radical innovation, but we honestly believe the idea has possibilities. It may even keep us all in business a few years longer! *The Management.*"

★ ★ ★

One executive who read the above notice thought the boss had gone a bit too far. "You're taking this setback too hard," he counseled. "Cheer up! Business will perk up! If you have a misfortune, look it right in the face and laugh at it!"

"I wouldn't dare," admitted the boss. "She outweighs me by thirty pounds."

★ ★ ★

What makes a woman march resolutely into a store to buy something? Margaret Kennedy lists these eight reasons: (1) Because her husband says she can't have it. (2) It will make her look thinner. (3) It comes from Paris. (4) Her neighbors can't afford it. (5) Nobody has one. (6) Everybody has one. (7) It's different, and (8) (Most likely) "Because."

★ ★ ★

A businessman, already rated a millionaire by his friends, continued slaving sixty hours a week, and hadn't taken a vacation in ten years. "Why do you keep on making more and more money?" demanded his doctor. "I'm just curious," explained the businessman, *to see if there's some income my wife can't live beyond.*

★ ★ ★

A representative from the U. S. Internal Revenue Department phoned the head of a big charitable organization. "I note," he said, "that a manufacturer named Ignatz Zilch reports that he donated ten thousand dollars to your charity last year. Did he?" "Not yet," was the jubilant reply, "BUT HE WILL!"

★ ★ ★

Returned traveler from the Caribbean reports that the American-Spanish dictionaries in rooms of the new, ultraswank, ultraexpensive international hotels conspicuously underline such phrases as "Is this deductible?" and "Is it O.K. to charge this to my expense account?"

★ ★ ★

The tax bureau at Albany received a letter from an anonymous taxpayer admitting he had cheated on his income tax for three successive years, and was so bothered by his conscience he couldn't sleep. His letter concluded, "I enclose fifty dollars. If I still can't sleep, I'll send the balance."

★ ★ ★

How to fight your way upward in the world of commerce is a subject fruitfully explored by Stephen Potter in his "one-upmanship." "Be the first in the office every morning," he advises, "the last to leave at night, never take a day off, slave through the lunch hour, and the inevitable day will dawn when the boss will summon you and say, 'I've been watching your work very carefully, Francis. Just what the hell are you up to, anyhow?'"

★ ★ ★

A plumber left a big party and climbed into a taxicab. "Take us to the Waldorf," he ordered the driver. "You're alone," the latter pointed out. "Where's your girl friend?" The plumber clapped a hand to his forehead. "Gadzooks," he exclaimed, "I've forgotten my wench."

★ ★ ★

Two Elm Street store owners had just negotiated sizable loans at the local bank, and were now eating lunch together. "I hope conditions improve soon," worried one. "If they don't, I guess I'll have to *rob* a bank." "If conditions don't improve soon," snapped the other, "I HAVE robbed a bank."

★ ★ ★

Gravely ill, and fighting for breath in an oxygen tent, a doughty old merchant sent for his only son, Ira, with whom he had not seen eye to eye for many a moon. Ira turned up promptly, however, looking very concerned.

"You're a good boy to come, Ira," wheezed the old man, "and before I die, I want to admit to you that maybe I've been too strict and set in my ways. I forgot too often that boys will be boys. But I'm making it up to you. When I'm gone, every cent I've got will be yours. So will you forgive me?"

A tear coursed down Ira's cheek. "Of course I forgive you, Papa," he said earnestly. "I forgive you for every insult you heaped on my head and every walloping you gave me. Pass on to the great beyond in peace, Papa! But first, isn't there one little thing I can do for you?"

"There certainly is," rasped Papa. "Take your big foot off that oxygen hose!"

★ ★ ★

A parting hint from sportswear king Alfred Shapiro: "Nothing improves a joke more than telling it to your employees!"

17. CAMPUS HUMOR

When Marcus Aurelius became Emperor of Rome in A.D. 161, and noted in his *Meditations* that "everything is the result of change," he could not have envisaged the flowering of the college humorous magazine.

For "change" is a word that does not exist in the lexicon of bright undergraduate editors. Stories that were good enough to make their fathers laugh in 1934, they reason—not to mention their great-grandfathers in 1891—should certainly suffice for a Freshman squirt with the appalling numerals "1963" on his cap! And, speaking as an old editor of the *Columbia Jester* myself, I think they're absolutely right.

So out of the yellowing files come old favorites in the endless struggle for revival.

To compound the slight to good Emperor Marcus' memory, one Midwestern editor risked another Pun-ic War by exhuming: Q. How did Aurelius get to Rome? A. The Stoic brought him. You'll have to be a Stoic yourself to survive these other collegiate remembrances of strings past.

"Coise it," muttered the villain, as the heroine wiggled out of the hold he had around the heroine's waist. "Wrong again," chortled the heroine. "It's a goidle."

"She's a nicely reared girl, don't you think?" "Right-o—and not bad from the front either."

PATRON TO WAITER: "I'll have some fish, but kindly omit the Napoleon. I refer to the bony part."

"I got shot while hunting last fall." "Have a scar?" "No, thanks, I don't smoke."

"What did Dad say when you asked for my hand?" "He fell on my neck and cried like a baby."

HE: "I'll have you know I play badminton." SHE: "Yes, and you play worse tennis."

AD IN CAMPUS DAILY: "*For sale*: Beautiful home overlooking nudist colony. Must sacrifice due to failing eyesight."

SOPH: "Now I know why my roommate's steady date reminds me of a switchboard. When she walks, all her lines are busy!"

A car pulled alongside a stranded coupe, and the kindly driver of said car called, "Outa gas?" "Nope." "Tire down?" "Nope; didn't have to."

Paul Revere paused at the first farmhouse he spotted in his famous ride and asked the colonial beauty who came to the door, "Is your husband at home?" "He is," she answered. "O.K.," ordered Revere. "Tell him to get up and defend himself. The British are coming." At the second, third, and fourth farmhouses virtually the same conversation ensued, but there was a variation at the fifth house. The wife who answered this time, incidentally, was the prettiest of all. "Is your husband at home?" began Paul Revere as usual. The wife answered, "No." Revere hollered, "WHOA!"

★ ★ ★

Asked to write an essay about Shakespeare's *Hamlet*, a sophomore at a Southern university was gratified to receive an "A" for his effort, but then was summoned to his professor's inner sanctum.

"My boy," began the professor, "you probably are not aware of the fact that I am a fraternity brother of yours—and spent my undergraduate days in the very chapter house you live in now. What's more, we used to keep a pile of old student essays on hand for consultation just as you do today. You have had the bad luck to copy word for word a paper on Hamlet that I happened to write myself."

"Now," continued the professor, "I suppose you're wondering why I gave you an 'A' on it. When I turned in the paper, the crusty prof I had only marked it 'B.' And I always have felt it richly deserved an 'A'!"

"I will describe that Williams boy I was out with last night in one sentence," volunteered the pert junior from Smith College. "He's a perfect gentleman from the word 'Stop.'"

* * *

A phone operator icily informed an importunate college boy, "I'm sorry, sir, but that number has been taken out." "I know darn well she's been taken out," wailed the boy. "What I'm trying to find out is: by whom?"

* * *

There's a junior up at Smith College whose face is very red these days. "Remember that backless, low-cut little dress I knocked 'em dead with at the Yale prom?" she prodded her roommate. "How could I forget it?" grinned the roommate. Confessed the junior, "I just discovered it's a belt!"

* * *

No subject is taboo for a collegiate comic—so long as there's a pretty girl mixed up somehow in the proceedings. They believe in having a chicken in every plot. Recognize any of these?:

The young actress whose Senior flame takes her to the best restaurants. "I just dote on him," she gurgles. "In fact, I table d'hôte on him."

The sorority sister who phoned her steady date to report, "We girls are playing a cutthroat game of poker. Tell me once more: does two pair of straights beat a flush house?"

The campus beauty who wandered into the woods with her boy friend to pick wildflowers. Her mother insisted upon going with them—so they picked wildflowers.

The daughter of a famous cornet player who was educated by a private tooter.

The lass, bound for her first prom, who was advised, "If at first you don't succeed, try a little ardor."

The cutie who went to a coed college to pursue learning but ended up learning pursuing.

★ ★ ★

There's an oddball student at U.C.L.A. who raises bees in his spare time. "Done well with your bees this season?" asked a kindly professor recently. "Yes and no," answered the student. "They haven't given much honey, but, on the other hand, they stung my mother-in-law."

★ ★ ★

"Sick jokes" we have in abundance this year: 1. "Hello, is this Toulouse-Lautrec? Your Bermuda shorts are ready." 2. "Tell the hospital people to rush that extra-wide bed into Room 7. We just picked up a guy who's been run over by a steam roller." 3. "Mom, what's a vampire?" "Shut up and drink your soup before it clots." 4. "How'd you puncture that tire?" "Ran over a milk bottle." "Didn't you see it?" "Naw. The kid had it under his coat." 5. (sickest of all) A lady's husband had severe heart trouble but couldn't afford the treatment indicated. Skies cleared when a famous doctor offered to perform the operation free on television. The couple signed the necessary waivers and the wife waited in an anteroom while the doctor went to work. Fifteen minutes later he told her grimly, "I'm sorry to say that your husband expired in the middle of the operation." The wife shrugged her shoulders and sighed, "Oh well, that's show business."

★ ★ ★

If the preceding stories have depressed you unduly, there's a silver lining to restore faith. Either students are growing more decorous and respectable than they were in my day, or the faculty advisers are inclined to greater leniency.

The fact remains that not one humor magazine editor has been booted out of college now in almost four days!

18. CANNIBALS!

It is said that an intrepid salesman once penetrated the jungle in Central Africa, bearded the chief of the fierce Mangbatu tribe there, and said, "I'd like to interest you in some frozen food." "You already have," the chief assured him. Whereupon the Mangbatus froze him and ate him for dinner.

Central Africa is almost the only region in the world where cannibalism is still practiced. The Mangbatus war intermittently with their neighbors, the A-Zandehs and the Fans, and the side that loses is definitely out of luck. When this diet becomes monotonous, the tribes forget their differences momentarily and go on a communal prowl for a succulent explorer or motion-picture director.

A relative of a great English poet laureate was rash enough to wander into this region once. The next day the chief was asking guests, "Tennyson anyone?" The tribes will never touch a missionary, however. They've learned they cannot keep a good man down.

★ ★ ★

A cannibal mother and her child scanned the heavens while a big airliner zoomed by. "What's that?" demanded the child. "It's something like a lobster," explained the mother. "You only eat what's inside."

★ ★ ★

Home from a trek through darkest Africa with his wife, an explorer confided to J. W. Cunningham that the highlight of the expedition was the day they were captured by a band of cannibals. The chief, luckily, proved to be something of an epicure. "I never eat a person who has passed the age of forty," he announced. "That was the moment," recalled the explorer, "that I heard my wife give her correct age for the first time in public."

★ ★ ★

OVERHEARD BY AN ALERT CANNIBAL REPORTER:

1. Chieftain to captured lepidopterist: "You must stick around for the festivities at tonight's banquet. You'll be profoundly stirred!"

2. Two African savages ran smack into Jayne Mansfield. "Just our luck," muttered one despairingly. "We have to be *head* hunters!"

3. Teen-age cannibal to his date: "Let's amble down to that old campfire and see who's cooking."

4. Chief's wife on the phone to her best friend: "Be sure to drop in Friday night. We're having the Joneses for dinner."

5. An "A" student in a cannibal school was suspended for ten days. His misdemeanor: Buttering up too many teachers.

★ ★ ★

In the heart of the African jungle, a very correctly attired English explorer was suddenly confronted by a sly-faced native urchin who whispered, "Ps-s-st! Would you like me to introduce you to my sister?" "Your sister!" exclaimed the Englishman, recoiling. "I wouldn't even drink your water!"

★ ★ ★

Dr. Albert Schweitzer, Nobel prize-winning samaritan whose hospital at Lambaréné, Africa, helps primitive people combat such dread tropical diseases as leprosy, malaria, and sleeping sickness, admits that his patients prove troublesome on occasion. One ate the ointment prescribed for a skin affliction. A second swallowed at one gulp a bottle of medicine supposed to last (three drops after each meal) for weeks. A third persisted in the belief that the doctor was a sacred leopard in disguise.

Despite everything, Dr. Schweitzer insists he would not exchange his jungle hospital for any other in the world.

★ ★ ★

A fellow named John Daly, on safari in deepest Africa, captured a ferocious lion, which he tamed, and named "Watson," or "Wats" for short. One day cannibals captured poor old Daly, bound him to the back of the lion, and led him down the jungle path. Daly quickly regained his wits, however, and dropped off this note for his companions to find: "Help! I'm a prisoner on Wats, my lion."

19. CHRISTMAS HOLIDAYS

Christmastime in New York is that magical season when the city's harsh jangle is muted to a joyous tinkle, when taxi drivers smile at cops, authors embrace publishers, and gossip columnists who have been printing poisonous rumors about their neighbors all year suddenly begin writing about the holly wreaths on orphanage doorways and the frost-decked branches in the parks.

In the Longacre sector of Manhattan, a group of well-known theatrical personalities invaded a dilapidated boardinghouse last Christmas season, intent upon bringing cheer to an old friend, proverbially unlucky, who once had been the most glittering star of them all. Knowing that he was too proud to accept anything more than a token gift, they rigged up a bogus raffle for a thousand dollars. The old actor was told that they would all draw slips from a hat, and that the man who drew the number four would win the thousand. To make sure the actor would win, a number four had been written on *every* slip in the hat.

They all drew slips and looked at them. The conspirators, of course, crumpled their slips and slipped them into their pockets, then waited for the actor to shout, "I've won!" But he never opened his mouth. Finally, they asked him what number he had drawn from the inside of the hat. He answered glumly, "Six and seven-eighths."

★ ★ ★

The day-before-Christmas festivities were particularly gay at P.S. 10, and the kindergarten teacher decided to conclude the program with a short inspirational talk. "The spirit of brotherly love and good fellowship rule in America not only at Yuletide but all through the year," she declared, "and that is because all of us are FREE." At this point a small boy in the back of the room protested vigorously, "I'm NOT free; I'm FOUR."

★ ★ ★

The manager of a department store toy section, bracing himself one December morning for the expected holiday rush, saw a determined kid dragging a heavy, odd-shaped sack across the floor. A companion was kicking it along methodically from behind.

The manager stopped the boys and said, "If you keep on getting in the way like this, Santa Claus is going to pass you by on Christmas morning."

The kid who was doing the kicking answered, "Who do you think we've got here in this sack?"

★ ★ ★

At Christmastime, a heavy-set gent in the toy department was obviously taken with a toy train that whistled, belched smoke, deposited milk cans, and, in fact, did almost everything but arrive at Grand Central Station forty minutes late.

"I'll take it," he said finally.

"Good show," approved the clerk. "I'm sure your grandchild will love playing with it."

"You're absolutely right," said the heavy-set gent thoughtfully. "I'd better have two."

★ ★ ★

Although it was the first day of May, the city of New York experienced a heavy and unseasonable snowstorm a few years back, and the Salvation Army thought it saw the chance to shoot some fine publicity pictures for use the following December in their annual Christmas drive.

They draped a pretty Salvation Army lass, recalls Bob Sylvester, and stood her out in fake snow on Fifth Avenue with a tambourine and a kettle on a tripod. They got just the pictures they wanted—not to mention $13.77 from absent-minded passers-by thinking of Christmas on May first!

★ ★ ★

Santa-Mental Season:

In a California town, a civic-minded resident set up on his lawn a floodlighted, papier-mâché Santa Claus in an elaborate sleigh drawn by six reindeer, and had all his trees and shrubs festooned with varicolored lights. The man who lived directly opposite contented himself with a single wreath in his window and a sign on his gate reading: "See our display across the street."

An Evanston, Illinois, group singing carols noticed that something was a wee bit out of kilter. It proved to be a new recruit, recently arrived from Mobile, Alabama. *She* was singing, "O, lil' ol' town of Beth-lee-hem."

In Salt Lake City a dilatory housewife bought a last-minute box of one hundred identical greeting cards, and, not even pausing to read the message inscribed thereon, feverishly dispatched them to the ninety-nine relatives and acquaintances whose own greetings already were displayed on her piano top and mantel. Some days later she accidentally picked up the one card of her own she had not mailed, and read what it said in a state of shock: "This little card is just to say, 'A gift you'll love is on its way.'"

In Wellesley, Massachusetts, a college professor informed his students that kissing under the mistletoe "originated with a Scandinavian myth." Giggled one of the girls, "That thertainly theemth reathonable."

In Philadelphia, a distinguished lady author had an embarrassing experience. She suddenly recalled a nephew she hadn't seen in years, and impulsively sent him a bubble-blowing set. He gravely thanked her by letter—adding that he has been a colonel in the U.S. Army for the past seventeen months.

And even behind the Iron Curtain certain Christmas amenities persist. Two surviving members of the Kremlin's innermost circle received a modest gift from an old comrade. The odd shape of the package prompted one of them to hold it up to his ear. An unmistakable ticking came from within. "That cheapskate Brombullekev," he sneered. "I'll bet this is the very same bomb *we* sent *him* last year!"

★ ★ ★

"So you want to know how to make a fruit cake for the holiday season?" beamed a TV personality on a morning show devoted to cooking and other kitchen activities. "O.K., let's go. We'll start by digging up a great big mixing bowl like this. You see it's fully four feet across. A sturdy canoe paddle for mixing and we're ready to pour in the ingredients. First, three pounds of dates. Next, two quarts of brandy. (Now, taste.) Four pounds of mixed nuts, two quarts of brandy. (Taste.) Three pounds dried plums (mix well). Three quarts brandy. (Taste. Say it's really getting that old flavor.) Now, two rounds raisins—uh two *pounds raisins*. Three quarts brandy. (Taste. S'wunnerful, huh?) Ten pounsh sherries, five quarsh branny. Make it ten! Wix mell (sorry) *mix well* and tashe. WOW! Two cans Ajax. Fifteen quarsh byooful, golden hooch. Tashe! HOT DOG! Lean over and take another ta . . . WHOOPS, there you go into the bowl! Stay there, Pa—s'glorious way to spend the holidays!"

★ ★ ★

From under the Christmas tree a wife called in to her husband, "Here's your most beautiful present. It took me weeks to find it."

"I'll be right in to look at it," said the husband.

"Wait a minute," cautioned the wife, "and I'll put it on."

★ ★ ★

A very rich, very exclusive couple at a New Year's Eve whoop-de-do were regaling friends with details of the sensational holiday week they had provided for their offsprings: the giant Christmas tree laden with trinkets; the fabulous presents; the round of theaters and parties; the special thirty-piece orchestra engaged to play for the last night of vacation.

Suddenly the wife gave an unearthly shriek.

"Wilbur! Wilbur!" she cried, "I just remembered. Our children never came home from prep school!"

20. CLOAKS AND SUITS

An enterprising immigrant succeeded beyond his wildest dreams when he reached these shores, but unfortunately was too busy to (1) Learn to read and write, and (2) Remember a promise to send for his wife the moment he achieved a respectable bank balance.

When the neglected wife wrote him a letter he had to ask a friend to divulge its contents to him. The friend, who had a voice like a foghorn on the *Queen Elizabeth*, read in a hoarse bellow, "'Why haven't you sent for me? I must have some money right away. Minnie.'"

The immigrant snatched the note angrily from his friend's hand, stuffed it into his pocket, and conveniently forgot it until a month later when he found himself seated next to playwright Mississippi Mahoney at a Book and Author luncheon. Again he asked, "Will you read my wife's letter to me, please?"

This time it was the soft, cultivated voice of the playwright that intoned, "'Why haven't you sent for me? I must have some money right away. Minnie.'"

The immigrant nodded with satisfaction. "Anyhow," he remarked, tearing the letter into shreds, "I'm glad to notice she's changed her tone."

★ ★ ★

Business was way below par in a certain men's furnishings shop, and the proprietor, in desperation, tried to haul in a passer-by. "I already have thirty-two suits in my wardrobe." "O.K.," proposed the proprietor. "I have another proposition. Bring the suits in and I'll make you my partner."

New ending to a rather old story: one merchant asked another, "Did you hear about Arthur Schmaltz selling Macy's a big bill and making ten thousand dollars' clear profit on it?" To which the other merchant replied, "It wasn't Arthur Schmaltz; it was Joe Gesicht. It wasn't Macy's; it was Marshall Field's. He didn't make ten thousand dollars; he lost ten thousand dollars. *And besides, it was I who told you the story yesterday.*"

★ ★ ★

"How's business?" inquired a customer of two partners in a dress-manufacturing house. "Well," one partner answered cautiously, "we're having our ups and downs."

When the customer had left, the other partner, silent until now, exploded, "I ought to punch you right in the nose. Holding out on me, hey? Since when have we had any ups?"

★ ★ ★

Mounting deficits provoked a real crisis in another textile firm, whose two partners decided that one must commit suicide to cut the overhead. The loser of the toss bravely climbed to the roof of the skyscraper, every floor of which housed a garment concern, and made the plunge. As he hurtled downward, he sneaked a look into the window of every floor. Passing his own firm on the fourth floor, he hollered to his partner, "Felix, cut the velvets!"

★ ★ ★

Mr. Boogle bought a bright green suit in a bargain basement but was back to exchange it the next day. "It won't do at all," he announced regretfully. "I put it on proudly this morning, but when I yawned waiting for the bus, two neighbors dropped letters in my mouth."

★ ★ ★

The owner of a big cotton mill contracted with a dress manufacturer to have his raw material converted into flashy summer dresses for the vacation season. The dresses were supposed to be delivered by May first, but there still was no sign of them on May fifteenth.

The frantic millowner phoned the converter long distance and shouted, "You're ruining me! I'll miss my whole market. Where are my dresses?"

"It's all your fault," the converter shouted back. "You were supposed to have your material in my hands in February. You were a full month behind in your delivery."

"Listen," interrupted the millowner, "I'm not interested in *my* behind. I'm interested in *your* behind!"

★ ★ ★

His textile business in the doldrums, and his daughter dating a "loafer" he had disliked at sight, the distressed Mr. Goldblatt went to consult the family physician. "Doctor," he implored, "give me something to soothe my nerves. For three nights now I haven't slept a wink: last night, tonight, and tomorrow night!"

★ ★ ★

"Mr. Lapidus," said the chairman of the charity drive, "you're the only man in this community who hasn't made a contribution, and I'm appealing to you personally to make our record a hundred per cent."

"Listen," said Lapidus, "my father has arthritis and hasn't worked in eight years. My brother is in the poorhouse. My sister has to scrub floors to take care of her eleven children. Not one of them has ever been able to pry a cent out of me. Now what do you figure *your* chances are?"

★ ★ ★

At the same fund-raising function, another wealthy cloak-and-suiter arose and announced in stentorian tones, "My name is Sam Schlepper and I'm the president of Maidright Dresses for Debutantes. One price, one quality for all: twenty-two dollars a dozen, 2 per cent off for cash. My address is 999 Seventh Avenue, three floors AND the penthouse. I'd like to donate to this worthy cause the sum of ten dollars—anonymously."

★ ★ ★

A favorite story in New York's busy garment district concerns the middle-aged manufacturer who confided to a crony at luncheon, "I had the funniest dream last night. I dreamed that I awoke suddenly, dressed without waking my wife, and went down to Coney Island, where I took ride after ride on the roller coaster." "I had a dream, too," recalled the crony, "and what a dream it was! First Marilyn Monroe walked in and threw her arms around my neck, and right behind her was Sophia Loren, also wanting to kiss me. Now what could I do with both those famous beauties at the same time?"

The first manufacturer was deeply hurt. "A fine friend," he said reproachfully. "With both Marilyn and Sophia there, why didn't you call me up?"

"I did! I did!" his friend assured him hastily. "But your wife said you were in Coney Island."

★ ★ ★

Ralph Purdy tells about a tailor who was trying to sell him a fall suit in a new hue. "This suit," he promised, "will perk up your appearance so that even your best friends won't recognize you. Just take a walk outside in it for a minute and see what it does for you." Purdy followed instructions. When he came back, the tailor shook him warmly by the hand and exclaimed, "Good morning, you beautifully dressed stranger! What can I do for you?"

★ ★ ★

A pants manufacturer was reciting his woes to a friend. "In January," he mourned, "I lost five thousand dollars. In February, I lost ten thousand dollars. March was the biggest blow yet. I lost fifteen thousand dollars. Can you imagine anything worse than that?" "Yes," nodded his friend. "*April.*"

21. COLLEGE DAYS

Just before commencement exercises at a famous New England college, the venerable doctor who had presided over the infirmary for forty years was disturbed in his garden by a student who complained, "There's something wrong with my hearing." "Can't you wait a few days till you get home and consult your family physician?" pleaded the old doctor. "No," said the student. "It's gotten so I can no longer even hear myself cough."

The doctor gave him a bottle of pills. "Take two after every meal," he ordered, and turned back to his roses. "Pills!" exclaimed the student. "Will they improve my hearing?"

"Not in the slightest," admitted the old doctor, "but they'll make you cough louder."

★ ★ ★

President McCracken of Vassar suffered grievous humiliation the day he was to award an honorary degree to Chief Justice William Howard Taft. The Chief Justice was an imposing figure of a man—three hundred pounds or so—and the car assigned to deliver him on the campus proved unequal to the job. Mr. Taft got halfway inside it—and stuck. McCracken and the chauffeur heaved and pushed, but could get him neither in nor out. Eventually they chopped the door away. The Chief Justice was a subdued speaker that day.

★ ★ ★

A famous Duke professor became annoyed at the restlessness of his graduating class one day and decided to preach them a little sermon on patience and self-control. "It's all a state of mind," he explained. "You simply must not allow yourselves to become upset or lose your tempers over mere trifles.

"To give you a concrete example, I call your attention to the fly that has just settled on the tip of my nose. Do I hop up and down with anger and excite myself by taking a wild swipe at the fly? No, gentlemen. I simply sit here calmly and wait for the fly to leave of its own volition."

At this precise moment, the professor let out a wild yell and jumped to his feet. "Blank, blank, blank," he cried. "It's a BEE!"

★ ★ ★

At Northwestern University, Dr. Paul Witty told of a student who needed psychoanalysis. Dismissed as cured by the analyst some months later, the student declared, "At least I'm happy now." "What were you before?" asked Dr. Witty. The student sighed, "Happier."

Witty also recalled the visit of a Freshman's father, a rough diamond, who was taken to the Pump Room for what obviously was the fanciest dinner of his life. He ordered a shrimp cocktail, but when it was placed before him, his face fell. "Hey, this is *sea-food*," he protested. "I thought a shrimp cocktail meant a small martini."

★ ★ ★

Harvard University is conceded to be one of the nation's greatest storehouses of knowledge, and its one-time president, the late Charles W. Eliot, had a ready explanation. "We're adding more knowledge every semester," he declared. "The freshmen bring us so much of it—and the seniors take away so little!"

★ ★ ★

Serious Harvard students of yesteryear strove manfully to win the approval of doughty Charles Townsend Copeland, one of the great English professors of all time. "Copey" marked up papers submitted to him so quickly that some students were convinced he read only the first few paragraphs and based his conclusions on insufficient evidence.

A senior, smarting under a scathing criticism, thought he had his tormentor dead to rights one day. "Professor Copeland," he announced in class, "I glued pages 22 and 23 of my manuscript together purposely—a fact that escaped your attention entirely. This proves you never read that far."

Copey answered calmly, "My boy, you don't have to eat a whole egg to know it's bad."

★ ★ ★

In the course of one midsummer vacation Professor Copeland decided to whip up an anthology of literary tidbits he particularly fancied (it was published under the title *The Copeland Reader*). Toward the end of his labors an acquaintance asked him, "How did you spend the summer?" Professor Copeland answered airily, "Just raiding and writing."

★ ★ ★

Two Harvard graduates were exploring an abandoned gold mine near Cripple Creek recently when from one shaft there suddenly came a dismal groan. "For heaven's sake," gasped one Cambridgeite, "who is there?" There followed another groan, and a weak voice rasping, "It's me." The Harvard man up front turned to his companion, and asked with a puzzled frown, "What do you think he's trying to say?"

★ ★ ★

A Yale graduate, perusing the want ads in a metropolitan journal, saw one that seemed promising. "Wanted," it read, "a bright Harvard man, or equivalent." The Yale man wrote to the box indicated, inquiring, "When you say you desire a Harvard man or equivalent, do you mean two Princeton men, or a Yale man working half time?"

★ ★ ★

Startled by a rumor (since officially denied) that Yale was going to throw open its doors to female students, irate graduate John

E. Robson, of the class of '52, penned these telling words for the *Yale Alumni Magazine:*

> Gentlemen:
> Can it be true what people say—
> That Yale's admitting girls?
> Will floors of campus barbershops
> Be littered now with curls?
> Will all Yale's ivy-covered peaks
> Soon echo with their strident shrieks,
> And chapel bells forever after
> Compete with screams of distaff laughter?
> Will windows now in future springs
> Be hung with dainty underthings?
> *Bright College Years* three octaves higher?
> Our fiscal need is not *that* dire!
> Will not our manly intellects
> Be clouded o'er with thoughts of sex?
> And possibly, in future years,
> The football team will wear brassières?
> Oh, comfort me and reassure
> That Yale will not become impure!
> If so, this vow I leave you with—
> I'll surely send *my* son to Smith.

★ ★ ★

In Philadelphia, *Holiday's* pictorial editor embellished an article on northern New Jersey with a two-page spread on student life at Rutgers. One photograph showed a student's room at a frat house. Reader response was almost instantaneous. A gent in Camden, fit to be tied, wanted his sign back or fifteen bucks in cash, the Hudson River Day Line demanded the return of the life preserver from the *Peter Stuyvesant,* and the Standard Oil people thought it would be nice if the student would come across pronto with the Esso globe hanging from the ceiling.

★ ★ ★

In Ann Arbor, an associate professor of literature realized how old he was getting when he asked his young daughter what she was studying. "Oh," she replied, "all about some jerk named Hitler."

★ ★ ★

CAMPUS SAGES . . . At the University of Michigan, Ben Fairless opined, "Speakers have been showering us with pearls of wisdom for centuries, and if all their valuable advice were laid end to end, it would still be just as good as new. Very little of it ever has been used." . . . Home economics prof at Arkansas: "If you don't want your children to hear what you're saying, pretend you're talking to them." . . . Advice to an economics class at Reed: "It pays to live within your means. Remember, a small part of what you earn still belongs to you." . . . A philosophy student at Tulane announced, "Frankly, I have nothing but contempt for both Aristotle and Plato." His professor observed amiably, "Not, I take it, the contempt which familiarity breeds." . . . A young instructor at a university rich in traditions and endowments was called to the mat by the dean who told him sternly, "We've been hearing rumors about you that we do not like. Once and for all, are you or have you ever been a member of the Communist party?" The young instructor answered, "I'm sorry, sir, but we're not allowed to say."

★ ★ ★

Two editors of a Cornell student newspaper, determined to prove the gullibility of people high in public life, once formed an organization to "rescue from oblivion" one Hugo N. Frye, "the father of the Republican party in New York." Invitations to a dinner commemorating Frye's birthday brought enthusiastic replies, dripping with regret, from the Vice-President of the United States, the Chairman of the Republican National Committee, and a dozen congressmen. The Secretary of Labor wrote: "It is a pleasure to testify to the career of that sturdy patriot who first planted the ideals of our party in your region of the country."

There was no such person as "Hugo N. Frye," of course. His name came from the then popular phrase, "You go and fry!"

Harvey Breit tells about a long-haired scholar from Wisconsin who insisted that Shakespeare's plays had been written by Queen Elizabeth. The eminent minister, Dr. Hugh Black, challenged him. "Surely," he scoffed, "you don't believe a woman could have composed such masterpieces." "You miss my point entirely," said the scholar. "It is my contention that Queen Elizabeth was a man."

It was a grim president of a coed college in Ohio who faced the student body after a "panty raid" had made page one of the local paper. "We are going right to the root of this evil and wave of irresponsibility," he thundered. "As of this morning the dean of women and I have decided to stop petting on the campus."

The press raised such a fuss when a big state university abolished the honor system during final examinations that the chairman of the board of trustees felt called upon to give an explanation. "We realized to our regret," he admitted, "that the professors had the honor and the students had the system."

An English prof at Vassar was impressing upon his Freshman class the advantages of acquiring a large vocabulary. "Say a word over out loud to yourself five times," he advised, "and it will be yours for life." A pert frosh in the front row closed her eyes and breathed ecstatically, "Walter, Walter, Walter, Walter, Walter. . . ."

Ed Barrett, dean of the Columbia School of Journalism, tells of the rich trustee who called a college president and said, "Send somebody over to address our home-builders' convention next

week, Sam. But please don't send anybody lower than a dean."
The prexy answered dryly, "There IS nobody lower than a dean!"

★ ★ ★

"Did you hear what that absent-minded Professor Mack did yesterday?" chortled Mrs. Green. "He sent his wife down to the bank and kissed his money good-by."

Mr. Green sighed heavily, and said, "The professor isn't as absent-minded as I thought!"

★ ★ ★

Craziest story of the month concerns a college student who couldn't live on the scale to which he was accustomed on the modest allowance doled out to him by his parents. Desperate to wangle a bonus from his father, he bethought himself of a dachshund named Man that was the old man's pride and joy, and wired him: "There's a professor here who can teach Man how to talk for two hundred dollars cash. What do you say?" Papa said yes—and wired the two hundred.

Convinced he was now launched on a sure thing, the rascally son squandered the two hundred, then wired Papa again: "For three hundred dollars more, professor guarantees to teach Man how to read and write." "Wonderful," enthused the father—and produced the cash once more.

Papa was waiting on the station when his son came home for spring vacation. "Where's Man?" he cried. "I can't wait to see him talk, read, and write."

"I have a disappointment, Father," said the student. "Yesterday I said to Man, 'Tomorrow's the day we go home and see the family. Won't that be great?' Man answered, 'I wonder if your mother's found out yet that your father's carrying on with that cheap blonde at the nightclub. What a ball we'll have dragging *that* into the open.' Well, Father, when I heard Man go on like that, I felt there was only one thing to do. I shot him."

Papa reflected for just a moment, then spoke as follows: "My boy, there is only one more thing I wish to know. Are you sure that blank-blank dog is dead?"

★ ★ ★

Two old college classmates met for the first time in years. "How goes it with you, Pete?" asked one. "Not good at all," mourned Pete. "My wife ran away with the letter carrier, my son is a juvenile delinquent, my bank failed, and all my teeth will have to come out." "Gosh, I'm sorry to hear that," sympathized the classmate. "What business are you in now?"

"Same old line," answered Pete. "Selling good-luck charms."

22. COMMUTERS

For some years a witty Philadelphian named Caskie Stinnett had been contemplating a book that would tear the lid off the commuting racket. A brief newspaper item, estimating that "over five billion hours are wasted each year by American people in commuting" finally galvanized him into action.

Were these wasted hours necessary, mused Stinnett, and why the heck were commuters willing to spend so much time on trains anyhow? The results of his researches is an amusing and informative compendium called *Will Not Run Feb. 22.*

Stinnett has determined that there *are* soul-satisfying ways to improve commuting hours. Finest of all is to walk down the aisle until you find a seat-hog who, despite standees, tries to keep a whole seat for himself by spreading newspapers, packages, and wearing apparel over the vacant half. Stinnett has perfected a lunge that not only wins him three-fifths of the seat, but knocks two packages on the floor and catches a destructive heel in the hog's trousers cuff at the same time.

Other pleasant—if dangerous—ways to kill time are:

1. See how much you can disturb the passenger ahead when you hurl your overcoat into the rack above you. Knocking off his hat counts three points; his glasses, five.

2. Count how many times you can leave the door open on a very cold day.

3. Tear items out of your newspaper and stuff them into various pockets until your seat companion surrenders and heads for another car. (A lady on the 8:27 from Mount Kisco accomplishes

spectacular results with a loaded charm bracelet that jingles and rattles every time she blinks her eyes.)

4. Leave your seat a full fifteen minutes before your train reaches its destination, and teeter uncomfortably in the aisle. Then see how many sheep—though they've made the trip hundreds of times before—follow your lead. (Average score: twelve.)

5. Study what to do every time the railroad files a new "rate schedule." (Draw up a petition of protest, circulate it through the car, form a protective committee—then pay the higher fare.)

★ ★ ★

Embittered commuters have compiled a few hints for conductors, too:

1. Adopt a general air of hostility and suspicion, remembering that a good train is an empty train. Smile only when a commuter discovers he's on the wrong train.

2. Turn on the heat on all cars on May 1, off on December 1. Be sure, too, that drinking water is well heated before train leaves the yards.

3. In punching tickets, nick commuter's fingernail.

4. Keep passengers guessing which end of the car you will open at the station. A few clever, misleading gestures will gang them up at the wrong end. Always choose the door, of course, that will give them the longest walk on an open platform when the weather is bad.

★ ★ ★

I must admit that I often enjoy my own safaris to and from my Westchester retreat, and that I've met some very pleasant and helpful conductors on that run, too. I recall one kindly old gent who was standing near my seat when a young trainman bustled up to report on the number of passengers. "What kept you so long?" asked the conductor. "Well," said the young fellow, "that big one-hundred-and-six-seat car took a long time to count—there were one hundred and three passengers in it."

"Son," the old man said, "I'll give you a tip. Next time count the three empties and subtract."

★ ★ ★

If you think the present-day commuter has troubles, cast your eye over this selection spotted by John McCutcheon, Jr., in an 1865 issue of *Popular Science Review:*

"It has sometimes happened to passengers to feel the floor of their carriage gradually crumbling away beneath their feet. They have no recourse but to await in a state of hopeless terror the moment when their last support shall be shattered asunder, hurling them bruised and maimed on the iron tramway, to be crushed and dismembered by the following carriages."

★ ★ ★

There's one commuter on the New York Central who is strictly barred from all bridge games. "He's the kind of player," explains a grim fellow passenger, "who calls a spade three spades."

★ ★ ★

When commuter Stone started filling his pipe, the little lady sharing a seat with him on the 4:50 plucked nervously at his sleeve. "Pardon me," she stated, "but tobacco makes me very ill." "In that case," suggested Stone benignly, still filling his pipe, "if I were you, I'd certainly give it up."

23. COPS AND ROBBERS

The world's most polite bandit waved his pistol at a bank's employees and customers and announced silkily, "Now, ladies and gentlemen, all those in favor of leaving these premises alive will kindly hold up their hands."

★ ★ ★

A banker in Minnesota asked the home-town police chief if he knew anything about a new applicant for the post of receiving teller. "I'll say this about him," replied the chief thoughtfully. "He's a gentleman to his fingerprints."

★ ★ ★

For an enlightening look into the thinking processes of a top criminal, I suggest this exchange between a prison investigator and the notorious bank robber and escape wizard, Willie Sutton. "Willie," the investigator asked him, "what makes you rob banks?" Without the slightest hesitation Sutton explained, "Just one reason, sir: that's where the money is!"

★ ★ ★

At a fashionable nightclub, a girl-about-town boasted to a friend in the powder room, "I had my nose bobbed for eight hundred dollars and already I've been taken for Kim Novak." "You've been taken all right," sneered the friend—"for eight hundred dollars."

★ ★ ★

Complainant in a police court demanded that a belligerent neighbor be arrested.

"Describe him," demanded the police officer. "Has he got a mustache?"

"I'm not sure," admitted the complainant. "If he has one, he sure keeps it shaved off."

★ ★ ★

PERSONAL NOTES FROM OUR BETTER PENITENTIARIES:

A Sing Sing librarian has thoughtfully renamed the Jules Verne classic: "Around the World in Sixty to Ninety Days."

The clean-up man in a prison baseball team line-up hit a rival pitcher's fast ball a country mile. He tore around first, zipped past second, rounded third, and headed for home—but they finally nailed him—between third base and the Mexican border.

A temporarily incarcerated member of the mob had a birthday gift sent to the "babe" he hoped was waiting faithfully for his release. The note enclosed read, "For my gorgeous hunk of stuff I send this genuine mink stole. Well, maybe it ain't genuine mink— but, honey, it sure was stole."

A con man's wife visited him faithfully once a month in the jail. One visit, he asked anxiously, "What's the news on the governor's pardon?" "It couldn't be better," she answered brightly. "He's getting out next Tuesday!"

The governor of a Rocky Mountain state phoned the warden of the state penitentiary and sneered, "I see there's been another jail break at your miserably run institution." The warden pleaded, "Keep your pants on, Guv. It was a mere slip of the pen."

★ ★ ★

A Jersey City newshawk has stumbled upon what must be the saddest sack in six states. His name (actually) is Peter Rabbit the Third, and he has fallen into the clutches of the law for misdemeanors on numerous occasions. "It's always the same story," he laments. "I'm getting along fine until one cop asks my name. When I answer 'Peter Rabbit' the trouble starts."

★ ★ ★

New York cops are used to just about everything, but one traffic officer was stopped cold at the sight of an old sedan parked on a side street with four occupants solemnly fishing out of its open windows. The man in the driver's seat furtively beckoned to the cop. "The poor nuts think they're going to catch some salmon here. I'm humoring them by playing along."

"You're in a 'no parking' area, buddy," interrupted the cop, "so you'll have to humor your nutty friends some place else."

"O.K., if that's the way you feel about it," nodded the driver— and pulled out a pair of oars.

★ ★ ★

"We're down to our last twenty-dollar bill," wailed a famous burglar's wife. "You'll have to produce some money fast." "All right, all right," grumbled the burglar husband, "but you'll have to wait till the bank closes."

★ ★ ★

A couple of sharpies spotted a fine-looking horse hitched in front of a feed store in Pennsylvania. One of them made off with the horse while the other hastily strapped himself into the harness. "Sure, I'm your horse," he told the astonished farmer when he returned. "A wicked witch put a hex on me and turned me into a horse. The spell just expired. And now I'll ask you to release me, if you please."

The farmer swallowed the tale without question. A week later, however, he spotted his fine horse up for auction at a neighboring county fair, and promptly bought it back. "Well," he whispered in its ear as he led it away, "I see she got you again!"

24. DEFINITIONS

Your name does not have to be Webster to qualify you as a definer of words. The list below, for example, was composed by a variety of otherwise sane citizens, not one of whom was related to the great lexicographer.

ABALONE—An expression of disbelief.

ACCUMULATE—A convenient way of asking, "Why are you so tardy?"

ACOUSTIC—What you use when you shoot pool.

ASPERSION—A donkey from Iran.

AUCTION—A place where you get something for nodding.

BACHELOR—A gent who comes to his office every morning from a different direction.

BARGAIN—Anything you can buy for only twice what it's worth. (Will Rogers.)

BILIOUS—The nauseous feeling you get when you open your mail the first of the month.

BORE—A person who has nothing to say—and says it.

BREVITY—The quality that makes cigarettes, banquet speeches, vacations, and love affairs bearable. (H. L. Mencken.)

CELEBRITY—One who works all his life to be famous enough to be recognized—then hides behind dark glasses so no one will know who he is. (Dudley Murphy.)

CENSOR—A self-appointed snoophound who sticks his noes into other people's business.

CENTAUR—A man with a horse where his pants ought to be.

CLEAVAGE—Something which excites disapproval in everyone but the audience. (Dore Schary.)

COBRA—A brassière for Siamese twins. (J. C. Furnas.)

COINCIDE—What you do when it starts raining.

COURAGE—A woman pedestrian bluffing a woman driver.

CROTCHETY—Wearing tight pants.

CYCLIC CHANGE—Getting off one bicycle and onto another.

DIPLOMACY—The art of saying "Nice doggie" till you can find a rock. (Wynn Catlin.)

DOLLAR—Something that can never fall so low as the means some people adopt to get it. (Bill Nye.)

EGOTIST—A man who's always me-deep in conversation.

EMBARRASSED—Emmy's lost her unmentionables.

EXPERIENCE—A comb life gives you after you lose your hair. (Judith Stern.)

EXPERT—A man who avoids errors as he sweeps on to the grand fallacy. (B. Stollberg.)

FAD—Something that goes into one era and out the other.

FANATIC—One who redoubles his energy when he has forgotten his aim. (Santayana.)

FATHER—A man whose daughter marries a man vastly her inferior mentally, but then gives birth to unbelievably brilliant grandchildren.

FIREPROOF—The boss's relatives.

GALAHAD—Former sweetheart.

GLADIATOR—What the cannibal said after he dined on the lady explorer.

GROSS IGNORANCE—144 times worse than ordinary ignorance.

GULCH—Birds who follow ocean vessels.

HIGHBROW—A person who enjoys a thing until it becomes popular.

HOCKSHOP—The loansomest place in town.

INTUITION—That uncanny second sense which tells a woman she is absolutely right—whether she is or not. (Harlan Miller.)

LOAFER—A fellow who is trying to make both weekends meet.

LANDLORD—Someone who'd rather sleep than heat.

MORON—Censors think girls should have.

OFF-DAY—The day after a day off.

OLD-TIMER—A man who remembers when the only problem about parking was getting the girl to agree to it.

ONE-HORSE TOWN—A place where all the lights on Main Street dim when you plug in your electric razor. (Paul Osborne.)

PATRIOT—A citizen who can whistle "The Star-Spangled Banner" while the tax collector is examining his books.

PERFECTIONIST—One who takes infinite pains and usually gives them to everyone around him. (Mary Wilson.)

PESSIMIST—An optimist on his way home from the racetrack. (Red Smith.)

PNEUMONIA—A slight cold handled by MCA.

POISE—The ability to sit calm and unperturbed in a barber chair, with your mouth full of lather, while the shine boy hands your new twenty-five-dollar hat to another customer. (Harvey Campbell.)

PREJUDICE—A device that enables you to form opinions without getting the facts. (R. Quillen.)

SCHNAPPS—Tries to bite you.

SPARTAN—A person who can eat just one peanut.

THONGS—What Thinatra things.

TIPS—Wages we pay other people's help.

TREE—An object that stands in one place for ages, then leaps in front of a wife who is driving.

UPPER CRUST—A lot of crumbs held together by dough. (Jean Webster.)

WOLF—A character whose park is worse than his bite.

ZOUNDS—Noises.

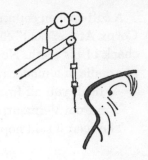

25. DENTISTS

A Texas oil trillionaire went to an honest dentist who told him, "Your teeth are in perfect shape. There's no work necessary. They don't even need polishing." "Start drilling, anyhow," ordered the trillionaire. "I feel lucky today."

★ ★ ★

"Painless dentistry is simple as chopping down a tree," a dentist explained to a burly logger. "You breathe one whiff of laughing gas, and poof! the tooth is out."

"Any extra charge for that stuff?" asked the logger dubiously. "Fifty cents extra," said the dentist.

"I guess the old way is best," decided the logger. "Go ahead, doc, and never mind how much it hurts."

"You're a brave man," said the dentist. "Open your mouth."

"Wait a minute," cried the logger. "It isn't me that's got the toothache; it's me wife."

★ ★ ★

Dr. Edward Pullman, the society dentist, is a rock-and-roll addict in his spare hours. Recently he was adjusting the drill in a pretty patient's mouth when he absent-mindedly inquired, "What speed do you prefer: seventy-eight, forty-five, or thirty-three and a third?"

Detecting some ominous decay in the molar of another glamorous debutante, Dr. Pullman brooded, "What is a place like this doing in a girl like you?"

Philosophizes Pullman, "There is nothing to promote the payment of an old dental bill like a new toothache."

A soft-spoken country boy from Alabama enlisted in the Marine Corps. At the "boot" camp he was sent to the dentist for a thorough check of his teeth. Never before had he seen the elaborate paraphernalia of a modern dentist's office, and he was terrified.

"Wheah you all from?" he asked the dentist, stalling for time.

"I'm from Vermont, and so is my assistant," said the dentist.

The recruit said hopefully, "Ah'm a Yankee, too."

26. DEPARTMENT STORES

They look so beautiful and lifelike, those plastic dummies used nowadays by exclusive specialty shops to show off their wares, that male strollers have become more devoted window shoppers than their wives!

Display dynamo Mike Gross needed a dozen glamorous female manikins for use with a set of posters he was planning, and when he was invited to inspect the factory where the manikins actually were made, he found time to toddle over—closely followed by me.

Our guide had a lot of emergency wires saved to show us.

The first one came from the owner of a lingerie shop in Algiers. "Four figures you shipped," it read, "arrived minus upper limbs. Send us arms—for the love of Allah."

The second was from an operator in Shreveport: "Last lot of heads too pale. Must these things go wan forever?"

The third complaint was most serious of all. "Head and legs of Miss Tuscaloosa are dazzling," admitted the sender, "but your fool shipping department forgot to include the body. My kingdom for a torso!"

By this time our guide had whisked us into the room where they stored spare parts, some of which were positively fascinating. "Watch this," he urged, as a group of workmen, clad in blue-zipper suits like the one Winston Churchill sported during the war, filed solemnly to their posts. The foreman struck a gong and asked, "Gentlemen, shall we join the ladies?" You could have heard a pinion drop.

Never were beautiful women made so quickly! "And now," promised the guide, "you'll see the flesh tints applied. It's the final stage."

From a shelf under the table each worker produced a spray gun and a can of pinkish paint. The foreman glanced around to be sure all was in readiness. Then he raised his own gun and pointed it at the figure nearest him.

"Brothers," he proposed solemnly, "let us spray."

★ ★ ★

An office worker came home sporting a new hat—which was fine except that it was three sizes too large and looked like it had been soaked in a tub of water. He confessed that he had picked it up at a bargain basement sale—and that he knew it looked terrible on him.

"So why did you buy it?" demanded his wife. "It was this way," explained the office worker. "When I tried it on and got a load of myself in the mirror, I looked too stupid to argue with the clerk."

★ ★ ★

Short-lived, thank heaven, was the inexplicable vogue for those hideous sack and chemise dresses. Department store buyers admit sadly they can't even give them away as premiums with pickle juice. Bob Hope summed up the male reaction to the chemise with, "When my girl puts on a dress, I want to know where she is in it." Arlene Francis donned one for a TV appearance, and then sought out her husband, Martin Gabel. "How do I look?" she demanded. "First," he countered, "tell me who you are."

Zsa Zsa Gabor gave the only sensible defense for the fleeting fashion that I ever heard. "I really enjoyed wearing a chemise dress," she purred, "because I looked so good when I took it off."

★ ★ ★

A Montreal housewife took a deep breath, and plunged fearlessly into a maelstrom around the special bargain counter in a big department store. She emerged an hour later, battered but triumphant, waving a long piece of white material. "I'll take this," she gasped. "You will not, madam," said a floorwalker firmly. "That's the cloth we use to cover the counter at night."

★ ★ ★

Remember Queen Salote, of the distant land of Tonga—a tall, majestic, seven-foot, ebony-black lady who stole the show at Queen Elizabeth's coronation in 1953? Pouring rain could not dim her expansive smile or the finery that she was sporting. Said finery, it has been revealed, didn't come from Tonga at all—not even from the South Pacific area. It was supplied, as a matter of fact, by R. H. Macy in New York!

Another unusual sale by Macy's (my informant is Margaret Harriman) was made to a Brazilian. He liked the looks of a live burro he spotted in a promotion stunt and insisted that it be sent to his plantation in far-off Brazil. Some weeks later, however, it was returned for credit. Wrote the burro-fancier: "When I saw it at my home, alas, it did not have the same appealing expression around the eyes."

★ ★ ★

It was in Macy's, too, that a loyal customer ordered a flagpole delivered to his Connecticut home so that he might fly Old Glory on July the Fourth. The first pole delivered by the store proved too short, so, after a considerable amount of telephoning, a new one was provided. This, alas, turned out to be too long.

The exasperated customer threw it into the back of his garage, and bought a pole just the right size in the nearest shopping center. After an hour of digging in the midday sun, he imbedded it firmly and headed for the nearest lake to cool off, pausing only to call Macy's again and order their oversized pole removed pronto from his premises.

Macy's were just as anxious as he was to terminate this aggravating and unprofitable transaction. Their truck zoomed over to the customer's estate with the speed of light. There was only one flagpole in sight, and, though it was rooted deep in the rich Connecticut soil, Macy's minions hesitated not. With a mighty effort, they yanked it out of the ground and carted it triumphantly back to New York.

The customer, they say, regained normalcy along about November.

27. DOCTORS

A nearsighted doctor broke his glasses one morning just before a new patient was announced. Hoping to bluff his way through, he boomed, "Glad to see you again Miss Er—Umpph. What seems to be bothering you?"

The young lady told her story while the doctor scribbled some notes on his pad. "Could be serious," he announced. "Better take off enough so I can examine you." When she reappeared, he poked an exploratory finger here and there and sighed, "Those ribs—sticking out that way—I don't like it a bit."

"Listen, Doctor," said the young lady, "if it's all the same to you, pay some attention to me—and stop fiddling with that Venetian blind."

★ ★ ★

Doc Brown's battered jalopy—a Model T, to be precise—was the subject for considerable merriment for the younger fry in front of the village drugstore. Doc Brown ignored the gibes as he climbed into the seat, then remarked amiably, "This car's paid for, boys. If you'll check with your parents, you'll discover that most of you ain't!"

★ ★ ★

A doctor diagnosed a patient's run-down condition as too much worry over money matters. "Relax," he ordered. "Just two weeks ago I had another fellow here in a dither because he couldn't pay his tailor bills. I told him to forget about them and now he feels great." "I know," said the patient glumly. "I'm his tailor."

★ ★ ★

The same pill-osophic physician ran into further trouble with a patient who obviously had been overeating. He advised, "Just cut out all starches and sweets and smoke one cigar a day." At the end of the fortnight the patient was back, looking simply terrible. "Cutting out the starches and sweets I could stand," he reported, "but that one cigar a day near killed me. I never smoked before in all my life!"

★ ★ ★

In his *Live Longer and Enjoy It,* Dr. Peter Steincrohn points out how much punishment the human body can survive. An average man can get along without his gall bladder, spleen, tonsils, and appendix, and survive the loss of one of two of his kidneys, one of his two lungs, two of his four or five quarts of blood, two-fifths of his liver, most of his stomach, four of his twenty-three feet of small intestine, and half of his brain!

★ ★ ★

MEDICAL MISCELLANY . . .

Small mishap at a local hospital last week. A new doctor sawed the arm off a patient. "What kind of operation do you call that?" asked a supervisor. "Operation!" gasped the doctor. "I thought it was an autopsy!"

Sign in a doctor's office in Worcester, Massachusetts: "Ladies in waiting room will kindly refrain from exchanging symptoms. It gets the doctor confused."

"Phew," sighed a relieved surgeon as he joined his colleagues in the hospital's executive dining room. "I sure performed that operation in the nick of time! Another hour and the patient would have recovered without it!"

There's one song that an expectant nurse down at the General Hospital keeps singing over and over these days: "Which doctor?"

Two overweight hypochondriacs (they had been exceeding the feed limit) sat down for a nice, long, hurt-to-hurt talk.

"A minor operation," explains Melinda Drake, "is an operation performed on somebody else."

"Beware of women doctors," warns Jerry Lewis. "One of them said my throat needed painting—but she couldn't decide on a color."

A teacher at P.S. 10 asked her class for the definition of a creek. The bright son of a doctor explained, "A creek is a river with low blood pressure."

The chiropractor was giving Mr. Uppercue a vigorous workout. "It's going to rain tonight," he predicted confidently. "I can feel it in your bones."

A worried industrialist had had a complete check-up at the local hospital. "What's the verdict?" he asked the head doctor anxiously. The head doctor, a cautious man, cleared his throat and said, "Let us put it this way, Mr. Higgins. If you were a horse, I'm afraid we'd shoot you."

★ ★ ★

Ollie James tells the story of a bright young doctor who was having a hard time getting a foothold in the community he had selected for his operations. So he hung a new sign outside his door which proclaimed, "A-Number-One Psychiatrist." And sure enough the very next morning a new client popped up.

She carried in her arms an American flag, a bowl of cherries, a glockenspiel, and a crate of chickens. She was attired in an evening gown, a miner's cap, and spiked baseball shoes, and she had a pair of skis strapped to her back.

"I see you have a problem," ventured our doctor.

"You bet I have," she agreed. "It's my brother. You will have to cure him."

"First," suggested the doctor, "I want to see how much help I can count on from you. Agility will be necessary. Suppose you strap on those skis and do a slalom from yonder filing cabinet to the top of your crate of chickens."

The visitor did as she was directed, but the crate splintered when she landed on it and the room was showered with chickens, cherries, and glockenspiels. The poor girl fainted dead away.

When she came to, the doctor was eying her speculatively from across his desk. "How long, madam," he inquired formally, "have you been subject to these fainting spells?"

★ ★ ★

Another new doctor opened a shiny office and decided he'd have the prettiest nurse in town. He found a lulu, too, and when she reported for work, told her enthusiastically, "You look so crisp and fresh in your new uniform! I'm going to call you 'Ivory' because you're 99 $\frac{44}{100}$ per cent pure."

An hour later, he changed her name to "Duz."

★ ★ ★

A patient was told by his doctor that an intricate and costly operation was mandatory. "You needn't worry about the cost," soothed the doctor. "Just pay me two hundred dollars down and fifty a month for the next three years."

"Sounds like buying a car," commented the patient.

"You're right," the doctor assured him. "I am."

★ ★ ★

An overweight grandmother, despite many warnings, insisted upon cheating on her strict diet. One time she went too far and had to be taken to the hospital. The only room available was in the maternity ward, and there Grandma was wheeled.

Her small granddaughter was stationed outside this room the next afternoon when a visitor stopped to inquire, "What are you doing here, little girl?" "It's my grandma," explained the little girl brightly. "She's been cheating again!"

★ ★ ★

A boss visited an ailing employee at the hospital, after having promised his wife he'd cheer up the poor fellow. "Now, Albert," he boomed reassuringly, "there's not a thing for you to worry about. Everybody at the office is prepared to pitch in and do your work —if we ever can figure out what in hell you've been doing."

★ ★ ★

Dr. Richard Gordon tells, in his book called *Doctor at Large*, of the day a gawky, teen-age girl came to his office, complaining that she coughed so steadily at night she couldn't sleep. Dr. Gordon asked her to strip, then put the stethoscope on her chest. "Now, then," he commanded, "big breaths!" The girl nodded proudly, and agreed, "Yeth, thir: and I'm only thixteen!"

★ ★ ★

Two genuinely disturbed inmates of a state mental institution were walking unattended on a crisp afternoon when one of them suddenly dove into the turbulent, icy waters of a river that bordered the grounds. Without hesitation, the other plunged after him and saved his life.

"A brave and wonderful act!" applauded the superintendent later. "Any man who does a thing like that obviously is completely sane. Tomorrow you may go home."

The inmate still was expressing his gratitude when a white-faced orderly whispered an urgent message into the superintendent's ear. "I'm afraid I have bad news for you," the superintendent told the inmate. "The man whose life you saved has hung himself."

"Oh, no," protested the inmate. "He's fine! *I just hung him up to dry!*"

28. DRINK

Three men who had indulged rather freely at a convention banquet were driving home together through the pitch-black night. Two were in the front seat, the other in the back.

Suddenly the driver asked the man in the back seat to look out the rear window and see who the crazy driver was behind them. "He's hanging too close on my tail," complained the driver. "For five minutes now he's ignored my waving to let him pass me. Besides, he only has one headlight on."

The man looked out the back, then almost jumped out of his seat. "No wonder he can't pass you," he cried. "He's on tracks!"

★ ★ ★

"Beg pardon," said the man at the door, "but would you care to contribute something to the Home for Hopeless Alcoholics?" "You bet," replied Mrs. Murphy promptly. "Come back about ten this evening and you can have Murphy."

★ ★ ★

One of Jeff Keates' funniest cartoons depicts a well-sozzled gent assuring his beefy hostess (with a tray of drinks in her hands), "Thanks, no. If I have too many of those things, I say things that I later regret, you old bat, you."

★ ★ ★

A lady vacationer sauntered into a Miami bar, and spotted a friend sipping a cocktail. "Ah, there, Marie," she called. "I see you're having one."

"Nonsense," frowned Marie. "It's just the cut of this made-to-order dress that makes me look that way."

★ ★ ★

A man who obviously considered himself a VIP ordered a round of drinks for everybody—including the bartender—in a swanky café—and then confessed he didn't have a dime. The bartender gave him a black eye and the heave-ho. The next night he reappeared, ordered drinks for everybody—the bartender included—and again admitted he was penniless. This time the bartender gave him a real working over before throwing him out.

Back came the fellow a third night and loudly ordered a round of drinks for everybody once more. "For me, too?" inquired the bartender.

"Certainly not," said the big shot loftily. "One drink and you're a raving lunatic."

★ ★ ★

Joe E. Lewis, nightclub entertainer supreme, once vowed to give up whiskey (that'll be the day!). "I'm switching to carrot juice," he explained. "I get just as loaded but I see better."

At Chicago's Chez Paris, an opulent guest at a ringside table offered Joe a bunch of imported grapes. "No sir," announced Joe emphatically. "You don't catch me taking my wine in pills!"

Lewis explains the curse of drink thusly: "Just one glass of whiskey makes you feel like a new man—but then the new man wants a drink, too! Despite the high cost of intoxicating beverages," he concludes, "a ten-cent drink of bourbon is still available in Las Vegas—as a recent autopsy shows."

★ ★ ★

A young gent who liked his liquor too much awoke one morning with a frightful hangover and one dime in his pocket. He bought a stamp, a sheet of paper, a pencil, and an envelope, and wrote his wealthy father: "This time I've hit bottom, Dad. I don't know where my next meal is coming from. If I can pull through this somehow, I'll never touch hard liquor again."

Just then, he spied a half-filled bottle of cheap gin next to the telephone. He downed it, then added this P.S. to his letter: "And so, Dad, if you need any help, just let me know."

* * *

Two old, old friends came to New York for a class dinner, and reserved a hotel room for the night before departing for the festivities. This proved to be a wise precaution. They woke up late the following morning with man-sized headaches—also a really impressive collection of bruises and one black eye apiece. They decided to seek out the bartender at the convention hall to discover what happened. He greeted them jovially with, "Well, well! I see you boys decided to make up!"

* * *

A shoemaker went out on a bender, and wound up in police court. Anxious to prevent his wife from hearing of his predicament, the poor fellow tried hard to talk his way out. The judge, not too busy, was content to let him talk on, but finally interrupted. "This new tale you've just concocted," he advised, "seems beneath standard to me. Shoemaker, stick to your last!"

* * *

A notorious drunkard-about-town was persuaded to take up yoga to pull himself together. After ten months of torturing long-unused muscles, he became quite proficient at it, too. "Has yoga helped him?" his wife was asked. "In one way," she answered. "Now he can get drunk standing on his head, too."

* * *

A kindhearted judge was commiserating with another put-upon wife. "Your husband really is a problem," allowed His Honor. "Has he ever tried Alcoholics Anonymous?" "I reckon he has, Judge," she nodded sadly. "That man'll drink anything!"

* * *

An old Kaintucky cunnel made his way with some difficulty to the breakfast table. As he lowered himself into his chair, his wife noticed that his hand was bandaged. "Just a matter of minor consequence at the club last night," he told her. "Couple of our younger members who have difficulty holding their liquor got a bit under the weather. One of them inadvertently stepped on my hand."

★ ★ ★

The late Irish poet Oliver Gogarty had an insatiable thirst, and explained his philosophy in one sentence: "There is no such thing as a large whiskey."

★ ★ ★

Classified ad quoted verbatim from the London *Times:* "Attention ship-in-bottle makers: I offer you my services gratis. I will accept full bottles of Amontillado Sherry, or Haig and Haig Whiskey, and return them ready for insertion of ship. Prompt, conscientious work guaranteed. Address Box DSK."

★ ★ ★

An unsuccessful contestant in a beauty contest returned home exhausted and disgruntled. A friend, attempting to console her, asked, "Was the competition very stiff?" "No," answered the contestant bitterly, "but the judges were."

★ ★ ★

A passel of tramps in the nation's capital successfully eluded the constabulary, and established headquarters for the night in the little park surrounding the base of the beautiful Washington Monument. Came dinnertime, and the tramps proceeded to cook their mulligatawny stew and roast their spuds.

A couple of inebriated gents paused to survey the proceedings. They were struck by the sight of the monument bathed in moonlight, with the tiny fires crackling at its base.

One of the inebriates finally shook his head and predicted sadly, "THEY'LL NEVER GET IT OFF THE GROUND!"

29. MR. EMERSON'S WISDOM

Editor Robert Linscott has cut down the million and a half words in Ralph Waldo Emerson's *Journals* for a Modern Library edition one tenth as long. A reader will not only be staggered by the wealth of material and the succession of brilliant thumbnail characterizations, but will realize anew that under Emerson's somewhat somber and flinty Yankee façade there sparkled a vein of precious wit and down-to-earth humor.

Emerson began making random entries in his journal in his junior year at Harvard, and contributed "one golden coin after another" through his lifetime to what he called his "intellectual savings bank." He never fully appreciated himself the warmth and humor of some of his entries. "What is called a warm heart I have not," he laments on one page, and notes on another: "Why has my motley diary no jokes? Because it is a soliloquy and every man is grave alone."

★ ★ ★

Here are a few of Emerson's devastating descriptions:

"What a notable green grocer was spoiled to make Macauley!"

"Napoleon III acquired such skill in the art of lying that you could not even depend upon the exact contrary of what he said."

"Alcott is a tedious archangel: a pail of which the bottom is taken out."

"William Lloyd Garrison is a tart Luther who neighs like a horse."

"The word liberty in the mouth of Mr. Webster sounds like the

word love in the mouth of a courtesan. All the drops of his blood
have eyes that look downward."

★ ★ ★

"Great geniuses," pointed out Emerson, "have the shortest biographies. Their cousins can tell you nothing about them." A man
who rode with the herd, and never stuck his neck out was never
his favorite. "Whoso would be a man," he proclaimed, "must be a
non-conformist"; also, "A foolish consistency is the hobgoblin of
little minds, adored by little statesmen and philosophers and
divines." "I like to have a man's knowledge comprehend more than
one class of topics, one row of shelves," he said. "I like a man who
likes to see a fine barn as well as a good tragedy."

★ ★ ★

Emerson dismissed one acquaintance with, "The louder he
talked of his honour, the faster we counted the spoons." "People
who wash much," he noted, "have a high mind about it, and talk
down to those who wash little. Morning bathers are haughty
scorners." "My cow," he complained, "milks *me!*"; estimated another time, "I have spent say $20 this year in wine and liquors
which are drunk up, and the drinkers are the worse. It would have
bought a beautiful print that would have pleased for a century, or
have paid a debt." "Every hero," he noted sadly, "becomes a bore
at last." "A man of no conversation," he urged, "should smoke."

I doubt that Mr. Emerson would have appreciated television.
"Hospitality," he wrote, "consists in a little fire, a little food—and
an immense quiet."

★ ★ ★

Reactions of the general public to the gyrations of the stock
market are fairly predictable. When a bull market is in progress
in Wall Street, investors and speculators consider themselves
financial wizards. But it is never their fault when the situation
turns sour. Wicked brokers and manipulators are held responsible
for their losses.

Ralph Waldo Emerson was no exception to the rule. And the stock market must have been skidding indeed when he made this waspish entry in his journal: "I took such pains not to keep my money in the house, but to keep it out of reach of burglars by buying stock. I had no guess I was putting it in the hands of these very burglars now grown wise and standing dressed as Railway Directors!"

30. ENGLAND, THEIR ENGLAND

Britain's trade balances aren't as favorable as once they were, and the sun, alas, sinks a little lower on its empire each day—but the British people are as fiercely proud, and loyal, and dependable as ever they were, satisfied that theirs is the only right way to do things because—well, that's the way they always did them. If you disapprove, that's your affair.

They tell about the parliamentary committee that was appointed at the end of World War II to effect repairs in St. Stephen's Chapel, damaged by a stray Nazi buzz bomb. (Miraculously, this was the only bomb that fell on any part of Parliament or nearby Westminster Abbey.)

England's tallest, straightest, and stanchest oaks, the committee knew, grew in Shropshire, and thither the members journeyed to make their selection. They thought they had completed their task, but then they spotted the finest tree of all—the veritable father of all oak trees—deep in Lord So-and-So's estate. They felt they simply had to have that oak, but the lord repulsed them. "The answer, I fear," he said, "is no—just as it was the last time some chaps from Parliament tried to make off with it." "When was that?" demanded the chairman stiffly. The lord answered, "1348."

★ ★ ★

There are not nearly enough seats in the House of Commons to accommodate all the members, so late-comers have their choice of perching on the steps or standing in the rear. Yet when the time came to rebuild the hall, it was Sir Winston Churchill who per-

suaded the committee not to have a single seat added. "Get them
here on time," he argued. "Let the late ones suffer."

Nor were the builders allowed to tamper with the very wide
aisle that separates the two opposing parties: Conservatives and
Labourites. That space was marked off centuries ago, so that hot-
headed adversaries, drawing swords, could barely reach the tips of
each other's weapons at full arm's length. Any member who steps
one inch beyond the designated borderline to this very day is declared out of order.

I must say that I was startled by the lack of decorum exhibited
by the current supposedly august House of Commons. The afternoon I was there, the attendance was comparable to our own
House of Representatives on a run-of-the-mill day. While the
Prime Minister was speaking, other members wandered in and out
without a by-your-leave, and several times the Labour opposition
interrupted with lusty boos. Obviously unperturbed, the P.M. concluded his remarks, took his seat, and calmly stretched his legs out
on the desk!

★ ★ ★

An editorial writer in London's sedate *Times*, while admitting
the harsh realities of Britain's weather, insisted that the forecaster could brighten everybody's outlook by more felicitous choice
of words. "Instead of the endless 'Cloudy, with bright intervals,'"
he proposed, "why not a more optimistic 'Bright, with cloudy intervals' from time to time? Not only would this sound more cheerful, but, who knows, the weather might actually improve a bit!"

★ ★ ★

The *Times* has been investigating another very important matter: the number of times a cuckoo can call without stopping. And
since a great many English people take their bird watching very
seriously, letters have been pouring in on the subject.

One reader in Tilehurst reported he had heard a cuckoo call
distinctly 121 times in succession. "A mere nothing," pooh-poohed

another reader from Leamington Spa. *Her* cuckoo had sounded off 205 times without a pause that refreshes!

A third reader counted over 300 successive cuckoo calls, but honorably disqualified himself when he discovered he was standing outside a clock factory.

A forlorn lass in London wrote the editor of an Advice-to-the-Lovelorn column: "I've been hopelessly in love for years with a peer of the realm, and follow him wherever he goes, but he won't even give me the time of day. Should I continue trying to make him date me?" The editor gave her an emphatic reply. "Obviously," she noted, "you have missed the boat. Why hang around the peer?"

The late Robert Sherwood, eminent playwright and wit, never quite knew how it had come about, but he found himself one day in a group of American tourists being herded through the Shakespeare country. The tour had reached Anne Hathaway's cottage in Stratford, and a painstaking guide was making a speech about every last object on the premises: "Here is the pot in which she brewed tea"; "Here is the bureau on which she kept her knitting," etc. The impatient Sherwood finally added an observation of his own: "And there is the chair in which she read her London *Times*. I can see her now the morning after *Hamlet* opened, scanning the review and muttering, 'Well, I guess the old so-and-so has another hit. . . .'"

It was a common interest in Shakespeare, notes Moss Hart, that prompted a learned scholar in England to conduct a twenty-year correspondence with another learned gent in New York, though never the twain had met. When the Englishman finally announced his intention to visit America, the New Yorker wrote: "You must be my guest."

"Impossible," regretted the Englishman. "I must now confess

that I have two heads—not to mention a tail three feet long. Damn inconvenient, too."

"I don't care how many heads you have," insisted the New Yorker. "You will stay at my house, and I will meet you at the airport."

"Sporting of you, I must say," enthused the Englishman. "And to make sure that you recognize me, I will be wearing a red carnation."

An American publisher, motoring leisurely through Britain, stopped for the night at a pleasant little place that bore the encouraging name of "Writer's Motel."

He liked it, too, but, while checking out the next morning, he asked the person in charge, "Where are all the writers? I didn't spot a single writer the whole time I was here." "Oh," was the answer, "Mr. Writer has gone to London and Mrs. Writer is visiting a sick aunt."

In his amusing book, *My Friends Look Better Than Ever*, Joseph Chase tells about a British admiral who waited until the ladies had retired at a dinner party, and then regaled the male guests with stories about the behavior of seals in the Arctic.

"When the bull seal waxes amorous," explained the admiral, "he comes out of the water on to a slab of ice and sets up a bellow that can be heard for miles. The female seals seem to find it irresistible. I believe I can imitate it for you."

The admiral bellowed lustily, the chinaware rattled, two glasses fell to the floor, and the admiral's wife burst into the room demanding, "Were you calling me, Sir Henry?"

★ ★ ★

David Niven loves to tell the story of the day he made his triumphant return to his exclusive Pall Mall club in London, after years of starring in Hollywood. A member who could have played Colonel Blimp without a bit of make-up looked up from his military journal and humphed, "I say, Niven. They tell me you're about to leave us." "On the contrary, sir," said Niven. "I'm just back. I've been in America." "Extraordinary," mused the member. "Never knew we had a base there." "But we do!" countered Niven. "It's called Fort Goldwyn and I was confined to barracks there for fifteen solid years." "Outrageous," grunted the member, turning back to his journal. "You must lodge a formal protest with the rules committee!"

★ ★ ★

An ex-GI revisited the town in England where he had been bivouacked during World War II. At the local inn he was joined by two hospitable brothers, the elder of whom said, "We like Americans here. Be our guest for dinner." "With pleasure," said the American. "You are just as friendly and generous as a duchess I met here in 1944. Beautiful old girl, with a great estate just over the hill there, and when I think of the things she did to entertain me . . ."

"What's he saying?" demanded one of the English fellows, who obviously was hard of hearing. His brother told him cheerfully, "He knows Mother!"

★ ★ ★

A man approached the inquiry desk of the very swanky Claridge's Hotel in London and asked, "Do you have special terms for commercial travelers?" The frock-coated dignitary behind the desk regarded him coldly and retorted, "We certainly have, you blank-blank blighter! Buzz off!"

★ ★ ★

Eamonn Andrews, who is the panel moderator of the "What's My Line?" TV show in Great Britain, lists some occupations that have never come along to plague John Daly and his American panel—yet, anyhow!

Here are a few: a pork pie raiser, chucker outer, bluebottle breeder, hare controller, skeleton beater, winkle washer, sagger maker's bottom knocker, haggis mixer, ship's husband, brandy snap curler, and a wuzzer.

These are real occupations, mind you! A pork pie raiser, for instance, is a cook of sorts and a winkle washer works in a fish establishment. For further information, you'll have to contact Eamonn Andrews, care of B.B.C., London.

★ ★ ★

"Danny Kaye and Bob Hope aren't the only American comedians who get to meet the big shots when they're in London," points out Jack Benny. "True, I wasn't summoned to visit the royal family—but here's how close I got to the very top: I was invited to dinner at Number 9 Downing Street!"

★ ★ ★

A very smug and complacent British actor disclosed airily to a New York reporter that he had attended both Oxford and Cambridge. "Why did you leave Oxford?" asked the reporter. "Pneumonia, dear boy," explained the actor. "Because you caught it?"

persisted the reporter. "No," admitted the actor. "Because I couldn't spell it."

★ ★ ★

Another British visitor—this one a scenic designer—in the course of an interview at the Waldorf, expressed a great enthusiasm for the game of squash. "Which," demanded an impish scribe, "do you consider most important: squash or sex?" The designer thought this over solemnly for a moment, then countered with, "Do you mean squash tennis or squash racquets?"

★ ★ ★

Two young English lads entered Eton on the same day—and loathed each other at sight. What's more, their hatred grew steadily more intense as they matured.

Years passed. One rose to the rank of admiral in the Royal Navy. The other became a fat, important bishop. Then one day they met at the Oxford railroad station.

The bishop scored first. He poked the admiral right in the middle of his array of gold medals and inquired, "Stationmaster, when does this train pull out for London?"

The admiral never batted an eye. "In twenty minutes, madam," he replied courteously, "but in your condition, should you be traveling?"

★ ★ ★

From a very early day, a part of the south transept in London's Westminster Abbey has been called the Poets' Corner, and here, in the walls and beneath the paving, have been interred the bones of England's greatest writers. An American lady stopped short one day and asked her guide, "But where is Tennyson buried?"

"Madam," he replied gently, "you're standing on him."

31. SEPARATE FABLES

Isak Dinesen is the pseudonym of a very distinguished Danish lady named Baroness Tania Blixen who lives close by Elsinore, the castle Shakespeare chose for the setting of *Hamlet*, and who has written three offbeat but emphatic best-sellers named *Seven Gothic Tales, Out of Africa* and *Winter's Tales*.

It is from the latter volume that I retell, with permission, the following fable:

There lived a doughty sea captain who was fiercely proud of just two things: his wife and his ship. And because he considered his wife the most beautiful thing in the world, he had a replica of her carved in wood for the figurehead of his ship. This aroused his wife's jealousy.

"You love this figurehead more than you do me," she accused. "Nonsense," he answered. "I think highly of it only because it looks like you. And it dances as giddily through the waves as you did the day you married me. But its back is always turned to me, you'll note—and when it's a kiss I'm wanting, it's to you in Elsinore I hurry home."

One day the captain performed a great service for a rich merchant in the Far East, who rewarded him with two very blue, very precious stones. These stones, the merchant hinted, were remarkable in many respects. To the captain, they suggested only his wife's blue eyes, and he promptly had them set into the face of the figurehead on his ship.

Back home for the New Year's celebration, he showed the stones to his wife—who thought that the use to which he had put them was utterly absurd. "What a pair of earrings they would make for me," she sighed, but he bridled at the idea. "No," he told her, deeply troubled, "and if you understood, you would not ask me."

The wife, unconvinced, waited only until the captain was called to Copenhagen, and then she had a local glazier remove the two stones, replacing them with bits of blue glass. "What he doesn't know will not hurt him," she reasoned. But she was wrong.

No sooner had her unwitting husband sailed off with a cargo for Portugal than the greedy lady discovered that her eyesight was failing. Nor could the finest doctors in Denmark be of any help to her. "Never have we heard of a similar case in this part of the world before," they told her. "There is no cure." "If only I could replace the jewels in that accursed figurehead," wailed the wife. "Did he not say they were my eyes?"

But the ship never did come back. Weeks later, word came that it had been wrecked off the coast of Portugal, and gone down with all hands aboard. "And here's the strangest part of the story," concluded the message. "In broad daylight, and on a sea smooth as glass, the ship ran straight into a mighty rock any mariner could see with his naked eye twenty nautical miles away!"

★ ★ ★

One night Adam came home very, very late indeed and found Eve in a temper under the Tree of Knowledge. "Late again," she pouted. "I'll bet you're carrying on with some dizzy blonde."

"Your accusation," countered Adam with dignity, "is not only outrageous but absurd. You know perfectly well there is nobody in this wide, wide world but you and me."

With this, Adam retired for the night. Something caused him to awake with a start, however. There, hovering over him, was Eve—painstakingly counting his ribs.

★ ★ ★

A triumphal feast was scheduled in a remote village, and, to insure adequate liquid refreshments, a great cask was constructed,

174 THE LAUGH'S ON ME

into which each villager agreed to pour one bottle of his very best wine.

"If I fill my bottle with water," reasoned one, "the dilution will be so slight that nobody will notice."

But when the feast commenced, and the cask was tapped, nothing but water poured forth.

Everybody in the village had figured alike: "My bit will not be missed!"

★ ★ ★

There once lived a rich merchant who had three friends. Two he esteemed particularly, the third he accepted with reservations. Accused of cheating on his taxes, the merchant was summoned to court. Naturally, he wanted a character witness, and went to the two friends he loved.

One, however, flatly refused to accompany him, the other volunteered to go only as far as the gate of the court. It was the friend he rated lowest who not only went willingly with him, but so ably defended him that he was acquitted.

In like manner, every man has three friends when Death summons him to appear before his Creator. The one he loves most—his money—cannot go with him a single step. The second—his relatives and neighbors—can accompany him only to the grave. It is his third friend, whom he esteems least—his good works—who goes with him before the Court, and obtains for him his eternal reward.

★ ★ ★

A famous Greek mathematician had all but perfected an equation that would solve the riddle of the universe, and win for him honors and riches too great to compute. "If only I could solve that last small point," he sighed.

"Go to the Wise Woman in Thebes," urged a friend. "Never has she failed yet to come up with the right answer."

So the mathematician set out upon the long and wearisome journey to Thebes, and lo! when he set eyes on the Wise Woman of

Thebes he found her to be the most luscious and beautiful creature he ever had seen.

"I can receive thee this day," she informed him in a husky, vibrant voice, "because my husband is out hunting. I can answer one question only. What will it be?"

The mathematician sighed ecstatically. "When," he asked softly, "will thy husband be returning from that hunt?"

32. FARMERS

The late Alben Barkley told about a farmer in the drought country who was able to survive only because a kindly storekeeper gave him unlimited credit. Then came good fortune: plenty of rain and steadily rising prices for the farmer's crops. He paid back his entire debt—but then the storekeeper never set eyes on him for a solid year. Next time they met, the farmer was driving a shiny, new car and he and his four sons were dressed up fit to kill. "How come," asked the storekeeper reproachfully, "that you now shop elsewhere after I carried you on my books for so many lean years?"

The farmer all but wept. "Goshamighty, Tom," he mourned, "I didn't realize you sold for cash!"

★ ★ ★

An anonymous friend mailed me the following little poem. I wish somebody could identify the author:

Grandmother, on a winter's day, milked the cows, slopped the hogs, saddled the mule, and got the children off to school; did a washing, mopped the floors, washed the windows, and did some chores; cooked a dish of home-dried fruit, pressed her husband's Sunday suit, swept the parlor, made the bed, baked a dozen loaves of bread, split some firewood and lugged it in, enough to fill the kitchen bin; cleaned the lamps and put in oil, stewed some apples she thought would spoil; churned the butter, baked a cake, then exclaimed, "For goodness' sake, the calves have got out of the pen," and went out and chased them in again; gathered the eggs and locked the stable, back to the house and set the table, cooked a supper that was delicious, and afterward washed up all the dishes;

fed the cat and sprinkled the clothes, mended a basketful of hose; then opened the organ and began to play "When you come to the end of a perfect day."

★ ★ ★

A farmer down in Delaware came into a big air-conditioning plant and said, "I want an estimate on the cost of installing an air-conditioning unit in my chicken coop. My chicks lay twice as many eggs in cool weather and I aim to eliminate that midsummer slump."

An alert salesman said, "How about figuring on a unit for your home at the same time?" "What good would that do?" countered the farmer. "My wife doesn't lay eggs."

★ ★ ★

In western Kentucky, writes Mel Clay, two miserable chicken thieves got delusions of grandeur and decided to steal a pig. Unknowingly, the porker they hustled into their beaten-up truck was a winner of three blue ribbons at state fairs, the pride and joy of its owner, Colonel Culpepper. The irate colonel alerted the sheriff, who hastily established road blocks on the state highway. The robbers blundered right into one of them.

They hastily attired the pig in one of their old coats, jammed a battered fedora down on its head, and propped it up between them on the driver's seat.

"Who are you three varmints?" demanded the sheriff, as they drove up to him. "I'm Abraham Lincoln Johnson," quavered one of the thieves. "I'm his brother George Washington Johnson," added the other. The sheriff turned his flashlight on the pig in the middle and barked, "And what's your name?" "Oink," answered the pig.

The sheriff grudgingly let the truck proceed on its way, but ten minutes later he still was scratching his head. "You know, Tom," he told his deputy, "that Oink Johnson is just about the homeliest man I've ever seen."

★ ★ ★

Herb Shriner boasts that a fireman in his home town has rescued at least a dozen girls but never got a single medal or promotion for his bravery. He rescued the girls from the fire chief.

★   ★   ★

The keeper of a general store in a small New Hampshire village bought a fresh stock from a Boston wholesaler, but neglected to pay for it. The wholesaler, his dunning letters ignored, wrote to the local banker to check on his customer's credit rating, to the county judge to ask for the name of the best lawyer in those parts, and to the station agent to make sure the goods had been delivered in the first place. Back came this note: "As station master I delivered your goods O.K., and as owner of the store, signed receipt for same. As bank president, I O.K. my credit. As judge, I recommend myself as the best lawyer in these parts. And, if I wasn't the pastor too, I'd tell you to go to hell!"

★   ★   ★

Who says those tight-lipped folks up New Hampshire way have no sense of humor? An inn in Plymouth, New Hampshire, advertises: "No, the Pilgrims *did not* land here. The *Mayflower did not* anchor in our harbor because we haven't any harbor. We're 483 feet above sea level—and a long way from the coast. But we do have many visitors and they're the kind who make us proud to have them around. Our weather is regular New England weather. Ninety per cent of all the weather in the world passes through our

Main Street every winter. It is then distributed to the weaker communities in diluted doses."

★ ★ ★

Frank Boyden, headmaster of the famous Deerfield Academy in Massachusetts since 1902, remembers when Deacon Greenough grew horseradish in a field adjacent to the school, and gave each lad a small bottle thereof when he departed for summer vacation. The bottles bore this legend: "If a boy loves a girl, that's his business. If a girl loves a boy, that's her business. But if they both love horseradish, that's *my* business."

★ ★ ★

A farmer in Iowa was riding his mule down a narrow lane when he came to an orchard full of ripe, luscious apples. From the mule's back, he reached up to pluck a few, but just then the pernickety mule bolted from under him, leaving him hanging perilously from a branch overhead. "Confound it," bellowed the owner of the orchard, who *would* happen along at that precise moment, "whatcha doin' up there in my tree?" "Nothing at all," soothed the quick-thinking trespasser. "I just fell off my mule."

★ ★ ★

SOCIAL NOTES IN THE GOOSE CREEK DAILY GAZETTE:
1. At the Odd Fellows' picnic Sunday, Mrs. Murchison won first prize in the ladies' rolling-pin throwing contest. She threw her pin ninety-nine yards.
2. Mr. Murchison won the one hundred-yard dash.

★ ★ ★

The proprietor of the general store in a tiny North Dakota hamlet was appointed postmaster. For three solid months thereafter not a single piece of mail emanated from the place. Not only local residents but government postal authorities demanded an explanation—and this was it: "THE BAG AIN'T FULL YET!"

★ ★ ★

Tip to weekend farmers by Herman Fox: "Don't throw away your empty seed packets when you've finished your planting. They frequently are just the right size for storing the crop."

★ ★ ★

Stuart Chase has a neighbor whose little crop of corn was ruined last summer because of a scarcity of rain. "We did everything possible to provoke a storm," he complained. "Left out the tennis rackets, washed the car regularly, planned picnics for the weekends, and invited guests from a hundred miles away—and would you believe it, in spite of all that, the darn sun went on shining without a cloud in the sky!"

★ ★ ★

John Straley tells about the city fellow who bought Seth Perkins' place in Hicksville. Two weeks later every one of his baby chicks was dead. "What did you feed them?" Seth demanded. "Feed them?" echoed the city fellow. "I thought the old hen nursed them!"

Later in the summer, Seth met the city man driving a load of hay and mopping his brow with a bandanna. "First time I've ever gotten this hot," he complained. "Mebbe," reckoned Seth, "it's the first time you ever sat on a load of burning hay!"

That's when Seth Perkins decided to run for state assemblyman. He had to shake hands with a hundred constituents a day—and because he had milked so many cows, he shook hands one finger at a time.

★ ★ ★

A farmer up in Maine owned that rarest of beasts, a talking pig, but he lacked the perspicacity to cash in on it. A visitor from Boston discovered the pig's unique gift by accident. "Gadzooks!" he exclaimed, "This pig can talk—and with a Harvard accent, at that." "Yup," agreed the farmer. "He's been shootin' off his mouth now for nigh on to three years." "But why have you never told anybody about this?" marveled the Boston man. The farmer sighed and said, "Well, I kept hoping he'd outgrow it!"

★ ★ ★

An elderly banker sold out his business for several million dollars and took up farming in a mild but expensive way. One of his costlier purchases was a lot of two hundred pigs and a prize boar.

The next time he visited New York, he told his old associates that the pigs hadn't been on his property ten days before he noticed a peculiar thing. The boar wasn't paying the slightest attention to a single one of the sows.

"Luckily for me, however," continued the banker, "a highfalutin veterinarian came along and suggested that I mix some special new vitamin pills in that boar's diet. And from the day he started eating them, he hasn't given those sows one moment's peace."

An ex-partner asked, "What's the name of those new vitamin pills?"

"I don't remember their name," confessed the banker, "but I'll tell you this. They taste like peppermint."

33. THE FIGHT GAME

The late Jim Jeffries, once heavyweight champion, liked to tell this story about his father: "Pa always hankered to be a successful farmer, but the fates seemed to plague him. When it wasn't bad weather, it was the bugs and pests. Then the nearby city of Los Angeles began busting at the seams, and people were always at Pa to sell them a little bit more of his farmland. Smaller and smaller the crops got, till Pa finally came to us, almost in tears, and said, 'Kids, we'll have to move somewhere else. The farm's plumb gone. All we got left is this roof over our heads, a ten-thousand-acre orange grove, and two million dollars in the bank.'"

★ ★ ★

Another famous titleholder, Jim Corbett, once met Steve Brodie, the man who jumped off the Brooklyn Bridge—but the meeting was not a rousing success. "So you're Brodie," enthused Corbett. "I've always wanted to meet the man who could jump over Brooklyn Bridge." "You got it a bit wrong, Mr. Corbett," explained Brodie. "I only jumped OFF that bridge." "What! only OFF the bridge?" exploded Corbett. "Why, any darn fool could do that"— and walked away.

★ ★ ★

"Spike" O'Shaugnessy, toughest hombre in the Five Points section, always swore that if he ever was blessed with a son, he'd raise him to be a heavyweight champion. Mrs. O'Shaugnessy finally produced a young heir for him, and the blissful "Spike" promptly dumbfounded his associates by naming the infant

"Clarence." His explanation was a simple one. "Wid a monniker like dat," smiled Spike, "de poor little so-and-so'll have to know how to fight by de time he's four years old."

★ ★ ★

"Butch" McGuire, the terror of the Ninth Ward, was over-matched in his bout with the middleweight champ, and was knocked cold in the third round after absorbing a dreadful beating. Coming to at length in his dressing room, Butch fastened a baleful eye on his manager, Slippery Sam Finnegan, and mumbled through a split lip, "Just you get me a return match wid dat bum, Slippery, and you'll see a real massacre. I'll knock your block off!"

★ ★ ★

Ex-pugilist Buddy Baer told Herb Stein there was no truth in the story that he and Brother Max, both of whom fought Joe Louis in their time, were scared to death of the Brown Bomber. "Max and I offered to fight him again," he insisted, "but the Boxing Commission wouldn't let both of us in the ring with him at the same time."

★ ★ ★

On his first professional appearance, an apprentice heavyweight was absorbing a dreadful shellacking. "Let him land a couple of wallops on your *left* eye next round," urged his compassionate manager. "Your face is getting lopsided."

34. FISH STORIES

Before the opening of a recent American League pennant race, Ted Williams, the famous Red Sox outfielder, went out on a fishing expedition with Benny Goodman, the eminent clarinetist, and the two of them came back with the biggest single day's catch of the season. One sailfish was such a whopper, in fact, that a stranger on the dock exclaimed, "The fellow who caught that fish is a dog-gone liar."

Every time he tells this story, admits Goodman, the size of the fish grows materially. "But when you're telling a fish story," he advises, "remember honesty is the best policy. Never tell a man more than you think he will believe."

★ ★ ★

"Fishing again," wailed the wife of another dedicated angler as he kissed his wife absent-mindedly farewell. "I do believe I'd drop dead if you spent one weekend at home with me." "Now, now," he countered. "No bribes!"

★ ★ ★

One of the country's most ardent and expert fishermen is ex-President Herbert Hoover. They tell of one day when he waited in vain, however, for a single strike, and then, to make matters worse, encountered on the way home a lad toting a wonderful catch of speckled trout. "Where did you get them?" exclaimed Mr. Hoover enviously. "I found the perfect spot," boasted the boy, obviously unaware of his questioner's identity. "You just walk down that lane marked 'Private' till you come to a sign saying 'Trespassers will be prosecuted.' Just beyond is a stream marked 'No fishing allowed,' and there you are."

* * *

My uncle Al, who knows all the anglers, writes from Florida about one fellow who boasted, "What a dream I had last night, men! I was out in the middle of a lake all alone with Marilyn Monroe." "Did the dream have a happy ending?" prompted Uncle Al. "Did it!" enthused the sportsman. "I caught a nine-pound big-mouth black bass!"

* * *

A gentleman came home from a weekend at Newport in a state of virtual collapse. "What have you been up to with those ritzy society folk?" asked his doctor. "Fishing through the ice," was the answer. "In August? What for?" scoffed the doctor. "Cherries," explained the gentleman.

* * *

Two fish were idly flipping their fins in the English Channel when a black shadow spread over the scene. "Must be a storm blowing up above us," hazarded one. "Nonsense," corrected the other. "That was only the *Queen Mary's* bottom."

Fish number one, visibly impressed, murmured, "God save the King!"

* * *

Ivan Sanderson's *Follow the Whale* is a whale of a book. These are samples of the facts it divulges: 1. There are fifty-one varieties of whales, counting dolphins and porpoises. 2. White-sided dolphins assemble in schools as large as two thousand. 3. Right whales are called right because they're the only variety that doesn't sink when killed. 4. Sperm whales can stay under water for an hour and a half, bottlenose whales for as long as two hours. 5. One bottlenose whale was found with the beaks of ten thousand cuttlefish in its stomach. 6. The largest whale ever measured was a female blue 113 feet long, with an estimated weight of 170 tons. 7. Whales make quite a racket. Not only as they "talk" incessantly under water but their stomachs growl prodigiously. A governor of Tasmania once complained that he had been kept awake all night by the "snoring" of inconsiderate whales in the sea outside his window!

* * *

Two solemn-visaged Vermonters went fishing one summer day in an old launch. For three hours neither of them moved a muscle. Then the one up forward became a bit restless. "Confound it, Seth," grumbled his companion. "That's the second time you've shifted your feet in twenty minutes. Did you come out here to fish or practice dancing?"

* * *

Cedric Adams tells of two dauntless fishermen who were trolling for muskellunge on a lake in northern Minnesota. The muskies were vicious that day, and snapping at everything—but they absolutely refused to be hooked.

"I say we quit," said one fisherman finally. "O.K. by me," agreed the other. "I don't mind them having Sunday dinner off my bait, but what gets me is when they shove their heads up, lean back on their flippers, and use my line for dental floss."

★ ★ ★

All day long Mr. Shaugnessy sat fishing from the end of the recreation pier, and all day long a stranger sat behind him, watching intently. Finally Mr. Shaugnessy turned and asked with sarcastic politeness, "Did it ever occur to you to do some fishing of your own?" "Never," admitted the kibitzer cheerfully. "I haven't the patience for it."

★ ★ ★

There was a paragraph in the sports section the other day about a fisherman in Cuba who, just like Ernest Hemingway's *The Old Man and the Sea,* hooked an enormous marlin from a small sailing boat and spent two whole nights and a day wearing him down before bringing him in.

That reminded me of a story Charlie Case, a great and original monologist, used to tell up and down the Keith-Orpheum circuit when I was a boy. Case claimed that he had been treed in the South by a snarling, bloodthirsty wildcat, and spent a long, harrowing night keeping just out of reach of his claws.

"I think I can safely say," concluded Case, "that I never was so tired of an animal in my life."

35. FLORIDA

Standing at a window on the top floor of the newly enlarged $20,000,000 Fontainebleau Hotel in Miami Beach, and gazing south at a maze of luxurious stucco palaces and swimming pools, it is difficult to realize that barely forty-five years ago this area was an almost inaccessible jungle wilderness.

The transformation of greater Miami is a story of typical American imagination and daring. Jack Kofoed tells it in *Moon Over Miami* and Jane Fisher implements it with *Fabulous Hoosier*, the life story of her late husband, Carl.

There wasn't even a trolley car in Miami until 1905. "The first one ran along Flagler Street," recalls Kofoed, "and adhered to no rigid schedule. If a lady waved her parasol, the accommodating motorman would back up four blocks to take her aboard. He'd also stop the car as long as ten minutes, smoking his pipe placidly while another rider did her morning shopping. About once every ten blocks, the car went off the tracks, and all the male passengers would have to get out to help the crew lift it back on to the rails."

When Carl Fisher, with John S. Collins and a few other hardy operators, surveyed Miami Beach in 1913, it was overrun with tangled, deep-rooted palmetto and mangrove trees. Alligators and snakes lurked in its treacherous marshes. The mosquitoes were most murderous of all.

But Fisher had only to discover, noted Will Rogers, that "sand would hold up a real estate sign, and that mosquitoes could be rehearsed not to bite you until after you bought." Two years and many millions of dollars later, a causeway linked the Beach with

Miami proper, and Lincoln Road had been hacked through the wilderness. (Recently, property on Lincoln Road has sold as high as ten thousand dollars a front foot!) Every tree, every flower, every blade of grass in Miami Beach had to be planted by hand.

In 1915, Carl Fisher offered six hundred feet of ocean frontage in the heart of Miami Beach absolutely free to anyone who would build a $200,000 hotel on it. Not one soul nibbled at the bait.

A few years later, on that exact spot, however, the Roney Plaza shot up at a cost of two million. And now there's talk of replacing it with a new edifice at ten times THAT figure.

For the 1959 season, Greater Miami Beach boasted 396 hotels, 79 motels, and 2,477 apartment buildings. Every year the hostelries have grown more fantastic and elaborate. But it's hard to see how they're ever going to top the Fontainebleau. With five acres of cabanas, three separate beaches (where you sometimes get even more sun than you've basked for), six imposing restaurants, two complete convention halls, a ballroom seating four thousand, and 847 flunkeys adding considerably to the general hubbub, it is entirely possible, though not recommended, to lose your wife on Tuesday morning and not find her again until Sunday night—without either of you ever leaving the premises.

In furtherance of the Gallic spirit, the management has thoughtfully printed all warning signs and directions in French. They feel it's no fault of theirs if not one guest or employee in twenty can understand what the signs mean. The sentiments of the first garbage remover who was confronted with the admonition, *"Defense d'entrer,"* have not been recorded for posterity. To most of the patrons, "Fontainebleau" means simply "Bring Money."

★ ★ ★

The owner of one big hotel and movie chain in Florida is named Schine, and Jack Paar is dying for him to take a horseback ride on a horse named Harvest Moon. Paar wants a photograph of this happenstance. The caption he has in mind for it, as you've undoubtedly guessed, is "Schine on Harvest Moon."

A man back from the Florida gold coast says that the tipping nuisance there has reached an all-time high. He phoned downstairs for a deck of cards on one occasion and the bellboy delivered them in fifty-two separate trips—one card at a time!

★ ★ ★

A doctor admired the names on some luxurious yachts tied up in Key Biscayne, Florida: fancy notions like *Sea Sprite, Moonbeam,* and the like. The one that really tickled him, however, was a neat craft labeled simply *The $28,500.*

★ ★ ★

An elderly, bejeweled lady in Florida was boasting about her two remarkable grandchildren. "Tell me, Mrs. Rosenwasser," interrupted another sunbather, "how old are your grandsons?" Mrs. Rosenwasser favored her with a grateful smile and replied, "The doctor is four and the lawyer is six."

★ ★ ★

Another proud lady had no grandchildren to boast about, but she never did stop talking about her unmarried son. "He's thirty-one, and a millionaire already, but it's because of me he never married," she told anybody who would listen. "He takes me everywhere. I'm his date at first nights in the theater and cocktail parties. He wouldn't dream of coming to Florida unless I come with him. Every day he goes to the most famous psychiatrist in New York—for fifty dollars an hour. *And who do you think he spends the entire time there talking about?*"

36. VIVE LA FRANCE!

On the wall of many a French restaurant, a sign reminds patrons that *"un repas sans vin est comme un jour sans soleil."* ("A meal without wine is like a day without the sun.") It's scarcely necessary. Standard equipment for workers in France—and Italy, too—when they set out to perform their day's tasks, is a loaf of fresh bread under one arm and a bottle or jug of wine under the other. More affluent citizens sometimes skip the bread.

The Frenchman defends his incessant wine bibbing—and it is indeed a habit easy to catch—by explaining that it's just the thing for the *foie* (the liver). But as Alexis Lichine points out in his definitive *Wines of France* he doesn't add that the wine makes it veritable child's play to eat the rich food that *does* cause the liver to act up. One sip of choice wine leaves the mouth perfectly clean and ready for another succulent morsel of just what the doctor has warned you not to eat.

★ ★ ★

There is an endless ritual—and highfalutin talk—in the selection of a proper wine and a proper vintage. Among connoisseurs, sending one bottle out of three back to the kitchen because it's "corky" or the wrong temperature is about par for the course.

There was one gourmet in Hollywood whose pretensions on the subject of wines became intolerable to his friends. To show him up, one went to extraordinary lengths. He searched the town for a bottle of the rarest and costliest French wine available, then poured its contents into an empty bottle of a cheap domestic brand advertised on TV at twenty-nine cents a quart. Then he asked the gourmet for dinner.

The mere sight of the twenty-nine-cent bottle made the gourmet turn pale, and when his glass was filled he looked wildly for the nearest exit. There was no escape, however, so, with the host and his wife watching intently, he took one small sip. Then he took another.

His reputation hung in the balance. He was equal to the test. He put down his glass very gently, smacked his lips, and said, "My dear boy, you never should have tried a juvenile trick like this. *You can't afford it!*"

★　★　★

A New York importer consulted the wine list at an inn in the château district of France, and was surprised to note that the wines of poor years were priced very much higher than those of good years.

"It is for your compatriots, who usually know nothing about wines," the proprietor explained readily. "Always they order the most expensive. Thus we sell them our poor wine—and save the best for our regular clients!"

★　★　★

At the age of ninety-four, a French playwright boasted that he still drank four bottles of wine a day and made love to three different women. "In recent months, however," he admitted sadly, "I've had to warn those women not to cough."

★　★　★

In this year's version of an oft-told tale, it's Brigitte Bardot who stepped out of a shower in her Paris Ritz suite and found a window washer gazing rapturously at her from his perch outside the bathroom. Miss Bardot was reportedly too stunned even to reach for her traditional towel; she just stared and stared. Finally, the window washer broke the impasse by hollering, in colloquial French, "Wassamatter, lady? Ain't you never seen a window washer before?"

★　★　★

A Parisian genius has invented a new version of that murderous Russian roulette game. It's called Shower Roulette. Six men have to take showers, and then are handed towels. In one of the towels is wrapped Brigitte Bardot.

And before bidding adieu to a fascinating subject, have you heard about the man from outer space who landed in Paris and told the first gendarme he spied, "I'll see your leader later. First, take me to Brigitte Bardot"?

★ ★ ★

One day somebody is sure to write a book about the Ritz Hotel in Paris. It dates back to 1892, when the gay Prince of Wales (later King Edward VII) summoned Charles Ritz and told him, "I want a nice, secluded little hotel in Paris where I can steal off for occasional—er, relaxation. It must have English service, American plumbing, and French cooking!"

Ritz went back to Paris and bought the Lauzun Palace, on the Place Vendôme. It contained only twenty apartments, the demand for which was so insistent that Ritz expanded less than two years later. He bought a structure on the Rue Cambon, built an arcade to connect it with the Lauzun Palace—and that's the way it's been ever since—two hundred rooms with a staff of 450 to give guests the kind of service they wish they were accustomed to. The Ritz has paid its stockholders an undeviating annual dividend of 7 per cent. To this day no electricity is allowed in the kitchen; the chefs claim it makes the *spécialités de la maison* taste different— and heaven forbid that anything come along to disturb the ritual established sixty-four years ago!

★ ★ ★

The Paris subway, called the "Métro," doesn't carry as many passengers each day as its counterpart in New York, but has several unique features worthy of comment. In the first place, it has "first" and "second" class compartments. First class costs a penny or two more and is equipped with cushioned seats. There are also special seats on every train set aside for invalids and la-dies expecting bundles from heaven—a fine idea that managers of American urban rail systems well might borrow.

Another excellent feature of the Paris "Métro" prevents pas-sengers from holding up a train at the last minute by trying to pry open half-closed doors. As a train enters the station, gates auto-matically shut at all entrances to the platform, so that only pas-sengers already on the platform can climb aboard. As the train pulls out, the entrance gates open again on now-empty platforms.

★ ★ ★

A tourist at the Louvre was surprised to see a veritable horde of students copying the famous original paintings on the walls. Tapping a guide on the shoulder, he asked, "Say, what do they do with the old pictures when the new ones are finished?"

★ ★ ★

Bill Feather quotes this despairing paragraph from the writings of the French artist, Jean Gabrial Domergue: "The world belongs to women. When a man is born, people ask how his mother is. When he gets married, people exclaim, 'Isn't the bride sweet!' When he is dead, people ask, 'How much did he leave her?'"

★ ★ ★

A couple of French tourists, winding up an extensive trip around the United States, passed an old folks' home. The inmates were rocking back and forth vigorously in their chairs on the porch. "*Regardez*, Clarinda," marveled the French husband. "These crazy Americans keep up their mad pace to the very end."

★ ★ ★

A beautiful young American girl in a shining red sports convertible got caught in the whirling jam of traffic round the Arc de Triomphe in Paris one afternoon. Around and around she went, unable to extricate herself and proceed on her journey down the Champs Elysées. Furthermore, a smiling gendarme who saluted her each time she circled past him added to her exasperation.

Finally she risked life and limb by braking to a halt and tearfully demanding of the gendarme, "You see what's happening to me. Why don't you help me get out of this mess?" "Ah, mademoiselle," beamed the gendarme. "You are so very beautiful I can hardly wait to see you come around again!"

37. THE GAMING TABLES

A bridge partner of expert Ely Culbertson once threw away a certain grand slam. Culbertson assured him, "I see big things ahead of you—all of them insuperable obstacles." When the game was over, he added for good measure, "You can fool some of the people all of the time. You're one of them."

★ ★ ★

Hal Sims, late bridge wizard, always insisted, "The one thing amateurs never will learn is that the best bid in a bridge hand very often is 'I pass.'"

★ ★ ★

Oswald Jacoby, another master of the game, was asked to comment on the play of a certain prominent book manufacturer. "I had given up on him," admitted Jacoby, "but about two years ago, his game suddenly took a turn for the better. He quit."

★ ★ ★

Three old card-playing cronies were plagued so consistently by a talkative kibitzer, they resorted to a subtle stratagem to rout him.

They invented a brand-new game, improvising as they went along. Thus, while the kibitzer looked increasingly bewildered, the dealer tore the deck in half, dealt three halves to one crony, seven to another, and kept the rest for himself. He then announced, "I have a mingle. I bet one buck."

The second player declared, "I've got a shnorkel. I raise you two dollars."

The third enthused, "You don't bluff me out. I have a farfel. I raise you both ten!"

At this point the kibitzer pulled himself together. He shook the third player's shoulder and hollered, "Are you nuts? With a miserable farfel, you got the nerve to raise a mingle and a shnorkel?"

★ ★ ★

Jerry D. Lewis, author of a tiptop collection of poker stories called *Dealer's Choice,* reveals that Hoyle—"whose name has become a part of our language as a synonym for the Supreme Court of Poker—not only never wrote any book of poker rules; he never played or even heard of the game!"

Hoyle, it seems, wrote a very successful book on whist, so when the publishers decided to bring out a poker rule manual, they merely appropriated the Hoyle name.

★ ★ ★

What are *your* chances of drawing a big hand in a poker game? Lewis asserts there are 2,598,960 possible combinations, and that you have:

1	chance in	649,740	for a royal flush.
1	" "	64,973	for a straight flush.
1	" "	4,164	for four of a kind.
1	" "	693	for a full house.
1	" "	508	for a flush.
1	" "	254	for a straight.
1	" "	46	for three of a kind.
1	" "	20	for two pairs.
1	" "	1¼	for one pair.

The man who has the best chance in a poker game, however, adds Lewis, is the fellow who's lucky enough to know just when to quit and go home.

★ ★ ★

On a transatlantic liner, a passenger allowed himself to be counted in on a high-stake poker game, protesting to the promoters that he hadn't touched a card in ten full years. Given the deck to deal, he weighed it absent-mindedly in his hand, and observed, "This deck is one card short!"

★ ★ ★

Underneath the broadwalk at a Gulfside winter resort, a dice game was raging. A newcomer joined the group, and patiently awaited his turn to "shoot." When it came, he planked a soiled ten-spot on the blanket, was promptly covered, uttered a few supplications to Lady Luck—and rolled the dice. Unfortunately for him, a third die rolled out of his sleeve, and joined the pair which already registered a five and a two. The third die stopped at six.

There was a moment of tense silence, and then the acknowledged leader of the game quietly reached out and slipped the third die into his pocket. Then he handed the original two to the shooter. "Go ahead and shoot, boy," he said, pulling out a razor. "Your point is thirteen."

★ ★ ★

When it comes to dyed-in-the-wool gamblers, you've got to hand it to Lady Godiva, insists Jimmy Durante. She put everything she had on a horse.

"Horses don't bother me nearly as much as bees," continued Durante. "A fellow I thought was my pal insisted on showing me his beehives. I stuck my face into one of those hives, and when those bees got a load of my schnozzola, the queen bee hollered, 'Run for the hills, boys: it's an anteater!' "

Durante also tells us he's figured out what to do in case there's ever an air raid while he's playing in Las Vegas. "I'll just hide under a slot machine," says Jimmy. "They ain't been hit for years."

★ ★ ★

A New Yorker, eager to test his luck at the gaming tables, flew to Las Vegas and taxied to a hotel on the "Strip." He handed the driver a twenty-dollar bill and said, "I hope you can give me change for this." The driver shot a reproachful look at his passenger and explained, "Out here, brother, a twenty-dollar bill IS change."

★ ★ ★

Joey Bishop was patronizing a quiet little hideaway at Las Vegas when a character suggested, "Come out to the swimming pool and let me demonstrate my new trick. I can stay under water for three hours." "Three hours!" echoed Bishop. "You'll drown." "Oh, darn," grumbled the character. "You know the trick."

To this story, Bishop adds the postscript, "Las Vegas is the only spot in the world where you'll find ladies with chinchilla wraps and diamonds fishing for nickels in a slot machine."

★ ★ ★

Even Las Vegas croupiers, hardened to big shots and staggering sums won and lost at the gaming tables, blinked their eyes when one luckless wit lost, on successive nights, $50,000, $75,000, and $90,000. "Good heavens," gasped one croupier finally, "where do you dredge up all that money you're losing? From a pump?" The gambler socked him right in the nose, snarling, "Don't you call my wife a pump!"

★ ★ ★

A group of top-level scientists took time off from their study of interplanetary rockets and missiles for a Las Vegas "vacation." One of them spent so much time at the roulette tables that a colleague grumbled, "Jones there is throwing away his hard-earned savings as though there was no tomorrow."

The man he addressed looked thoughtful. "Maybe," he commented finally, "Jones *knows* something!"

38. GHOSTS

Do I believe in ghosts? Well, I'm not *sure*. Neither are you.

Deep down in the souls of the most sophisticated of us lurks an abiding fear of the supernatural which all the discoveries of scientists cannot eradicate.

One of the country's most celebrated scholars, being interviewed on television, pooh-poohed the very idea of ghosts for ten minutes, but then, when asked point-blank if he would sleep alone in a house reputed to be haunted, replied hastily, "Not on your life. *Suppose I'm wrong?*" Of course, the scholar may have been influenced by the fact that he was talking on a ghost-to-ghost network.

★ ★ ★

Vincent Starrett tells about a young man in China, a long time ago, who had been asleep in the guest house of a lonely country estate, and awoke with a start to find a beautiful woman in the room with him. She was sitting at a dressing table, humming tunelessly, and combing her long black tresses. Suddenly, without warning, she lifted her head from her shoulders and set it on the table before her!

The young man rushed screaming to the living room, where four strangers were playing mah-jongg. "What's the matter?" asked one of them. "Matter?" echoed the distrait young man. "I woke up to find a mysterious woman in my room—and she just took off her head and put it on the table!"

"Is *that* all?" scoffed one of the players. "Why, *every one* of us can do that, too."

And they did—all four of them!

A she-ghost complained that a certain he-ghost was getting a trifle too familiar. "Don't be angry," he begged. "I'm simply doing what comes supernaturally."

★ ★ ★

Financier Bernard Baruch is one of many notables who likes to tell spooky stories—when the spirits move him. He was rattling off a series of them at his plantation in Hobcaw, South Carolina, one evening, and the eyes of an impressionable young retainer grew bigger and bigger as the session progressed.

Along about midnight, a guest named Ed Smith asked the retainer to take a message down the road a piece. Very reluctantly, the boy stepped out into the starless night, whistling valiantly. When Smith heard him returning, he stole behind a tree in the yard and emitted a bloodcurdling "Ooooo."

The boy stopped dead in his tracks. "Is that you, Mr. Ed?" he quavered.

The long wail was repeated.

"Mr. Ed," decided the boy, "I know that's you—but I'm going to run anyhow!"

★ ★ ★

A man named Devlin had waited until the last moment to catch his plane for California and he kept glancing at his watch as the taxi whirled him out to Idlewild Airport. He didn't notice the camera on the back seat of the cab until he was almost at the field.

It was a foreign make, obviously expensive. Twenty of the roll of thirty-six pictures had been exposed. There was no time for long explanations to the driver. Devlin put the camera with his own luggage, thinking, "I'll watch the classified ads in the New York paper I see every morning. Someone's bound to claim it."

But nobody did. After a decent interval, Devlin had the reel developed. The man who handed him back the pictures had a strange look on his face, Devlin thought. Outside the store, he looked at the prints himself.

They had been shot from different angles, but all were taken, obviously, at the same place.

They showed Abraham Lincoln delivering his speech at Gettysburg.

★ ★ ★

A sagacious farmer in Vermont, feeling that his end was near, instructed his wife, "I want to be buried nekkid, Effy. I know where I'm headed, and I won't need any clothes down there."

Some days after his demise, his ghost flitted through a keyhole and tapped his startled widow lightly on the shoulder. "Effy," it whispered, "I'll need my suit and heavy overcoat after all. There are so many well-heeled folks in Hell these days, they had to put in air-conditioning!"

39. GIRLS

"Yes, sir," boomed the father of the town's richest—and ugliest
—girl, "the man who marries my daughter will certainly get a
prize." Cautious bachelor Erskine asked politely, "May I see it?"

Colonel Corncrib, of Ottawa, Illinois, divides Womankind into
five ages: From 1 to 10, the GOOP age; from 11 to 15, the HOOP
age; from 15 to 50, the SNOOP age; from 50 to 70, the DUPE age;
and after 70, the STOOP age.

More poetic—and long-winded—Hindus have this conception of
what constitutes a "perfect woman": "Take the lightness of the leaf
and the glance of the fawn; the gaiety of the sun's rays and the
tears of the mist; the inconstancy of the wind and the timidity of
the hare; the vanity of the peacock and the softness of the down on
the throat of a swallow. Add the harshness of a diamond, the sweet
flavor of honey, the cruelty of the tiger, the warmth of fire, and the
chill of snow, the chatter of the jay and the cooing of the turtle-
dove. Melt and mingle these ingredients and woman is the result."

★ ★ ★

Arch Armed knows a girl who is the closest thing to Abbe Lane:
she looks like Xavier Cugat.

Joe E. Lewis, on the other hand, thinks that his new girl has
early American features: *she* looks like a buffalo.

Garry Moore advises that you always can size up a nice girl by
the sweet nothing-doings she whispers in your ear.

Arthur Hornblow says that his beautiful bride, Leonora, learned just two French words on their honeymoon in Paris. One was Van Cleef, the·other Arpels.

Edith Head, famed Hollywood dress designer, suggests, "Your dresses should be tight enough to show you're a girl, and loose enough to show you're a lady."

Allan King believes that "the girl who doesn't gossip has no friends to speak of."

Maggie O'Flaherty comes up with the perfect gift for a girl who has everything: penicillin.

Charles Boyer believes "A boy becomes a man at twenty-one, whereas a girl becomes a lady at a moment's notice."

And Robert Q. Lewis has made a minor change in an old nursery rhyme: "Mary had a little lime; she also had some gin. And everywhere that Mary went, was where she thought she'd bin."

★ ★ ★

At the Miss America contest, the fair representatives of the states of New Hampshire and Alabama met in the dressing room. "We might as well face it," sighed the miss from New England. "Men are all alike." The Alabama beauty smiled her agreement, and murmured, "Men are all Ah like too."

★ ★ ★

It was bound to happen sooner or later. Jimmy Durante met a girl whose nose was even bigger than his. "It's meant a fortune to me," said Jimmy, "but I imagine it's a cause of some embarrassment to you. Why don't you get it fixed?" The girl wailed, "You don't understand, Mr. Durante. I've *already* had it fixed."

★ ★ ★

In a manual for bachelors called *The Little Black Book,* authors Caldwallader and Nudnick give this advice to huntsmen stalking their prey: "In the seclusion of your apartment when things are progressing nicely and your overtures are being reasonably well received, it is essential that interruptions be avoided. A vital trifle to keep in mind is the young lady's handbag. *It should always be kept well out of her reach.* In that magpie's nest, which is a woman's purse, lies a veritable arsenal of defense weapons: comb, powder, lipstick, nail file, cigarette holder, etc.—so immobilize her and do not permit her to fence and parry with any of the above articles of war."

★ ★ ★

A debutante hadn't returned home from a date with a new boy friend by 3 A.M. and her parents were becoming frantic. Then the phone rang, and the father ran to answer it. It was the debutante daughter, who explained hastily, "There's not a thing to worry about. I'm perfectly safe. I'm in jail."

★ ★ ★

Three lonesome-looking lasses sat alone in a bar and grill, gossiping idly over cups of coffee. Finally one was summoned to the phone—and brightened at once. "That'll be great," she was overheard saying. "I'll meet you under the clock at the Biltmore. Shall we say eightish?" Then she left the bar.

Now came a call for the second girl. "Of course I'm free for dinner," she enthused. "Call for me, please. Make it about nineish."

That left the third girl all alone. Finally she couldn't stand it any longer. She turned toward a group of male diners in the rear of the room and inquired plaintively, "Tennish, anyone?"

★ ★ ★

THE LASS ROUNDUP:

1. The Sioux City siren who treats her gentlemen callers like dirt. She hides them under her bed.

2. The Newport News nymph who had kissed so many sailors her lips moved in and out with the tide.

3. The Bronx bombshell who called her poodle "Shakespeare." "After the Bard of Avon?" she was asked. "Oh, no," she explained. "After Shakespeare Ginsberg, my drama coach."

4. The Beverly Hills bride who made a slight change in the wedding ritual. She kept the bridal bouquet and threw the groom away.

5. The Charleston charmer who, upon hearing that Hugh O'Brian, TV's Wyatt Earp, was vacation-bound for Lake Louise and Banff, enthused, "That sounds wonderful, but how do you Banff?"

6. The Carolina chorine who admitted, "I've ditched that fellow I adored last month. He was just a passing fiancé."

7. The Philadelphia flapper who mused, "What I like are the quiet things in life—the folding of a hundred-dollar bill, for example."

8. The Baltimore beauty at a neighborhood movie who got so annoyed with the attentions of the gent in the next seat that she changed cars four times.

9. The Dallas dreamboat who tapped the arm of an oil tycoon and whispered coyly, "How much did you say your name was?"

10. The Mobile model who refused to marry a senile millionaire. She dreaded the thought of old age creeping up on her.

11. The Smith Sophomore who was ecstatic about her newest romance. "It's the funniest thing about how we met," she gurgled. "We were introduced!"

★ ★ ★

The published extract of the diary of Kay Nelson, a lovely, accomplished, and perceptive lady, gives an interesting insight into a girl's way of filling a hope chest.

In June, Miss Nelson bought a pair of white Bermuda shorts and a gray checked shirt for $14.98.

In July, she bought a gray flannel skirt to go with the shirt ($35).

In August, she bought shoes and a handbag to go with the blouse and skirt ($90).

In October, she bought a fashionable black dress to go with the shoes and handbag ($260).

In November, she bought a platinum mink stole to go with the dress ($1,000).

In December, for Christmas, she's trying to promote a gray convertible ($4,600) to go with the mink stole.

For ten minutes, I racked my brain trying to think of whom Miss Nelson reminded me. Suddenly, in a blinding flash, it came to me. My own wife, Phyllis!

★ ★ ★

Have you heard about the dashing millionaire sportsman who just bought his best girl a bikini bathing suit? He's looking forward to seeing her beam with delight.

★ ★ ★

"Am I the first girl you ever kissed?" she whispered softly in the back porch swing. "That's quite possible," admitted the legal light who was enjoying her caresses. "Were you in Atlantic City in 1937?"

★ ★ ★

"Willie," chided a ten-year-old lad's uncle, "isn't it about time you had a girl?" "Golly, no," said Willie emphatically, and stomped off to have a catch.

The little girl from the house next door smiled to herself and said softly, "They're always the last ones to know!"

40. GOLF

A noted psychologist's wife asked him why he never would let her play golf with him. "My dear," he admonished her, "there are three things a man must do alone: testify, die, and putt."

★ ★ ★

An accident led to the beginning of golf, to hear Fred Beck tell it. One fateful day a Scotsman took a wild swing at a sheep, cut under it, and accidentally connected with a small, round rock which was so cleanly hit it went sailing down the fairway. He took another whack at the stone, which this time hit his mother-in-law. Delighted, he cried, "Hey, Mac, watch me swat this one into yonder rabbit hole." There was no more sheepherding done in those parts that day. The game of golf was launched at 11:10, the first lie about a score at 11:22, and the first golf joke at noon sharp.

★ ★ ★

The late George Gershwin was an avid golfer. Playing on a links in Miami Beach with which he was unfamiliar, he couldn't get going one morning, registered a 9 on the first hole, and an 8 on the second. "I can't figure out what I'm doing wrong," he fretted. His caddy volunteered, "Mister, you just ain't got rhythm."

★ ★ ★

A chap who loved his weekend golf was laid low by an attack of grippe. After a fortnight of rest, he was all set to resume play when he suffered a relapse. "Why can't you play this time?" grumbled his constant opponent on the links. "Let me put it this way," said the stricken one glumly. "My trouble is an overlapping grippe."

Jones had just flubbed his fourth shot in the same trap one Sunday morning. "The way I'm playing golf," he muttered disgustedly, "I might just as well have gone to church."

★ ★ ★

"I Love Lucy" established not only the fame of Desi and Lucille but producer Jess Oppenheimer as well.

The latter was playing a round of golf, using a ball with his name stamped clearly upon it, when he hooked a drive onto an adjoining fairway. As he dashed over to retrieve it, another player calmly picked it up and put it in his pocket.

"Hey," yelled Oppenheimer, "you're picking up the wrong ball, aren't you?"

The player examined it judicially, then answered, "Nope. This is what I've been playing. An Oppenheimer!"

★ ★ ★

An Oklahoma oil tycoon appeared at a local golf links to make a fourth followed by a servant pulling an adjustable, foam-cushioned chaise-longue behind him.

"Are you going to make that poor caddy lug that couch all over the course after you?" he was asked.

"Caddy, my eye," explained the oil man. "That's my psychiatrist."

★ ★ ★

Harpo Marx is telling about a round of golf President Eisenhower had in the South, with a young Negro lad caddying. The President flubbed a drive and the caddy opined, "Mister, you sure goofed on that one." When the President followed with a hook into the woods, the caddy said, "Jeepers, that's even worse!"

Just then another caddy hastily whispered that the lad was toting the clubs of the President of the United States. So when the President sank a long, tricky putt, his little caddy had a chance to make amends. "Mr. Lincoln," he enthused, "that was a beauty!"

★ ★ ★

Prize golf alibi of the year was pulled by neophyte Allan Wilson —of the Washington Wilsons. After whiffing his tee shot three times, he glowered at his companions and announced, "Somebody has been cracking walnuts with my driver."

★ ★ ★

There's a tricky three-par hole on the golf course at Pebble Beach, California, that occasionally drives even the experts to distraction. A tongue of the Pacific Ocean surges in between the tee and the green, and only a well-directed two hundred-yard drive can keep a player out of serious trouble.

Almost as disastrous as a drive into the briny is a hook shot on to the beach below the green. Bing Crosby found his ball there one windy day, and wasted seven shots trying to lift it up onto the green. The eighth try almost made it, but then began rolling back, picked up speed, and hit Bing in the stomach.

Crosby tossed his wedge to the caddy and said, "That settles it, son. When your ball starts to hit back at you, it's time to quit!"

★ ★ ★

George Burns persuaded his wife Gracie to come to the links with him one morning. "Care to take some lessons?" he suggested. "No, thanks," she replied. "I learned yesterday." George did show her how to sink a twenty-footer from the back of a great Dane. He called it "putting on the dog."

★ ★ ★

One of Palmer Hoyt's golfing cronies has a tiny idiosyncrasy. Every time his ball lands in the rough, he nudges it back onto the fairway with his foot. For his birthday, they gave him a shoe with a number nine iron inside. "I've been playing with him now for twenty-one years," recalls Hoyt, "and he hasn't had a bad lie yet."

★ ★ ★

At a Catskill resort, a vacationer encountered a frail, rabbinical old man with a long beard, who identified himself as the head dietician, making sure that meat and milk were not served at the same meal.

Came February, and the vacationer went to Miami, where he met the same old man. "What brings you South? The sun?" he asked. "No, same thing as in the Catskills," said the old man. "I'm in charge of the dietary laws here now."

In June, the vacationer took a trip to Israel, and in Tel Aviv he ran into the old man for the third time. "I suppose you're still taking charge of the dietary laws?" he nodded.

"Oh, no," the old man replied. "Here I'm the golf pro."

41. HILLBILLIES

A traveling salesman lost his way in the feudin' country near the Blue Ridge Mountains. He finally found refuge with two hillbillies who never had been more than a mile from their primitive shack in all their lives.

When the salesman left the next day, he left a portable radio set as a token of his appreciation for their hospitality. That evening one of the hillbillies, out of curiosity, fiddled with the radio dials, and accidentally tuned in to a speechmaker at a political rally.

At bedtime the politician was still talking over the radio, and the two mountaineers didn't know how to turn off the flatulent speaker. In desperation one mountaineer picked up an ax and struck the set. The voice stopped. However, it had only jarred the set and in the morning the second hillbilly was awakened by organ music coming from the radio. He woke his pal.

"You know that windbag you killed last night, Zeke?" he said. "Well, they're burying him today."

★ ★ ★

A gaunt mountaineer in West Virginia courteously permitted two New York tourists to hunt on his land. "Only one thing I ask in return," he said. "It's possible you'll stumble on a still near the top of yonder hill. If you do, I'll ask you to bring me back a jugful or two."

The hunters found the still all right, but had barely picked up the jugs before bullets started whistling over their heads. They fled down the hill and panted, "Your still is being raided!"

The mountaineer calmly bit off a chew of fresh tobacco. "I guess I neglected to tell you," he admitted, "that that still ain't mine."

★ ★ ★

A rugged Kentuckian got himself all mixed up in World War II, and after five months in the European front lines, wrote this letter to his wife back home: "Dear Nancy: I been a-gittin' yore naggin' letters all along. Now I want to tell ye, I'm damn tired of them. For the first time in my life I'm a-fightin' in a real big war, and I want you to let me enjoy it in peace while it lasts. Yours, etc."

★ ★ ★

A tough old mountaineer had been missing for five days, and his wife finally decided to look for him. She found him in a thick clump of bushes, looking rather peaked. "Suppertime, Paw," she ventured. "Yep," agreed the mountaineer. "Well then," she continued, "ain't ye comin' home?" "Nope," said he. "Why not?" said she. "Becuz," he said with finality, "I'm standin' in a bear trap."

★ ★ ★

A hillbilly and his ten-year-old son came down to a big city for the first time. The boy was thunderstruck by what he saw, and asked countless questions, not a single one of which his father could answer. Finally, the boy said, "Paw, I'm sorry if I'm so dumb.

Hope you don't mind me asking all these fool questions." "Go right ahead, son," said his father heartily. "That's the only way you'll ever learn things."

★ ★ ★

In the Tennessee hills, a character known as "Uncle Zeb" allowed as how he had the smartest durn horse in all the U.S.A.

"I was riding him one day in a lonely stretch of country," he recalled, "when he suddenly stumbled. I fell and busted my hip."

"Don't tell me," scoffed a tourist, "that the horse reset your hipbone."

"Nope. But he did grab me by the belt, drag me home, then gallop seven miles to fetch a doctor."

"Wonderful," conceded the tourist.

"Not so wonderful," corrected Uncle Zeb. "The dangburned crittur brung back a *horse* doctor!"

★ ★ ★

A Kentucky mountaineer married a beautiful fourteen-year-old girl, but admitted to his paw and maw that he had a big problem to face. "What do I do now?" he pondered. "Take her on a honeymoon, or send her to camp?"

42. HISTORY

Richard Carrington, in *A Guide to Earth History*, makes this startling observation: "Let us imagine that, by some magic, the whole of earth's history could be compressed into a single year. On this scale, the first eight months would be completely without life. The following two would be devoted to the most primitive of creatures. No mammals would appear until the second week in December.

"Man, as we know him, would strut onto the stage at approximately 11:45 P.M. *on December 31.* The age of written history would occupy little more than the last sixty seconds on the clock!"

That ought to help you reduce current world problems to the proper perspectives!

★ ★ ★

Richard Armour has written his own History in a volume named *It All Started with Europe*. He starts doling out his pun-ishment in the days when channel swimming was not yet a standard pastime ("because the English Channel did not yet exist") and carries through to the era of the bikini, or invisible bathing suit, whose wearers "fear only Neptune—because of his habit of zooming up from the depths of the sea with his pitchfork held on high."

En route you will encounter many a noble Roman in his toga ("the sack of Rome"), the Toudors and the Fourdors ("inventors of the station wagon"), Egyptian ras ("so indispensable a part of college cheers"), and Genghis Khan (whose "collection of concubines was widely known as the Golden Horde").

Mr. Armour hints that his next safari may carry him to Turkey, where "a rolling stone gathers no mosque."

★ ★ ★

The great lovers of history, observes Bertrand Russell, would be looked upon as juvenile delinquents today. Helen of Troy, for instance, was exactly twelve years old when Paris carried her off to Sparta.

★ ★ ★

For four solid days it had been pouring rain in prehistoric Britain. One hirsute cave dweller viewed the weather disgustedly and told a neighbor, "Explain it any way you like, but I say we never had atmospheric disturbances like this until those blank-blank scientists started fooling around with bows and arrows."

★ ★ ★

A king and queen of yore thought the world of a certain mischievous jester, but he risked the royal ire one day by venturing, "An apology can sometimes be worse than an insult."

"Either prove that," commanded the king, "or off you go to be beheaded."

After dinner, His Majesty happened to bend over, and the jester landed a lusty kick on the royal posterior. As the king straightened up, purple with rage, the jester explained, "Pardon me, Sire. I thought you were the queen!"

When I was a lad, elocution teachers were fond of making their charges recite a touching poem that began "The boy stood on the burning deck"—with appropriate gestures. Behind the teacher's back, we shouted parodies, some printable, some not. One I vaguely remember began: "The boy stood on the burning deck, eating peanuts by the peck."

The poem was based, as a matter of fact, on an actual historic sea battle: Nelson's successful attack upon the French fleet at Aboukir in 1798. The French flagship, *l'Orient*, took fire, and the blaze lit up the entire bay. Officers begged the little favorite of the ship, the captain's son, to board a lifeboat, but he insisted upon staying in the exact spot his father had assigned to him—not realizing that his father had been mortally wounded, and could give him no further instructions.

Sadly the officers rowed away without him—and, just before the whole ship blew up, saw him steadfastly rooted to his position on deck, waiting for his father to tell him what he must do next.

★ ★ ★

Skeptics who always suspected there was a lot more going on than met the eye in the private lives of those ultrarespectable, strait-laced hypocrites of Queen Victoria's day are chortling over the revelations in Cyril Pearl's *The Girl with the Swansdown Seat*. Fancy ladies in London a century ago, maintains Mr. Pearl, concealed not only skeletons (and lords) in their private closets, but magnificent "conveniences" as well, decorated with genuine jewels and rarest materials. The one with the "swansdown seat" belonged to a doxy named Skittles, who knew a couple of thousand tricks or two, did she, about how to separate a heap from the goats. Mr. Pearl says there were some eighty thousand "soiled doves" like her in London at the time, and that almost all of them were faring considerably better than virtuous maidens toiling for the starvation wages characteristic of the Industrial Revolution. It's different today, of course.

Peter Fleming recalls that on the fateful day in World War II when Hitler unleashed his greatest air armada on London, and blitzed the gallant British for six solid hours, "The staid London *Times*, in moments of crisis perhaps the greatest character-actor on the stage of public life in England, faithfully recorded the discovery in an air-raid shelter in Euston of a Great Crested Grebe!"

★ ★ ★

An American who had gazed upon the majestic sweep of the Mississippi and Columbia rivers could not hide his disappointment when first he saw the River Thames from his London hotel window. "Is that dinky little stream the one I've heard so much about?" he grumbled. "You must remember," his English guide reminded him, "that the mighty rivers you have in America are merely water; the Thames, sir, is liquid history!"

★ ★ ★

Ollie James knows a proud citizen who can trace his ancestry clear back to the Boston Tea Party. His great-great-grandmother was the last bag thrown overboard.

★ ★ ★

HAIL TO THE CHIEF!:

All thirty-three men who served as President of the United States have been American-born, though Martin Van Buren, number eight, was the first born under the American flag.

Only three Presidents first saw the light of day west of the Mississippi: Hoover (Iowa); Truman (Missouri); and Eisenhower (Texas). Eight Presidents were born in Virginia; seven in Ohio.

Average age of Presidents taking office: fifty-four; at death: sixty-seven. W. H. Harrison, at sixty-eight, was the oldest President; Teddy Roosevelt, at forty-two, the youngest. Harrison's administration—one brief month, was, of course, the shortest; F.D.R.'s (who else?), twelve years, one month, eight days, the longest. Tyler had the most children (fourteen).

Lincoln was the tallest President (6 feet, 4 inches); Taft, who tipped the scales at well over three hundred, the heaviest; and

Madison the smallest, a bantam just over five feet, who weighed barely a hundred pounds after a heavy dinner.

Andrew Jackson was the first President to travel by train, Teddy R. the first to fly while President, Ike Eisenhower the only one to hold a pilot's license. Harding was the first to speak over the radio, Coolidge the first to broadcast an inaugural address, Eisenhower the first to appear on television.

James Polk was the first successful "dark horse"; Franklin Pierce probably the best friend of literature (two of his intimates were Hawthorne and Longfellow).

John Quincy Adams was the only bald-headed man ever elected President of the United States; Buchanan our only bachelor President; Andrew Johnson the only one who never spent a day in a schoolroom. His wife taught him how to read and write!

There exists one photograph of Ulysses Grant minus his beard. When his wife requested a profile for a cameo, he misunderstood, and under protest shaved off his whiskers.

James Garfield, most scholarly of Presidents, could write simultaneously in Latin with one hand, in Greek with the other. Ben Harrison and his wife, terrified of newly installed electric lights in 1891, let them burn all night, rather than risk a shock by touching the switch.

Taft was the only President—so far, anyhow!—who also served as Chief Justice of the Supreme Court. Taft also was the first, but not the best golfer in the White House, and began the practice of tossing out the first baseball in the season's opener.

Ulysses S. Grant's first name actually was Hiram; Grover Cleveland's first name was Stephen; Woodrow Wilson's first name was Thomas.

There was one U.S. President who never cast a vote: Zachary Taylor.

And Herman Hover, of Hollywood, hoping fervently that 1960 will break the jinx, points out that, beginning with 1840, each and every President elected in the twentieth year following died in office! They were William H. Harrison, 1840; Abraham Lincoln,

1860; James A. Garfield, 1880; William McKinley, 1900; Warren
G. Harding, 1920; and Franklin D. Roosevelt, 1940.

★ ★ ★

Some visitors down south indulged in an "escorted tour of famous Civil War battlefields." The driver-guide was very eloquent:
"Here's where a handful of Alabama boys knocked the stuffings
out of ten thousand Yankees," or "Three regiments of New York
infantry got licked here," or "This is where an Atlanta platoon captured nineteen thousand Yanks and killed as many more."

A Boston lady who grew more and more indignant as the tour
progressed, finally interrupted. "Didn't the North win just one
battle in this war?" "No, ma'am," was the answer. "Not while I'm
driving this bus they didn't!"

★ ★ ★

Up in Massachusetts, in the charming town of Deerfield, there
is another venerable citizen who likes to show visitors the local
sights. His pride and joy is a neat monument marking the spot
where the original settlers had a bloody encounter with the
Indians.

"Who won the battle?" asked one visitor innocently. The venerable citizen regarded him with some disgust, then answered
slowly, "Well, sir, the Indians didn't build the monument."

43. HOLLYWOOD

These new Hollywood stars with strange names like Rip and Rory and Tab and Rock are all very well in their way, but for gentlemen of advancing years like myself, they'll never achieve the glamour and the outrageous audacity of old roisterers like John Barrymore and W. C. Fields.

Playwright Harry Kurnitz tells about a turbulent luncheon party at which the late Mr. Barrymore, "The Great Profile," was regaling two cronies, Ben Hecht and Gene Fowler, with choice details of recent amatory exploits. Mr. B. was not only specific in his references but pronounced each syllable with that resounding and pear-shaped clarity he had learned in his apprentice days. A pair of tourists and their wives could not help overhearing at an adjoining table and were not amused. In fact, they were horrified. The husbands yelled over to Mr. B. to cease and desist.

This, of course, provoked only a fresh and even more explicit outburst from the perverse Mr. B. The tourists' wives fled for sanctuary and the tourists—two hundred pounds apiece on the hoof—rolled up their sleeves and advanced upon Mr. Barrymore. Fowler and Hecht jumped up to break their path, but Barrymore proclaimed grandly, "Stand aside, men! Let the peasants present their petition."

So Fowler and Hecht stood aside—and the peasants knocked Mr. Barrymore's block off.

★ ★ ★

A cherished legend on the Paramount lot concerns the day when the irascible W. C. Fields, tired of having Baby Le Roy steal scene after scene right from under his nose, spiked the moppet's orange juice with a slug of bathtub gin. When Baby Le Roy fell sound asleep, Fields roared, "The kid's no trouper! Send him home!" Well, Baby Le Roy, now grown to manhood, says it ain't true! Interviewed by Don Freeman in San Diego, Le Roy insisted, "I've seen lots of photographs of Fields and me when I was a baby, and the expression on Bill's face radiates genuine love!"

Bingo! Another illusion shattered!

★ ★ ★

W. C. Fields's classics revived by Don Freeman: 1. The day he described a tiny and peculiar bird to Charlie McCarthy. "It sounds mighty small," admitted Charlie. "Do you need glasses to see it?" "Yes, indeed," said Fields. "At least three or four." 2. The time Gene Fowler discovered Fields in his garden, a quart of martinis in one hand and a long whip in the other. With each swig he would lash his whip at a passing swan. "Don't look aghast," he rasped at Fowler. "The so-and-so hissed at me!"

★ ★ ★

If you are interested in the beginnings of the motion picture industry, there's a plaque next to the doorway of 151 West 34th Street, New York (now part of Macy's), that should intrigue you. It reads: "Here the motion picture began! On the night of April 23, 1896, on this site in Koster and Bial's Music Hall, Thomas A. Edison with the 'Vitascope' first projected a moving picture. In commemoration of this event, this tablet is here affixed by the Motion Picture Industry, 1938."

★ ★ ★

Spyros Skouras, powerful motion picture tycoon, still speaks English with a thick Greek accent. He tells this story on himself: "For a long time my assistant, Ulric Bell, had trouble with his hearing, but I couldn't persuade him to try a hearing aid. Finally, however, he got one and I asked him if he could hear me. 'Yes, I can, Mr. Skouras,' Ulric answered, 'but now I don't understand you!'"

★ ★ ★

David Selznick produces motion pictures. He also sends memos to members of his staff—about thirty a day when he's in robust health. Underlings read the memos, too—if they want to stay on the payroll.

One day an aide discovered that he had duplicated an order—a slight error that would cost Selznick about ten thousand dollars. Hastily he sat down to write a note to his boss.

"Dear David," it began. "In reply to your memo of tomorrow . . ."

★ ★ ★

Nunnally Johnson caught George Jessel in one of his rare moods of despondency on a gray day in Hollywood. Then Jessel was told he was wanted on the phone. "Cheer up," counseled Johnson. "That's probably Sam Goldwyn offering you a fortune to produce a new picture for him." "Not only will it not be Sam Goldwyn," predicted Jessel darkly, "but I will rip the pocket of my new coat coming out of the phone booth."

★ ★ ★

Of the countless stories going the rounds about the late Mike Todd, the one that I think catches the bravado and gusto of the man best concerns the day he was aboard a reconstructed paddle-wheeler making shots for *Around the World in Eighty Days*.

Glancing behind him, Todd noticed hundreds of seagulls circling in the air. "Why are they following us?" he demanded. "Gulls always follow ships at sea," explained the captain. "They're after food—the garbage we throw overboard." "Garbage!" echoed the outraged Todd. "No seagulls following a boat of *mine* are going to eat garbage. Throw them some decent food. Mike Todd goes first class!"

★ ★ ★

A movie producer confided to a scribe, "I've got a new mystery film coming up with the greatest surprise ending you ever saw. The butler did it." "What's surprising about that?" scoffed the scribe. Explained the producer, "There's no butler in it!"

Irving Lazar, inimitable and unstoppable Hollywood agent, known as "Swifty" to his friends, is as famous for the big words he uses as the gorgeous wardrobe he sports. One day he casually slipped the word "egregious" into one of his typical London-to-Hollywood telephone marathons. "Don't use words you can't define," cautioned playwright Moss Hart at the other end of the phone. "I can define 'egregious' perfectly," answered Lazar. "I learned it while I was looking up the meaning of 'eclectic.'" "What were you doing looking up 'eclectic'?" wondered Hart. "My dear boy," snapped Lazar haughtily, "I look up 'eclectic' all the time!"

★ ★ ★

BABES IN THE HOLLYWOODS:

1. A crooner whose last four records had sold over a million looked out at his swimming pool one morning, and rang for his butler. "Jeeves," he yawned, "the pool needs restocking. Order a couple of dozen blondes."

2. Danny Thomas tells about a Hollywood pair who were rapturously happy for years. Then they met each other.

3. Three diminutive kiddies in Beverly Hills decided to play house. Said the first, "I'll be the papa." Said the second, "I'll be the mamma." Said the third, "I'll be the divorce attorney."

4. Dinah Shore tells about two sound-effect men who engaged in a furious hassle at her studio. It seems they were stealing each other's thunder.

5. "I wouldn't say he's exactly drunk," mused a Hollywood comic about a supposed pal, "but every time you close the door to his dressing room, the whole studio gurgles."

6. Phil Silvers tells of a friend on the Coast who went in to see the studio chiefs with a hard-luck story and an urgent request for a raise. He didn't get the raise but they bought his story.

7. There's a luscious movie queen in Hollywood half the men in town want to marry. The other half already have.

8. One of the new starlets broke off abruptly with her boy

friend. "He was too unpredictable," she pouted. "One day I'd think I was in love with him, and the next day I wouldn't."

9. David Niven ran into a shoestring producer and asked him how his latest picture was faring at the box office. "I'll be perfectly honest with you," the producer replied. "I won't answer."

10. A Hollywood sob sister found the mother of a reigning, well-developed screen princess becomingly modest. "My little girl," admitted the mother, "is just like any typical young American lady who earns more than two million dollars a year."

★ ★ ★

A young novelist's first best-seller was up for grabs to the highest bidder in Hollywood. One producer, enthusiastic personally, but worried that the public might not be in the mood for a distinctly "downbeat" novel, decided to leave everything to a Univac machine. The producer, three yes-men, and the author accordingly gathered to watch while the galley proofs were fed, one by one, to the electronic marvel, and the red, green, and amber lights began flashing in mad profusion. Halfway through, the author could stand the suspense no longer. "How am I doing?" he demanded hoarsely. "It looks like you're in," whispered one of the yes-men encouragingly. "The Univac just sent out for another package of popcorn!"

★ ★ ★

Cary Grant, who, along with Frank Sinatra, Marlon Brando, and Bill Holden, is just about the hottest male property in Hollywood today (typical contract for a single picture: $500,000 in cash against 10 per cent of the gross!) is not the one to sit idle while he awaits the director's pleasure on a set.

Toiling recently on a new picture for Alfred Hitchcock, Grant and costar Eva Marie Saint spent their spare moments concocting a novel kind of menu, including such odd but delectable tidbits as Mixed Emotion, Curried Favor, Cheese It, Stuffed Shirt, Sour Puss, and Frozen Asset.

Hitchcock added Buttered Up, Lettuce Alone, Fat Chance, Crisp Manner, and Slice of Life.

Another top director, Stanley Donen (of *Indiscreet* fame) contributed Grilled Suspects, Chicken Out, Bitter Tears, Hot Diggety, and Humble Pie.

A technician tried to chisel his way into the act with Aw Come On Turnover, but was promptly banished from the set.

★ ★ ★

The debonair Cary has another compilation to which you'll want to add your own two cents' worth. He calls it "Unlikely Couples," and typical nominations include Grace and Emmett Kelly, Jane and Bertrand Russell, Marie and Woodrow Wilson, Dolly and Guy Madison, and Grant and Natalie Wood.

Get it? Then there are Grandma and Park Commissioner Moses, Dorothy and Fess Parker, Esther and Tennessee Williams, Betsy and Barney Ross, Lena and Trader Horn, Faye and Ralph Waldo Emerson—and Emi and Cary Grant!

★ ★ ★

Another parlor game that's keeping babes in Hollywood from watching too many horse opreys on TV challenges contestants to identify famous screen stars from a list of their actual, or original, names.

How many of these celebrities do *you* recognize? 1. Ella Geisman. 2. Arthur Gelian. 3. Norma Baker. 4. David Kaminsky. 5. Tula Finklea. 6. Bernie Schwartz. 7. Margarita Cansino. 8. Archibald Leach. 9. Doris Kappelhoff. 10. Dino Crocetti. Answers: 1. June Allyson. 2. Tab Hunter. 3. Marilyn Monroe. 4. Danny Kaye. 5. Cyd Charisse. 6. Tony Curtis. 7. Rita Hayworth. 8. Cary Grant (thought we'd fool you!). 9. Doris Day. 10. Dean Martin.

One can understand how Claudette Chauchoin became Claudette Colbert and how Virginia McMath became Ginger Rogers, but Issur Danielovitch into Kirk Douglas and Spangler Brough into Robert Taylor were sleeper jumps for fair!

Maybe the last two got their cue from one Iosif Dzhugashvili.

By the time *you* heard tell of him, of course, he was Joseph Stalin!

★ ★ ★

A Hollywood babe managed to latch onto an inconspicuous part in a great screen epic. The director was an exacting fellow, however, with an unlimited bankroll, and the projected two-month shooting schedule stretched out first to four months, then to six. Finally the bored "actress" inquired plaintively of a columnist, "Say, who do you think I'd have to romance to get *out* of this darn picture?"

★ ★ ★

Life in Hollywood is like this: a big bad man-about-town was having difficulty persuading a sweet thing to go home and hear his hi-fi set. "Look," he implored, "how long have I known you?" "About three-quarters of an hour," she estimated coyly. "All right then," he stormed. "Have I ever lied to you?"

★ ★ ★

On one of those lots with forty-two sound stages (thirty-nine now devoted to TV), a writer from Westport gained an audience with a hard-to-pin-down studio head, was told he had exactly two minutes to outline the plot of his proposed screenplay. The writer was disgruntled but game. He finished his synopsis in two minutes flat, scarcely pausing to take breath. The studio head snarled, "That's the lousiest story line I've heard so far this year. Get out and stop impeding the wheels of progress."

"Hold on," interrupted the writer. "That outline I gave you wasn't my story. It was Shakespeare's *Hamlet*. I'll tell you *my* story when you've got more time!"

★ ★ ★

A famous movie queen agreed to lead the Thanksgiving Day parade in a Southern city, but canceled by telegram at the last minute. This is how the local gazette handled the story.

First day: Miss Fifi Whosis, reigning beauty of the screen, will be our guest this year.

Second day: The ravishing Fifi Whosis, irresistible siren of Hollywood, tells the secrets of her beauty.

Third day: Fifi Whosis, who will lead the parade day after tomorrow, will live up to her reputation for charm and affability, and sign all autographs.

Fourth day: Fifi Whosis, fifty-three-year-old former motion picture actress, has canceled her appearance in our fair city.

★   ★   ★

What does Marilyn Monroe really think of all those revealing photos of her the studios send out by the thousand? This is what she told Pete Martin when he was gathering copy for his book, *Will Acting Spoil Marilyn Monroe?*: "Who's to say what picture is too revealing and what one isn't? The censors kill practically everything taken of me and the ones that do get through are usually retouched. After one sitting they killed twenty-eight of thirty poses of me. The question is: does a girl show too much cleavage? It seems to me they ought to worry if she *doesn't* have any. That really would upset people! I just don't understand people who expect girls to look like boys!"

Marilyn was guest of honor at a football coaches' luncheon one day and charmed all the guests by reminding them, "I bet I've devised more defensive plays than the whole lot of you put together!"

★   ★   ★

Herb Stein caught a glimpse of Anita Ekberg in a very low-cut gown at a Hollywood prevue, and was informed by a companion, "She comes from one of the Scandinavian countries." "Yes, I see," agreed Herb appreciatively. "Jutland, no doubt!"

★   ★   ★

When Zsa Zsa Gabor slipped on the ice during a personal appearance tour in Canada, the physician summoned discreetly reported, "Miss Gabor's fall bruised her somewhat and slightly injured her otherwise."

Zsa Zsa, never at a loss for a few thousand words, insists that she never takes gifts from perfect strangers—then adds, "But who's perfect these days?"

★ ★ ★

Jayne Mansfield's fan mail included this poignant appeal from a starry-eyed admirer in Tokyo: "Honorable Missie Mansfield: Please mail me your honorable photograph as soon as possible and as honorably naked as possible."

Another Mansfield item (from a source we admit is not too reliable) has it that she just finished reading a book about the Einstein theories, and commented, "That Einstein was twenty years ahead of his time. He had a lot of my ideas."

★ ★ ★

A cocky sailor from one of our new atomic submarines is boasting that he's gone clear around the world—not to mention under the North Pole—with "Lana Turner on his arm." He adds, "It's the best job of tattooing I've ever seen!"

★ ★ ★

A young actor with a name five syllables long won a big part in a new movie and promptly had his name changed to Flash Upton. The picture was a smash, and the actor won rave notices and a new contract. Ensconced in his new fourteen-room penthouse, he gave a great housewarming party, and thoughtfully named his old mother the guest of honor.

Everybody showed up but Mamma, and the actor was frantic with worry. Finally he went to the lobby to speak to the doorman. "You didn't see a little old lady come in here at any time?" he asked anxiously. "There was one," recalled the doorman. "She's been sitting patiently over in that corner for about three hours now."

It was Mamma all right. "Mamma," he cried, "you've had me in a state! Why didn't you come up to my apartment?"

"I wanted to, my son," she told him with tears in her eyes, "but I couldn't remember your new name!"

44. HORSES

"I have an excellent, if quick-tempered, friend named Ben," writes Robert Griffin of Atlanta, "who never had been on a horse in his life, but he was darned if he was going to let the stablemaster know that on the first day of his winter vacation. So off he cantered on a nag, looking unconcerned as you please. He did fine, too, till he tried to stop the horse. It paid no attention to him whatever. When it finally trotted back to the stable of its own accord, Ben was sore as a boil. 'This confounded creature absolutely refuses to stop when I tell him to,' he hollered. 'I want my money back.' 'I'm a very busy man,' replied the stablemaster, 'and I have no time to listen to your tale of whoa.'"

★ ★ ★

One of the features of a small-time rodeo group that toured Oregon and Washington was a grizzled cowboy named Pecos Pete who could gallop across an enclosure and pick up a handkerchief with his teeth en route. The stunt always got a big hand.

One night, however, Pecos Pete made a slight miscalculation. He swung down from his saddle at the proper instant all right, but he came up without the precious handkerchief. A concerted sigh went up from the audience. Pecos Pete reddened with shame.

The ringmaster had to think fast. He seized the mike and bellowed, "You ain't seen nothing, folks. Pecos Pete will attempt the same death-defying feat again—and this time, he will pick up the handkerchief *and his teeth* at the same time!"

★ ★ ★

Help-wanted ad in a Chicago paper, inserted by the owner of a fashionable Arizona dude ranch: "We need an experienced ranch hand immediately. Guitar player. Sideburns. Must have Southwest accent. We'll teach you to ride."

★ ★ ★

A horse who had won a gallop poll in a dozen TV "Westerns" in a single week neighed to a colt in the next stall, "All this churning of the midnight soil is wearing me down. I no longer know wither I'm coming or going." "You can't continue this way," agreed the colt. "Why not consult your veterinarian. He'll probably prescribe a complete rest." "Not a chance," sighed the horse wearily. "He's also my agent."

★ ★ ★

The late comedian Joe Frisco used to pass out racing tips to all and sundry, including the bank teller where he cashed his checks. Since most of the tips were worthless, the teller was soon deep in the hole, but Frisco kept telling him, "Just keep doubling your bets and sooner or later you're bound to catch up with things."

"Sure enough," chortled Frisco to a friend, "a nag I told him about came in first and paid 13 to 1!"

"Did that make the teller even?" he was asked.

"Naw," admitted Frisco. "The warden wouldn't let him use the phone!"

★ ★ ★

Joe Frisco was as impecunious as he was witty, but he took it for granted that his better heeled friends would provide for him. Nor did they ever let him down. One Thanksgiving season, he persuaded Bing Crosby to give him twenty dollars "for a turkey." The same afternoon, Bing spotted him at his usual haunt: the ten-dollar window at a racetrack. "You here!" exclaimed Bing in mock astonishment. "Where's that turkey you wanted?" Joe explained, "He just came in sixth."

★ ★ ★

In racing circles, a current whimsy has it that a confirmed plunger lost everything at the track but his bus fare home. He waited at the entrance for twenty minutes until a bus finally lumbered into view. It was marked Number Two. He looked at his ticket. It was good only for Number Seven.

He tore up his ticket and mused forlornly, "I can't even bet on the right bus!"

* * *

The children in a certain school in Boston instituted a drive for funds to build a new statue of Paul Revere. The father of one of the kids was a celebrated ex-jockey, and, though he was far wealthier than most of the other parents, he refused to contribute a single penny. "It's not that I'm stingy; you know that," he explained to his boy. "It's just that I never had any use for that bum Revere. He gave his horse a bad ride. He went wide at Lexington."

* * *

A gent who spent most of his business hours trying to pick the winning nags at racetracks all over the country called his doctor in some alarm. "It's my wife," he quavered. "She seems to think she's a racehorse. She's snorting and whinnying and chewing up all the grass on our front lawn." "Probably her reaction to your endless talk about horse racing," guessed the doctor. "Bring her over this afternoon and I'll examine her." "O.K.," agreed the gent. "I'll gallop her over right after lunch."

* * *

A Kentucky horse-fancier admitted to a friend that he was so anxious for his new hopeful to win his first race, he surreptitiously fed it six mint juleps in the paddock. "Did it win?" asked the friend. "No," admitted the owner, "he came in last. But he sure was the happiest horse in the race!"

* * *

One of the unhappiest kids in Westchester County is the boy who desperately craved a horse for his birthday. His parents deemed him just a bit too young for a real horse—the birthday was his fourth—and gave him a rocking horse instead. But the boy took one look at it, kicked it violently, and burst into tears.

"What's wrong, son?" demanded the dismayed father. "Don't you like your rocking horse?"

"I should say not," wailed the boy. "I want a horse made of *horse!*"

45. HOTELS

It was Benjamin Franklin who pointed out that "God helps them that help themselves," and a certain gentleman may have had these words in mind when he strode up to the desk of a popular mountain resort and demanded a room on the eve of the busiest weekend of the year.

"Got a reservation?" asked the clerk.

"Who needs a reservation?" scoffed the gentleman. "I've been coming here now every year for ten years, and never before did I have a reservation."

"Sorry," snapped the clerk, not looking sorry at all, "but this year we are absolutely filled up, and you don't have a reservation, you don't get a room."

"Listen," said the gentleman, "suppose I told you President Eisenhower was coming here tonight. For him, I bet, you'd find a room all right."

"Of course, for President Eisenhower——" began the clerk, but the gentleman interrupted him. "So I'm telling you President Eisenhower *isn't* coming tonight," he shouted triumphantly, *"and you can give me his room!"*

★ ★ ★

A timid little lady from Des Moines, whenever she checks into a strange hotel, always locates the fire escape the moment the bell-boy has deposited the bags in her room. One day she couldn't find any such exit, and when she had reached the last door at the end of the hall, jerked it open to see where it led. There, majestically seated in the bathtub, was a red-faced Englishman with a walrus mustache.

"Pardon me!" exclaimed the timid little woman, flustered beyond belief. "I'm trying to find the fire escape."

She had gotten back as far as the door to her own room, when the Englishman, dripping wet and with a towel ineffectually draped around his middle, came paddling up behind her. "Where," he gasped, "is the fire?"

★ ★ ★

Conrad Hilton spent a night at the Conrad Hilton Hotel in Chicago, asked for a bill when he checked out in the morning. He gave it back to the cashier after scrawling his signature across the bottom. She studied it a moment, then asked, "Tell me, Mr. Hilton, with what organization are you connected?"

★ ★ ★

"There's a suspicious-looking character in Room 716," a hotel manager told the house detective. "Better check on him pretty carefully."

When the house dick returned the manager inquired, "Find any of our towels in his suitcase?" "No," admitted the detective, "but I found our chambermaid in his grip."

★ ★ ★

Tourist-hungry motel managers have persuaded numerous authorities to change their villages' names lately. Who would think, for instance, of lingering in a hamlet named Dishwater Pond, New Hampshire? The name was changed, very wisely, to Mirror Lake. Similarly, in the twinkling of a town council's edit, Mosquito, Oregon, became Troutdale, Bee Pee, Kentucky, blossomed out as Chevrolet, and Mole Hill, West Virginia, was reborn as Mountain View.

★ ★ ★

On the beach near the newest hotel in Havana, the wife of a vacationing businessman came up with a conch shell and held it to her husband's ear. "Do you hear the sound of the waves inside the shell?" she asked. "Nah," grumbled the businessman. "The only thing *I* hear is fifty-five dollars a day—without meals!"

★ ★ ★

The resident manager of a sedate Philadelphia hotel was horrified to discover that a suite had been given for a long weekend to a couple who had registered as "W.E.R. NOTMAN AND WIFE, NORFROM, CONNECTICUT."

★ ★ ★

A well-dressed out-of-towner was registering at a swanky hotel when a beautiful blonde suggested, "How would you like to take me out this evening?" "How much?" asked the knowing stranger. "Fifty bucks," said she. "I'll give you five," he countered. "You are a cheap palooka," she decided, "and I no longer yearn for your company."

Later the stranger's wife appeared upon the scene, and he was escorting her across the lobby when the blonde once more hove into view. A broad grin lit up her face and she whispered in his ear, "See what you get for five dollars?"

★ ★ ★

A sloppy-looking, unshaven gent lumbered up to the registration desk of a big hotel, demanded the best suite available, and, with a great flourish, signed his check-in card with a big "X." As an afterthought, he pulled the card back from the clerk and added another "X." "This one," he explained, "stands for doctor of philosophy."

★ ★ ★

A cowboy in town for the rodeo shambled up to the desk of a fleabag hotel on a side street and said, "Gimme one of your two-dollar rooms, please." "Sorry," said the desk clerk. "Our minimum rate has been doubled. Those rooms are four dollars a night now." "What a gyp," grumbled the cowboy. "Whose bright idea was that?" "The new owner's," sighed the desk clerk. "This hotel has changed hands." The cowboy slung his duffel bag over his shoulder, and exited, declaring, "Tell the new owner this hand has changed hotels."

★ ★ ★

A lady wanted to spend a month at a new resort hotel but before packing her trunks took the precaution of writing the hotel manager to be sure dogs were permitted in the hostelry. It developed that the manager had a couple of dogs he was very partial to himself. This is the note he sent the lady:

"Dear Madam: I have been in the hotel business for some twenty-eight years. Never in all that time have I had to call the police to eject a disorderly dog at 4 A.M. Never once has a dog set the bedclothes afire by carelessly throwing away a lighted cigarette. Never has one dog stolen my towels, bedspreads, or silverware. Of course your dog is welcome at my hotel. Sincerely, The Manager.

"P.S. If the dog will vouch for you, you can come, too."

46. HUMOR

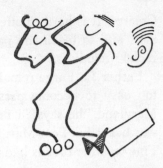

Professional funny men and scholars have been striving for years to define and isolate that most elusive thing, "Humor." The deeper they probe into its wellsprings, however, the more tiresome they become. I remember with a shudder one learned gentleman who covered over three hundred pages some years ago explaining exactly what caused people to laugh. Wolcott Gibbs, a noted wit in his own right, inspected the result with dismay. His review consisted of a single sentence: "Mr. So-and-so has got American humor on the ground—and is breaking its arm."

Fred Allen once told a university class: "I am often requested to define laughter but I cannot. Daniel Webster says, 'Laughter is a movement of the muscles of the face, especially the lips, with a peculiar expression of the eyes, indicating merriment.' Mr. Webster must have been thinking of an adult. In a baby that would signify gas. Then there was Nietzsche, the eminent German philosopher, who wrote: 'Man is the only animal that laughs; man alone has suffered so excruciatingly that he was compelled to invent laughter.' But what happened to Nietzsche after he made that remark? He died insane!"

★ ★ ★

"It takes no great talent," is the timely reminder of Father John La Farge, "to spread suspicion, fear, and hate. The tools are always at hand, the audience ready, and a halo of holy zeal is always easily adjusted to any ambitious writer's brow. On the other hand, it is tough going when you are striving to build up the full strength, spiritual and temporal, of man according to the image of his

Creator. It is hard to offer no panaceas to encourage healthy humor, and to teach the patient conquering of one's personal and
racial prejudices."

Father La Farge remains, however, a confirmed optimist. "It's
too easy to become pessimistic like my friend, Mart Jones, in
Maryland," he says. "I once remarked to Mart that the weather
was beautiful. Poor Mart answered dolefully, 'I hate fine weather.
Fine weather breeds bad weather.'"

AMERICA'S TWO GREATEST LIVING HUMORISTS

When I lecture at universities and colleges I almost invariably
am asked who I think are the greatest American humorists alive
today. My answer is always the same. In my opinion, James Thurber and E. B. White are so far ahead of the pack that their closest
pursuers are mere specks on the distant horizon.

Almost every literate person has read some of the writings of
Jim Thurber. "The Secret Life of Walter Mitty," "The Catbird
Seat," and "The Night the Ghost Got In" are probably his best-
known stories, but millions have chuckled over his countless other
pieces—and his fantastic drawings, too. Thurber art leans to "huge,
resigned dogs; determined and sometimes frightening women, and
globular men who try so hard to think so unsuccessfully." Harold
Ross, famed founder of *The New Yorker* magazine, once complained, "Thurber's women don't have any sex appeal." Marc
Connelly reminded him, "They do for Thurber's men!"

E. B. White, it seems to me, never has received quite the homage
that is his due. Much of the best material in the early years of *The
New Yorker's* "Talk of the Town" department was by him, though
it was unsigned. His *Here Is New York*, which catches the whole
essence of Manhattan in fifty-four short but masterly pages, was
written in a single humid midsummer afternoon in a cramped hotel
room. His *Charlotte's Web* is, I think, one of the best books of the
century. It's always hard to decide whom it delights most: the
children who listen to it, or the parents who read it aloud. I expect

I'll receive a lot of letters from irate readers for this, but I truly believe *Charlotte's Web* is a greater book than *Alice in Wonderland*.

In private life, Thurber and White are devoted friends, and, as a matter of fact, collaborated on a book called *Is Sex Necessary?* way back in 1929. Both men, like so many other distinguished humorists, are shy and introverted, a far cry from the "hail fellows well met" uninitiated persons expect "funny men" to be.

Thurber is his own most severe critic. He admits he rewrote one of his recent books "fifteen or twenty times" and threw away 200,000 words! "Once," he recalled, "my wife started to read the manuscript aloud at a party, but she didn't get very far. Somebody hissed. It was I."

It's no accident that E. B. White's two most successful books concern animals (*Stuart Little* is about a mouse, and the heroine of *Charlotte's Web* is a spider). "Animals are a weakness to me," admits White. "Maybe this doesn't explain why I wrote *Charlotte's Web*, but I can't tell why I sneeze either. A book"—and who is there to say him nay?—"is a sneeze."

"The world likes humor," E. B. White points out, "but it treats it too patronizingly. It decorates its serious artists with laurels, but its wags get only Brussels sprouts. I'm sure there isn't a humorist alive who doesn't recall the day when someone he loved and respected took him anxiously into a corner and asked, 'When are you going to settle down and write something serious?'"

Bearing out Mr. White's assertion, neither the Pulitzer Prize Committee nor the National Book Awards jury ever has given a top prize to a recognized humorist! If either would like to make amends for this glaring oversight, I suggest they take a long and earnest look next year in the direction of James Thurber of Ohio State and Elwyn Brooks White of Cornell!

★   ★   ★

Back of the desk in playwright Moss Hart's sumptuous new study, neatly framed, is this quotation by E. B. White: "I sometimes doubt that a writer should refine or improve his work by so much as a dictionary. One thing leads to another and the first thing you know, he has a stuffed chair and is fast asleep in it."

★ ★ ★

"Humor," philosophizes Rosalind Russell, "is like this. If you see a lady you know is the mother and sole support of five kids walking down the street, and she takes a pratfall, you'll feel pretty terrible and rush over to see if she's hurt herself. But if a rich, overdressed, overfed, worthless old dame slips on the same banana peel, and takes exactly the same fall, you'll think it uproariously funny. A lot of factors enter into the things that make people laugh."

★ ★ ★

Ben Cole, of Indianapolis, tells about a local senator who once sent a long humorous quotation over to the sages of nearby De Pauw University, and requested the author's name. For hours the savants pored through reference volumes without making the slightest headway. "There just doesn't seem to be any record of that quotation," they admitted finally. "That's fine," was the senator's unexpected response. "I wrote the darn thing myself. Just wanted to be sure nobody had said it before me."

★ ★ ★

A distinguished San Francisco attorney named Nat Schmulowitz has delved back into ancient Greek sources to prove that some of the jokes Broadway columnists claim to have "originated" are often more than two thousand years old!
A Few Examples:
1. A professor tried to train his jackass to get along without eating, by gradually cutting down on his feed. When the animal dropped dead of starvation, he said, "An irreplaceable loss! Just when he had learned not to eat, he died."
2. A professor met a friend and exclaimed, "I heard you had died." "But you see I'm alive," smiled the friend. "Impossible," decided the professor. "The man who told me is much more reliable than you are."

3. A braggart in a crowded marketplace saw his neighbor, just in from the country, and cried, "Hello! How goes it on my great sheep ranch?" The neighbor cried back, "When I left, one sheep was lying down, the other one was standing up."

★ ★ ★

Stoddard King, who wrote the lyrics of "A Long Long Trail," proclaimed his love for humor that was well seasoned in this poem, called "An Antiquarian Dissents":

> The good, new jokes come bravely out
>   To face a bitter age;
> They wander timidly about
>   And go upon the stage.
> But even though we hear them sprung
>   By experts and with zest,
> We do not like our jokes too young—
>   The bad old jokes are best.
>
> No tombstone-graven epitaph
>   Records the jokes of yore;
> We love most heartily to laugh
>   At gags we've heard before.
> They rouse us to a merry bray
>   As they go tottering by—
> Though new jokes greet us every day,
>   The old ones never die.
>
> Shoot if you must this old gray head,
>   But spare Joe Miller, please;
> And do not offer me instead
>   A fresh, unripened wheeze.
> Devote such time as you can spare
>   To new-coined humor's quest,
> But I shall still depose and swear
>   The bad old jokes are best.

★ ★ ★

Gilbert Highet, in a stimulating radio talk on "Nonsense," offered as a perfect modern example this excerpt from the late Robert Benchley's *Another Uncle Edith Christmas Story*:

"Everyone on board," continued the old salt pork, "felt that something was wrong. We were at that time at Lat. 78, Long. 78, which canceled each other, making us right back where we started from."

"Don't tell me that we are back at Nahant again," said little Philip, throwing up.

"Not exactly Nahant," said Uncle Edith, "but within hailing distance of a Nahanted ship."

"You just used Nahant in the first place so that you could pull that gag," said Primrose, who up to this time had taken no part in the conversation, not having been born. . . .

★ ★ ★

A pompous gentleman once asked the sharp-tongued British actress, Mrs. Patrick Campbell, "Why do you suppose it is that women are so utterly lacking in a sense of humor?"

"God did it on purpose," Mrs. Campbell answered without batting an eyelash, "*so that we may love you men instead of laughing at you.*"

47. HUNTING

Judging by the number of licenses issued, over half a million American men must have considered duck hunting their favorite sport last year, although poet Ogden Nash derided the breed as "Mighty men with gun and pluck, hoping to outwit—a duck!"

The late W. C. Fields announced flatly that all duck hunters were crazy. The irascible comedian indulged in the sport just once in his life. His host couldn't understand why he had accepted the invitation at all until the time came to awaken him at 3 A.M. "Get up at 3 A.M.," roared Fields. "I thought you said 3 P.M.!"

The following morning Fields did no hunting. Along about noon, he wobbled into the town's one saloon and anxiously clutched the arm of the bartender. "Did I come in here last night," he inquired, "hand you a hundred-dollar bill, and then spend it all on liquor?" "You did," nodded the bartender. "Thank heavens," cried Fields happily. "I was afraid I had lost it."

Incidentally, Fields gave the bartender his gun, too.

★ ★ ★

Out in Wahoo, Nebraska (birthplace of Darryl Zanuck), there's a hunter of great repute named Bill Behrens. One morning Behrens spotted a wild blue goose flying past his house, and honked hopefully at it. Apparently the goose liked his voice, because it checked its flight, honked back, and hovered above the house until Behrens got his shotgun and climbed into his car.

Because hunting is illegal within Wahoo City limits, Behrens kept honking until he drove out into the open country. There he got out of the car, gave one final honk, and dispatched the silly goose.

Have you heard about the brave hunter who came back to camp with his hands full of splinters? It seems he caught a timber wolf bare-handed.

Another nimrod wound up a day in the woods by demanding three clothes brushes, explaining to the attendant, "That was a dirty trek."

Alfred Hitchcock tells of a huntsman who was stranded in the heart of the vast African desert when his jeep broke down. To his surprise there materialized from nowhere an immaculate Oxfordian Englishman who led him to a beautiful villa, equipped with all the latest gadgets, and insisted, "You must be my guest until spare parts for your jeep can be brought down from the coast." He then produced his wife and daughter, both young and dazzling enough to be sisters.

For five nights, the hunter stayed in the villa, and on each of them, once everything was still, he had a charming, generous, and silent visitor. Was it the wife or the daughter? Neither by word nor glance did either give a sign during the day.

The jeep eventually was repaired and the hunter made his goodbys. "Tell me," he asked his host at the moment of departure, "why do you all live here in the midst of a wasteland like this?"

"We have a secret misfortune," the host explained reluctantly. "We have another daughter whom you did not meet. She is a leper."

★ ★ ★

In the trophy room of an Adirondack lodge there's a bulletin board listing the names of the intrepid members, along with their most noteworthy hunting accomplishments. Opposite the name of Monte Marmaduke III is the notation, "Killed: thirty-four cases of Scotch."

★ ★ ★

Old Grandpa Heimerdinger, confined to a wheelchair, hadn't walked a step for seven full years—but one thing he was bent on doing before he died. He wanted to hunt just one more bear. Accordingly, the first time he was left alone with his two young grandsons, he persuaded them to give him his gun and wheel him deep into the woods, some ten miles away.

Suddenly a huge grizzly lumbered directly into their path. The two brave lads promptly left Grandpa in his wheelchair and hot-footed it, screaming, back to town. Their mother was putting her car away when they got there. "Grandpa has been et by a grizzly bear," they wailed.

"Stop yelling," advised their mother. "Your grandpa got home five minutes before you did."

★ ★ ★

They tell of a hunter named Shephard
Who was eaten for lunch by a lephard.
Said the lephard, "Egad,
You'd be tastier, lad,
If you had been salted and pephard."

★ ★ ★

A famous big-game hunter was captured by African savages and imprisoned in a hut tastefully decorated with the shrunken, preserved heads of previous victims. A year later he managed to escape, however, and made his way to the nearest settlement, where he phoned his wife.

"I had given you up for lost," she sobbed.

"Never mind that," said the hunter. "Just rush me some new clothes. I'm in rags. I'll need a suit, size 40, a shirt, size 16, and some shoes, size 10B."

"And oh, yes," he added. "I'll need a hat, too. Size one."

48. INDIANS

When the white man began pushing the Indians around in America, notes Frank Wortman ironically, the Indians were running things in distressingly primitive fashion: no taxes, no national debt—and women doing most of the work. The white men, of course, soon put a stop to *that* sort of nonsense.

Underestimating the Indians, as a matter of fact, has been the general fashion for far too long in this country. Kids of my generation were brought up on one-reel movie atrocities in which the Indians were always the arch-villains, pillaging and scalping—and too few teachers reminded us that, far from being the aggressors, these were people fighting desperately to protect their homes and families against ruthless white invaders. The situation has improved slightly today, but we still prefer to laugh at the gaucheries of one Indian in a thousand who has struck oil and is riding around in a big limousine and forget the desperate plight of the other 999.

★ ★ ★

Are the Indians really as taciturn and sharp-eyed as they have been pictured? Earle Dexter, who has worked with the Navajo tribe for twenty years, thinks yes. In his book, *Doors Towards the Sunrise,* he tells about a government official who made a long-winded address to the tribe, then rashly requested an audience reaction. An old patriarch rose slowly to his feet and shattered the pretenses of the speaker in exactly six words: "Much wind! Heap dust! No rain!"

★ ★ ★

Back in colonial days, a fur trader named William Johnson learned the Mohawk tongue, married an Indian princess, and prospered. Johnson did his best to understand the complicated thinking processes of his Indian friends. Their dreams, he realized, were particularly important. If one Indian dreamed that the tribe was in danger of attack, the entire tribe would break camp and move a hundred miles away.

One day Johnson was trying on some richly laced suits, which he had imported from Europe at great expense. An Indian chief saw them, and announced, "Sir William, I dreamed last night that you received some suits, and gave every one of them to me as a gift." Unhesitatingly, Johnson gave the suits to the chief—but the next day was back at his side to report, "Last night it was my turn to dream. I dreamed that you gave me as a gift three hundred acres of that Mohawk land."

The chief, game to the end, gave Johnson the land, but concluded sadly, "After this, Sir William, I will never dream with you again. You dream too hard for me!"

★ ★ ★

The "picturesque" Indian of today, daubed with war paint and adorned with feathers, is a concession to the tourist trade. Visitors to one reservation showed their disappointment too strongly when their "redskin guide" turned out to be a U.C.L.A. Junior with a conservative blue serge suit and a crew cut. They didn't like what the wild braves were saying. That mistake will not be repeated.

The U.C.L.A. student, incidentally, was carrying in his wallet a check from a big magazine for a humorous article entitled, "The Ute's Companion, or How Aboriginal Can You Get?" As further refutation to the notion that the taciturn redskin lacks a sense of humor, there's the story of an Indian who sends up smoke signals in the desert with a fire extinguisher strapped to his side. His explanation: "Me misspellum word, me can erasum."

★ ★ ★

Back from a trip through the wildest stretches of Utah and Arizona, a publisher whose hobby is visiting National Parks recalled one day when his horse came to a sudden stop. Injun trouble. "They bobbed up from nowhere," explained the publisher.

"Suddenly they were in front of us, behind us, to the right of us, to the left of us!" "What did you do?" asked a friend anxiously. "What could we do?" shrugged the publisher. "We bought some blankets."

★ ★ ★

A tourist in New Mexico spotted a fine earthenware jar in an Indian souvenir depot and asked, "How much?" "A hundred dollars," answered the Indian proprietor. "Nonsense," exclaimed the tourist. "I'll give you twenty-four bucks for it."

"Listen, wise guy," said the Indian disgustedly, "bargains like Manhattan Island you're not going to get any more!"

★ ★ ★

A Washington big shot was tendered a banquet by an Indian tribe intent upon getting his approval for a bill that would benefit them. They gave him the works. He was particularly impressed by the chief's elaborate costume.

"That's a beautiful piece of mink attached to your belt," said the big shot. "Where did you trap it?"

The chief was just winding up to tell a whopper when his squaw spoiled everything. "Trap nothing," she hooted. "He cut that off my old fur coat."

★ ★ ★

Nat Benchley, aided and abetted by such pale-faced culprits as Marc Connelly, William J. Barker, and Gwyn Steinbeck, has compiled a list of Indian songs which will make your scalps tingle. Here are a few of the more gruesome details:

Algonquin Buy a Paper Doll That I Can Call My Own.

Cheyenne, Cheyenne Harvest Moon Up in the Sky.

Osage Can You See.

I Navajo I Could Love Anybody—

I'll Be Down to Get You in Apache, Honey.

Aztec the High Road and You Take the Low Road.

Oswego Marching Through Georgia.

Life Is Just a Bowl of Cherokees.

Say It Isn't Sioux.

Seminole Cow Hand from the Rio Grande.

Ol' Rockin' Cherokee's Got Me.

You Took the Pottawattamie That Once Was the Hottawattamie So Why Not Take All of Me?

Are you still conscious? Do you wish to contribute a few Piutes of your own? No reservations; no admittance fee.

Comanche Faithful!

49. INGENUITY

Many a hostess has to call upon her ingenuity and resourcefulness when her dear husband suddenly turns up with four unexpected guests for dinner or a disaster destroys the peace in the kitchen.

Take the time Mr. and Mrs. Calvin Coolidge entertained friends at a Thanksgiving dinner in their Northampton, Massachusetts, home. The maid entered the dining room, bearing aloft a magnificent, golden-brown turkey. Then, alas, she slipped and fell on her face, while the turkey skidded clear across the floor.

That's when Mrs. Coolidge showed her mettle. "Never mind, Mary," she soothed, seemingly unperturbed. "Just take this turkey back to the kitchen and bring in the other one."

★ ★ ★

A farmer whose income depended entirely upon the size of his potato crop ran afoul of the law and was sentenced to sixty days in jail right in the planting season. His furious wife wrote to tell him: "Now you're in the clink, I suppose you expect me to dig the field and plant the potatoes. Well, I ain't going to do it." He answered: "Don't you *dare* dig up that field. That's where I hid all the money and the guns." A week later she wrote again: "Somebody at that jail must be reading your mail. The cops were here and dug up the entire field. What do I do now?" Back from the contented prisoner came his final message: "Plant the potatoes."

★ ★ ★

On a Florida beach, a remarkably stout gentleman lolled in a reinforced deck chair and watched with unconcealed admiration while a bevy of bathing beauties, also unconcealed, gamboled on the golden sands. "I thought you came here to reduce," sneered an acquaintance who had just worn himself out on the golf links.

"That's exactly what I'm doing," beamed the stout gentleman. "I walk eleven miles every morning to watch!"

★ ★ ★

A cost-cutting storekeeper in New Hampshire raised the paper-towel dispensers in his washroom a foot and a half above their former niche. Now when a customer wants to dry his hands he has to reach so high that water runs down his sleeves. Probably he cusses a bit—but he uses only one of the storekeeper's towels instead of three.

★ ★ ★

There are three competing dress shops right in a row on the main street of an Alabama city. One morning the merchant on the right put up a sign proclaiming, "Unprecedented Fire Sale." The merchant on the left countered with "Absolutely Final Bankruptcy Clean-out." The merchant in the middle hung up a very simple announcement indeed. It read "Main Entrance"!

★ ★ ★

A couple of adjoining barbershops in Miami Beach did a bit of sign posting, too. One announced: "Why pay $1.50 for a haircut? We'll do the job for fifty cents less!" Two hours later the other hung out this sign twice as big: "We guarantee to repair dollar haircuts."

★ ★ ★

From Harry Hershfield comes the story of a lady who went to a delicatessen for some corned beef. "How much?" inquired the clerk. "Never mind how much. Cut!" ordered the lady. After several slices, the clerk asked, "Is this enough?" "No. Cut, cut," she demanded impatiently. After watching him intently while he sliced some minutes more, she finally queried, "Is this the center of the corned beef?" "Yes, lady," he replied wearily. "Ah hah," nodded the lady. "Now give me ten cents' worth of that part."

A jeweler in Wisconsin had been robbed three times, and the police had arrested nobody. The next time, he vowed, he would catch the marauder himself. He rigged up a camera, designed so the thief would snap his own picture in the act of robbing the store. As bait, he put a tray of cheap costume jewelry, an imitation watch, and two one-dollar bills in front of the camera. Alas, the thief, on his next visit, ignored the cheap jewelry, the watch, and the two dollars—and disappeared into the night with the jeweler's three-hundred-dollar camera.

★ ★ ★

A wild-eyed gent had the U.S. Patent Office in a dither the other day demanding protection on what he termed "The greatest invention of the decade." It turned out to be a cake of soap ten feet long. "You couldn't even lift a thing like that to lather yourself," scoffed a clerk. "You don't have to," replied the great inventor triumphantly. "You just climb on top of it and slither up and down!" . . . Colonel Francis Duffy has devised a square bath tub for people who don't like to leave rings. . . . Dave Garroway has all but perfected a silent alarm clock for folks who like to oversleep and a cork anchor for chronic drifters. . . . And Marine "Sandy" Winnick wins first prize for the most ingenious line of the year. Approaching a beautiful redhead at a service dance in San Diego, Sandy informed her gravely, "I'm compiling a new national telephone directory. May I have your number, please?"

★ ★ ★

Starlet Terry Moore had an alibi ready when she appeared very late for a TV rehearsal on a day the streets of Manhattan were glazed with ice.

"Every time I took one step forward," she wailed, "I slipped back two."

"If that's the case," inquired her unmollified director, "how did you manage to get here at all?"

"I discovered a way," explained Terry. "I just turned around and started back home!"

A Stamford commuter was just leaving the house to make his customary train when his wife requested him to detour through the kitchen and give the maid a severe dressing down. "But I thought you were delighted with her?" he demurred. "I am," said the crafty wife, "but this is her morning for beating the rugs, and she does a much more thorough job when she's angry."

Just to prove that all those fabulously rich operators you hear about are not concentrated in Texas, Peter Lind Hayes has a story about a prominent member of the breed who hails from Mobile.

This Mobillionaire was gazing out over the harbor of Portofino in Italy one morning when a magnificent yacht sailed into view. It carried a crew of twenty-six and had ample accommodations for sixty passengers. Our hero rose to the occasion like the true Southern gallant he was.

"I'm going to buy me that yacht for my old mammy," he told the startled captain. "Tell me how much it is, and then sail it right over to Mobile in time to surprise Mammy on Christmas morning."

"But this is preposterous," objected the captain. "It is now December 20. How can we possibly sail across the Atlantic in time?"

"Okay, sonny boy," said the Mobillionaire affably, pulling out his wallet. *Fly it over.*"

★ ★ ★

In a primitive town two hundred miles south of the Rio Grande, a tourist noticed a native squatting lazily in the shade and asked him, "Could you tell me the exact time?" The native yawned, reached up to his burro, idling in front of him, and lifted the animal's tail. "Senor," he announced, "ees exactly 10:37 A.M." Then he promptly went back to sleep.

The tourist, intrigued, walked a few steps to the plaza at the end of the street, checked with the big clock on the cathedral tower, and discovered that the time indeed was 10:37 A.M.

Returning that way some hours later, he observed that neither the native nor his burro had moved six inches. Again he requested the time. Again the native lifted the burro's tail, and politely droned, "Ees exactly 4:51 P.M." Again the cathedral clock verified his calculation.

"This is amazing," marveled the tourist. "Would you mind telling me how you can ascertain the exact time by merely lifting that fool burro's tail?"

"Ees simple," the native assured him. "When I leeft tail, I can see clock on cathedral tower."

50. INSURANCE

The object of a good insurance salesman is to sell you so many different kinds of policies you can't afford to do any of the things that might give you a chance to collect.

There *are* insurance men, however, with hearts of gold, and not one paragraph of tiny print in their souls. One follows clients to see that they take no chances that aren't covered in their policies. His motto is, "Block that stunt!" Another rounded up every man he could find who was over ninety-eight and wrote liberal policies for them. The home office finally caught up with him and demanded, "What's the idea of giving insurance to these antiques? Are you trying to bankrupt us?" "It's the law of averages," maintained the agent. "Look up the figures yourself. You'll see how few people of ninety-eight or over die each year."

★ ★ ★

An insurance agent received this inquiry from a lady in Wichita: "If I take out one of your special policies on my husband's life, exactly what will I get if he dies?" The agent, a stickler for accuracy, replied, "If he dies naturally, ten thousand dollars. If he dies accidentally, twenty thousand dollars. If he dies intentionally, thirty years."

★ ★ ★

A persuasive insurance broker in Rhode Island thought a neighbor's massive, ferocious-looking dog was a good reason for the neighbor to take out a fat policy. His powers of persuasion carried the day—and not a moment too soon—for the neighbor, anyhow.

The policy had barely been signed when the dog made a leap for the insurance broker and bit him.

⋆　⋆　⋆

A policy purveyor who had experienced a run of miserable luck finally persuaded a secretary to summon her boss to the phone. "I don't suppose you're in the market for some additional life insurance?" began the salesman. "Why, yes, I am," replied the prospect. "How large a policy would you suggest?"

"Excuse me, sir," stammered the salesman. "I must have the wrong number!"

⋆　⋆　⋆

Pyke Johnson, of Doubleday, had to choose between two old college chums when it came to selecting a policy. "One was named Budd, the other Walter," recalls Johnson, "so I thought it best to string along with Walter." His reason? He figured Budd was slicker than Walter.

⋆　⋆　⋆

Insurance agent E. B. Bowers, of Columbia, South Carolina, has found that a touch of Oriental courtesy speeds payments by delinquent premium payers. Here's his pitch: "Esteemed Policyholders: Kindly refrain from joining illustrious ancestors while insignificant premium reposes unpaid in offending pocket, since meantime honorable family, not insurance company, is holding the burlap."

⋆　⋆　⋆

At an annual roundup of agents for a big insurance company this spring, the president suddenly cried, "On your feet, everybody! Look at the bottoms of your chairs!" The startled agents jumped up, and found on the seat of every chair a crisp new dollar bill.

"Keep the dollars, boys," smiled the pres. "I just wanted to demonstrate that the time has come when you've got to get out of your chairs if you want to make a buck."

51. IRELAND

In the good old summertime, when there are no new shows opening on Broadway for drama critic Brooks Atkinson to make or
break with his pungent reviews, he relaxes with his lovely wife
Oriana in some foreign clime. One summer the Atkinsons chose
Ireland, and the story of their happy peerin' in Erin is told in Mrs.
Atkinson's bouncy *The South and the West of It.* I particularly
enjoyed her report on the birth and blossoming of one of the Em-
erald Isle's major sources of revenue: the Irish Sweepstakes.

Do you be believing that these Sweepstakes are an old established thing, steeped in tradition? Get along with you! They came
into being only twenty-nine short years ago, and the mastermind
who deserves sole credit for the show is one Joseph McGrath, of
Ballsbridge, Dublin.

Mr. McGrath had begun life as an accountant, and soon made
himself known to the British. So well known, in fact, that they
clapped him into jail for his part in the bloody Easter Rising of
1916. When the Provisional Government was set up, appreciative
countrymen named McGrath Labor Minister.

It was a chance visit to an Irish hospital that altered the destiny
of Joseph McGrath in 1930. He found the hospital in deplorable
state—equipment inadequate, staff shockingly underpaid. Most of
its funds were provided via a local lottery. McGrath didn't like the
setup. He liked it even less when he discovered that almost all the
other hospitals in Ireland were depending upon similar sloppily
handled lotteries for revenue to keep them going. Why not one
whopping lottery, reasoned McGrath, in which all the medical

centers could share? When he persuaded authorities to legalize his super-Sweepstakes project, he knew he was headed for the glory road.

The first Sweepstakes fund amounted to $1,169,238, and fully one-third of it went to the impoverished hospitals. That proportion has been maintained, and slightly bettered in fact, ever since. Mc-Grath and his staff receive only reasonable fixed salaries. The rest goes to winners. By 1956, the prize booty was up to more than five and a half million dollars, with sixteen first prizes alone worth $140,000 apiece, and thousands of other "consolation" awards. The hospitals received over four million dollars, the government over $600,000 in taxes. It's gotten so that it's almost a pleasure to be sick in Ireland.

Everything connected with the Sweepstakes draw, reports Oriana Atkinson, is so honest and aboveboard that even Willie Sutton, the famous authority on breaking open American banks, couldn't figure a way to beat the game. Over four million sweeps tickets were sold in 1958 at about a pound apiece. Of course, none of them was sold in this country. That would be illegal. Winners in America were given their tickets by bighearted leprechauns from bosky dells on the shore of Loch Derg and Benny's Drugstore just off Sixth Avenue. Banshees and dullaghans give away sweep tickets, too, but should be avoided at all costs. Your true leprechaun lives in a bluebell and speaks only Gaelic.

Illegal though it be to purchase a Sweepstakes ticket, the tax department has generously stepped forward to share the spoils with winners—in a ratio of anything up to 8 to 1. Then, by the time creditors and forgotten relatives have moved in for their share of the kill, winners are lucky if they come out even. This teaches them such a lesson they don't go out hunting for another leprechaun for several hours.

★ ★ ★

After swabbing floors at the Ninth National Bank for over twenty years, Bridey Clancy suddenly became rich. She won a

$50,000 sweepstake! Envious friends crowded round her and begged, "Whatcha gonna do now, Bridey? Buy a mink coat and a Cadillac? Go to Europe? Sure you'll be throwing up your job."

"That I won't," promised Bridey. "I like that job. But this I'll say: me attitude ain't going to be the same! Lord help that fat vice-president if he gets in the way of me mop!"

★ ★ ★

James Cagney tells of an Irish bartender whose wife had just died. Determined that she be properly "waked," he summoned friends from miles around. The whiskey flowed, and there was much ado.

On the morning the funeral was to be held, the man went to his closest friend and said to him, "Dinny, if you think there'll be a bit of fun in it, I'll keep her another day!"

★ ★ ★

Another Cagney favorite concerns the Englishman who boasted a bit too much in an Irish pub, and came out a very bad second in the fracas that ensued. "Not only that," he mourned to the judge a while later, "but as I was coming to, I heard one of my assailants suggest, 'Let's throw him out of the window.' 'Not good enough,' amended the other. 'Let's take him up a flight.'"

★ ★ ★

An Irishman was bowled over by a Dublin bus, and promptly sued for £100,000. Carried into court on a stretcher, he testified he had been unable to move one muscle since the accident. The jury burst into tears and awarded him the full £100,000, without leaving the courtroom.

The attorney for the bus company was not so impressed. "Hennessy," he thundered, "I believe you're a faker. I'm going to follow you twenty-four hours a day, and if you so much as waggle one toe . . ."

"You're a hard, unfeeling man," protested Hennessy, "and to prove your suspicions are unfounded, I'll tell you exactly what I'm going to do when I'm carried out of this room. An ambulance will take me to the ferry for England. Another will take me to the ferry for Calais. There I'll be placed aboard a train for Lourdes. And at Lourdes, me boy, if you're still following me, you're going to see the darndest miracle in the past two hundred years!"

★ ★ ★

The butcher in a seaside town in Cork was a bit too fond of the bottle. Twice a year, as a matter of fact, he went off on a monumental bender, and since he was the only butcher about, everybody had to live on fish until he reopened his shop. A tourist came to the local inn for a two-week visit just after one of the butcher's benders got under way, and was outraged to be served nothing but fish for luncheon and dinner on four successive days. On the fifth day he took one look at the luncheon menu, and announced, "I'm leaving." "You're booked for a fortnight," protested the proprietor, "and only four days have been ticked off. Where do you think you're going?" "Thanks to the food you served me," said the tourist grimly, "I am going up the river to spawn."

★ ★ ★

A wealthy American checked into the same inn that summer, and told the proprietor, "For dinner this evening I'll want a clear soup, salmon mayonnaise, a rare steak, strawberries and cream, and coffee." The flabbergasted proprietor exclaimed, "Begor, sir, if we had all them things, we'd have ate them ourselves!"

52. SUNNY ITALY

"Plenty big-shot Americans arriving Rome airport this season," chauffeur Joe Cestarni assured me. "Great fellows for conversation, too. Sixty-eight per cent tells me, 'Rome wasn't built in a day.' Twenty-four per cent begin, 'All roads lead to Rome.' Sixteen per cent say, 'When in Rome, I guess I better do what Romans do.'"

"That adds up to 108 per cent," I pointed out.

"Extra 8 per cent the worst kind," nodded Joe. "They say all three!"

I soon learned I was one of the most fortunate tourists ever to land in Rome. "You will see the ruins of the Forum in full moonlight," Joe told me. "Furthermore, there is big, wonderful pageant at St. Peter's tomorrow. And, third, you are sitting in same limousine occupied exclusively for last four days by Gary Cooper!"

To show my appreciation, I gave Joe Cestarni a brand-new story for his repertoire—the one about the ancient Roman who proposed to a friend, "Let's burn down Rome before that Nero gets around to it. I'm all for eliminating the fiddle man."

"Ever heard that before?" I demanded. "Yesterday," grunted Joe. "*Twice!*" Then he told *me* about the time Julius Caesar's wife Calpurnia came up with a new recipe for pizza pies. "Did you like them?" asked Brutus. "Et tu, Brute," answered Caesar.

Joe Cestarni and I declared a truce at this point.

★ ★ ★

Another recent visitor to Rome was Sir Laurence Olivier. While there, he attended a full-dress reception, and found himself standing next in line to a very elegant, stiff-backed Italian duke. After fifteen minutes of silence in this position, Olivier felt that some polite remark was in order. He pointed admiringly at the duke's ornate gold cuff links and inquired, "Cartier?" The duke answered coldly, "Cellini!"

★ ★ ★

Two young girls, obviously American, were conversing in front of Rome's Grand Hotel when an older lady interrupted to ask, "How can I get to the Colosseum from here?"

"Take the first turn to the left," answered one girl, "and keep going. You can't miss the Colosseum. It's just across the street from the souvenir and record shop!"

★ ★ ★

Two ladies from Montreal toured Italy by motor last summer and inevitably pulled up before the famous Leaning Tower of Pisa. While they were parking their car, a uniformed attendant appeared, handed them a pink ticket, and collected a hundred lire therefor. When the ladies returned to their hotel, they asked the concierge, "Who gets the money collected for parking near the Tower?"

The concierge examined their pink ticket, smiled, and explained, "There's no parking charge in Pisa, ladies. What you did here was to insure your car against damage in the event that the Leaning Tower fell on it."

★ ★ ★

In a New York neighborhood dominated by citizens of Italian extraction, it is the annual custom to parade a fine, life-size statue of St. Rosco through the streets. In the midst of one of these celebrations, the procession paused a moment to rest, and an indignant Irish spectator took advantage of the opportunity to proclaim to all and sundry that St. Patrick had it all over St. Rosco in every conceivable way, shape, and form.

Several Italians took issue with the Irishman, who finally got so angry he picked up a stone and heaved it, neatly knocking off the head of the statue. "That just goes to show you," he bellowed triumphantly to the stunned Italians. "If that had been St. Patrick, he'd have ducked!"

53. KIDS

I visited my son Chris in prep school recently and was struck by a few changes that had been effected since I was a boy. Mine were the days, for instance, when automobiles had no tail fins but could fit in a garage, and when, since only the headmaster had a car and students hitched rides on the back steps of ice wagons, the parking problem was not so acute.

Then, too, some girls and boys as young as twelve actually had learned to read and write. Nor was there anything like TV to dim the allure of the movie palace down the block. Don't tell *me* there's any beauty on television to compare with Norma Talmadge or Anita Stewart!

And how the dances have changed in the past few decades! I don't mean the steps and rhythms so much as the rules governing procedure. Half the fun of going to a dance when I was an adolescent was the hope that, by "cutting in" on a pretty girl just imported to the group, you might acquire a new love for "life"— or at least the next fortnight. If you were stuck with one girl for longer than a single swing around the floor, you either would feign a nosebleed or wave a dollar bill behind her back in the hope of promoting a relief patrol.

None of that indiscriminate stuff today! "Going steady" is the thing. Seventeen-year-olds, having solemnly exchanged frat and sorority pins, dance together for the entire evening, and never dream of changing partners once. How, without a series of dramatically different "crushes," can they tell what kind of a husband or wife they actually prefer?

My son Chris points out loftily that "kids need security more now than in the simple old days." Something to do with pressures of the missile age, and a couple of years of military service after college cutting down the leeway for experimentation. "Got to get your course set early, Dad." Maybe he's right.

There have been a few changes in vocabulary, too—not radical, mind you—just enough to make you wonder if your son is speaking English. "Listen carefully," he suggests, "or you won't be 'entirely with it.'"

When a prep-schooler announces that something is "casual," he means it's simply colossal. "Let's get on the stick" is his way of urging "Get a move on." He'd be truly mortified to be overheard greeting his parents as Mom and Dad; today it's a condescending, "Hi, fans."

An uncomplimentary gibe is a "wicked slash." When it strikes home you moan, "Get the Band-aids." A fellow looks "grubby" when he's dressed carelessly—especially when the gruesome effect is deliberate. A "well-fed tie" (plenty of food spots on it) is the first essential for a true "grub."

"We were just hacking around," is the standard reply for any parent rash enough to ask, "What were you doing all day (or evening)?"

"Jap," means an unexpected, tough exam. And "shafted" is the word that has replaced "gypped." Next time your young hopeful tells you "Did I get shafted on that Jap?" you can know he's just achieved an "F" in a test sprung by some unfeeling professor on the very afternoon he had been planning to brush up on racing dives and turns in the swimming pool.

"But yesterday," I quoted gravely, "the words of Caesar might have stood against the world; now lie they there, and none so poor to do them reverence."

"That's a wicked slash," approved my son Chris. "It's real casual."

★ ★ ★

One of Wendell Willkie's first jobs was teaching school in Coffeyville, Kansas, where he hit upon a novel way to make the basic doctrines of the Declaration of Independence clear to his students. "I'm giving each of you three common, everyday buttons," he told them. "Imagine that the first represents Life, the second Liberty, and the third the Pursuit of Happiness. Tomorrow I'm going to ask you to produce the buttons and tell me what they stand for."

The next day one lad sadly reported that one of his buttons was missing. "Here's Life and here's Liberty," he said, "but Ma sewed the Pursuit of Happiness on my pants."

★ ★ ★

One of the troubles of the day, observes Mr. C. N. Peace, is that once we came upon the little red schoolhouse, whereas now we come upon the little read schoolboy.

★ ★ ★

At a conference on education, a vote-conscious state senator boomed from the speaker's platform, "Long live our teachers!" From the back of the hall came the query, *"On what?"*

★ ★ ★

It's Charlotte Bradford's notion that schoolteachers petition for higher salaries at the wrong time of the year. "If they'd wait till the beginning of August—just past halfway in the kids' summer vacations—to make their plea, parents would give them anything they asked on the first ballot!"

★ ★ ★

Television has changed schoolboys and girls a lot—but they've never come up with a substitute for that good old game of post office. A group of enthusiastic kids were playing it recently at a party, when a boy and girl shut themselves in a closet and didn't come out. "Come out of there," ordered the host's mother finally. "We can't," the boy called back. "We have our braces hooked!"

★ ★ ★

Did you know that the official word for a pupil learning the alphabet is "abecedarian?" Well, little Heathcliff was one abecedarian who couldn't get to first base. His mother put a small clock in front of him and threatened, "When that clock strikes seven, either you know that alphabet, or you get no dinner."

Heathcliff took no chances. He swallowed the clock. His frantic mother summoned the doctor, who reported in surprise, "It doesn't seem to be bothering him." "It's *me* who's bothered," screamed the mother. "Every time I wind it, he bites my finger."

★ ★ ★

When a kid tells his parents, "I didn't hit him. I just sort of pushed him," or "I didn't do a thing," he REALLY means he just walloped his younger brother. On the other hand when he hollers "M-O-M-M-Y," he means that his younger brother has just walloped *HIM*. This information comes from a real authority: Mr. Robert Paul Smith. Smith also has the translation for a twelve-year-old girl's wails, "I wish I was dead." She plans to lie on her stomach on her bed in her room all afternoon, refusing all nourishment except a carton of soft drinks, three boxes of chocolate crackers, and a jar of cocktail onions.

★ ★ ★

A young mother in Milwaukee, exhausted from her daily chores, lay down on her couch to steal forty winks. Half asleep, she felt one of her youngsters patting her face and was drowsily pleased by this unexpected display of affection.

Then the doorbell rang. She jumped up with a start to admit a delivery man from her husband's favorite liquor shop. He looked at her so queerly that when he had gone, she rushed over to a mirror to inspect herself.

Her face was completely plastered with green trading stamps!

★ ★ ★

Jean Roath writes about a small-town drugstore she visited while motoring through Wyoming. The store was chock-full of happy youngsters consuming banana splits and other hard-to-digest concoctions. In the center of the group sat a sunburned old cowhand in blue jeans, flannel shirt, and sombrero.

"I'm just an old feller having myself a time," he explained happily. "Many's the time I used to come to town to get drunk, but now I find I get a much bigger kick out of buying the kids all the ice cream they can eat!"

★ ★ ★

There's a lady in the suburbs who is determined that, when her twelve-year-old son Herbert grows up, he will be not only a Fred Astaire, but a Winston Churchill as well. With that end in view, she marches him to dancing school every Wednesday afternoon, and furthermore sits grimly at the ringside to see that he not only pushes little girls around the room, more or less in tune with the music, but engages them in conversation at the same time. Herbert takes an exceedingly dim view of the entire procedure.

Last Wednesday, Herbert was executing what he fondly believed to be a foxtrot with a brand-new dancing partner when he caught his mother's signal: "Engage her in conversation!" He took a deep breath, and gallantly informed his lady fair, "Say, you sweat less than any fat girl I've ever danced with!"

Herbert won't have to go back to that dancing school for quite a spell.

CHILDREN OF DISTINCTION

BOYS . . .

1. The eight-year-old lad who was asked by his grandfather, "What is the first thing you notice about a girl?" The lad—wise beyond his years—promptly replied, "That all depends on which direction she's facing!"

2. Peter, who, like all six-year-olds, abhorred washing, and came

to the dinner table one evening with elbows black as pitch. Sent back to the bathroom for repairs, he dawdled there so long that his mother called, "How are you coming, Pete? Elbows clean yet?" "Not clean," he called back triumphantly, "but I've got them to match."

3. The 150-pound ten-year-old who won the part of Cleopatra in a school play. "But why," asked his mother, "did they give such a part to the huskiest lad in the class?" "They had to," explained the boy cheerfully. "It was my snake!"

4. The youthful scion of an elegant family who came home to report that a rambunctious classmate in school had dared to call him a sissy. "What did you do?" demanded his indignant father. The scion answered, "I hit him with my purse."

5. The boy scout who admitted to his father that his daily good deed was not quite up to snuff this once. "I helped an old lady across the street like you suggested," he said, "but she got hit by a taxi."

6. The nine-year-old who, asked by his teacher to name the four seasons of the year, came up with "Football, Basketball, Baseball, and Vacation."

7. The young teen-ager who was discovered by his mother in a cutthroat poker game. What's more, his stack of chips was sadly depleted. "Look, Mom," he said sadly, "no hands!"

8. The kid from Texas who got all the way to the finals of a national spelling bee but then lost out because he couldn't spell "small."

9. The ornery young sprout in a one-room mountain school whose teacher was endeavoring vainly to explain the word "feet." Finally she urged, "Now, boy, just tell me what a cow has four of that I only have two of." The sprout told her—and that's why he was expelled from school.

10. The smart aleck who had to give a sentence containing the words "Highway Cop." He earned a nice fat "F" with his "Highway cop wid a headache every Sunday morning."

GIRLS . . .

1. Lucinda, who, at the age of ten was given a check for twenty dollars by her parents and told to open an account at the savings bank. Officials there gave her an application blank that included the question, "Have you had an account previously elsewhere, and if so, will you please print here the name of the bank?"

Lucinda gave the problem due thought, then laboriously spelled out, "Yes. Piggy."

2. The little girl at boarding school who was asked by the staff psychiatrist, "Do you ever get homesick?" "Yes, sir," she answered, "but only when I'm home."

3. The twelve-year-old lass who was asked to pass on her mother's new evening gown. She exclaimed with enthusiasm, "Gee, Mom, it makes you look just like a princess—a very old princess."

4. The little girl on TV who announced, "The one I want to be when I grow up is Marilyn Monroe—because she's famous all over."

5. The honest seven-year-old who admitted calmly to her parents that Billy Brown had kissed her after class. "How did that happen?" gasped her mother. "It wasn't easy," admitted the young lady, "but three girls helped me catch him."

6. The little girl who assured her teacher, "Of *course* I know how to spell banana. I just never know when to stop."

7. The moppet who was showing a playmate her older sister's bedroom. "She's sixteen," said the moppet ruefully. "I was promised her room one day, but she never married."

8. The three sophisticated young ladies, all approximately eight years old, who were discussing what they hoped to be when they grew up. The first one wanted to be a movie queen and play opposite Marlon Brando. The second wanted to be a nurse who discovered marvelous new serums. The third was most emphatic of all. "I," she announced, "want to be a widow."

9. Judy, who was leading her young friends in the kitchen in a symphony banged out on pots and pans. "I wish Mom would hurry and make us stop," she grumbled. "This noise is killing me."

10. The promising seven-year-old who was given the difficult assignment in class of describing the taste of chocolate ice cream in a single sentence. "Chocolate," she explained (and let's see *you* do better!), "tastes the opposite of vanilla."

AND THEIR PARENTS . . .

1. The mother who demanded of her seven-year-old, "What are you reading?" "A story about a cow jumping over the moon," was the answer. "Throw that book away at once," commanded the mother. "How often have I told you you're too young to read science fiction?"

2. The very cagey mother who assured her recalcitrant youngster, "You'll just *love* this new breakfast food. It tastes just like a grasshopper."

3. Mrs. Goombleheimer who boasted, "My son Arthur is smarter even than Abraham Lincoln. Arthur could recite the Gettysburg Address when he was ten years old. Lincoln didn't say it till he was fifty."

4. The most cautious mother of the month. When her kid asked, "Can I go outside and watch the solar eclipse?" she grudgingly conceded, "O.K., but don't stand too close."

5. The knowing father who really had his children fighting over their new encyclopedia by revising their index titles to "*Armstrong* to *Boone, Cheek* to *Cheek, Desi* to *Lu, Ode* to *Marilyn, Rock* to *Roll,* and *Says* to *You.*"

6. Will Rogers' ma. When he was ten she had trouble persuading him to tuck in his shirttails in school or when company came to dinner. She sewed lace around the bottom of every shirt he owned. It worked wonders.

7. The exasperated father who yelled upstairs to his errant off-spring, "O.K.! This is the last time I'm going to tell you for the last time!"

8. The resigned P.T.A. mother who speculated, "Whatever is going to become of these children of today—in the unlikely event their neighbors let them grow up?"

9. The parents' group in Chicago that has opened a children's art school, dealing only with the primary colors. It's called—what else?—"Three Little Pigments."

10. The mother of little John Charles, who found his first report card distinctly encouraging. "John Charles is a bright, alert lad," was the comment, "but I believe he spends too much time playing with the girls. However, I am working on a plan which I believe will break him of the habit."

John Charles's mother acknowledged receipt of the report and added this note of her own: "Let me know if your plan works, and I'll try it on his father."

★ ★ ★

Boys and girls have adopted enthusiastically a game introduced by Steve Allen. Steve provides you with the answer; you must deduce the question.

EXAMPLES:

1. *Answer:* Mount Whitney, Mount Olympus, and Mount Sinai.
   Question: Name two mountains and a hospital.
2. *Answer:* Cleopatra, Mata Hari, and Florence Nightingale.
   Question: Name three dead women.
3. *Answer:* Washington Irving.
   Question: Who was the first President, Sam?

★ ★ ★

Herman Hickman, late football coach and commentator, had a sentimental streak almost as wide as he was. Here's his favorite poem, authorship unknown, which he was ready to recite at the drop of a referee's whistle:

A Little Boy Prays for His Dog

Dear God,
> They say my dog is dead;
> He had the softest little head;
> He was so good, he'd always do
> Most anything I told him to.

Kind God,
> Sometimes he'd chase a cat,
> (He wasn't often bad like that),
> And if I called him back, he came
> The minute that I said his name.

Please God,
> If he feels scared up there,
> Won't You please let him sleep somewhere
> Near You? Oh, please take care of him,
> I love him so! His name is Tim.

★ ★ ★

A bank robber was reported driving like mad somewhere in Virginia, and every sheriff in the state was alerted to watch for him. Taking no chances, one conscientious sheriff decided to stop every car on the road and cross-examine its occupants. The dowager in a sleek limousine took this amiss. "By what authority do you presume to stop this car?" she demanded angrily.

The sheriff took his badge out of his pocket to show the lady—and blushed violently. The badge was a tin affair marked "Space Ship Patrol." His nine-year-old son had switched badges.

★ ★ ★

H. Allen Smith tells about a suburbanite mother who returned from a shopping tour to find this note from her eight-year-old on her bureau: "Hi, Mom. While I was in school today our cat came all apart in the garidge. Love, Harold." She rushed out to the "garidge" to find that the cat had given birth to a litter of kittens. Another young writer of notes informed her favorite editor, "I still find your magazeen very educashunal, but please let us have less about monsters and more about werewolves."

★ ★ ★

Admirably concise was this missive airmailed by a twelve-year-old in camp: "Dear Pop: Please write often even if it's only a couple of dollars. Love, Jason."

And another lad who didn't believe in wasting words synopsized Longfellow's *Evangeline* in exactly sixteen words: "Evangeline was a beautiful girl who had a boy friend. Eventually she had to leave town."

★ ★ ★

Time to tell your young fry the facts of life? You might borrow a leaf from Donald Ogden Stewart, who wrote his pride and joy as follows: "Dear Boy: Now that you have reached the magic age of fourteen, the time has come to tell you about the bees and flowers. There is a male bee and a female bee, although I haven't the slightest idea which is which. As for the flowers—we get ours from the Plaza Florists, Inc. Well, that takes care of *that*. Write soon. Affectionately, Father."

★ ★ ★

The doctor gazed pensively at the gawky teen-ager who sat drooling over a picture of Elizabeth Taylor. "Your son," he consoled the anxious parents, "is entering into a developmental phase in which he is simply ga-ga over the female sex. This phase will last about seventy years."

★ ★ ★

Ernest Blevins made this stern New Year's resolution: "Be more patient with my son Tom. No matter how irritating he is, I must remember he is sixteen, and going through a most exasperating period of adolescence." By accident, Mr. Blevins then came across his son Tom's set of new resolutions. Topping them, and underlined, was "Try to be more patient with Dad!"

54. LADY DRIVERS

It was in 1954 that Tom Merrill, vice-president of the State Farm Mutual Insurance Company, in Bloomington, Illinois, threw a bombshell into the ranks of male automobile drivers. Elaborate tests, he declared, had proven conclusively that female drivers were by no means the bad and reckless drivers they (and their cars!) were cracked up to be.

In fact, added Mr. Merrill, housewives ranked twenty-eighth best in a list of sixty-four occupational classes in the safe handling of private passenger cars.

A lot of flabbergasted male drivers haven't believed a single statistic ever since. And now these doubting Thomases may once more rejoice! No less an authority than the U.S. Bureau of Public Roads has rallied to their defense.

Twenty-eighth safest, these lady drivers, eh? The Bureau, working hand in hand with the Massachusetts Registry of Motor Vehicles, checked the average cost of accidents in the Bay State. It was $4,300. And hear this: For men the average was $3,800. For women drivers the figure vaulted to $8,200! (These figures were compiled from the records of a million and a half motorists, traveling over eleven billion miles.)

The reasons for the startling discrepancy? They're anybody's guess, though one defensible theory is that women possibly panic more completely in a crisis, and cannot react quickly enough to minimize the damage.

★ ★ ★

That theory, incidentally, was advanced by Mr. Theodore Willing, of Niagara Falls, New York, who added, "My definition of a reckless driver is a man who lets his wife drive." What soured Mr. Willing, apparently, was the manner in which Mrs. Willing extricated herself from a very tight parking jam one afternoon. She turned on her ignition, stepped angrily on the accelerator, and plowed straight into the car in front, folding it like an accordion. Reversing gears, she then crumpled the car behind her even more effectively. By this time the Willing machine itself was a thing of shreds and patches—but Mrs. W. was positively triumphant. "Climb in," she ordered her goggle-eyed spouse. "*Now* we have room to get out!"

★ ★ ★

Motorcycle officer George Blake, operating out of Baltimore, spotted a young lady driving one of those underslung foreign jobs at something better than ninety miles an hour. Overtaking her with difficulty, he motioned her to pull over. "I guess you're giving me a ticket for speeding," she pouted. "Who said anything about speeding?" countered Officer Blake. "I'm charging you with flying too low!"

★ ★ ★

Horace Young, of White Plains, confesses that his wife is in a decidedly run-down condition, having run down seven pedestrians in a space of four days. One of her victims, incidentally, was a cop on a bicycle. Mrs. Young was knocked speechless; the cop, spokeless.

Gracie Burns once told her husband George why she consistently ignored red traffic lights. "When you've seen one," she scoffed, "you've seen them all."

Donald Lausch, of San Antonio, writes that his wife has been awarded a badge of merit for donating five pedestrians to the municipal hospital. She also wound up the week by driving up the side of a building. "It gave us a bad moment," adds Mr. Lausch, "because there was another lady motorist coming down."

But Howard Goodman, of Waukegan, is well satisfied with the progress *his* wife is making in her course on auto driving. "Six more lessons," promises Goodman, "and I'm going to put the door back on our garage."

★ ★ ★

Here are four safety slogans from other lands, collected by Francis Duffy, designed to slow up rattlebrained speed demons of either sex:

1. *Lassan jars, tovabb erst.* (Hungary: "Go slower; get farther.")

2. *Un automovil esta siempre tan borracho como el que lo guia.* (Mexico: "An automobile is always as drunk as the man driving it.")

3. *Vorsicht ist keine Feigheit, unvorsichtigkeit kein Mut.* (Germany: "Caution is not cowardly, and carelessness is not courage.")

4. *'N kat het sewe lewens, 'n voetganger net sen.* (South Africa: "A cat has nine lives, a pedestrian only one.")

Here in the U.S.A., mechanics in the Chrysler plant in Detroit have coined a safety slogan of their own: "It takes a lot of nuts to hold an automobile together—but only one nut to tear it apart!"

★ ★ ★

One of the most eloquent summaries of the traffic situation in New York was delivered by the lovely French film star, Leslie Caron, the first time she was caught in a typical mid-Manhattan jam-up. She calmly turned off the gas in her car, shrugged her shoulders, and observed, "How wonderfully you have ze traffic organized here in New York. *Nussing whatever moves!*"

55. LECTURERS

John Mason Brown is one of the nation's most talented and successful lecturers today, but when he was first breaking into the game he experienced the usual difficulties. In one hall, where miserable acoustics added to his troubles, people started slipping out long before he was finished. Only a handful was left when an attendant slipped him a note marked "urgent." Brown paused in his peroration to read it. "If you ever finish," it said, "please turn out the lights, lock the door, and leave the key with the cop on the corner."

★ ★ ★

John Cameron Swayze tells about a time when he was engaged to address a ladies' luncheon club on the subject of Chinese history and philosophy. He did his best, then asked the chairwoman, "Why did you ask me to make China my subject?" "We wanted the talk to be appropriate," was the explanation. "We are now going to serve a chow mein luncheon."

★ ★ ★

Emily Kimbrough was about to deliver a lecture recently when a workman appeared on the stage, waving a screwdriver and beckoning the chairlady. There followed a hasty conference, whereupon the chairlady brushed past Miss Kimbrough and told the standing-room-only audience, "I'm sorry to say there will be a slight delay. Word has just been given me that there is a screw loose in our speaker."

★ ★ ★

Author Lynn Sumner uses this introduction to warm up his lecture audiences: "It's a great pleasure to speak in this auditorium—

a word derived from two Latin roots: *audio,* I hear—and *taurus,* the bull."

* * *

"Mighty hoaxes," Henry L. Mencken once pointed out to an audience of journalism students, "from little acorns—and an astonishing assortment of other nuts—grow and grow."

In several learned reference volumes, Mencken cited as an example, in recurrent newspaper articles, and even in senatorial speeches recorded in the Congressional Record, the following facts about the invention of the American bathtub have been dutifully listed:

1. The first American bathtub was introduced by Adam Thompson, on December 10, 1842, to a group of derisive friends in Cincinnati, Ohio.

2. Recovered from their first shock, doctors denounced the bathtub as a menace to general health, and Boston prohibited its use entirely except on medical prescription.

3. Virginia hastily levied a tax of thirty dollars on every bathtub sold within its borders, and a bill banning the use of bathtubs entirely in Philadelphia from November 1 to March 31 was defeated by the narrow margin of two votes.

4. No bathtub was allowed inside the White House until 1851, when President Millard Fillmore bravely dunked his limbs in one of the fiendish contraptions.

There is only one thing wrong with these interesting statistics: they are completely untrue from beginning to end. Mencken admitted that, in one of his more playful moods, he had invented them from whole cloth for a piece that appeared first in the New York *Evening Mail* for December 28, 1917.

When he saw to his amazement that his fabrication was being taken seriously (even his own Baltimore paper printed it as fact), Mencken tried desperately to convince everybody he had perpetrated what he thought would be a harmless hoax. But he was too late.

President Fillmore's bathtub seems destined to go down into history with President Washington's cherry tree!

* * *

Elizabeth Shenck, of the Lee Keedick Lecture Bureau, solemnly avers that she has sent speakers to every city, town, and hamlet in the U.S.A., including Ash, Kan.; Fiven, Tenn.; Odear, Me.; Shoo, Fla.; Noahs, Ark.; Dinah, Mo.; Carpet, Tex.; Kay, O.; and Whis, Ky.

* * *

George Bernard Shaw lectured in Dublin one day, and, as was his wont, riled the audience by telling them a lot of things they didn't like to hear. "If you would devote the money to dentistry that you throw away attempting to revive Gaelic," he thundered, "it would do you more credit."

The audience booed and jeered, but Shaw waited patiently till the hall was quiet again. "If you do that again," he threatened, "I'll continue this lecture in the Gaelic tongue you all profess to want— and then not one person in this hall will have the faintest notion of what I'm saying."

For the balance of his talk, you could have heard a pin drop.

* * *

A portly old party spoke earnestly and lengthily at a high school graduation, and, since a very small part of the audience was listening to him, the harm done was negligible. The principal, afraid that the distinguished guest's feelings might be hurt, buttered him up when the ceremony was concluded.

"I deeply enjoyed your account," he purred, "of how you climbed the ladder of success, rung by rung. I take it that you are now a very wealthy man."

"On the contrary," the speaker assured him. "I haven't got a bean. But can I climb ladders!"

* * *

After an interminable speech in the chapel, a saddle-sore Dartmouth Sophomore wrote:

> I love a finished speaker:
> I really, really do.
> I don't mean one who's polished.
> I do mean one who's through.

★ ★ ★

At M.I.T., they tell of a bumbling old mossback who delivered a speech at Yale. "Every letter in your university's name stands for something," he announced. "The 'Y' is for 'youth,' the 'A' is for 'ambition,' the 'L' is for 'loyalty' and the 'E' is for 'endeavor'—and I mean to say a few words about each of these subjects." Two hours later he completed his peroration, most of his audience having sneaked out or fallen asleep in the course thereof. "Does anybody wish to add anything to what I have said?" he inquired rashly. "I do," proclaimed a student in the front row. "Let us just give thanks you aren't speaking at the Massachusetts Institute of Technology!"

56. LEGAL LIGHTS

A charming lady whose books I publish is outraged because, though her lawyer is admittedly brilliant, he isn't "half so cute" as James Stewart in *Anatomy of a Murder*.

Being the author of best-selling novels, hit plays, and a couple of superduper Hollywood spectacles, this lady, of course, has special need of top-drawer legal assistance. Not only do literary contracts run to fifteen and twenty pages of single-spaced type these days, but the successful author is a sitting duck for lawsuits, plagiarism suits, libel suits, invasion of privacy suits, breach of contract suits, and heaven knows what else. When hit notices are printed, vultures trying to get in on the kill are never far behind.

Often the author has been slaving for as long as ten years over a seven-hundred-page novel, compressing into its pages all the highlights of his lifetime. He may never write another hit, because he's told everything he knows in this one (something the income tax people, incidentally, refuse to take into consideration). His own lawyer, plus the legal department of his publishers, have combed telephone directories and lists of every description to make sure his characters have fictitious names.

Then lightning strikes. The Book-of-the-Month Club and *Reader's Digest* Condensed Books empty pots of gold into his lap, and what bloated plutocrats are left in Hollywood fly East to wine and dine him at the Pavillon.

Let him enjoy it while he may, for bingo! a Marmaduke Blintz, graduate of six asylums, hits him with a plagiarism suit, and furthermore, that name he conjured for his villain—Outgo J. Schmierkase—wasn't such a smart idea after all. It develops there really *is* an Outgo J. Schmierkase, living in a remote mountain hamlet, who feels that the use of his name in the author's work has damaged his career as third assistant keeper of the county jail washroom to the tune of three million clams.

The distracted author runs back to his lawyer—and the lawyer's wife runs to order a chinchilla coat.

A wildly improbable literary libel suit attracted an overflow audience recently. The novel under fire was one of those earthy, four-letter-word affairs, and when the judge ordered the defendant's lawyer to read it aloud to the jury, it was a caution to hear the immaculately groomed legalite reel off billingsgate as though it were a sonnet by Elizabeth Browning.

At one point the hero called the villain a very bad name. The lawyer winced, then read the line in such a subdued tone that a juror in the second row couldn't hear. "What's that you said?" he interrupted. The lawyer repeated, "I said, 'You're a blank blank blank.'"

The juror thought for a moment that the lawyer was addressing him personally and threatened to bust him in the nose, but the judge restored order and everybody went peacefully to lunch.

Jockeying for a friendly judge is part of the day's work for a capable trial lawyer. In his book *My Double Life*, Newman Levy tells how his father, one of the shrewdest lawyers of all time, shuddered to discover that one of his defendants was scheduled to be tried before a brutally severe judge named Goff.

Nor could he wangle a postponement. "We are going to trial Monday, and that is that," ruled Judge Goff.

On Monday, however, lawyer Levy announced suavely in court, "I am sorry to inform Your Honor that my client had an emergency appendicitis operation last night, and is now in Roosevelt Hospital."

The suspicious judge sent his own personal physician to the hospital to check the facts. He found that the appendix had indeed been removed; what he did not discover was that it was a perfectly healthy appendix.

The case was tried before a more lenient judge some months later, and the defendant was acquitted. "The appendix," chuckled lawyer Levy, "was no use to him—but the adjournment was."

★ ★ ★

HEARD IN COURT:

1. A lawyer tore excitedly into court and asked that a new trial be granted a client found guilty the day previous. "I've uncovered new evidence," declared the lawyer. "Of what nature?" asked the judge. "My client," explained the lawyer, "has an extra six hundred dollars I only found out about this morning."

2. Accused of bigamy, a very wealthy businessman hired a crack lawyer to defend him, and won a speedy acquittal. "You're a free man again," the lawyer told him. "Go home to your wife." "Splendid!" enthused the acquitted. "Which one?"

3. Judge Frank Smathers writes that the most disarming appeal he ever heard a defense attorney direct at a jury was: "My client may talk like a fool and act like a fool. But do not be deceived, gentlemen. He really *is* a fool!"

4. A prisoner, just sentenced, told another judge, "I am not as filthy a rat as Your Honor [here he coughed discreetly] takes me to be." The judge glared and barked, "An extra thirty days for not putting your words closer together!"

5. "How did the explosion occur?" testified a qualified witness in court. "The reason is clear. The engineer was full and the boiler was empty."

6. A magistrate fastened a beady eye on a defendant and thundered, "Well, why did you take the $100,000?" "Your Honor," whined the defendant, "I was hungry."

7. A character in Ventura, California, found the perfect method recently for talking himself out of jury duty. "I know it's unpatriotic," he told the judge, "but you just gotta excuse me from jury duty on this drunken driving case." "Why?" snapped the judge. "I'm the defendant," explained the character. He was excused.

8. A very beautiful girl approached a police lieutenant in the Broadway sector and said, "My ex-boy friend, who's a heavyweight contender, is threatening to break into my apartment and beat me up. I think I ought to have police protection." "Say the word," consoled the lieutenant, "and I'll send a couple of my patrolmen home with you. Personally, however, I think you'd be safer with the heavyweight contender."

★ ★ ★

In *Life with Fiorello* biographer Ernest Cuneo tells about the day a righteous New York alderman protested that ladies of the evening were being allowed to collect city relief funds. Mayor La Guardia thundered, "I thought this was a question settled two thousand years ago, but I see I was wrong. Sergeant-at-Arms, clear the room so this big bum can throw the first stone!"

★ ★ ★

The judge in an Omaha divorce court had a tough case with a stubborn, unyielding man and wife who refused even to look at each other in court. "O.K.," conceded the judge. "Go through with the divorce, but understand that everything you possess will have to be divided equally." "What about our three children?" demanded the wife. "That's something you'll have to figure out for yourselves," said His Honor. The wife made a sudden decision. She seized her spouse by the collar and ordered, "Come on home, you lug." To the judge, she threw over her shoulder, "We'll be back next year—with *four* children."

★ ★ ★

It was a pretty sensational murder trial, and most of the population of the county seat was in the courtroom when the jury filed in to deliver its verdict. "Your Honor," announced the foreman, "we want to make this trial as fair and merciful as possible, so before announcing our decision we'd like to ask the defendant a single question." "Proceed," said the judge. The foreman turned to the prisoner and asked politely, "Sir, do you prefer AC or DC current?"

★ ★ ★

When humorist James Thurber was in Bermuda, the doings in the magistrate's court fascinated him. One defendant had been jailed by the complaint of a girl friend. She charged he had assaulted her. He said it was just a "platonic argument." "How come," demanded the magistrate, "that if it was only a platonic argument, the girl was naked as a jay bird when the police arrived?" The defendant looked the magistrate straight in the eye and explained, "I guess I must have knocked her naked during the argument."

★ ★ ★

Another highlight in the Bermuda court came when a woman demanded a divorce. Her grounds? "Judge," she said, "I have reason to believe my husband is not the father of my last child."

★ ★ ★

The late Clarence Darrow once was having the devil of a time pinning a hostile witness down to some semblance of a coherent story. Challenged directly, the witness whined, "How can you doubt my word, Mr. Darrow? I am wedded to the truth." "Ah," nodded Darrow with a significant side glance to the jury, "and how long have you been a widower?"

★ ★ ★

A Pine Street lawyer has just received a letter from a stranger who obviously has a magnanimous streak. "I know you specialize in drawing wills," the letter began. "If the time ever comes when you cannot think of a beneficiary, I want you to feel free to use my name."

★ ★ ★

Accused of making off with a couple of nice, plump chickens from Colonel Rasmussen's hen house, Old Jeff waxed righteously indignant, and declared that he needed no lawyer: he would defend himself in court!

The magistrate's eyes twinkled, and he asked, "Old Jeff, do you want to ask your accuser any questions?"

"Yes, *suh*," said Old Jeff emphatically. Pointing a gnarled finger at Colonel Rasmussen, he demanded, "Colonel, did you *see* me go into that hen house?"

"I certainly did," maintained the Colonel.

"Did you see me *come out?*"

"No, I can't say that I did," admitted the Colonel.

"Your Honor," said Old Jeff simply, "there am my defense. I am still in that hen house."

57. LETTERS

Hanging over the head of every vacationing businessman—an ominous, black cloud, marring an otherwise sun-drenched landscape—is the certainty that his desk, when he reluctantly returns to same, will be brimming over with a mountain of miscellaneous correspondence.

Eighty per cent of it, furthermore, at a conservative estimate, will be scarcely worth opening: old advertisements, dubious requests for donations, invitations to dull parties long since given, etc.

The late Henry Mencken confessed that he only opened his mail "when he was in the mood." And he had a happy formula for answering controversial letters. "Dear Sir (or Dear Madam)," he would reply, "you may be right!"

Celebrities are accustomed to a daily ration of "nut" letters. Most of these letters are very flattering, some wheedling, and a scattered minority downright vicious. The latter generally add up to "How dare you disagree with me? Get lost!" The most insulting letters invariably come from cowards who do not sign their names.

Garry Moore, one top TV star who is always ready to fight for his convictions, has devised a wonderful system for coping with poison penmen who *do* identify themselves. He mails the offending missive right back to the sender with this note of his own: "The enclosed letter arrived on my desk a few days ago. I am sending it to you in the belief that as a responsible citizen you should know that some idiot is sending out letters over your signature. Cordially . . ."

★ ★ ★

When a scandal breaks in Hollywood, the whole world is buzzing about it twenty-four hours later. Some time ago, for instance, a beautiful but impulsive star was falsely accused of inexcusable behavior in a public place, and over eleven hundred presidents of women's clubs promptly wrote indignant letters to her studio, demanding that she be blacklisted forthwith.

This is the form-letter reply with which the astute head of public relations at the studio put a quick end to the disheartening episode:

"Dear Madam: We too have heard echoes of the shocking incident to which you refer. We have been longing to take summary action, but until now have been unable to put our hands on a single piece of tangible evidence to substantiate the rumors. Since we realize that a woman of your standing would not make a serious charge of this nature without absolute proof, we beg you to forward same that we can proceed without further delay."

To date, the studio has not received a single reply.

★ ★ ★

The tax authority of a New Jersey town received this letter from an irate Italian resident:

"Sir: I got your letter about what I owe. Now be pachant. I ain't forgot you. When I have the money you will get paid. But if this was the first Judgment Day and you was no more prepared to meet your maker than I am to meet your account you sure would go to Hell. Trusting that you will do this, I remain . . ."

★ ★ ★

This letter was received by the editor of a big family magazine:
"Sir: My wife was about to divorce me until she read your touching article about the evils of a broken home. Now she says she is going to stick to me through thick and thin. Please cancel my subscription."

★ ★ ★

On the wall of the Drama Department of a Chicago newspaper is a framed copy of this poignant appeal:

"Please send me a few pictures of stars in bathing suits or less for my wall as I am sixty-five years old and haven't felt this good in years."

★ ★ ★

The problem of superfluous mail is aggravated by tycoons who suffer from chronic cases of dictationitis. I know one who thinks nothing of composing a six-page epistle—single-spaced—to complain to the manufacturer that a ten-cent almond bar he purchased that morning did not contain the usual number of nuts. To complicate the problem, he paces erratically about the room as he dictates, chewing the while on a corner of his handkerchief.

The secretary has learned how to cope with her boss. Out of every thirty letters he dictates, she discards as worthless at least eight —and simply doesn't type them. She then waits until ten minutes before he has to dash to catch the 4:50 to plank the mail on his desk for signature. In his haste he doesn't notice how many of his priceless words have been lost for posterity. The secretary proudly figures that in one year she has saved the U.S. Post Office the trouble of delivering two thousand absolutely useless letters.

(Note by Mr. Cerf's secretary: Methinks my boss is waxing autobiographical!)

★ ★ ★

For those who *must* correspond frequently, there is reproduced below an ingenious "Handy Dandy Little Giant Mail Answering Form" calculated to save infinite hours of penmanship or pecking on a typewriter. It was devised by a gregarious New York *bon vivant* and globetrotter named Irving Hoffman, and promptly adopted by such eminent citizens as Groucho Marx and Abel Green. Copy it yourself, if you will, with Mr. Hoffman's compliments, altering clauses to suit your own nefarious purposes.

HANDY-DANDY LITTLE GIANT MAIL ANSWERING FORM

☐ No. ☐ Yes. ☐ Maybe.

☐ Congratulations.

☐ You're wonderful. ☐ You're welcome.

☐ Thank you. ☐ Get well soon.

☐ I'll call you. ☐ Call me.

☐ Mr. _____ is out of town.

☐ Mr. _____ won't be back.

☐ Enclosed find check.

☐ Mr. _____ has been declared a mental incompetent. Your communication has been forwarded to his attorney.

Mr. _____ is not equipped to handle your problem. You should consult:

☐ President Eisenhower. ☐ Rodgers & Hammerstein.

☐ Ernest Hemingway. ☐ Marilyn Monroe.

☐ Dorothy Dix. ☐ E.Z. Personal Loan Co.

☐ My Uncle Max takes care of all my insurance.

☐ I do not need a new car.

☐ Out to lunch. ☐ Lunch is out.

☐ You have paid me the highest compliment a woman ever paid a man—but I am not worthy of your love.

A fine thing about the Handy Dandy Answering Form is that, armed therewith, you can give a friend an occasional well-earned pat on the back with virtually no effort whatever. There never can be enough of THAT kind of mail!

"If we suddenly discovered," the late Christopher Morley once observed, "that we had only five minutes left to say all we wanted to say, every telephone booth would be occupied by people trying to call up other people to stammer that they loved them."

Why wait until the last five minutes?

58. LIMERICK LANE

The twenty-five limericks that follow are: (1) reasonably new; (2) reasonably clever, and (3) clean enough to reprint in a family periodical. Four beautiful secretaries helped me to select them from a mountain of over seven thousand submitted for possible publication in my weekly Cerfboard in *This Week* magazine.

1. Said a calendar model named Gloria,
   "So the men can enjoy real euphoria,
   You pose as you are
   In Jan., Feb., and Mar.,
   Then in April they wanna see moria!"

2. She married a fellow named Leicester.
   With triplets the Lord one day bleicester.
   Les looked at that trio
   And shrieked, "One, two, three-oh,
   I wonder whatever posseicester?"

3. From Number Nine, Penwiper Mews,
   There is really abominable news:
   They've discovered a head
   In the box for the bread,
   But nobody seems to know whose.

4. An Indian maiden, a Sioux,
   As tempting as fresh honeydioux,
   Liked to show off her kneezes
   As she strolled past tepeezes,
   And hear the braves holler, "WIOUX! WIOUX!"

5. An old maid who came from Vancouver
Won a man with this adroit manouver:
She jumped on his knee
With a paean of glee
And now nothing on earth can remouver.

6. Mourned a limerickondite medic (before he had read this
particular roundup, of course):
A limerick packs laughs anatomical
In a space that is most economical
But the good ones I've seen
So seldom are clean—
And the clean ones so seldom are comical!

7. A dentist named Archibald Moss
Fell in love with the dainty Miss Ross,
But he held in abhorence
Her Christian name, Florence,
So he renamed her his Dental Floss.

8. Said a cat, as he playfully threw
His wife down a well in Peru,
"Relax, dearest Dora:
Please don't be angora;
I only was artesian you."

9. A resident of Hong Kong, probably riding in a limerick-
shaw, was in such haste to submit the following, he sent it by
cable:
There was a young girl named Irene
Who was chosen as Stock Exchange Queen
For, as duly reported,
She was successively courted
By Merrill, Lynch, Fenner, and Beane.
Informed that the famous Wall Street house had changed its
name to Merrill, Lynch, Pierce, Fenner, and Smith, the mortified
poet charged, "They did it on purpose to louse up my limerick."

10. In GONIA once, which is PATA,
    A CLYSM occurred that was CATA,
    A GINEER that was EN
    Lost his TURE that was DEN
    In a TORIUM there that was NATA.

11. According to experts, the oyster
    In its shell—or crustacean cloister—
    May frequently be
    Either he or a she
    Or both, if it should be its choice ter.

12. A young trapeze artist named Bract
    Is faced by a very sad fact.
    Imagine his pain
    When, again and again,
    He catches his wife in the act!

13. Wrote a swain to his gal in Saskatchewan:
    "If you'll wear my ring, I'll dispatchewan
    By parcel post when
    In some five-and-ten
    If the clerk turns his head, I can snatchewan."

14. A frisky young maiden in Glasgow
    Gave a party that proved a fiasco.
    At ten-thirty, about,
    The lights all went out
    Through a lapse on the part of the gas co.

15. When twins came, their father, Dan Dunn,
    Gave "Edward" as name to each son.
    When folks said, "Absurd!"
    He replied, "Ain't you heard
    That two Eds are better than one?"

16. Almost everybody commits at least one limerick at some low point in his career. The late Heywood Broun, for instance, perpetrated:

There was a young man with a hernia
Who said to his surgeon, "Gol dernia,
When improving my middle,
Be sure you don't fiddle
With matters that do not concernia."

17. A quiet young lady called Snookie
    At betting was quite a smart cookie.
    Before every race
    She went home to her place
    And curled up with a very good bookie.

18. A certain young lady named Hannah
    Was caught in a flood in Montannah.
    As she floated away,
    Her beau, so they say,
    Accompanied her on the piannah.

19. An impetuous swordsman from Parma
    Was lovingly fondling a charma.
    Said the maiden demure,
    "You'll excuse me, I'm sure,
    But I *think* you're still wearing your arma."

20. There was a young lady from Gloucester
    Whose husband once thought he had loucester.

But he found her that night
In the icebox, locked tight;
We all had to help him defroucester.

21. My stenographer's notable glamour
Couldn't quite compensate for her gramour.
She got me so ired
That I told her, "You're fired!"
Now I wish she was back again, damour!

22. Said a fellow from North Philadelphia
To his girl, "When I saw ya, I fellphia.
It was love at first glance,
But 'twill last, this romance,
Till the church bells are ringing a knellphia."

23. Miss Fanny, a dream from Bryn Mawr,
Acquired a sleek, long-fyn cawr.
Her control was superb
Till she parked at a curb:
Then Fanny stuck out too dyrn fawr!

24. Concerning the bees and the flowers
In the fields and the gardens and bowers,
You will note at a glance
That their ways of romance
Haven't any resemblance to ours.

25. In conclusion earnest Elmo Calkins beseeches:
Pray search this wide land with a glimmer stick,
For there must be some lad at his primer quick,
Who when pressed can supply
A lot better than I
An acceptable rhyme scheme for limerick.
This I'd like to see myself!

59. MAGICIANS AND MIND READERS

I always have been a pushover for mind-reading acts—the kind where a lovely lady sits blindfolded on stage and identifies objects her husband borrows from the audience as he circulates swiftly up and down the aisles.

The name on a business card? The serial number on a ten-dollar bill? The incredible contents of a debutante's handbag? These things are child's play for the blindfolded lady with the X-ray eyes —especially if she and her glib partner have rehearsed their pre-arranged code properly.

In the good old days of Keith vaudeville, the lady was sure to get a laugh by suddenly leveling a finger at a bald-headed patron in a front row and shrilling, "I am reading your mind right now, mister, and if you don't look out, I'm coming down to slap your face." Today, of course, the level of the comedy is infinitely higher: lines like "That gentleman on the aisle in the third row comes from Idaho, I see. Well, Boise will be Boise."

★ ★ ★

The cleverest, most-difficult-to-detect "mind-reading" routine I ever have "caught" is performed by Lucille and Eddie Roberts. My first encounter with the talented pair was at a hotel in Miami Beach so new it hadn't even changed hands yet. When Lucille correctly read the name on a sheet of my scratch pad, I took it as a trick of the trade, but when she added a precise description of the layout and location of my place in Mount Kisco, I was genuinely flabbergasted. In her dressing room later she finally admitted that she

and Eddie live exactly one block from us, and that on a clear day
they can see me writing a Cerfboard column from their front
porch!

"Of course, there's no magic in our act," laughed Eddie Roberts.
"It's the result of long, agonizing months of study and rehearsal.
Unless we achieve perfect co-ordination and teamwork, the illusion we seek to create is shattered. Every word I speak is part of
an elaborate code that we must change constantly to avoid detec-
tion. It's a kind of verbal shorthand. Not only the words, but every
inflection of my voice conveys information to Lucille."

★ ★ ★

In *The Great Sebastians,* playwrights Crouse and Lindsay provided Alfred Lunt and Lynn Fontanne with fat parts as a couple
of nimble-witted mind readers, not unlike the Robertses. To make
their performances convincing, the Lunts mastered a code of their
own. They also were aided by an accomplice who spotted actual
celebrities in the audience before curtain time. Thus equipped,
Lynn Fontanne read these celebrities' minds to a fare-thee-well.

Novelist Edna Ferber is not likely to forget the night Miss Fontanne, blindfolded, told her the exact menu of the dinner she had
hosted before coming to the theater. This proved not only that the
Lunts were brilliant mind readers, but that they had not forgotten the details of a heart-to-heart telephone conversation with
Miss Ferber's cook.

★ ★ ★

Unhappy was the mind reader who performed all the way from
Hoboken to Hong Kong in the past year. "I took my wife along
everywhere," he reported, "but it was no use. She always found
her way back."

★ ★ ★

When master magician John Mulholland is on tour, his laundry
tickets cause a stir in hotels along the way. One Chicago laundryman, for instance, phoned to protest, "There must be something

wrong with your tabulation, sir. How can any man's wash consist of 1 pair of shorts and 122 handkerchiefs?"

★ ★ ★

Peter Lind Hayes tells about a magician who arrived at a millionaire's estate for a weekend, carrying a bag of props with his other luggage. A butler unpacked everything while he lunched, so when he went to his room he found in one drawer, impeccably laid out, three decks of marked cards, a stiletto, a collapsible birdcage, a revolver, and two sets of false teeth.

★ ★ ★

At the last magicians' convention, one magicmaker asked another, "Say, whatever happened to that blond wife of yours you used to saw in half every performance?" "Oh, we split up some time ago," was the answer. "Now she's living in Boston and San Diego."

60. MATRIMONY

A young machinist and his bride, honeymooning on the shore of a New Hampshire lake, were caught in a canoe in a sudden violent squall. The machinist, scared within an inch of his life, resorted to prayer. "Save us," he implored, "and I vow to give up smoking, drinking, gambling . . ." "Don't go too far, darling," interrupted his bride hastily. "I think I hear a motorboat coming to rescue us."

★ ★ ★

Henny Youngman knows a lady who finally has hit upon a sure-fire method of getting her good-for-nothing husband out of bed and off to what he laughingly refers to as work every morning. "All I do," explained the lady, "is throw the cat on his bed." "How does that get him up?" asked Youngman. "It's a cinch," chuckled the lady. "He sleeps with the dog."

★ ★ ★

In Texas they tell about an all-male dinner which wound up with half the assemblage too boiled to navigate. One of the more sober participants was holding forth on marital infidelity, and concluded, "One class of women are least trustworthy of all, and that's the gals with brown eyes."

A listener admitted, "I've been married nine years, and haven't the faintest idea what color eyes my wife has got." With that he rushed home, and, finding his wife retired, carefully pried open one of her eyelids. "By the great horn spoon," he shouted. "Brown!"

With that his neighbor, Cuthbert Brown, crawled out from under the bed and admitted, "Yup, it's me, all right. But how in heck did you know I was here?"

★ ★ ★

The language of one classified ad in a newspaper of unquestioned integrity brooked no misinterpretation. "Air-conditioned, full-equipped Cadillac," it read, "in perfect condition, for sale at fifty dollars." A bargain hunter hastened to the address given, and demanded of the lady who opened the door, "You the one offering that Cadillac?" "I am," she said, and led him to the automobile—a beautiful thing in every respect. "Here's the fifty," said the man hastily. "Now what's the catch?"

"No catch at all," explained the lady patiently. "I'm simply carrying out the provisions of my late husband's will. He provided that his new Cadillac be sold at once—and the entire proceeds be turned over to his secretary."

★ ★ ★

HUSBANDS . . .

Two old college mates met after several years. One said glumly, "I've a tough row to hoe, Jim. My wife's always trying to keep up with the Joneses." "You're lucky," snapped the other. "Mine's trying to keep up with the Rockefellers."

A wealthy textile man in Greenwich proudly exhibits to callers a closet full of woolen cloth and bolts of silk, explaining, "Rich as she is, my wife insists on making all her own clothes." Next he shows guests five live alligators in the patio. It seems she also makes her own handbags.

A henpecked gent threw out his chest about a quarter of an inch and announced, "This morning I definitely laid the law down to my wife." Candor, however, compelled him to add, "She repealed it."

"It's the little things that break up marriages," insists Jimmy Starr. "Little blondes, little brunettes, little redheads." Adds Victor Moore: "Marriage is a two-way proposition. Show some consideration for your wife. Let her out of the house occasionally. Send her out to wash the car."

This is a story of a man who may well be the stingiest in all New York. His doctor told him it was imperative for his wife to get some sea air—so he fanned her two weeks with a herring.

Myron Cohen tells of a merchant who came home unexpectedly and found his wife in the arms of his best friend. He looked at the friend reproachfully and sighed, "Max! I must! But you?"

In San Mateo, a harassed husband assured his wife, "If we keep on saving twenty more years at our present rate, when I retire we'll owe $2,000,000!"

"My wife is progressing splendidly with her new reducing diet," reported a long-married man happily. "Tuesday she disappeared completely."

In Tyler, Texas, an old oil driller heard that his wife had been rushed to the hospital. He hastened to her side, then asked the doctor, "What ails her?" "We're not sure," frowned the doctor. "May we have your consent to perform an exploratory operation?" "Nothing doing," roared the driller. "Ain't nobody going to wildcat on my wife!"

★ ★ ★

AND WIVES . . .

"I hear," a wife told her husband when he got home from the club, "that all those drinks you had this afternoon didn't agree with you." "Where did you get that erroneous information?" demanded the husband. "Oh," she retorted airily, "a little burp told me."

A wife in Wichita had a great deal of trouble with her complexion. Her druggist husband suggested a new facial cream so effective, he promised, it would take the wrinkle out of prunes. The lady applied the cream faithfully. Today her complexion is still terrible—but she certainly has the smoothest prunes in Wichita.

"I am fully aware that a great many husbands snore," grumbled a new lady patient to a doctor, "but my husband is a ventriloquist, and he snores on both sides of me at the same time!"

A newly married society gal surprised even herself one morning by getting up to serve her husband breakfast. Gratified, he kissed her on the top of the head and announced, "My darling, you are the eighth wonder of the world." "Be that as it may," warned the wife, "but don't let me catch you fooling around with any of the other seven!"

Mr. Green looked up from his newspaper in time to see his wife dashing out of the front door. "Going shopping?" he called after her. "I haven't got the time," she called back. "I'm just going to get a few things I need."

Seth Parker and his bride, Betsy Lou, told friends their honeymoon had been dreamy—but they're still riled about the sign they found on the back of their automobile the evening of their marriage day. It read: "Amateur Night."

There's a platinum-tressed sexpot out in Movieville who insists on observing all the rules in the etiquette book. When her fifth husband passed away, for example, she ordered black olives in her martinis for a solid month.

Mrs. Toplitz was up till all hours the other night removing some spots from her husband's trousers—two ten-spots and a five.

In Stamford, Connecticut, Whitney Darrow, Jr., heard a well-turned-out young matron confide to an intimate, "It's lucky I spent Rud's bonus in advance this year. He didn't get one."

Mr. and Mrs. Halloran were celebrating seventy-five years of wedded bliss, and a nosy reporter asked Mr. Halloran the secret for such exemplary marital felicity. "We settled everything the day we were married," beamed Mr. Halloran, "and it's been a joy ride ever since. Mrs. Halloran was to make all the minor decisions and I was to settle the major ones." "Sounds fine," admitted the reporter, "but what exactly do you consider minor decisions?" "Oh," said Mr. Halloran, "whether I keep a job or not, where we live, how we bring up the children, where and when we take vacations —things like that." "And the major decisions left to you?" "Big things, my boy," beamed Mr. Halloran. "Who's to be President of the United States, where we stand on Berlin, how to handle the Soviet, the hydrogen bomb. . . ."

★ ★ ★

Mme. Zaza Horntoot, the gypsy fortuneteller, stormed into the police station to report the disappearance of her husband. "You gypsies swear you can find everything in the cards," needled the police sergeant. "How's for locating your husband that way?" "Give me fifty cents," proposed Mme. Zaza, "and I'll do it!"

★ ★ ★

Tough old coot in the Imperial Valley got fed up with having his wife rifle his pockets every night. He got hold of a couple of rattlesnakes, and slipped one into each pants pocket before climbing into bed.

His wife strolled in some minutes later, looking mighty riled.

"Been digging for my money again, hey?" he asked, with elaborate unconcern.

"Yeah, but you're even more broke than usual," she complained. "I looked in both your pockets and there's not a thing in them but snakes."

★ ★ ★

"For three weeks," complained a blond wife to her crony, "I couldn't find my husband. I was getting worried enough to consider notifying the police when bingo! he turned up." "Where did you find him?" asked the friend. "One evening," explained the wife, "I got a sudden impulse to go home—and there he was!"

61. MUSIC

On fashionable East Sixty-fifth Street, just off Park Avenue, New York, a luxurious private house is occupied by a prominent socialite and businessman named Jules Glaenzer.

Some years ago, Mr. Glaenzer invited a small but select group to his house for dinner. One of the guests was Judy Garland, the singer; another, Richard Rodgers, composer of *Oklahoma* and a half-dozen other great musical shows.

It was a hot summer's evening, and all the windows were wide open. When Dick sat down at the piano, and Judy belted out a few introductory melodies, it is reasonable to suppose that every passer-by on Sixty-fifth Street paused at least momentarily to enjoy one of the most spectacular free concerts of the season.

Four young people went even further. Glaenzer's butler reported, "There are two young soldiers with their girls at the door. They want to know if they can listen to the music at closer range."

There was a war going on at the time, and Glaenzer said promptly, "Ask them to come up." The two infantry privates may have been nineteen; their girls were even younger. Silently, they accepted introductions to the assembled party, grouped themselves around the piano—and the impromptu concert was resumed.

If Dick Rodgers ever wrote a song that Judy doesn't know—verse as well as chorus—Dick never has been able to discover what it is. She remembers incidental production numbers he has forgotten himself, and can render unfalteringly refrains he composed for a boys' club when he was sixteen and the first number he wrote with Oscar Hammerstein for a Columbia Varsity Show. (It is a myth that Rodgers met Hammerstein only after the death of his former collaborator, Larry Hart; the two boys belonged to the same college fraternity chapter—along with myself—some thirty-five years ago.)

At any rate, Judy sailed through virtually the entire Rodgers catalogue that summer evening at Jules Glaenzer's house, and, as is her wont, did not spare herself in the process. It was only when her voice became fuzzy around the edges and Dick complained that his back was beginning to ache that the concert was declared over.

It was then that the first comment came from the visiting quartette since their entrance an hour previous. They had sat silent and starry-eyed through the entire recital, giving no indication that they recognized a single person in the room. Now, however, as they arose to leave, there was a note of sadness in the voice of their spokesman—the lad who had explained their intrusion in the first place—as he assured Mr. Glaenzer softly, *"Nobody ever will believe this story."*

Fifteen minutes later, they still were standing at the curbstone across the way, looking up at the Glaenzer drawing room, as though, by this time, they no longer even believed the story themselves.

★ ★ ★

Think you can name the top song hits of the past fifty years? *Variety,* "the bible of show business," lists them as follows: "In the Shade of the Old Apple Tree," "Schooldays," "Casey Jones," "Alexander's Ragtime Band," "I Want a Girl," "Waiting for the Robert E. Lee," "St. Louis Blues," "Over There," "God Bless America." On behalf of "White Christmas," I demand a recount.

★ ★ ★

Deciding that he needed a new rash of publicity, that old favorite conductor, Vincent Lopez, hired a young Broadway character who swore he could plant items in every column in town. Lopez awaited results in vain for a fortnight. Then the young man burst in and cried elatedly, "Well, boss, we've got the lead-off item in the hottest column in the business tonight!" Gratified, Lopez turned to the column indicated. The first item read: "What ever became of Vincent Lopez?"

★ ★ ★

A maestro with decided notions of his own put together an orchestra consisting of forty-eight strings and one drummer. Came the evening of the big premiere. The maestro had just raised his baton when the impatient drummer banged on his drums and crashed his cymbal.

The maestro dropped the baton. "O.K.," he snarled. "Who's the wise guy?"

★ ★ ★

Have you heard about the overenthusiastic band leader? He hired more men than he could wave a stick at. One musician, however, soon was dropped. Every time he opened his mouth, he put his flute in it.

The band's theme song was composed by the Russian master, Shostakovitch. Its title, of course, was "Shostakovich Small by a Waterfall."

★ ★ ★

Opera lovers in the good old days were less demanding than audiences of 1959. The music was all that mattered then, and fourth-rate scenery, threadbare costumes, and even three-hundred-pound sopranos lumbering about the stage as "fairy princesses" were accepted without protest.

Mme. Schumann Heink, famed Austrian contralto of yesteryear, was the soloist at a Chicago concert, but, because of her girth, had difficulty squeezing her way to the podium via a narrow aisle between the violins and 'cellos. One helpful musician whispered, "Why don't you try going sideways?" The broad-beamed diva answered despairingly, "Can't you see I *haff* no sideways?"

Lovely Lily Pons changed all that. She proved that a very big voice could come out of a very trim package. After one of her early appearances, a critic exulted, "At last! A Carmen who weighs less than the bull!"

Maria Callas admits that a strict diet enabled her to shed forty pounds—and sing better than ever.

★ ★ ★

A brash American soprano made her debut at the famous opera house in Milan. The applause was so tumultuous that she had to sing her big aria seven times. She then blew kisses to the audience and announced tearfully, "You've made me the happiest girl in all the world. But I'm so exhausted I can give you no more encores."

From the top balcony came a stern voice: "You'll go right on singing that aria till you get it right!"

★ ★ ★

The price of fame: A great orchestra conductor, young, handsome, adored by the "weaker" sex, had a date with a charmer late one night that he wanted to keep a dark secret. He pulled up his coat collar, jammed his hat down over his ears, and in a disguised voice told the driver of a cab the address he sought.

Arrived at his destination, he paid the fare, then began looking in vain for the entrance to his beloved's abode. The driver watched him with deep interest for some moments, then called out, "If it's the same girl you visited last Tuesday, maestro, she's two doors to the left!"

★ ★ ★

An Italian orchestra director's son was the only kid in his class to identify a selection played by the school orchestra as a composition of Paganini. "Your father's training, I suppose," beamed the teacher. "No seen my pop in six months," protested the kid. "I read it here on the music." The teacher looked. It said, "Page nine."

★ ★ ★

One of the late Maestro Toscanini's favorite stories about himself concerned the day on tour when a plump, rosy-cheeked young chambermaid caught his fancy. Pulling a pair of tickets out of his pocket, the Maestro said gaily, "Tell me, my dear, how would you like to go to the concert—in six-dollar seats—tomorrow night?" The maid continued dusting for a moment, then inquired, "Is that the only night you get off?"

★ ★ ★

Toscanini once played host to Yehudi Menuhin. The latter was in the middle of a violin sonata when a phone in the hall began to ring. Toscanini motioned to Menuhin to continue playing, picked up a pair of scissors, cut the phone wire in two, then leaned back happily once more to listen to the music.

62. THE NAVY

To the home of Don Addis, of Hollywood, Florida, came a group from the U.S. Navy, to rehearse for a benefit a special rendition of "Anchors Aweigh." For a climax, each man was trained to pop up and sing one word of the song in rapid succession.

Grumbled the commander, "Very shabby performance! I got a glimpse of the sailor who stood up and sang 'Anchors' and he was a mess." Replied his aide, "He wasn't the worst. You should have seen the one that got 'Aweigh'!"

★ ★ ★

The wife of a submarine commander gave birth to a beautiful baby girl in the Norfolk Hospital while her husband's craft was patrolling Far Eastern waters. This is the cable she sent him: "Ahoy, skipper. New craft successfully launched at seven bells. Tonnage: eight pounds. No periscope. All shipshape. That is all we hope. Love. Mary."

★ ★ ★

A candidate for a naval commission was undergoing an oral examination.

"Tell us," said the chairman of the board, "what kind of animals eat grass?"

The candidate didn't answer; just fidgeted with his necktie and turned red.

"Come now," urged the chairman. "Surely you can answer a simple question like that. I will repeat: What kind of animals eat grass?"

"Animals!" exclaimed the candidate with obvious relief. "I thought you said 'admirals'!"

★ ★ ★

Helen McKay, after observing the hazards to which U.S. Navy personnel are exposed on the Place Pigalle in Paris, warned, "It's *c'est la vie,*/ and *c'est la guerre,*/ But most of all/ *C'est la* beware!"

★ ★ ★

Old navy men should appreciate J. R. Sertchek's story of the ensign who demanded a house with washrooms on every floor. "I put my faith squarely in that old proverb," he explained: "Two heads are better than one!"

★ ★ ★

"What was the rank of that navy man you were dancing with all evening at the country club?" demanded an anxious mother. "I'm not sure," answered the daughter coyly, "but, judging by his actions, I'd say he was a Chief Petting Officer." (Sounds like a wolf in ship's clothing!)

★ ★ ★

In Annapolis, a midshipman obviously destined for big things was asked by a visiting admiral, "Name three of the great naval figures in our history." Without hesitation the midshipman replied, "Farragut, Jones—and, beg pardon, sir, but I didn't quite catch your name."

★ ★ ★

There turned up in the Navy a recruit who had neither a first name nor a middle name: just Jones—plus initials R.B. The government took a dim view of this unusual nomenclature and entered his name officially as R (only) B (only) Jones. Sure enough, when RB's first pay check came rolling in, it was made out to Ronly Bonly Jones!

★ ★ ★

The new recruit at a Great Lakes training camp had just been put over the obstacle course: through a thick, tangled patch of forest, across an ice-cold, swift-running river, and under a maze of wicked barbed wire. "Well, boy," grinned a diabolical petty officer, "how do you like being a sailor?" "Shucks, mister," answered the recruit innocently, "where I hail from, we gotta go through country like this just to get to the barn!"

★ ★ ★

Two angry young members of the downbeat generation went to the shore to witness the flight of an experimental navy jet. In the course of same, the button was pressed on a new automatic ejection seat, and the copilot floated lazily to earth.

"Jeepers," exclaimed one of the downbeat boys. "Dig that crazy toastmaster!"

★ ★ ★

An old joke had it that the way the kiddies in Las Vegas learned to count was, "One, two, three, four, five, six, seven, eight, nine, ten, Jack, Queen, King." Now they've shifted the scene to Cape Canaveral. *There* the bright young things recite, "Ten, nine, eight, seven, six, five, four, three, two, one, zero, Oh, damn!"

★ ★ ★

The Navy decided to put a live mouse in the nozzle of a new rocket they were testing and borrowed one from the Harvard Laboratory. The rocket was put into orbit without a hitch, and for three months whirled dizzily around the globe in outer space. Then it returned to earth, and lo and behold, the mouse marched out in the very pink of condition.

Returned to the Harvard Laboratory, this mouse became, of course, the hero of the hour. "What's it like," demanded a spokesman for the stay-at-home-mice, "to go spinning for three months in outer space?"

"I'll tell you one thing, fellows," admitted the hero-mouse nonchalantly, "it's better than cancer!"

63. NEWSPAPERS AND MAGAZINES

Many years ago, an elderly New York merchant who had made his fortune, and sought only tranquillity for the balance of his life, settled in the far-off Pacific island of Tahiti. There were no planes or cruise ships in those days. Once a month a tramp steamer dropped anchor long enough to deliver supplies—and fulfill the merchant's subscription to the New York *Tribune,* his one link with the civilization he had forsworn.

All his life, the merchant had methodically read one newspaper every day, and he did not propose to change the habit now. His fresh supply was piled carefully in a closet, and, as usual, he read one issue every day—exactly four months after publication date.

No matter how intrigued he might be with some front-page story, the thought of peeking at the next day's issue (lying within arm's reach) to see how it turned out was simply unbearable to him!

★ ★ ★

Why, wonders editor Jim Fox of Jamestown, is every murderess and female hoodlum featured in stories circulated by wire services described as "beautiful" or "attractive"? He examined closely, for instance, the picture of an ax-wielding husband killer labeled "attractive mother of three" and discovered she looked in reality "like five miles of bad road."

Editor Fox has now decided how the news services operate in these cases:

"Attractive" means: buck teeth or no teeth at all, ratty hair, and a figure like fifty pounds of potatoes, badly sacked.

"Pretty" means: as bad as "attractive," but the subject is a few years younger and not quite so dirty.

"Beautiful" means: probably as bad as "pretty," but the light's so bad you can't really tell whether it's a picture of Sophia Loren or Boris Karloff.

★ ★ ★

Overheard at a local press club: "He's the kind of editor who expects his photographer to get both the start and finish of a hundred-yard dash!"

★ ★ ★

The late Emile Gauvreau, editor in his day of some of the most flamboyant and sensational tabloid newspapers ever published, ruefully summed up his own career in this one sentence: "I was part of that strange race of people, aptly described as spending their lives doing things they detest to make money they don't want to buy things they don't need to impress people they dislike."

★ ★ ★

It is the profound belief of veteran newsman Gene Fowler that the most important thing a young, would-be journalist can learn is how to pad an expense account so expertly that the most suspicious managing editor will O.K. it. "Many a fine wardrobe and fully stocked liquor closet," maintains Gene, "has been the reward of a finagler who knew just when and how to submit a phony expense tab."

Fowler's rep was so well established in his salad days on a New York paper that, when an explosion was heard rocking Jersey, a frightened owner stuck his head out of his private office and cried, "Don't send Fowler across the river to cover that story. He'll buy the ferryboat!"

★ ★ ★

A political reporter came back to the city desk after interviewing a senatorial candidate. "What did the old boy have to say?" inquired the editor. "Not a darn thing," grumbled the reporter. The editor nodded and ordered, "Keep it down to two columns."

★ ★ ★

Frank Brookhauser claims he has a neighbor in Philadelphia named Hubert B. WOLFESCHLEGELSTEINHAUSENBER-GERDORFF. Mr. W. (heaven forbid that we have to repeat in full!) is, logically enough, a typesetter, having realized, no doubt, that nobody else could ever get his name into print correctly.

★ ★ ★

The elderly foreman of a local newspaper's composing room up and eloped one day when the Algonquin Round Table was still going strong. Everybody sent congratulatory wires. Alexander Woollcott's contained just one word: "STET."

★ ★ ★

Paul De Kruif, distinguished bacteriologist and author of *Microbe Hunters*, reached the finals of a rural checkers tourney last summer, but was roundly trounced by farmer Hawkins, who thus captured the crown for the seventeenth consecutive year. The local paper's headline for the event was "De Farmer Takes De Kruif."

★ ★ ★

The editor of a small-town newspaper had a sign over his desk that read "Obituary Editor." In due course, his son took over the post, and had the sign duly changed to "Son of Obituary Editor."

★ ★ ★

Three darn fools out of four, maintains the editor of the Echo Valley *Vigilant*, will sign any petition that is stuck under their noses. To prove his point he printed a circular beseeching the state governor to burn the bridges on the only two roads leading into town, and to fine every citizen twenty thousand dollars. He collected sixty-three signatures the first hour.

★ ★ ★

Do you think it's easy to bring out a newspaper once a week in a small town? Listen to this sob story from the Star Valley (Afton, Wyoming) *Independent:*

"Publishing a small paper is no picnic.

"If we print jokes, people say we are silly; if we don't, they say we are too serious.

"If we stick to the office all day, we ought to be out hunting things to write about; if we go out and try to hustle some news, we ought to be on the job in the office.

"If we don't accept contributions, we don't appreciate genius; if we print them, the paper is full of junk.

"If we edit the other fellow's story, we are too critical; if we don't, we're asleep.

"If we clip things from other papers, we're too lazy to write them; if we don't, we're stuck with our own stuff.

"Now, like as not some guy will say we swiped this from some other paper. . . . We did, and admit it."

★ ★ ★

Provocative ads culled from the classified columns of small-town gazettes:

1. "Lost: Will the gent who picked up a fur coat at Inspiration Point last night please return the redhead that was in it. No questions asked."

2. "Will the person who took a slice of chocolate layer cake from the police commissioner's office please return same. It is part of the evidence in a food-poisoning case."

3. (In California) "For sale cheap: swimming pool swum in only twice by an old lady from Altadena."

4. "Mexican burro for sale. Name your own price. Can be seen evenings in my back yard or heard within a radius of three miles any morning about 6 A.M."

★ ★ ★

Old Judge Elkins had been the owner and editor of the Frogville *Gazette* for thirty-two years, and in all that time, he insisted, he had lost money both in circulation and advertising. Outside job-printing jobs, he added, weren't what they used to be, either. "Where do the profits come from then?" he was asked. The judge winked and said, "Every issue we make at least ten typographical errors—and sell 'em at a nice price to them smart-alecky city magazines."

★ ★ ★

James Thurber is an avid hunter of typographical boners. This one, culled from a paper known more for fifth-rate columns than first-rate news, is just about his favorite: "Among the first to enter the airplane was Mrs. Clara Adams of Tannersville, Pa., lone woman passenger. Slowly her nose was turned around to face in a southwesterly direction. Then, like some strange beast, she crawled along the grass."

★ ★ ★

An Iowa weekly printed this note on its first page recently: "We were the first journal in all Iowa to announce the destruction in Des Moines by fire of the block-long —— Paint factory. We are now first again to inform our readers that the report was utterly without foundation."

★ ★ ★

A West Virginia newspaper reproduced a photograph of a counterfeit ten-dollar bill that had found its way into the community, hoping that by bringing it to the attention of its readers there would be no recurrence. The next day the photograph of the bill, carefully clipped from the newspaper, was passed without question in the local grocery store.

★ ★ ★

If you want to know the "ten best" of anything at all—football players, Hollywood sirens, barbers, ways of eating spaghetti—all you have to do is pick up a newspaper or magazine, because there are a lot of people who seem to make a living compiling these lists. I even know a fellow who's working on the "ten best letters in the alphabet"—but it's said he has an "X" to grind. A movie magazine last year gave its idea of the "ten happiest marriages in Hollywood." Unfortunately, by the time the issue hit the stands, four of the marriages had gone phfft!

★ ★ ★

An English newspaper offered substantial prizes to contestants who submitted answers to this question: "Who are the happiest people on earth?" The four answers that captured top prizes were:

1. A craftsman artist whistling over a job well done.

2. A little child building sand castles.

3. A mother, after a busy day, bathing her baby.

4. A doctor who has finished a difficult and dangerous operation, and saved a human life.

★ ★ ★

A kid reporter on his first big assignment was watching the sun set behind the gaunt mountains back of Las Vegas. He tapped an old croupier on the shoulder and said, "Beg pardon, but that *is* the west over there, isn't it?" The croupier assured him, "Son, if it isn't, you've just scored the biggest scoop since the Johnstown Flood!"

★ ★ ★

Rolfe Peterson, the life of every party in Salt Lake City—in fact, in all Utah, is in cahoots with a writer of an advice-to-the-lovelorn column named Pamela Cardiac. Here's a letter, adds Rolfe, that Pamela received recently:

"Dear Pamela: Ever since my husband saw a movie called *Moby Dick* he has been driving me to distraction. The movie impressed him so deeply that he went right out and bought a harpoon. He waves it around all the time hollering, 'Thar she blows!' The other night while I was watching TV he let go of the harpoon and knocked out our picture tube. I'm afraid he'll harpoon me next. What can I do? [Signed] Landlubber."

Pamela was equal to the occasion. She promptly answered: "Dear Landlubber: This is probably just one of the many troublesome stages men stumble through during middle age. I'm confident it will blow over—pardon me—pass over. Here's how you can help. Some night when he's sound asleep, holler, 'Thar she blows' in his ear. Then, when he stirs, add, 'Pull, men, pull! The monster's turning on us!' Then rock the bed violently and shout, 'Look out for his tail! He's knocked a hole in the whaleboat!' Then empty a bucket of cold water over him. A pinch of salt stirred in beforehand will add to the realism.

"When he's fully awake I'm sure he'll have lost a good deal of his enthusiasm for whaling. Meanwhile, be of good cheer, look on the bright side, and don't let him have a clear shot at you. [Signed] Pamela Cardiac."

★ ★ ★

The late Harold Ross, founder of the *New Yorker* magazine, editor until his untimely death, and the man who singlehanded made it one of the greatest successes in journalistic history, was a restless, perpetually inquisitive genius who "read the Encyclopaedia Britannica for fun," and was one of the few souls who "could pace up and down while he was sitting still at his desk."

It was Ross who persuaded Raoul Fleischmann, of the baking Fleischmanns, to invest an original fifty thousand dollars in the venture, and then pony up a cool half-million more before it turned the corner. It was Ross too who persuaded brilliant people like Thurber, White, Benchley, and Dorothy Parker to contribute pieces for a fraction of what the established slicks would have paid them. Ross invented the "profile," too. The going rate in the early days was $150 tops, for which the writer had to check and recheck his facts, and write and rewrite until Ross was satisfied. Nobody ever resigned.

Making a top-ranking author rewrite a piece three or four times is a well-nigh impossible task, but Ross possessed the magic formula. Across the top of, let us say, the third rewrite he would pencil, "This piece is too good not to be perfect!"

Dorothy Parker labeled Ross "a professional lunatic." Russell Maloney noted that "Ross considered perfection his personal property, like his hat or his watch." One editor complained to Ross, "Every week you holler that the new issue doesn't contain a single laugh." Snarled Ross, "This week there are fewer than ever!"

★ ★ ★

Cartoonist Charles Addams, who leans toward the macabre in most of his famous drawings, is seriously considering eliminating people with two heads from his future productions. He explains, "Too many angry letters from the two-headed set."

★ ★ ★

Frances Lobert points out (though I don't quite understand what I am supposed to do about it) that the more ads a magazine carries, the duller its editorial content becomes. Miss Lobert also thinks less space should be devoted to the extramarital didoes of

Hollywood film stars. "Let's face it," declares Miss Lobert. "Sex is there to stray!"

★ ★ ★

"The thing I like best about those new sexy magazines on the stand," observed Jones, Yale '59 (a keen student of printing, by the way), "is all the beautiful off-color plates."

★ ★ ★

A magazine on gardening received a request for information from a faithful subscriber with a signature that insured immediate attention from the editor-in-chief. The letter was signed "Constant Weeder."

64. NIGHTCLUBS

Boniface H. D. Hover claims that a nightclub proprietor must possess these five minimum requirements: (1) The friendliness of a poor relation. (2) The docility of a defendant with no defense. (3) The memory of an elephant. (4) The philanthropy of a Carnegie, and (5) (most important of all) a wealthy father who is an idiot.

★ ★ ★

A beautiful, languid young lady who spent most of her waking hours in El Morocco, the Stork Club, and the Richelieu was finally talked into a weekend at Niagara Falls. "I couldn't believe what I saw," she enthused upon her return. "The water was flowing like champagne!"

★ ★ ★

Four newcomers on the nightclub beat have names designed to intrigue you: Miss Page Wunne, Miss Eartha Quake, Miss Pepper Mint, and Miss Norma Vinson Peal. Miss Peal's ad in a theatrical weekly concludes, "Have sweater. Will ravel."

★ ★ ★

Helen Morgan, the singer whose rendition of numbers like "Why Was I Born?" and "He's Just My Bill" brought tears to the eyes of thousands of hardboiled hijackers in the speak-easy days, has become famous all over again since her life story, or a vague facsimile thereof, was re-created both on TV and the screen. In real life, Miss Morgan came to a tragic end. "The only things worth while in life," she told a reporter in one of her soberer moments near the finish, "are fish in the sea, children playing in the sun—and those stars on the brandy bottle."

★ ★ ★

Orson Welles recently played an engagement at a Las Vegas nightclub, but possibly his act was deemed a bit too highbrow for the assembled crap shooters and slot-machine manipulators, because his audiences were seldom large. Welles told one sparse assemblage, "I am a producer, director, writer, and actor. Isn't it too bad there are so many of me and so few of you?"

★ ★ ★

NIGHTCLUB NOTABLES . . .

The girl in the line who claims she's two-thirds married. That is, she's willing, and so is her mother.

The stripper who boned up on English literature for three months, entered a TV quiz contest, and walked off with a check for fifty thousand dollars—proving that you can make much more grinding than you can bumping.

The indiscreet, lovely lass who anchored at a ringside table. "There," nodded the knowing maître d'hôtel, "goes a good time who's been had by *all*."

The censor—a killjoy who always has a grind to ax.

The tap dancer who explained, "It's only natural that I be fastidious. Papa was fast, and Mamma was hideous."

The mean old cops who threw an artiste into jail for taking too much off. She was taking it off her income tax.

The notorious gold digger who strutted into Chez Paris oozing diamonds from every pore. "Trouble with that girl," opined a lass with less taking ways, "is that she's getting too big for her brooches."

★ ★ ★

Joe E. Lewis recalls a thoughtful boss for whom he toiled in the freewheeling Capone era in Chicago. "I'll never forget," says Joe, "the day the good man heard I was stranded in Glencoe and sent a car for me. Luckily I jumped out of the way in the nick of time."

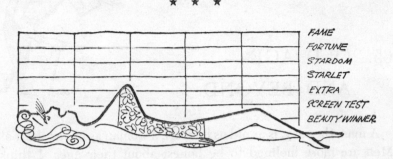

FAME
FORTUNE
STARDOM
STARLET
EXTRA
SCREEN TEST
BEAUTY WINNER

The conversation at a popular Hollywood restaurant turned to a highly publicized, highly curved new glamour girl. "They say she's going to go far," reported a producer. "She can't miss," agreed his girl friend. "She's already halfway there!" About another movie starlet, the word has gone forth that she likes staying up until the "*oui*" hours.

In a nightclub, a beautiful blonde snuggled up to her escort and whispered, "How's for giving me a diamond bracelet?"

"My pet," replied her companion (Dorothy Kilgallen suggests he may have been listening to John Daly too often on "What's My Line?"), "extenuating circumstances compel me to preclude you from such a bauble of extravagance."

"I don't get it," confessed the blonde.

"That's just what I said," agreed her companion.

65. OLD AGE—
AND BEYOND

A man, they say, is as old as he feels; a woman as old as she looks. Men are more inclined to be honest about their ages, I think—particularly when the statistics are there for everybody to check in Who's Who. But as Diane de Poitiers pointed out, the years that a woman subtracts from her age are not lost; they are added to the age of other women.

★ ★ ★

Sir Winston Churchill, probably the greatest man alive, wears the mantle of his age with unequaled grace and equanimity. When he was seventy-five, he harumphed, "I am ready to meet my Maker. Whether my Maker is prepared for the great ordeal of meeting me is another matter." On his eighty-second birthday, a young photographer told him, "I hope I may have the privilege of taking your picture again when you're a hundred." "No reason why you shouldn't," said Sir Winston cheerfully, "if you continue to look after your health."

★ ★ ★

"Doctor," pleaded an old gaffer, "you've got to help me. Here I am ninety years old and still chasing girls." "What's wrong with that?" laughed the doctor. A tear trickled down the old gaffer's cheek. "I chase them," he confessed, "but I can't remember why."

★ ★ ★

A character actor confided to a pal, "I'm almost sixty-five years old, have saved half a million, and have fallen madly in love with a dashing young blonde of nineteen. Do you think I'd have a better chance to have her marry me if I told her I'm only fifty?" "I think you'd have a better chance to land her," said the pal frankly, "if you told her you're eighty!"

★ ★ ★

In 1933, when he was forty-two years old, a canny Scottish doctor named James Mackintosh sat down and wrote himself a letter. It contained "a bit of friendly advice," and was not to be opened until his sixty-fifth birthday.

"Certain undesirable tendencies in your character and outlook are already apparent," he warned himself bluntly, "and I have little doubt that they will become more marked as you grow older.

"You will become even more talkative," he predicted. "Do try to curb this fault, lest it lead to a final inability to learn anything. Try *really* to listen to others occasionally—not just turn your head and make gestures which have become automatic.

"Secondly, avoid prying into the affairs of young people, even on the plea (for self-justification) that you are doing it to help them.

"Thirdly, neither pose as 'that dear old man,' hoping to hear murmurs of how young you are in spirit, nor choose to ignore the fact that you are now sixty-five and on the point of retirement. For heaven's sake, do not persuade yourself you are a special case. When the time comes, clear out.

"If you have kept mind and body active, a world of new interests and activities lies before you. You can sharpen three rare and beautiful qualities, too: courtesy, integrity, and tolerance. By tolerance, I mean a mind that is still open, still able to understand and sympathize with the point of view of others. Now remember . . ."

On his sixty-fifth birthday, Dr. Mackintosh read his letter thoughtfully, then wrote himself this answer: "My dear Mackintosh: Thanks for your letter of thirty-three years ago. A little solemn, I thought—but then, of course, you were addressing a man old enough to be your father . . . I shall try humbly to follow your friendly advice."

Dr. Mackintosh thereupon retired as dean of the London School of Hygiene and Tropical Medicine—a post he had held with great distinction for more than a decade.

★ ★ ★

Browsing in a Washington Square bookshop, Peter Lind Hayes caught sight of an impromptu open-air chess tourney in progress in the park opposite, and went over to investigate. One decrepit old codger, so frail and weather-beaten he scarcely could move the chessmen, nevertheless cleaned up every opponent with such ridiculous ease that Hayes scarcely could believe his eyes.

"Pop," he asked, "to what do you owe your amazing stamina and clarity of mind?"

"Sensible habits," quavered the victor. "Every day since I was fourteen I've imbibed two quarts of whiskey, used beer for a chaser, and made love to a different girl in the afternoon and evening."

"Amazing," marveled Hayes. "How old are you?"

The answer was, "Going on twenty-two."

★ ★ ★

A Chillicothe undertaker has twisted a familiar airline slogan for his own purpose: His sign reads, "Pay now; go later."

★ ★ ★

Very much against his will, philosopher Voltaire was conned into speaking a small eulogy over the body of a deceased acquaintance whom he had loathed for years. Said Voltaire, "Here lies a man who was a sturdy patriot, a gifted writer, a loyal friend, and a faithful husband—provided, of course, that he is really dead."

★ ★ ★

General Omar Bradley has revived the story of the timid old Vermont spinster who breathed her last in Devonshire, and whose body was sent back for burial—as per her last wish—in the churchyard of her home town. When her nephew there opened the casket, however, he beheld not the placid features of his aunt Effie, but an English general in full regimentals who had died the same day. Frantically, he cabled the general's heirs to ask for suggestions.

Back came this cable: "Bury the general quietly. Aunt Effie interred at Westminster Abbey this morning with six brass bands and full military honors."

★ ★ ★

From the department of philosophy at Columbia University comes the tale of a righteous sage who departed this life at an advanced age and awoke before the pearly gates. Heaven welcomed him with appropriate ceremonies. Some years later, his trusted disciple followed in his steps, and looked him up in Heaven. He was found under a spreading cypress tree, with a gloriously beautiful damsel in his lap. "I am glad, revered teacher," said the disciple, "to see you have won your just reward." "Reward nothing," grumbled the sage. "It's *her* punishment."

★ ★ ★

I think you'll like this anecdote told to me by Warren Wire, of Los Angeles. "Last Christmas," he writes, "my daughter and son-in-law and their six-year-old Steven were among our guests. After dinner, we watched a football game on television, and that led to a general discussion of sports.

"One said he liked prize fights best; another golf; a third baseball. Somebody finally asked young Steven what kind of sport he liked best. He looked in turn at everybody in the room, then came over and threw his arms around me, and said, 'MY GRAN'PA.'"

66. OVERSEAS TRAVEL

New guidebooks to every place from Toledo to Timbuktu are a dime a dozen these days, but the familiar, red-bound, kept-up-to-date Baedekers continue to outsell them. Karl Baedeker didn't know what he was starting when, in Coblenz, Germany, in 1830, he issued a guide to the surrounding Rhine country. It proved so reliable, thorough, and popular, he began branching out to foreign climes, soon had his snoopers poking their noses into inns and hostelries in every corner of Europe.

Success did not affect Herr Baedeker's methods. He remained suspicious of the reports turned in by his own agents, preferred traveling incognito, and digging up the facts himself. As A. P. Herbert put it, "Kings and government may err, but never Mr. Baedeker."

All Baedeker guides contained a note that should carry off a prize in any and all contests for classic understatement: "When traveling, ladies add considerably to the expense."

★ ★ ★

A major headache for Frances Knight, trim, dynamic director of the U.S. Passport Office, and her staff, is the army of careless tourists who lose their passports—sometimes in the darnedest places!—and are deeply grieved if they don't get replacements immediately. One dear lady I know succeeded in losing her passport twice in a single day. She left it behind in a Paris hotel room in the morning, and then, after a justifiably enraged husband drove back eighty miles to retrieve it, inadvertently flushed it down a drain in Geneva that evening!

The youngest applicant for a passport in the past year was exactly one week old (he didn't apply personally); the oldest a man of ninety-two, making his first trip out of the United States, and rarin' to get on his way. A third applicant wrote in the square marked "purpose of trip": "I've got to get away from it all, especially interference." He turned out to be an angry, unsilent young gentleman of twelve, tired of parental advice.

Frances Knight recalls with particular pleasure the young miss who submitted with her passport a photograph of herself in a WAC uniform. Since she no longer was in the service she was requested to submit a photograph out of uniform.

This, obviously, was a girl who believed in obeying orders. Her next picture revealed her definitely out of uniform—in fact, naked as a jay bird!

★ ★ ★

Too many Americans, abroad for the first time, are so busy doing what they've been told to do that they miss not only the flavor and charm of the places they visit, but the heady excitement of discovery as well.

There's the sad case of a St. Louis couple, for instance, who worried lest they be dressed improperly for their evenings aboard ship. "Everybody dresses for dinner on a luxury liner," their travel agent assured them, so the first evening aboard they emerged from their cabin arrayed to the teeth. It is not the custom to dress the first night out, however, and they were dismayed to discover they were the only ones wearing evening clothes.

"That agent is cuckoo," they declared, and the second night they appeared in sports clothes. This time everybody else was dressed formally. So the third night, they reverted to evening clothes—forgetting it was Sunday, when nobody dresses up. Wrong again!

Determined to get into step before it was too late, they abandoned formals for the fourth night, which was the captain's gala, with all other first-class passengers wearing their very gladdest rags. And, to make their record complete, they donned evening clothes again for the fifth night, only to learn that informal garb prevails the evening before a ship docks. By striving to follow advance instructions, instead of finding things out on the spot for themselves, this couple succeeded in being wrong five times out of five.

★ ★ ★

To prove to my wife that I know the duties of a father when she points them out to me, I took my two sons, the summer they were sixteen and twelve, respectively, to Europe. In exchange, they taught me the lyrics of six current rock-and-roll hits. Fortunately these lyrics are interchangeable. Often, in fact, they're better that way. The boys were chanting a new Elvis Presley classic as they deplaned in Rome. "Your bambinos very talented!" enthused our porter. "They speak Bulgarian."

The behavior of children aboard a transatlantic plane, notes Art Buchwald, conforms to a certain pattern. A sturdy lad generally refuses to buckle his safety belt, but makes up for this by tripping the stewardess as she is explaining how to use the life belt properly. Furthermore, once the plane is safely aloft, he *does* fasten his belt. It then takes his parents and several unselfish passengers to get it unfastened. Later, after wolfing his own meal, by staring intently at others while they eat, he usually winds up by devouring three extra pieces of cake, several cups of salad dressing—and getting sick. "Lindbergh had the right idea," concludes Buchwald. "He flew the Atlantic alone."

My younger son Jonathan was determined to take pictures with his brand-new camera while we were twenty thousand feet above the Atlantic, but since he had his camera set for five feet the pictures did not turn out too well. Jonathan had a further discouraging habit of forgetting to turn the film in his Kodak after he had snapped a picture. In this manner he probably was one of the first men alive to get the Alps, the Colosseum, and the Leaning Tower of Pisa on a single negative.

My older son Christopher also went through Italy and France with fun and camera. Chris, furthermore, used a light meter. When conditions were favorable, he could get an extremely accurate reading inside of twenty minutes. Aboard a steamer in the Bay of Naples, he decided to snap a gull in full flight with Mount Vesuvius in the background. Unfortunately, when he was ready to take the picture, the gull had just made a landing in West Philadelphia.

In Rome, I decided to show the boys some of the famed sculptures and paintings. They were properly appreciative. Jonny wrote in his diary: "Dad took us to the Borghese Gallery this morning, where I had the most boring hour I ever spent in my life."

The boys did have one big moment in Italy, when my wife, seeking to find the button that would put the room lights out in Naples at 2 A.M., pushed down all of them on the buzzer next to her bed. Shortly thereafter, our room was invaded by the porter, the waiter, the maid, the 33rd Infantry, and the Fire Department.

In Florence, I met an old classmate in a dither because that morning he had seen a lot of costumed movie actors playing baseball. "That's no longer unusual," I remarked. "With so many Americans roaming around these days, you're likely to see a ball game in progress most any place in Italy." "Not like this one," insisted my friend. "Napoleon was playing third base."

★ ★ ★

Dore Schary, movie producer and author of *Sunrise at Campobello*, was in Italy that summer, too, and told me of a friend who had taken her nine-year-old son to Venice for the first time. Anxious for the boy to be properly dazzled by his initial visit to the famous Piazza di San Marco, she suggested that he keep his eyes closed till they reached its center.

Directly in front of spectacular St. Mark's church, she said, "Now! Open your eyes and tell me what you see."

The boy, very truthfully, answered, "I see Dore Schary." Mr. Schary was standing directly in front of them.

★ ★ ★

Sailing home aboard that superb ship, the *United States*, we were enthralled by the travelogue of an American Ambassador, just back from a tour of the Far East. A high spot of his trip was an address he made to a large audience of women, urging that they fight for equal rights for their sex. The women were delighted with his remarks—so much so, in fact, that they bought an eighteen-year-old girl and presented her to him as a gift.

67. PHOTOGRAPHY

A wily society photographer has developed an effective method for collecting overdue bills from celebrated female patrons. With each past-due statement he encloses an unretouched proof—the most unflattering he can find—of the customer, plus this note: "I am sure you have an adequate reason for neglecting to pay this bill. To save both of us embarrassment I will gladly call the account balanced if you in turn will permit me to blow up the enclosed excellent picture of you and feature it in my window display." The lady generally shows up the very next day, cash in hand.

★ ★ ★

Patron saint of the art of photography in America was George Eastman, who, fabulously wealthy though his Kodak company made him, never got over fretting over the most minute details. Thus, when he presented his home city of Rochester with a six-thousand-seat theater, he summoned the architect to tell him he had figured out a way to add two seats to the orchestra floor.

When the architect expressed surprise that Mr. Eastman could bother about two extra seats in an auditorium already planned to hold six thousand, Eastman replied sternly, "Each of those extra seats would net thirty cents a show, and if there are six shows a week, that's $3.60 for the two of them. At the end of a fiscal year that means $187.20—which, incidentally, is exactly 6 per cent interest on $3,120 for a year. Do you care to explore this further?" The architect hastily assured Mr. Eastman, "I'll take your word for it, sir."

★ ★ ★

When great sports events are in the making, you can bet that a competent photographer will be on hand to record them for posterity.

Early automobile races, for instance, were unostentatiously photographed by Henry Ford himself. The inventor quietly tucked the prints away in his files, and nobody knew they existed until they were uncovered a few months ago.

And when the first game of baseball as we know it today was played on June 19, 1846, a photographer, all dressed up to kill, was fortunately on hand—at a discreet distance from the diamond. The challengers were a team of "gentlemen amateurs," known as the New York Knickerbockers. Their opponents simply called themselves the New York Club. The game was played at the Elysian Fields, a summer resort just outside Hoboken, and, although the Knicks insisted on playing under their own rules, they were clobbered 24 to 1. Their lead-off man, Davis, furthermore, lost his temper to such an extent he was fined six cents for swearing.

Closer and closer to the action crept baseball photographers in the years that followed. The ultimate occurred at Griffith Stadium in Washington. A runner was poised on third base, and lit for home to score the winning tally after the batter had lofted a towering fly to right center. Catcher Rick Ferrell braced himself for the throw from the outfield at the same moment that an eager-beaver cameraman, determined to show how good he was, wriggled directly behind him to catch the action at home plate.

The ball and the runner arrived simultaneously. Ferrell made a wild stab and slapped the ball on the photographer's nose just as the runner's slide sent the camera flying ten feet in the air.

The camera was deposited in the nearest ashcan, the photographer was carted off to the hospital, and the runner was declared out for failing to touch home plate.

★ ★ ★

Fabulously successful movie producer Cecil B. De Mille long made a habit of assigning three separate camera crews to film elaborate sequences, thus assuring at least one print perfect enough to save the staggering cost of shooting whole scenes over again.

One spectacle called for a herd of wild elephants to stampede through thousands of extras and demolish a village it had taken studio carpenters four weeks to build. De Mille prudently stationed one camera crew in the foreground, one at the site of the doomed village, and a third on a hilltop in the distance. Because of the magnitude of the operation, he shot off a cannon to initiate action.

The crowds screamed. The elephants charged. The village crumbled. A beaming De Mille cried out, "Cut," and headed for the cameraman nearest him. "Get it?" he demanded. "The roar of that cannon deafened me so," was the crestfallen reply, "I never shot one inch of film."

The cameraman at the village drew a blank too. "Those darn elephants bowled over my entire equipment," he reported. "I was lucky to escape with my life."

"Stop worrying," consoled De Mille. "My man on the hill up yonder had a perfect view of all the action. I'm sure he covered it for us." He drove way up the hill and found the man standing attentively next to his camera.

"We're all set to roll, C.B.," he cried happily. "Any time you're ready!"

★ ★ ★

A crack Hollywood cameraman reluctantly devoted an entire day to shooting "artistic" stills of a callipygian but spectacularly untalented new screen personality. She threw all his fifty proofs contemptuously aside and pouted, "You never photographed my best side."

"How could I?" said the cameraman grimly. "You were always sitting on it!"

68. A PIPE DREAM THAT CAME TRUE

Pittsburgh is famous for its steel, Rochester has its Kodaks, and Detroit its automobiles. Washington, Missouri, concentrates on a single industry, too, and, while it may seem on the inconsequential side to uninitiates, it's made many a citizen in those parts independently wealthy. Washington, Missouri, is the corncob pipe capital of the universe.

It all began on a sultry summer day in 1869, when a farmer named John Scharnke wandered into woodworker Henry Tibbe's shop with a bagful of corncobs and a new idea, possibly borrowed from the Indians. "I'd like for you to turn some pipe bowls from these cobs on your lathe," he said. Tibbe added some reed stems to the bowls, and the two innovators sampled the finished products.

"The sweetest smoking this side of paradise!" enthused Tibbe, who forswore woodworking from that day forward, and concentrated exclusively on the production of corncob pipes. In 1878, his process was patented, and his fortune had gone up in smoke—up to about a quarter of a million dollars, in fact.

Today over ten million corncob pipes a year are produced by three factories in Washington, Missouri. Incidentally, these are the only factories of their kind in the world. Their business was given a new impetus in the tumultuous twenties, when glamorous Marilyn Miller, unchallenged queen of the Ziegfeld Follies and New York's Plaza Grill, announced unequivocally, "I like a man who smokes a corncob pipe!"

Even critic and curmudgeon Henry L. Mencken eschewed cigars

and acquired a sweet-tasting corncob after that—to the vast disgust of his epicurean publisher, Alfred A. Knopf, who has never been seen to puff a less expensive weed than a two-dollar pure Havana!

History's pages are crammed with other famous folk who reached for a corncob instead of a calabash. Rachel Jackson, wife of President Andrew Jackson, was probably the first prominent lady to puff away (explaining blandly that her doctor thereby promised her relief from a persistent bronchial affliction). Mayor Fiorello La Guardia, General Douglas MacArthur, and French hero Marshal Foch were also confirmed corn cobblers. Foch was initiated by an American liaison officer—a native, by chance, of Washington, Missouri.

In World War II, the American soldier again became the top salesman for corncob pipes throughout the world. Wrote one GI stationed in the Pacific to the head of one of Washington's factories: "Please rush me another dozen corncob pipes. With one I can trade for a pig, with two for a wife. With three I think I can even get a canoe."

Mark Twain often was seen with a corncob pipe clenched in his mouth. "If you grow wheat just to get the chaff, you're crazy," was one of his pronunciamentos, "but if you grow corn to get the cob, you're smart." "Giving up smoking my pipe," he also liked to explain, "is the easiest thing in the world. I've done it a hundred times."

How long does a corncob pipe last? Well, some months ago, an old spendthrift from Rockford, Illinois, returned a ten-cent pipe to the factory, demanding a new one in exchange. "I've only used this pipe seven years," he protested, "and it seems to me it hasn't held up so good." When received, the pipe had been wired together, the burned-out bottom had been replastered, and the stem was nailed on.

69. PLAYWRIGHTS
AND PRODUCERS

THE MEN BEHIND THE RUNS

Intricate indeed are the ties that bind those friendly enemies, Broadway playwrights and the producers who transform their brain children into reality. They cannot live without each other, and in their hearts they cherish a mutual if grudging respect, but, like a married couple of thirty years' standing, they know just how to sink an occasional harpoon where it will hurt the most.

In Ben Hecht's *Charlie*, an affectionate memoir of his old friend and collaborator, the late Charles MacArthur, there is a hilarious account of how MacArthur sought to prevent David Belasco, producer of his *Lulu Belle*, from mutilating and rewriting the original script. The big crisis came when Belasco decided that a page of dialogue from the star part, played by Lenore Ulric, had to come out.

The cries of anguish uttered both by Miss Ulric and MacArthur could be heard beyond the sound barrier. The Old Master—as Belasco liked to call himself—suddenly restored quiet by raising a hand and intoning, "Children, there will be a recess for ten minutes while I commune with the spirit world."

The cast watched in wonder while Belasco paced up and down the aisles of the empty theater, smacking his forehead occasionally with his palms. Suddenly he strode back upon the stage. "I've discussed my proposed cuts," he announced solemnly, "with Charles Frohman, greatest producer of us all, who died so gallantly when the *Lusitania* went down some years ago. Mr. Frohman listened to both sides of the argument and then said, 'David, go ahead and make the cuts.' Children, we cannot now disappoint Charles Frohman!"

"How," despaired Charlie MacArthur, "could you argue with such a wonderful, unbelievable ham? We gave in!"

★ ★ ★

Sam Goldwyn, dean of producers in Hollywood, remembers the day he raised Mary Pickford's salary to two thousand dollars a week. Those were the years, of course, when the bite of the income tax bug was not so deadly, and Miss Pickford was in Heaven. In Heaven, that is, until her coworker in the United Artists vineyard, Mr. Charles Chaplin, joined Miss P. and Mr. G. and casually remarked that *his* take-home pittance that year would total $670,-000! The clincher, furthermore, was yet to come. "I guess I could have gotten more," reflected Chaplin with the suspicion of a tear in his eyes, "but you both know what a terrible businessman I am!"

★ ★ ★

When you're slaving over the monthly budget, does the rock-and-roll of your teen-ager's records disturb your concentration?

If you're trying to read the evening paper, does the sound of your wife's voice prattling over the phone to a friend with whom she's just spent the entire afternoon in person get on your nerves?

If so, take a tip from the late, great Hungarian playwright, Ferenc Molnar: stop trying to change the habits of your family, and take careful stock of your own neuroses!

Molnar did his best work when the noise around him reached its greatest intensity. That's what his lovely widow, actress Lily Darvas told me. *The Swan* was written in a crowded, all-night café in Budapest, she says. He polished off the tenderest, most delicate scene while a scantily clad singer was braying a torch ballad just a few feet away.

"Poor Ferenc didn't get rich from *The Swan*, despite its success all over the world," recalls Miss Darvas. "Gilbert Miller, acting as agent for a picture company, bought it outright for something like eight thousand dollars. Later Mr. Miller did present him with a beautiful gold, diamond-studded cigarette case. Molnar always said it was the most costly gift he ever had received."

When Molnar set out to write *Liliom*, he decided to change his ways. At great expense, he fixed up a private study, on the quiet garden side of his house, replete with ornate desk, massive leather chairs, and rich, squishy carpet. He stayed in it faithfully—for about three days.

Then he cried, "This silence is driving me mad," and fled back to the New York Café, on the shore of the Danube, where Hungary's leading literary and theatrical lights were wont to congregate. There Molnar demanded a stack of menus, and began the first draft of *Liliom* on the backs and margins thereof. Three weeks later it was finished.

Like a surprising number of other famous authors, Ferenc Molnar never learned to typewrite. He carried a pocketful of different colored pencils about with him, and switched from red, to blue, then green, as he progressed with his scripts. "Believe it or not," says Lily Darvas, "he wrote the last lines of *The Swan* on the back of a book of paper matches!"

★ ★ ★

Thornton Wilder's play, *The Skin of Our Teeth*, delighted the eggheads, but proved exceedingly mystifying to "tired businessmen" in search of a simple evening's entertainment. One such gent appealed to his wife after the final curtain. "I wish you'd tell me exactly what this darn play was intended to accomplish." "Why, George," she told him, "Wilder was trying to epitomize the problems and the pitfalls confronting the human race from the beginning of time to the present day."

"Shucks," grumbled the husband, "there must have been more to it than THAT!"

★ ★ ★

Harry Kurnitz, renowned playwright and wit, began his career as a violinist in Philadelphia, and still starts fiddling at the slightest provocation. "I particularly love to play gypsy music in night-clubs," he admits. "When I've had a few drinks, some ancient urge rises in me. Too few drinks, I'm inhibited. Too many, my fingers refuse to function. But there's a period of about forty seconds between the two stages when I'm pretty good."

One of Kurnitz's favorite violins was purchased from the fiddler

who used to play sad songs to inspire Gloria Swanson when she was emoting before the camera in Hollywood's good old silent days. "I pick up this instrument," muses Kurnitz, "and, before I know it, I'm playing 'Hearts and Flowers'!"

Lawrence Langner, distinguished and longtime director of the Theatre Guild, is more absent-minded than the proverbial college professor.

Most recent of innumerable Langner anecdotes concerns the day that excellent young actor, Richard Kiley, importuned Langner to release him from a contract for a one-shot appearance on a

TV show. A more advantageous opportunity in Hollywood had presented itself. Langner was sympathetic, but said, "I can only let you go if a suitable replacement is found in time. I'll do my best for you."

Sure enough, he called Kiley some days later and said, "You're in luck. I found a perfect substitute for you last night. He was on some other TV show. In fact, he reminded me of you."

"What was the name of the show?" Kiley asked apprehensively. Langner told him.

"I thought so," sighed Kiley. "That was I."

70. POLITICS

Arthur Hadley's *Do I Make Myself Clear?* is a primer of basic Washingtonese that no visitor to the nation's capital can afford to overlook. Without Hadley to interpret, how could you know, for instance, that when a practiced politico says, "This has been a matter of principle to me since childhood," he means "It's a deal"? "My answer is a definite and final no" is congressional slang for "For the present I'm against it." "A multimillion-dollar giveaway program" means "no money being spent in my district." "The press has not been entirely accurate in its presentation of this affair" is the politician's way of saying "They've caught me lying." And "I am receiving information from businessmen and labor leaders all over the country that the provisions of this law have proved grossly unfair" simply means "My brother-in-law is in trouble!"

★ ★ ★

The candidate for a minor political office in western Texas was renowned for his absolute honesty, and, sure enough, here is the report on expenses of his campaign that he filed along about November 20: "Lost 1,349 hours thinking about the election. Lost two front teeth and a piece of left ear in a personal encounter with my opponent. Donated one beef, four shoats, and six sheep to county barbecues. Gave away 2 pairs of suspenders, 4 calico dresses, and $3 in cash. Kissed 126 babies, walked 977 miles, shook hands with 2,344 people, told 10,000 lies, got bit by 91 dogs, and talked enough nonsense to fill 400 volumes. And, after all that, I was only elected by a 53 majority!"

★ ★ ★

What, demands Bob Sylvester, have the following gentlemen got in common: Elbridge Gerry, George M. Dallas, William R. King, Hannibal Hamlin, Henry Wilson, William A. Wheeler, Thomas A. Hendricks, and Garrett A. Hobart? Well, for one thing, all of them were Vice-Presidents of the United States!

★ ★ ★

You often hear people ask who would take over should both the President and Vice-President of the United States pass away—and surprisingly few people know the answer. According to a statute passed on June 25, 1948, in an emergency of that kind, the Speaker of the House would succeed to the presidency. If there be at the time no Speaker, or, should he fail to qualify, the President pro tempore of the Senate, the Secretaries of State, Treasury, Defense, the Attorney General, Postmaster General, the Secretaries of Interior, Agriculture, Commerce, and of Labor succeed to the office in that order.

★ ★ ★

Senator Theodore Green, frugal millionaire Democrat from Rhode Island, has perfected a rare and effective technique for winning votes. He gives his taxi drivers, waiters, and barbers no tips at all, then tells them, "Be sure to vote Republican!"

★ ★ ★

The late Alben Barkley, lifelong Democrat, once defined a "bureaucrat" as a "Democrat who holds an office that some Republican wants." He added that, when the Republicans say they want to stabilize the farmer, they mean "foreclose on all his stock and move him into the stable." A Republican in the audience got square with the then V.P. by observing that the Democrats were like an iceberg: "10 per cent visible, 90 per cent submerged, and 100 per cent at sea."

★ ★ ★

"You might be interested," suggests Gerald W. Johnson in his book *Peril and Promise* "to discover who was the most successful of all our Presidents, measured by the ability to do everything he promised. It was James K. Polk!"

Polk promised that if he was elected, he would acquire California, settle the Oregon dispute, lower the tariff, establish a sub-treasury, and retire at the end of his first term. He was elected—and accomplished every one of his five major aims. No one ever has even approached that record since.

* * *

Back in 1892, when Adlai Stevenson's grandfather was hitting the whistle stops of the Northwest in his campaign for the vice-presidency, he ran into a local hassle in the state of Washington. Some citizens were insisting that the tallest peak in the Cascades be named Mount Tacoma. Others were equally determined that it be known as Mount Rainier. Inevitably Mr. Stevenson's opinion was sought—so he worked out a deal with the engineer of his special train.

"When I am Vice-President," he would declaim, "I will not rest until this crowning beauty of the great state of Washington is appropriately named. And I am in complete agreement with the worthy gentlemen who insist that that name be ——" At this juncture the engineer would blow a mighty blast on his whistle, and, while its echo was still reverberating, the train would tootle off for the next stop. Mr. Stevenson never did finish that sentence.

* * *

All-time dean of political spellbinders was William Jennings Bryan. Early in his career, Bryan rejoiced in the sobriquet, "The Boy Orator of the River Platte"—and with good reason, jeered a rival, adding, "The River Platte is four feet deep and five miles wide at the mouth."

At the height of his popularity Bryan returned to Nebraska to make a speech. Not only the whole of Omaha turned out for it, but farmers from fifty miles around. Only half the audience could squeeze into the auditorium. Bryan's manager told him, "There are at least five hundred folks outside in their buggies and wagons pining for a word from you. You can't send them away disappointed."

"Find me something to stand on and I'll address them when I've finished inside," said Bryan.

All they could find, unfortunately, was a fertilizer-spreader (that's a nicer name than is usually applied to it!), and of course all the farmers chuckled when Bryan climbed up on it. He was equal to the occasion, however. "My friends," he began cheerfully, "this is the first time in my life I have ever spoken on a Republican platform!"

★ ★ ★

When Teddy Roosevelt was campaigning in the West, a delegation of prim ladies urged him to come out openly against a candidate for the Senate from Utah who was a power in the Mormon Church. "Ladies," said T.R., "I prefer a polygamist who does not polyg to a monogamist who does not monog."

★ ★ ★

Teddy Roosevelt coined many Americanisms that have become part of our language. Examples: pussyfooter, weasel words, lunatic fringe, muckraker, square deal, and malefactors of great wealth.

Another T.R. quote supplied by Hermann Hagedorn, director of the Theodore Roosevelt Centennial Commission: "A typical vice of American politics is the avoidance of saying anything real on real issues, and the announcement of radical policies with much sound and fury, and at the same time with a cautious accomplishment of weasel phrases each of which sucks the meat out of the preceding statement."

★ ★ ★

Timely political squib, from the files of the immortal Will Rogers: "They took me in to meet President Harding, and I said, 'Mr. President, I would like to tell you all the latest jokes.' 'You don't have to, Will,' he answered. 'I appointed them.'"

★ ★ ★

Ethel Barrymore has written about any number of famous men she met in her busy career, but the one who obviously surprised her most was none other than Calvin Coolidge. Obviously she had expected a solemn, taciturn sourball. Instead, she recalled, "Mr. Coolidge made me laugh very, very much. He had an enormous sense of humor he deliberately hid from the people. In fact, he confessed to me, 'I have a feeling the American public prefers a solemn ass for a President. I guess I'll go along with them.'"

★ ★ ★

Shortly after he moved out of the White House, Calvin Coolidge sought recreation and rest at a famous resort hotel. He was pleased with the service and surroundings, but appalled by the bill at the end of his first week.

Seeking the cashier for an explanation of some items on the bill, he recalled some unmailed letters in his pocket. "I'll need some two-cent stamps," he told the cashier's assistant. "Sure thing, Mr. President," said the clerk cheerily. "How many do you want?"

"That depends," said Mr. Coolidge cautiously, "on what you charge for them here."

★ ★ ★

In the 1936 presidential election, when Alf Landon bagged only Maine and Vermont, a friend toted up the returns and sighed, "Tough luck, chief, but I guess the people have spoken." "That they have," admitted Landon ruefully, "but they didn't have to speak quite so loudly."

★ ★ ★

Franklin Delano Roosevelt certainly never lacked self-confidence at crucial moments, but I personally witnessed an exhibition of extraordinary modesty on his part. Invited to visit with him in his White House study shortly before the outbreak of World War II, I found him busily writing his name on the flyleaf of every book in his personal library. He was completely surrounded by piles of volumes.

When I asked the reason for this methodical labor, the President explained, "Visitors to the White House don't seem to realize these books are my personal property, and not the government's. They pilfer them as souvenirs." It never had occurred to F.D.R. that his personal autograph would make every book a hundred times more tempting to souvenir hunters!

★ ★ ★

In the heat of a whirlwind speechmaking tour in the deep South, Franklin Roosevelt once posed for a photograph in a seersucker suit. The late Robert Sherwood admired the result and requested an autographed copy for his study. F.D.R. sent it to him with this inscription: "Here's that seersucker picture, Bob—with affection from the sucker to the seer."

★ ★ ★

Franklin D. Roosevelt told this story on himself at many a dinner party: "A son introduced the new deacon to his father, who was both slightly deaf and a stanch Republican. 'Pa,' said the son, 'here's our new deacon.' 'New DEALER?' echoed Pa. 'No, new deacon,' repeated the son. 'He's a son of a bishop.' That pleased Pa, who agreed happily, 'They all are.'"

★ ★ ★

Herbert Hoover was making his way to the Chicago convention hall in 1952 when a red-faced character jumped past the safety rope and slapped him resoundingly on the back. "Hiya, Herb, old boy?" he chortled. Then, turning to a crony as Mr. Hoover moved angrily along, he boasted, "What did I tell ya, Joe? I never forget a face!"

★ ★ ★

A reporter followed a campaigning senator for three grueling days through the mountainous country of the Southeastern backlands. The senator was well past sixty, but, in those three days, he delivered eighty-one major speeches. "You amaze me," confessed the reporter at the end of the tour. "Here you've delivered eighty-one speeches in three days, and you appear fresher and more full of pep than when you started. How do you do it?"

The senator chuckled. "I didn't deliver eighty-one speeches, my boy," he remarked. "I delivered one speech eighty-one times!"

★ ★ ★

The collector of taxes in a Westchester community asserts that, from a political point of view, his family must be the most mixed up in the country. "I'm a Republican," he explains. "My wife's a Democrat, my kid's wet, my cow's dry, and my cat's on the fence."

★ ★ ★

A tub-thumping politician blew into Dallas and explained the razzing the papers had been giving him by orating, "These heah reporters ain't such bad fellers but they draw such big salaries they ain't in sympathy with plain folks like me."

One reporter duly quoted this statement, then added, "Other hilarious remarks by the speaker were . . ."

★ ★ ★

Thurston Morton tells a story of a political campaign in which, by accident, the Republican and Democratic congressional candidates met at the same time in a town with only one large auditorium.

The sheriff, who had to sweep out the courthouse, told the candidates they'd have to have their meetings at the same time because he didn't intend to sweep twice in one day.

And it was up to this sheriff to introduce the opposing candidates. He arose and said, "I want to present to you a man who, above anyone, has the welfare of each and every one of you at heart. More than anyone I know, he is devoted to our great and glorious state of Kentucky. He understands, as no other man, the problems of our great nation; I know of no other who is so expert in for'gn affairs, economics, education, taxation. . . ."

Then the sheriff turned to the candidates and asked: "Which of you polecats wants to talk first?"

71. PSYCHIATRY

There was a resident in a swank Park Avenue apartment who fancied that a live alligator was lurking outside his penthouse every morning. "Darnedest hallucination I ever heard of," admitted his psychiatrist, "but if anybody can cure you, it is I." Five visits later, the doctor felt he had made astonishing progress, and it was with a jaunty step that he came round for Visit Number Six. There was no sign of the patient, however, so the doctor made inquiries of the building superintendent.

"Haven't you heard?" sighed the superintendent. "When poor Mr. Jones came out of his penthouse yesterday afternoon, an alligator ate him."

★ ★ ★

An obviously distressed gent staggered into a psychiatrist's office and begged, "Doctor, you've got to help me. Every night I dream I'm marooned on a desert island with a dozen blondes, a dozen brunettes, and a dozen redheads—each one more beautiful than the rest." "You sound like one of the luckiest men alive," marveled the psychiatrist. "What do you need help for?" "My problem," sobbed the patient, "is that in my dream I'm also a girl."

★ ★ ★

A bemused Park Avenue analyst was compelled to ask a new client to repeat what he just had said. Complied the patient, "I said that for some reason people don't seem to like me. Pay attention, you overpaid fathead!"

★ ★ ★

Herb Stein met a Los Angeles psychiatrist who drank too much and saw pink Oscar Levants.

★ ★ ★

An indignant lady charged into a psychiatrist's office to demand, "You'll have to take my husband in hand—but quick. He's convinced himself he's a big-league baseball manager and keeps throwing baseballs at me."

"Why don't you order him to stop?" asked the psychiatrist.

"I'm afraid to," admitted the lady. "He keeps threatening to trade me to Philadelphia."

★ ★ ★

"My problem is my son," a lady announced to a new psychoanalyst. "He spends the entire day making mud pies, then eating them."

"That's not too serious a problem," the analyst assured her. "The same preoccupation pops up repeatedly in child behavior."

"Well, I don't like it," snapped the lady, "and neither does his wife."

★ ★ ★

"What do you mean, psychiatry hasn't helped me?" an indignant believer snapped at his skeptical wife. "A year ago when the phone rang, I wouldn't answer it. Today I answer it whether it rings or not."

★ ★ ★

A mixed-up industrialist who's been haunting psychoanalysts for seven years explained to his accountant, "It's not the cost of the analysis that bothers me; it's all the loose change that slips out of my pockets while I'm lying on the couch!"

★ ★ ★

A Chicago psychiatrist encountered a challenging problem in the person of a patient who was absolutely convinced he was in love with an elephant. After endless sessions on the couch, the analyst convinced the poor fellow it all had been a hallucination. "O.K., so I'm cured," nodded the patient weakly, "but now I've got another problem you must solve for me." "What now?" asked the analyst wearily.

The patient demanded, "Do you happen to know somebody in the market for one mighty big engagement ring?"

★ ★ ★

A neurotic movie queen was overjoyed when a psychiatrist rented her home in Palm Springs. "At last," she chortled, "I've got him lying on MY couch!"

★ ★ ★

An immaculately dressed but obviously distressed patient stretched out on a psychiatrist's couch for his first session, and began, "First, a word about my present status in life. I live with my family on a forty-acre estate with a tennis court, swimming pool, private golf range, and five-car garage. I also own a town house, yacht, and helicopter. My son is at Groton, my daughter at an exclusive finishing school outside Washington. And my wife, who adores me, is beautiful, and consistently voted one of the ten best dressed women of the year."

"Sounds like a perfect setup," said the analyst enviously. "Why do you need me?"

"I've got to know how to keep going," admitted the patient, "without lowering my standards. You see, my salary is only fifty dollars a week."

72. PUN-AMERICAN
CONFERENCE

The Pun-American Conference opens a new session by bestowing upon literateur Edmund Fuller, of Kent, Connecticut, first prize (a copy of *The Story of Bridey Murphy* and a calendar for 1928) for his double pun about a gentleman who brought home food for his dog. It was an Italian dish, compounded of flour, cheese, and tomatoes, and the thoughtful master tilted it against a door to make it more accessible for the lazy pooch. Then he summoned his wife and told her cheerfully, "There's no longer any need for you to plan that sight-seeing trip to Italy next summer. Here, before your very eyes, is the leaning Pizza of Towser." Wow, sir!

★ ★ ★

Mrs. R. A. Henry, weary of fractured French, thinks it's time for some splintered Spanish, and starts the ball rolling with

I COMO NO! — Let's listen to Eddie Fisher.

MUCHAS GRACIAS — The lawn needs mowing.

LA SOPA ES FRIA — Sample box of soap.

ESTOY LISTO — Santa Claus's notebook.

ESO SI — Fill 'er up.

LO SIENTO — Cheap perfume.

AL CINDAD — So long, Pop.

★ ★ ★

Joe Onsrud tells about a Wisconsin trapper who came to town to buy a case of soft drinks and a copy of *Of Human Bondage*. He left both on a table in a lunchroom and wandered about for a while. When he came back, the book had disappeared. "You having some trouble?" asked the proprietor. "I sure am," answered the trapper. "I've found my pop but I've lost my Maugham!"

★ ★ ★

An intrepid hunter in the lush jungles of Ceylon was so intent upon bagging a treacherous leopard that, in the excitement, his false teeth fell out. Ever since the poor man has been searching for his bridge on the River Kwai.

★ ★ ★

In feudal England, stouthearted Lord Elford complained, "Every noble in Britain but me has a moat around his castle. I want *two* built—and I want them fast." Elford's serfs (no relations) refused at first, but found a company of tough-looking bow-and-arrow boys mighty persuasive. "O.K.," conceded the leader of the serfs, "we dig you the moats."

★ ★ ★

John Dutt, of Huron, Ohio, tells of a golf club faced with an all-too-familiar problem: the ladies, who had all week in which to play, insisted on hogging the course on weekends as well. Things reached such a pass that infuriated men's foursomes began a weekly game of skill to see who could hit a ball closest to the gals without actually creaming them. The idea was, of course, to irritate the dear girls enough to make them quit entirely or at least wave the faster males through.

Word of these shenanigans finally reached the chairman of the greens committee, who promptly posted this sign at the first tee:

DRIVE CAREFULLY!
THE WIFE YOU SHAVE MAY BE YOUR OWN!

★ ★ ★

Katheleen Hempel, of El Kador, Iowa, knows a farmer named Schubert. What's more,

Schubert had a horse named Sarah.
He drove her to the big parade.
And all the time the band was playing
Schubert's Sarah neighed.

★ ★ ★

David Hulburd saw an unfortunate state assemblyman rendered *hors de combat* when his wife socked him on the head with a heavy glass lampshade. "There's one lady," pointed out Mr. Hulburd, "who conks to stupor."

★ ★ ★

The trustees of the Barcelona Zoo read that there were only thirty-four whooping cranes left in the United States and determined that they must have one before the breed became extinct. Never mind what Spanish wiles they had to exercise to fulfill their ambition; suffice it to say that a whooping crane was dispatched via air freight in due course, and consigned to the Barcelona Zoo.

Alas, when the fool bird arrived at the Barcelona airport, he flatly refused to debark, and the broken-hearted trustees had to return empty-handed to their zoo.

The moral of this story is that cranes in Spain stick mainly to the plane.

★ ★ ★

It was in Barcelona, too, according to S. K. Jaynes, Jr., of Richmond, Virginia, that a mammoth celebration was planned to honor the memory of Don Quixote de la Mancha. Unfortunately, the dancing master discovered suddenly that while he had twelve hundred beautiful maidens available for the gala, only nine hundred *caballeros* had volunteered.

It was the mayor of Barcelona who remedied the situation. Mounting his faithful Arabian steed, he galloped to the home of his great, good friend, the mayor of the neighboring city of Tarragona. "I need your help," he announced bluntly. "HOW ARE YOU FIXED FOR BLADES?"

★ ★ ★

Malcolm Ferguson of West Concord, Massachusetts, has encountered, of all things, a Chinese professor of geometry who dearly enjoys his work. To Ferguson he confided happily, "I love, I love, I love my wife, but oh, Euclid."

★ ★ ★

Clifton Fadiman, renowned critic and TV star, recalls a small boy who delighted in meeting Patrolman O'Reilly on the same corner each morning. He would buy a doughnut and feed it regularly to O'Reilly's grateful horse. One morning the horse would have none of the doughnut, however. "What's wrong with Brownie today?" asked the puzzled urchin. To which O'Reilly replied, "Oh, this isn't Brownie. This is a horse of a different cruller."

★ ★ ★

"I double dare you," writes an exceedingly rash St. Louisan named "Cubby" Baer, "to print the ten most groan-provoking puns you've heard in the past six months." No Cerf has refused a double dare since Jack Benny was thirty-eight years old.

Try the following, Mr. Baer, for sighs:

1. Remember the little Dutch boy who held his finger in a hole in the dike until the break could be repaired and thus saved the country from inundation? Florian Sybeldon, of Royal Oaks, Michigan, has discovered what the boy said when grateful citizens pressed him for a speech: "Please, not tonight, folks. I've had a tough day at the orifice!"

2. Carl Testa, of Los Angeles, has learned somehow of a lady in far-off Tibet who smelled something burning one day, and rushed out to the barn, moaning, "Oh, my bakin' yak!"

3. Mexican's alibi when charged with pushing his wife over a precipice: "Honest, Judge, I was just trying tequila!"

4. Professor William Parker, of Indiana University, suggests that the New York schools now devoted to recalcitrant and incorrigible students be designated P.S. de résistance.

5. In Boston, Dick Harrington ran into one of those fuss-budgets

who's always making mountains out of molehills. When he makes a mistake, of course, it's a butte.

6. An old Mississippi showboat captain had eleven children and thirty-two grandchildren. This was one man who bred his cast upon the waters.

7. A suspiciously well-dressed panhandler tried to pry Eddie Cantor loose from a ten-dollar bill at a broadcasting studio. "Not to you, you mountebank," stormed Eddie. "You look prosperous enough to take a de luxe tour of the West Indies." "Alas, no," mourned the panhandler. "Beggars cannot be cruisers."

8. A kindly Iowan visited a neighbor who was making butter, so he pitched in and helped. The next day the neighbor returned the call, and said, "Now I want to help you. One good churn deserves another."

9. K. M. Linhoff, of Long Beach, California, reports that a crook broke into his pigpen last week. "Now," he concludes mournfully, "I haven't got mahogany more."

10. In San Antonio, confides paronomasian (I had to look it up, too) Keith Elliott, two cooks in a drive-in restaurant were told by the boss to water the soup when the supply ran low. Their pride hurt and their honor impugned, they still had to carry out the order. And how did they address the soup? "We who are about to sigh dilute you."

And that ought to hold Mr. "Cubby" Baer for a while!

★ ★ ★

A certain Mr. Chan collected teakwood miniatures as a hobby, but began to notice that they were disappearing, one by one, in the dead of night. Furthermore, muddy footprints on the floor seemed to indicate that the culprit was a small, barefoot boy.

Determined to put an end to all this, Mr. Chan hid himself in the corner of his shop one night. His vigil was rewarded. In came the thief—and it turned out to be a black bear, who promptly started loading up with teakwood. A peculiar feature of this bear: instead of claws, he had the feet of a little boy.

What could be more natural under the circumstances than the agonized cry from the victim: "Hey, there! Where do you think you're going, oh, boy-foot bear with teaks of Chan?"

★ ★ ★

A hunter in Tsarist Russia persuaded a lady of noble birth to accept his suit. For their wedding supper he shot a wild boar. "My love," he apologized, "I know you are accustomed to caviar, champagne, and roasted peacock, but this is all . . ." "Enough," she interrupted. "I care not what I eat so long as we are together." Inspired by his bride's gastronomic heroism, the hunter immediately composed the opera that was to immortalize his name: "Boar Is Good Enough."

★ ★ ★

Miss Kitty Enton, who lives away off in Surrey, England—although she may be asked to move after this story appears in print—tells about an old squire who loved to putter about his garden, attended by a cockney gardener who worshiped the ground on which he puttered.

Two sailors hove into view one day, and the bolder of them hollered, "Hi, Pop, what kind of a tree is that you're spraying?"

"It's a peach tree," said the squire.

"You're wrong," countered the two sailors together. "It's a pear tree!"

The cockney gardener was not used to hearing his master disputed. He shook his finger angrily at the sailors and exclaimed, "'E knows fruit, salts."

★ ★ ★

Two old Yale classmates met at a reunion and recalled a siren from Vassar they both had dated in the good old days. "I saw her at a country club dance last week," sighed one. "Her figure is more sylphlike than ever." "Yes," answered the other resentfully, "and I'll bet she's still keeping it to her sylph, too."

★ ★ ★

I was dining the other evening at the home of Miss Madeline Fraser, a VIP of the San Fernando Valley, when, without warning, she whipped out a papyrus containing the following story and demanded that I print it. What could I do. Miss Fraser was the hostess. I was merely aghast.

"DEER girl," chortled OWL man Conley, "my pa's sister in TURKEY—you know, my FEZ-AUNT—finally came through and mailed me that hundred BUCKS she owed me."

"WALLABY a son-of-a-gun!" chortled Mrs. Conley. "OCELOT of DOE. How's for GIBBON some to baby?"

"I let my secretary BURRO it," admitted Mr. Conley SHEEP-ishly.

"That peROCside CHEETAH! EWE did this on PORPOISE," shrilled his outraged wife. At tense moments like this she frequently lapsed into a French patois she had picked up in LYONS. "I MOOSE keel her one day," she snarled. "No wonder ze loafers WEASEL at her from street corners! Her dress eet ees always too low: ZE BRA show!"

"OSTRICH to the facts," suggested Conley wearily, "and POS-SUM of those GNU spareribs you've been cooking. I declare, that recipe ought to be triple-starred in the next BULL-etin of Miss Duncan HYENA'S!"

Completely mollified, Mrs. Conley beamed, "I could eat a PLAT-TER, PUSS, myself! But BEAR in mind that Duncan is not a miss. He's a MON, GOOSE!"

CUR-TAIN

★ ★ ★

In darkest Africa, explorer Henry Morgan uncovered an ebony-hued gentleman who did everything backward. At the annual festival where his tribe would gather on the left bank of a river and exchange wives—a quaint local custom—this contrary gentleman invariably turned up on the right bank of the river. Why? Because he didn't know which side his bride was bartered on.

Henry also accepted the challenge that he couldn't invent a pun on the word "hippopotami." He riffled through the pages of Shakespeare and came up with "Oh, what a rogue and hippopotami."

73. QUICKIES

Many *aficionados* of the neatly turned phrase will assure you that no joke worth retelling should exceed forty words. This theory always has been abhorrent, of course, to ink-stained wretches who write on space rates, and particularly enraged the late Alexander Woollcott, who grew rich embroidering three-line wisecracks into six-page essays.

This section is specially tailored for those who read while they run, and like their stories short and snappy.

★ ★ ★

A reigning movie queen awoke one morning with a ringing in her ears—so she got an unlisted ear.

Hermann Schnapps is the name of one of the town's trustiest winetasters. He's unsteadily employed.

★ ★ ★

Colonel Corncrib is embarked upon nothing less than a brand-new alphabet book. It begins, "A is for ATOM, and if it's turned loose, the twenty-five other letters will be of no use."

A prominent television sponsor just dropped his summer replacement. His wife came back to town.

"Comes the end of November," sighs Jack Benny's Rochester, "and I can always tell the exact moment Mr. Winter knocks on the door: my janitor finally turns off the steam heat!"

Cheer up, counsels L. S. McCandless. You can still use a dime for a screwdriver.

You must have heard about the cowardly counterfeiter. He still has the first dollar he ever made.

Too bad about that inspector at the mattress factory. He was discharged for falling awake on the job.

Dallas millionaire Dealy decided to take up fishing. So he bought a dollar rod, a dollar reel—and the Gulf of Mexico.

Banker Schucat admits to disciples, "It isn't often I risk a verbal encounter with my wife, but when I do words flail me."

Author Joey Adams was the victim of a freakish accident. His wife Cindy demurred at crossing the street to buy him a pack of cigarettes, so he ran over himself.

Many tried-and-true fairy tales have had to be revised for kiddies of the TV age. One of them now begins: "Once upon a time there were three bears: the small size, the regular size, and the giant economy size." Another: "Once upon a time there was a farmer who made a fortune out of the wild oats on his farm. He caught a millionaire sowing some with his daughter."

A novel complaint has been registered by toilers at the U.S. Mint. They want to make less money.

"It's not always wise to organize your life so that you avoid your father's mistakes," warns Rev. Edward Rogers. "All that usually happens is that you make your grandfather's mistakes."

Boris Karloff, at a small motel, explained, "My demands are modest. I just want a small place to hang my hat and a few friends."

A librarian pointed proudly to a patron exiting with four books under her arm. "That lady," boasted the librarian, "gets more out of a mystery novel than any other reader in town. She begins every whodunit in the middle, so she not only wonders how it will come out, but also how it began."

A customer in a big department store asked the very Irish porter, "Do you know where the Chintz Room is?" "That I do," he replied promptly, and pointed to a door labeled "Men."

"The honeymoon is over," sighs Robert Wagner, "when the bridegroom stops helping with the dishes—and does them by himself."

A mother found her young daughter curled up with a book, and crying her pretty little eyes out. "Such an unhappy ending," wailed the dear child. "The heroine dies on the last page and the man has to go back to his wife."

One lady driver has found a foolproof way to avoid parking tickets. She just removes the windshield wipers. . . . Another lady, after a long luncheon with the "girls," staggered into a taxi, pulled a card out of her purse, and told the driver, "Take me to that address." "That's not an address," he corrected her. "That's a picture of you in a one-piece bathing suit." "So all right," she nodded haughtily. "Drive me to the beach."

"My garden was such a success this year," boasted a gentleman farmer, "that my neighbor's chickens won first prize at the poultry show."

"If I had my life to live over," sighs comedian Lew Parker, "I'd live over a saloon."

"Golly," exclaimed a husband, "this liniment makes my shoulders smart." Suggested his wife, "Why not rub some on your head?"

A Purdue graduate returned home from his twenty-fifth class reunion in a very chastened mood. "My classmates," he told his wife sadly, "have all gotten so fat and bald they didn't even recognize me."

74. QUOTATIONS

DR. KONRAD ADENAUER: An infallible method of conciliating a tiger is to allow oneself to be devoured.

LOUIS AGASSIZ: Every great scientific truth goes through three stages. First, people say it conflicts with the Bible. Next, they say it has been discovered before. Lastly, they say they have always believed it.

SHOLEM ALEICHEM: If somebody tells you you have ears like a donkey, pay no attention. But if two people tell you, buy yourself a saddle.

BUGS BAER: Alimony is like buying oats for a dead horse.

AMBROSE BIERCE: Acquaintance is a degree of friendship called slight when its object is poor or obscure, and intimate when he is rich or famous.

JOSH BILLINGS: Consider the postage stamp. Its usefulness consists in the ability to stick to one thing till it gets there.

DALE CARNEGIE: Success is getting what you want; happiness is wanting what you get.

MAURICE CHEVALIER: When you hit seventy, you eat better, you sleep sounder, you feel more alive than when you were thirty. Obviously, it's healthier to have women on your mind than on your knees.

WINSTON CHURCHILL: Eating words has never given me indigestion.

PETER FINLEY DUNN: When ye build yer triumphant arch to yer

conquerin' hero, build it out of brick—so the people will have some-thin' convenient to throw at him as he passes through.

WILL DURANT: Truth always originates in a minority of one, and every custom begins as a broken precedent.

ANATOLE FRANCE: If fifty million people say a foolish thing, it is still a foolish thing.

BENJAMIN FRANKLIN: The first mistake in politics is the going into it.

BENJAMIN FRANKLIN (upon discovering electricity): Ouch!

OLIVER ST. JOHN GOGARTY: We are part of what has gone before. Parcels of the past guide us. What we call the present is only a suburb of the past.

TOM GRIFFIN: One good turn usually gets the whole blanket.

HEINRICH HEINE: Why admire a rose as an aristocrat? Admire the democratic potato. For centuries it has nourished nations.

OLIVER HERFORD: Actresses will happen in the best regulated families.

E. W. HOWE: If you want to know how old a woman is, ask her sister-in-law.

CORDELL HULL: Never insult an alligator till after you have crossed the river.

DEAN JOHNSON: Duty is a task we look forward to with distaste, perform with reluctance—and brag about afterward.

C. F. KETTERING: If you want to kill any idea in the world today, get a committee working on it.

THE KINGFISH (Remember Amos and Andy?): Relatives is like radishes. Just when you think you has heard the last of them, there they is again.

JOE E. LEWIS: Conditions have gotten so bad in transportation they tell me the Mississippi River now only runs three times a week.

LIN YUTANG: All women's dresses are merely variations on the eternal struggle between the admitted desire to dress and the un-admitted desire to undress.

ABE MARTIN: You can tell how healthy a man is by what he takes two at a time—stairs or pills.

ABE MARTIN: It's impossible to enjoy doing nothing thoroughly unless you have a very great deal of work to do.

GEORGE JEAN NATHAN: I drink only to make other people interesting.

BILL NYE: If you could kick in the pants the fellow responsible for most of your troubles, you wouldn't be able to sit down for six months.

ROLFE PETERSON: When you think you're going down for the third time—just remember: you may have counted wrong.

GEORGE PHAIR: The difference between horse races and political races is that in a horse race the whole horse wins.

WILLIAM LYON PHELPS: A man can always borrow trouble. It's the only thing for which he needs no collateral.

WALTER PITKIN: A man wrapped up in himself makes a mighty small package.

WILLIAM PITT: Necessity is the plea for every infringement of human freedom. It is the argument of tyrants.

G. D. PRENTICE: About the only person I ever heard of who wasn't spoiled by being lionized was that Bible character Daniel.

TERRY RATTIGAN: There are a powerful lot of strings to a man's life: apron, heart, purse, and harp.

LOWELL REDELINGS: Money doesn't talk these days. It just goes without saying.

WILL ROGERS: Politics has got so expensive that it takes a lot of money to even get beat with. Card playing can be expensive, too, but so is any game where you hold hands.

GEORGE BERNARD SHAW: England and America are two countries separated by the same language.

GEORGE BERNARD SHAW (Modestly): I often quote myself. It adds spice to the conversation.

EDWARD SHELDON: God will look you over, not for medals, diplomas, or degrees, but for scars.

SYDNEY SMITH: The best way of answering a bad argument is to let it go on.

HAL STEBBINS: A good listener is usually thinking about something else.

JONATHAN SWIFT: The best doctors in the world are Dr. Diet, Dr. Quiet, and Dr. Merryman.

SIDNEY TREMAYNE: Letters that should never have been written and ought to be immediately destroyed are the only ones worth keeping.

MARK TWAIN: By trying, we can easily learn to endure adversity —another man's, I mean.

MARK TWAIN: Never meddle with old unloaded firearms: they are the most deadly and unerring things that have ever been created by man. You don't have to have a rest; you don't have to have any sights on the gun; you don't have to take aim, even. You just pick out a relative and bang away at him, and you're sure to get him. A youth who can't hit a cathedral at thirty yards with a cannon in three-quarters of an hour can take up an old empty musket and bag his grandmother every time, at a hundred.

And here are a few eipgrams of OSCAR WILDE's you may not have encountered before:

If one could only teach the English how to talk and the Irish how to listen, society in London would be more civilized.

Nowadays most people die of a sort of creeping common sense, and discover when it is too late that the only things one never regrets are one's mistakes.

An idea that is not dangerous is unworthy of being called an idea at all.

Murder is always a mistake. One should never do anything that one cannot talk about after dinner.

The difference between literature and journalism is that journalism is unreadable and literature is unread.

75. RAILROADS

Readers interested in the early days of railroading will do well to consult August Mencken's *The Railroad Passenger Car*. "Rails in the 1870's," recalls Mencken, "were constantly coming loose, and occasionally one of them would curl up through the floor of the car and transfix a passenger." Following an attempt to get some rest in an Erie sleeping car of the period, Horace Greeley protested to the head of the road, "I was left gasping like a netted fish on a hot sandbank."

Passengers in those days, in fact, rather expected an accident somewhere along the line. Porters instructed folks how to "place themselves, laying great stress on the importance of sitting diagonally in order not to receive the shock directly on the knees when the anticipated collision ensued."

★ ★ ★

Old railroad buffs tend to get misty-eyed at mention of one of their favorite roads—the old Jupiter and Lake Worth line on the eastern coast of Florida. Passengers referred to it fondly as the Celestial Road because the four stations on its eight miles of track bore the names of Jupiter, Venus, Mars, and Juno!

Another tiny railroad, still in operation, is known as the Ma and Pa. Officially, it is the Maryland and Pennsylvania, and runs between York, Pennsylvania, and Baltimore.

In the good old days, when our railroads were actually allowed to make a little money, annual passes were handed out rather freely to political bigwigs, newspaper VIP's, etc. Of course they were stamped "non-transferable," but that was just an invitation to petty skulduggery.

Historian B. A. Botkin tells of a day when the conductor on an L. and N. express collared a journalist who flashed a dubious pass, claiming airily, "I'm the Frank Smith for whom this pass was issued all right. I work for Colonel Henry Watterson." "That's just fine," exulted the conductor. "Colonel Watterson happens to be in the next car forward. We'll see if he can identify you."

The journalist figured that the jig was up, but to his surprise, the colonel nodded, "Yes, that's my man Smith. Sit down here, my boy." When the defeated conductor had departed, "Smith" started to say thank you, but his companion silenced him. "Compose yourself," he smiled. "I'm not Colonel Watterson. I'm traveling on a borrowed pass, too!"

★ ★ ★

Latest thing to be modernized and "prettied up" is the old railroad caboose. Bill Feather reports that the Thrall Car Manufacturing Company of Chicago has created a caboose that has as many trimmings and de luxe features—including bay windows, air conditioning, and electric gadgets—as a 1960 de luxe auto trailer. Roads that have acquired some of these new cabooses include the Burlington, Lackawanna, Great Northern, Milwaukee, and Frisco.

★ ★ ★

Are you confused by the elaborate series of signs and symbols in a typical railroad timetable? Caskie Stinnett adds a few to make things even worse:

T — Stops on signal to discharge card players carried through last three stations by mistake.

XX — No diner, but sandwich man boards train en route with sandwiches left over from southbound trip.

† † — Change for Chicago train. This train usually misses connection. (Stay at Roadside Inn. Advt.)

C/O — Stops only to discharge passengers who think they can

make better time by telephoning wives to for Pete's sake climb into their station wagon and come and rescue them.

★ ★ ★

The passenger in Upper Berth Number 7 ps-s-s-ed the conductor and asked, "Will you please bring me a glass of water?" "That's the tenth glass of water you've demanded in the past twenty minutes," protested the conductor. "I never heard of anybody drinking so much water."

"I'm not drinking it," said the passenger. "My berth is on fire."

★ ★ ★

A blizzard was raging in Iowa, and a railroad locomotive was stalled by the snow. A section foreman struggled up to the engineer, who was standing beside the track beating his arms across his chest.

"Hi, Tom," called the foreman. "Where's your fireman?"

"He's up in the cab," answered the engineer. "Poor guy got knocked unconscious by a piece of flying ice. Serves him right, I guess. He tried to spit against the wind!"

★ ★ ★

A graduate of the Lewis School for Stammerers met a friend aboard an accommodation train of the Boston and Maine and asked where he was heading.

"I'm g-g-going to the L-l-lewis School to c-c-cure my s-s-stammering," explained the friend.

"G-g-great," enthused the graduate. "They'll c-c-cure you for sure. They c-c-cured me!"

★ ★ ★

A frail, timid lady was crying hysterically in the aisle of a Pullman car. There was a mouse in her drawing room, it seemed.

The porter and conductor finally calmed her. Furthermore, she was absolutely right. There *was* a mouse in her drawing room. She had brought it aboard herself—in a shoebox—and released it when she deemed the moment ripe.

The railroad police maintain a protective section to round up just such petty chiselers as the frail little lady. She had collected "nuisance fees" from a dozen railroads for this same "mouse" dodge before they got wise to her little act.

★ ★ ★

A businessman bound from New York to the Middle West climbed aboard one of those economy-minded railroad trains, sat down at a clothless table in the diner and demanded a three-inch sirloin, smothered in mushrooms, béarnaise sauce, and French fries. The waiter eyed him pityingly and commented, "Are you ordering, sir, or reminiscing?"

★ ★ ★

An English lady, aboard an international train that originated in Switzerland, grew very fidgety as her train neared the border. She had struck up an acquaintance with a very friendly fellow passenger earlier in the journey, and now confided to him, "I mean to smuggle in this wristwatch I'm wearing, and I don't mind telling you I'm nervous as a cat about it."

A customs inspector marched into the compartment in due course and smiled, "I don't suppose either of you has failed to declare any dutiable objects." Almost casually, the man pointed to the lady's watch and said, "I believe you'll find our friend here has overlooked that little bauble."

The watch was confiscated, while the lady dissolved into tears. When the train was in motion again, she demanded of her informer, "How could you be such a swine?"

The man pulled a valise out from under his seat and opened it, revealing a cache of at least a hundred shiny, new watches. "Don't take it so hard, lady," he advised. "Help yourself to any two of them!"

★ ★ ★

Nine-year-old Marion, taken by her parents for her first transcontinental rail journey, was thrilled when the train plunged into a long tunnel in the Rockies. When it finally emerged at the other end, Marion exclaimed, "Look, Mom! It's tomorrow!"

76. RELIGION

Bernard Baruch's best-selling autobiography includes not only his recollections of world-famous personages, but affectionate stories of the simple folk he met down at his Carolina plantation.

One thing that impressed him about his servitors in the South was their fortunate faculty for making their religion meet their exact needs, accepting this and rejecting that. One old gentleman, for example, suddenly felt the time had come to be taken into the bosom of the church.

"Abraham," warned his parson, "you must have faith. Do you believe everything in the Bible?"

"Yes, suh," insisted Abraham.

"Do you believe the story of Jonah and the whale? And Daniel and the lions? Those hungry African lions what hadn't a thing to eat? Daniel, you know, walks right into their den, and slaps 'em in the face, and they don't do nothing to him."

"If that's what the Bible say, I believes it."

"And do you believe the story of the Hebrew children in the fiery furnace? They walks right into that furnace, steps on the hot coals, and they ain't even singed."

"Not even singed? A regular fire?"

"Right! Not even singed."

"Deacon," said Abraham, "I don't believe that."

"Then you can't be taken into the bosom of the church."

Abraham sadly picked up his hat and shuffled toward the door. Looking back, he added, "And, Parson, I don't believe that story 'bout Daniel and the lions, either."

★ ★ ★

Another parson down South lost every penny of the church funds gambling on the horses, and then lit out. A posse was organized to track him down.

"Gonna lynch him when you find him?" the leader of the posse was asked. "I should say not," he replied. "We're gonna bring the varmint right back here—and make him preach it out."

★ ★ ★

A chap named Charlie took an active part in just about everything that was going on in his pleasant little home town but church services. Try as she would, his wife just couldn't seem to talk him into attending services on Sunday morning.

One Sunday, however, she broke down his resistance, and even persuaded him to greet people at the door. He hailed almost everybody by their first name, until the church was filled and the services about to begin.

At the last moment a straggler appeared. Charlie shook his hand, told him how glad he was to see him in church, and expressed the hope he'd be back the following Sunday.

"I'll be back all right," the straggler assured him cheerfully, then walked down the aisle and up into the pulpit to start the services.

★ ★ ★

The new young preacher of a Texas congregation slaved over his first sermon, and marched off to church with high hopes. To his consternation, however, only one lone man had turned up to hear him. "What am I supposed to do now?" inquired the crestfallen preacher.

"I'm just a simple cowhand," responded the lone parishioner, "and don't know too much—but if I took a load of hay to the pasture and only one cow showed up, I sure would feed her."

So the preacher went through with his carefully prepared sermon just as though the church was packed. At its conclusion he asked his single listener, "How did I do?"

"Well," was the answer, "like I said, I'm only a cowhand, but if I took a load of hay to the pasture for a herd of cows and only one cow showed up—I sure wouldn't give her the whole load!"

★ ★ ★

Two goldfish, relates Walter Cronkite, were swimming around and around in a glass bowl. One announced crankily that he had become an atheist. "Fine, fine," scoffed the other. "Now just explain to me who changes the water in this bowl!"

★ ★ ★

The Baptist minister had come for Sunday dinner and six-year-old Susan Mae was dressed up in her very best for the occasion. All went well until the minister asked Susan Mae what she wanted to be when she grew up. "A dog," she announced. Susan Mae's mother yanked her out of the room, gave her a piece of what for, and marched her back to the minister's side. "Susan Mae is ready to give you a sensible answer now," she reported.

"That's splendid," said the minister. "What is it you really want to be when you grow up?" he coaxed. Susan Mae glared at her mother and declared, "A pony."

★ ★ ★

The Johnson family—*père, mère,* and seven offspring—were an estimable brood, but sadly delinquent in their attendance at the Baptist Church. Joe Garretson, of Cincinnati, tells how the good ladies of the church called on the Johnsons in an attempt to remedy the situation. The Johnsons maintained that they couldn't come to church because they didn't have the clothes.

The Baptist ladies thereupon fitted them out in fine style, but the following Sunday not one Johnson turned up at church. The Baptist ladies went round indignantly to demand how come. "We put on all those fine clothes you sent," explained Mrs. Johnson, "and we looked so elegant we went to the Episcopal Church!"

★ ★ ★

Skeptics have pooh-poohed every great advance of science and every outstanding invention. Autos, radio, television, movies—

none of them were practical, to hear the standpatters tell it. Eighty years ago a bishop in the Middle West preached a sermon castigating visionaries who dared predict that one day men would fly through the air like birds. "Flight is reserved for the angels," thundered the good bishop, "and to say men will fly is downright blasphemy."

The name of this bishop, incidentally, was Milton Wright. He had two sons, one named Orville, the other Wilbur.

★ ★ ★

George Ade, motoring in Indiana, ran plumb into a convention of ministers one evening. When they discovered Ade's identity, the ministers clustered round him to shake hands. One asked, "How does a humorist of your stamp, sir, feel in such reverend company as this?" "I feel," admitted Mr. Ade, "like a lion in a den of Daniels."

★ ★ ★

A progressive parson in Phoenix, Arizona (where the tempera ture hovers around the one hundred mark most of the summer), has a reminder for his congregation that has upped the attendance record week after week. "Ho, ho, my friends," he nods cheerfully, "so you think it's hot HERE?"

★ ★ ★

A kindly country parson who had just married a young couple had a parting word for the groom: "Son, God bless you. You're at the end of all your troubles." A year later, the groom returned to the scene of the crime and moaned, "What a year I've gone through! And you're the man who told me I was at the end of my troubles."

"So I did, son," smiled the parson. "I just didn't tell you which end."

★ ★ ★

Rep. Harold Cooley, of North Carolina, tells about a preacher who grew concerned about the spiritual welfare of a pretty, young, and frivolous widow in his congregation. Meeting her on the street one morning, he assured her, "Last night I prayed for you for two solid hours." The young widow dimpled and said, coyly, "Why, Reverend, you needn't have gone to all that trouble. If you had just called me on the phone, I could have been over in fifteen minutes."

★ ★ ★

The noted clergyman, Dr. S. Parker Cadman, received one morning a letter from a youth upstate, inquiring, "Is it possible to lead a good Christian life in New York City on eighteen dollars a week?" "My dear boy," replied Dr. Cadman, "that's about all you *can* do."

★ ★ ★

A spry old party of eighty suddenly decided to marry a blond (and avaricious) maid of seventeen. The clergyman took one look at the pair, and observed, "The font is at the other end of the church." "What do I want with the font?" queried the old gent. "Oh, I beg your pardon," said the clergyman, with a straight face, "I thought you had brought your grandchild to be christened."

★ ★ ★

The archbishop had preached a rousing sermon on the beauties of married life. Two buxom Irish ladies left the church feeling uplifted and contented.

"'Tis a fine sermon His Reverence gave us this morning," observed one.

"That it was," agreed the other, "and I wish I knew as little about the matter as he does."

★ ★ ★

"King Solomon," declares a little girl in Sunday school, "is my favorite character in the Bible—because he was so kind to ladies and animals." The startled teacher demanded, "Who told you that?" "Nobody told me; I read it myself in the Bible," asserted the little girl. "It says Solomon kept seven hundred wives and three hundred porcupines."

★ ★ ★

Robert Goodrich writes about an elderly gentleman, ambling through his garden, who overheard his granddaughter repeating the alphabet in an oddly reverent sort of way. "What on earth are you up to?" he asked her.

The little girl explained, "I'm praying, Grandpa. I can't think of exactly the right words, so I'm just saying all the letters, and God will put them together for me, 'cause he knows what I'm thinking."

★ ★ ★

The late Alben Barkley told the story of a certain minister who was fired summarily by his board of deacons, and put up a powerful protest. "Didn't I argufy?" he demanded. "Didn't I magnify? Didn't I glorify?" "Yes," admitted the deacons, "you argufied, you magnified, and you glorified real good, but you never told us wherein. And we're out to get us a preacher who will tell us wherein."

★ ★ ★

Jim Hawkins harks back happily to the time a social-climbing lady found herself seated at a big public dinner between a noted bishop and an equally famous rabbi.

"I feel as if I were a leaf between the Old and the New Testaments," she announced coyly—interrupting the bishop just as he was about to make a telling point. The bishop, distinctly annoyed, eyed her coldly and remarked, "That page, madam, is usually blank."

★ ★ ★

An Irish priest up Boston way delivered a number of fiery sermons denouncing the British, and was finally ordered by his superiors to lay off at once. Grumpily he steered clear of the subject for a month, then announced that he was going to tell the story of the Last Supper.

"Our Lord," he reminded his listeners, "told His disciples that one of them would betray Him. The venerable Peter asked, 'Is it I, Lord?' Our Lord answered, 'It is not.' In turn, Thomas, John, James, and the others asked the same question and received the same reply.

"Then Judas Iscariot arose from his chair, looked shiftily about the room, and asked gruffly, 'Bli' me, I si, Guv'nor, is it I?' "

★ ★ ★

George Jessel gets credit for the story about the devout Catholic girl who fell desperately in love with a Jewish lad. "Teach him the virtues of Catholicism," counseled her mother. "Make a convert of him!" "That's just what I'll do," promised the girl, and she set to work with a will that very evening.

The Jewish lad proved an easy convert. He waxed more and more enthusiastic as the days went by. Suddenly, however, one day before the wedding, the bridegroom called all bets off. "What happened?" cried the distracted mother.

"I oversold him," wept the girl. "Now he wants to be a priest!"

★ ★ ★

An old Polish immigrant was regaling a rapt audience with the story of how, in his flight from abroad, he, his wife, and children were pursued by wolves across an icy lake. In the middle of the lake, the ice cracked and the sleigh sank like a plummet. "And what do you think God did for us in this hopeless situation?" inquired the old man reverently. "Thanks be to Him, the whole story is a lie from beginning to end!"

77. RESTAURANTS

One thing most people of the theatrical and television worlds, regardless of their nationality, have in common is a fondness for a late-evening snack at a friendly and unpretentious delicatessen. An omelette with knockwurst before retiring may not be just the thing for the digestion, and pastrami and dill pickles undoubtedly cause some pretty weird dreams in the small hours of the night, but, to a performer who has been giving his all before the footlights, they seem to be as soothing as a mother's lullaby.

Bill Paley, head man at C.B.S., often spurns the superlative restaurant of the Ritz in Paris in favor of a delicatessen he's discovered not a hundred steps from the Place Vendôme. Jack Benny, in London, hails as his proudest discovery a side-street restaurant that features blintzes and cheese cake that would make "even Mr. Lindy's mouth water."

Lindy's itself, a New York institution, is equally famed for its wonderful food and its star-spangled clientele. Here Damon Runyon lingered by the hour to engage flavorsome Broadway characters in rewarding conversation (the end result being *Guys and Dolls*). Here, at a single table, you can see half a dozen television stars—Gleason, Berle, or Durante, perchance—swapping quips and insults.

Here it was, too, that Jack Pearl (Vas you dere, Sharlie?) played a reprehensible trick on the management. He bought a whole pound of prime corned beef at a butcher shop, and had it concealed on his person when he ordered a corned-beef sandwich at Lindy's. When his sandwich was put before him, he took one bite, then surreptitiously inserted the extra beef he had bought previously. Summoning the headwaiter, he inquired blandly, "How can you afford to put so much fine beef in a single sandwich?"

The headwaiter took one look at the overstuffed sandwich, did a bit of rapid mental calculating on the net cost of the meat therein, and headed for the kitchen with murder in his eyes.

★ ★ ★

It was at another de luxe delicatessen in the white lights district that a waiter planked down an apple pancake in front of Miss Merle Oberon and announced defiantly, "Well, that's the last one of those things I'll serve today." "What's the matter?" asked Miss Oberon indulgently. "Have you run out of apples?" "No," explained the waiter, "but the kitchen's on fire."

★ ★ ★

A very nice gentleman had finished his dinner in an exclusive Fifty-second Street restaurant when he was horrified to discover he didn't have enough money in his wallet to pay the bill and customary tip. "Don't let this predicament upset you," soothed the understanding waiter. "I'll just add up this little old bill over again."

★ ★ ★

Two advertising tycoons, dining in an expensive restaurant that befitted their expense accounts, fell into a violent argument. One beckoned a waiter to ask, "Could you lend us a dime to settle a bet?"

The waiter produced the dime, the coin was flipped, the argument settled—and eventually the check was produced. One item thereon startled the tycoons—even though they were only signing the agency's name. It read "Loan of a dime: twenty-five cents!"

★ ★ ★

One big branch of a national restaurant chain showed a sudden sharp and inexplicable decline in receipts, and inspectors were sent on the double to investigate. "Everything seems in perfect order," they reported, frankly puzzled. "We kept a close eye on all three cash registers, and every sale was accurately rung up."

That's how management discovered the gimmick. There were supposed to be only *two* cash registers. The cashier had thoughtfully installed a third register of his own.

★ ★ ★

For eighteen years Mr. Lipschitz had lunched at the same restaurant, and his order never varied: a plate of borsch and a package of soda crackers. The waiter never bothered even to ask what Mr. Lipschitz wanted: he put the soup and crackers in front of him, and not a word was spoken by either.

Suddenly, one noon, Mr. Lipschitz called over the headwaiter and announced, "I want you should taste that borsch!" The headwaiter was nonplused. "For eighteen years now we've served you that same borsch and never heard a peep out of you," he protested. "Nevertheless," Mr. Lipschitz insisted, "today I want you should taste it."

The headwaiter shrugged his shoulders, leaned over to taste the borsch, then said, "But where's your soup spoon?"

Mr. Lipschitz smiled triumphantly, lifted a finger, and said, "Ah HAH!"

★ ★ ★

Keith Elliot tells about the fellow who wandered into a roadside barbecue and inquired, "Do you serve stewed tomatoes here?" The proprietor answered cheerily, "Sure, Bud. Bring her in!"

★ ★ ★

Here's a diet that really will work—complete in four short words: "No more, thank you."

★ ★ ★

Steve Allen says one of the greatest hazards he ever has encountered in a restaurant is the "Brush-off Type" who skips over to your table to give you an effusive greeting, but is always looking around to make sure he's missing nothing else. For instance:

BRUSH-OFF. Hi, Steverino! Great to see you. How's the wife?

STEVE. She just broke her leg.

BRUSH-OFF. Wonderful! Glad to hear it! (Waves to somebody six tables away.)

STEVE. Compound fracture.

BRUSH-OFF (Spotting another celebrity). You must be mighty proud.

STEVE. She's suffering terrible pain.

BRUSH-OFF (Waving). Whaddyaknow? Congratulations! (Bowing) Where you staying?

STEVE. Yankee Stadium.

BRUSH-OFF (Rushing off to greet Zsa Zsa Gabor). Wonderful. I'll call you! 'Bye now. . . .

★ ★ ★

The Toronto *Star's* expert on dining out reported that a man in a very expensive restaurant took one look at the prices on the menu, then said to his girl friend, "What will it be, my plump little doll?"

★ ★ ★

At one of New York's most exclusive—and expensive—French restaurants, a young lady lost her garter, and an observant movie agent, always the gentleman, rushed to pick it up for her. "What," he asked coyly, "do you call this thing?" "It's my garter, of course," she replied. "Fancy that," said the agent. "Everything's so infernally high at this joint, I thought it might be your necklace."

★ ★ ★

In a Paris café, at 3 A.M., the last guest in sight sat sleeping at his table. The charwoman said to the proprietor, "I've seen you shake that old fool and wake him up five times. Why don't you make him go home?"

"Nothing doing," answered the proprietor cheerfully. "Every time I wake him up he asks for his bill and pays it."

★ ★ ★

In Hollywood, Jack Benny reported that he had taken his wife Mary to a new restaurant so expensive they don't even dare to print the prices on the menu. "You know I'm not stingy," said Jack. "That's just my show business character. But when I got the check —fifty-eight dollars for dinner for two—I sat there flabbergasted. The waiter must have thought I had fainted, so he threw a glass of water in my face.

"That was another three dollars."

★ ★ ★

John Straley recalls a gruesome incident in the dizzy cycle of life around Wall Street. An old restaurant there has displayed under glass a ham and cheese sandwich that was whipped up on the day the establishment threw open its doors in 1872. A cleaning woman inadvertently removed the glass case for cleaning the other day, and a zealous waiter served the eighty-four-year-old sandwich to a hungry customer.

"What's all the excitement about?" demanded the customer in the hospital yesterday. "It tasted just like every other sandwich I've eaten in that joint!"

★ ★ ★

A rabbi visited his favorite Jewish restaurant, and was astounded when a Chinese waiter came to take his order. Furthermore, the Chinese waiter spoke Yiddish!

When he left in the direction of the kitchen, the rabbi summoned the proprietor and said, "Where on earth did you dig up a Chinese waiter who can speak Yiddish?"

"Ss-s-sh!" urged the proprietor in a conspiratorial whisper. "He thinks he's learning English!"

★ ★ ★

A Bostonian whose business necessitated frequent trips to New York divided his patronage among a half-dozen first-class midtown restaurants, but, no matter what other delicacies were proffered on the menus, he invariably demanded a double order of snails.

"You have a one-track appetite when you come to New York," chided a friend. "Don't you have snails in Boston?"

"Of course we have," said the Bostonian, "but up there we don't seem able to catch them."

★ ★ ★

A man who had been a waiter all his life was breathing his last. "I'll be on the other shore of that River Styx," he told his wife, "waiting for you. If ever you want to talk to me badly enough, I'll come back, I promise."

Some weeks after the waiter had died, his wife decided she must speak with him again, and sought the assistance of the town's leading spiritualist. "Just knock on that table," advised the spiritualist, "and he'll hear you." So the wife knocked once, then again—more loudly—but absolutely nothing happened. Then she really hammered on the table, hollering, "Morris, you just come here quick—or else."

There was a flash of lightning and a roar of thunder—and Morris stood before her big as life. "Morris," she said reproachfully, "you heard me knocking. Why didn't you come?"

Morris explained simply, "It wasn't my table."

78. RICH MAN, POOR MAN

Jay Gould, one of the shrewdest and most ruthless stock manipulators Wall Street ever has known, was summoned one day by the rector of his church. "I've saved thirty thousand dollars in my lifetime," said the rector, "and I'd like you to tell me what stock I should buy with it." Jay Gould made a suggestion, the rector acted upon it—and six months later he was wiped out. "You gave me terrible advice," he told Gould, "and now my whole thirty thousand dollars has gone down the drain." "I'll restore your faith," volunteered Jay Gould. "Here's a check for forty thousand."

"I have one more confession to make," said the flabbergasted rector. "I'm afraid I passed on your market tip to several members of this congregation."

"Of course you did," agreed Gould cheerfully. "They're the ones I was after."

★ ★ ★

A Wall Street broker ate too big a lunch and dropped dead of heart failure. Just before going out he had dictated a letter to his secretary that, he said, was "the most important, probably, I've ever written in my whole life." The distracted secretary decided that she had better mail it, but, before dropping it down the chute, she added this postscript: "It may interest you to know that I died since I wrote the above."

★ ★ ★

A crystal gazer, to be worth her salt these days, has to be exceedingly well versed in many fields. The *Wall Street Journal* tells of one member of the crystal-gazer guild, located on the Atlantic City boardwalk, who was approached by a client seeking financial advice. The medium was equal to the occasion. "Sell your fifty thousand Anaconda at once," she counseled. "Then buy five thousand Du Pont and twenty thousand Big Steel, hold them three days, sell and put the whole wad into General Electric. That will be two bucks, please, and, for fifty cents extra, I'll tell you what to do with your over-the-counter securities."

★ ★ ★

WALL STREET EXTRAS:

The plunger who complained, "Since I lost my last cent, half my friends no longer speak to me." He was asked, "How about the other half?" "They," was the reply, "don't know it yet."

The gray-haired customers' man who asked the office manager, "Say, have I told you about the stunt my grandson pulled on me last week?" "No, you haven't," replied the office manager quickly, "and thank you very much."

The brokerage house head who gave this pep talk to his staff: "One day as I sat musing, sad, lonely, and friendless, a kindly voice came to me from out of the gloom, counseling, 'Cheer up, things could be worse.' And so, gentlemen, I cheered up—and sure enough, things got worse."

The trader who made a killing in the market. He shot the manager of an A & P.

The bank president who told an applicant, "You have made a very good impression on me, and I hereby appoint you the loan arranger." The applicant whooped, "Hi-ho, Silver!"

The paunchy stockbroker who assured an inquisitor, "Of course I'm not trying to corner the market. I've got trouble enough these days cornering my secretary."

★ ★ ★

A lady investor explained the secret of her successful operations to a gentleman friend. "I just look at a company's balance sheet," she stated. "If the total assets and the total liabilities are exactly the same, I know everything's all right."

★ ★ ★

Another lovely lady, recently widowed, was introduced to the mystery and excitement of playing the stock market, but, after dabbling for some months, she had this complaint to register with her broker: "It seems that every time there's talk of a panic, every stock I have goes down!"

★ ★ ★

The wail of an inexperienced investor in the stock market (as recorded in *Punch*):

I bought a little bunch of shares;
Into the sky,
High, high, above the price that I
Had paid for them I saw them fly.

Up, up they soared in steady rhythmic flight,
To my delight;
Poised gracefully, they hovered there awhile,
Waiting the time
When they should further climb.

There came a day at last
When all the economic sky was overcast;
My shares just folded up their golden wings,
Poor silly things,
And nose-dived, falling, falling
To earth. It was appalling.

I have them yet, looking, I fear in vain,
For that bright day when they shall soar again,
I will not sell them. Anyhow
Nobody wants them now.

★ ★ ★

Here are two rare and priceless bits of advice to those of you who like to dabble in Wall Street, passed on by Bernard Baruch, one of the most successful speculators of all time:

1. If you are holding a lot of stocks, and the market slips into a persistent decline, "sell to the sleeping point." That is, sell enough stocks so that you no longer will be tossing about in bed worrying, no matter how far down the market may go. "When we are worried," counsels Baruch, "it is because our subconscious mind is trying to telegraph us some message of warning."

2. It may be wise to periodically turn into cash most of your speculative holdings and virtually retire from the market for a while. This enables you to get a fresh, objective outlook on overall conditions. "No general," concludes Baruch, "keeps his troops fighting all the time, nor does he go into battle without some part of his forces held back in reserve."

★ ★ ★

A stockbroker with very questionable ethics talked an uninitiated sucker into buying five thousand shares of a phony oil stock at fifty cents a share.

A week later the broker reported, "You're lucky! That stock has just doubled in price!" "Buy me another five thousand," ordered the sucker.

A few days later the broker was on the phone again. "That stock's going wild," he exulted. "It just hit two dollars a share!"

"That's enough for me," decided the sucker. "Sell all I've got at the market."

"*Sell?*" echoed the broker, stunned. "To WHOM?"

★ ★ ★

A couple of forlorn tramps sat on a bench in Central Park while the sun slowly set behind the Jersey shoreline. "Have you eaten?" asked the first tramp wistfully. "Ah, yes," answered the other with a sigh. "Quite often!"

★ ★ ★

"All I need is one more dollar," whined a panhandler, "to get my book published." "That's a new approach," admitted his well-dressed prospect. "What's your book called?" "I'm naming it *1000 Easy Ways to Make Money*," said the panhandler. "So how come you must beg?" asked the prospect. "This way," the panhandler assured him, "is one of the easiest."

★ ★ ★

One derelict met another at a Bowery flophouse and reported sadly, "I ran into poor old Bozo Hannegan the other day and he sure had a pinched look." "Too bad," sighed the other. "What do you think was the cause?" "Well, for one thing," explained the first, "he was handcuffed to a cop."

★ ★ ★

A tramp knocked warily on the door of a moderately large residence, and bowed meekly when a powerful lady answered the summons. "Sure and what does a miserable runt like you be comin' 'round to bother me about?" she demanded with an obvious Harvard accent.

"If you'd be so kind," said the tramp humbly, exhibiting a small object in the palm of his hand, "I'd like to get a coat sewed onto this button."

★ ★ ★

A beggar accosted a lady with a time-honored, "Can you spare a quarter for a starving man?" The lady fumbled with her purse, whereupon the beggar urged her sharply, "Hurry up, lady. I'm double-parked!"

79. SALESMEN

A tight-fisted sales manager was carefully checking the expense accounts of his travelers, moaning and tearing his hair as he spotted typical "swindle sheet" items.

One made him yell for his assistant. "Look at this burglar's claim," he demanded. "How can you spend nine dollars for food in a single day in Sandusky, Ohio?"

"It's easy," answered the assistant cheerfully. "You just skip breakfast."

★ ★ ★

A very beautiful young lady was taken on by a vacuum cleaner company to demonstrate and take orders on a new lightweight model, and justified the move by turning in a sheaf of orders that doubled those of experienced salesmen on the staff. "How do you do it?" marveled the manager. "Nothing to it," she laughed. "I just address my sales talk to the husband in tones so low that the wife doesn't dare miss a single word."

★ ★ ★

A millionaire manufacturer told his star salesman, "Marry one of my three daughters and I'll make you a full partner. Here are two of them. The third will be along any minute." The salesman, trained to make instantaneous decisions, snapped, "I'll take the one that's coming."

★ ★ ★

"I'm afraid I wasn't cut out to be a traveling salesman," sighed a young college graduate after his first five-week-long trip through the Midwest. "All that happened was no orders to speak of, and an insult at practically every account I visited."

"That's funny," mused the veteran sales manager. "I was on the road for over thirty years. I had my samples flung out of windows, I was thrown down flights of stairs, I had my ancestry questioned by phone operators and office boys. But insulted? Never!!"

★ ★ ★

Top price for the day at a recent auction was reached when the auctioneer shouted, "Sold! To the little lady with her husband's hand over her mouth."

★ ★ ★

"A star salesman," proclaimed Walter Chrysler, "needs something more than charm and perseverance. He needs imagination. Let me remind you that the stinger of a bee is only three one-hundredths of an inch long. The rest of the twelve inches is pure imagination."

★ ★ ★

There always have been lots of ways of selling furniture, but a cagey couple in Flatbush have hit upon what sounds like a brand-new one. They rent a neat and accessible apartment and load it with furniture. Then they take ads in the papers saying: "We must move out West. All furniture sold at enormous sacrifice." Bargain hunters appear by the score and strip the place clean, paying approximately what they would at any regular store. As soon as the last chair has been sold, the couple refurnish and begin the cycle all over again.

★ ★ ★

A real estate broker in Denver was trying to sell a big tract of Colorado property sight unseen to an Eastern operator. "My client wants a place that's pretty high up," said the Easterner. "How high is this property?" "I couldn't say exactly," admitted the broker, "but it's just eight hundred miles to Pike's Peak—and it's downhill all the way."

★ ★ ★

Another realty salesman had just closed his first deal, only to discover that the piece of land he had sold was completely under water.

"That customer's going to come back here pretty mad," he predicted to his boss. "Shall I give him his money back?"

"Money back?" roared the boss. "What kind of a salesman are you anyway? Get out there and sell him a motorboat."

★ ★ ★

In Lisbon, an international spy had built up a nice little business selling top-secret information simultaneously to the governments of Britain, Italy, France, and the Soviet. A clever operative from the U.S.A. named Gordon Gordon offered him double his usual fee to get in on the same service. "I cannot," said the spy regretfully. "I love America the best, but my typewriter, she make only four carbon copies!"

★ ★ ★

A Baltimore supply house sent a salesman to bag an order from a hot prospect in Denver, telling him he could run up an expense account "within reason." Here's the tab he turned in:

> Plane fare: $200
> Taxis, etc.: $30
> Hotel room and food: $110
> Man is not made of wood: $50.

★ ★ ★

A young hustler spotted a rangy Texan, obviously in the chips, at a hotel bar and engaged him in what he hoped would prove a rewarding conversation.

"A millionaire, I'll bet," he grinned.

"Right nice of you to mention it, son," drawled the Texan. "A millionaire—and how!"

"Oil or cattle, I suppose."

"You drew a blank that time, son."

"Real estate then."

"On the nose, son. Some years back a smart salesman talked me into buying thirty-seven acres."

The young hustler's face fell a bit. "That doesn't sound like much in those wide-open spaces," he sniffed. "What do you call your place?"

The Texan answered quietly, "Downtown Dallas."

★ ★ ★

A dapper salesman stopped his new convertible to pick up a blonde at the roadside. "I'm a salesman," he told her for openers. "What do you do?" "Not a thing," she replied. "I just escaped from the state mental hospital." "Well, I——" began the salesman, then shifted to, "Say, can a girl like you ever have children?" "Why, of course we can," she answered mildly. "If we didn't where would all the salesmen like you come from?"

★ ★ ★

Bargaining with a Mexican salesman is a fine art, and requires infinite finesse. Ernest Blevins tells of one astute peddler who approached an American foursome with a tray of beautiful silver bracelets, all priced at a thousand pesos. One of the American ladies had been in Mexico long enough to negotiate intelligently and, after extensive bargaining, enjoyed to the hilt by both parties to the transaction, acquired a bracelet for exactly two hundred pesos.

"Now that's a genuine bargain," enthused the second lady. "I'll take a bracelet too at the same price."

"No, no, señora," protested the peddler. "For you we start over again."

★ ★ ★

No well-known figure—yet—has been identified as:

1. The sales manager who told an assistant, "You're the smartest fellow I've ever had in here; you work sixteen hours a day; and my customers are crazy about you. So I'm obliged to fire you. It's men like you who go out and start competing companies."

2. The salesman whose alibi for being three days late for an appointment was, "You'll have to excuse me. I'm just recovering from a slight case of whiskey."

And 3. The observant old field man at a cocktail party whose eyes feasted on a recently arrived blonde. "Gad," he exclaimed, "she was just made for that dress—but personally, I think, she should have held out for a mink coat."

80. SCOTCH TAPE

Make way for Sandy MacKenzie, aber-dean of Highland raconteurs, with a bagpipeful of stories from the Firth of Forth (or is it the Forth of Firth?).

High on the MacKenzie honor rolls you'll find:

MCINDOE of Inverary, outstanding Scottish wolf, who lured a lass up to a penthouse to see his etchings—and sold her six of them.

FRASER of Fraserburgh, who threw discretion to the winds and sent a telegram. When the girl at the inquiry desk told him there was no charge for the name, he assured her, "I know I may not look it, but I'm an Indian chief, and my name is "I-Won't-Be-Home-Till-Monday-Morning."

BURNS of Blairgowrie who told a companion, "I dine out now and then, but I never go to the same restaurant twice." The friend said, "I don't tip either."

COLQUHOON of Clydebank, who, visiting a skyscraper on Wall Street, noted that the cornerstone bore a date in Roman capitals: MCMIV. "Ha," chortled Colquhoon, "I dinna know McMiv, but I see he's got his name on one of yer tallest buildings!"

CAMPBELL of Colonsay, who, along with his chum McTavish, decided to swear off whiskey forever. McTavish thought it prudent, however, to keep one bottle in reserve in case of illness. Campbell reached the end of his endurance in three days. "McTavish," he moaned, "I'm not a well man." "Too late, Campbell," replied his friend. "I was verra sick myself all day yesterday."

MILTON BALLANTRAE of Buckhaven, who tells so many old jokes they've renamed him Miltie Edinburghle. Back of the counter of his pub he hung this sign: "In case of hydrogen bomb, keep calm, pay your check, and run like hell."

CAMERON of Cromarty, who hired a boat, and took his girl for a row on the loch. It started to rain, finally came down so hard that Cameron muttered, "We're getting drenched. I wish our hour was up!"

JOHN MCCAMMON of St. Louis—yes, St. Louis—whose dog, he says, eats nothing but cantaloupe—a veritable melon collie. When McCammon drives through Connecticut after a pun like that, adds Ellen Pierce, they probably make him use the Demerit Parkway.

Millionaire MONTGOMERY, who was entertaining a couple of beautiful girls on his yacht when an icy wind suddenly blew up. Montgomery called down to his crew, "Is there a MacIntosh down there big enough to keep a couple of young ladies warm?" "No," came the answer, "but there's a MacPherson here who's willing to try."

MCGREGOR of Glasgow, who turned down a free whiskey and soda! The unprecedented event took place on the third tee at the Wee Whippendee Golf Club, where the Scotsman was executing a couple of practice swings. "I'll nae drink when I'm driving," he explained, sadly but firmly.

Sportsman SANDERSON of Selkirk, who presented his parson with a fine string of pickerel, but warned him with an ill-concealed chuckle, "Those fish were caught on Sunday, Parson. Perhaps yer conscience won't be lettin' you eat them." "My boy," replied the parson, reaching for the string, "there's one thing I know: these pickerel were not to blame!"

MCTAVISH of Tiree, who made a surprise appearance at a notions counter and purchased a dozen thimbles. The clerk observed, "It looks like you're anticipating a lot of sewing." "Not sewing," amended McTavish. "Drinking."

It's the Scots themselves who circulate the stories highlighting their frugality and caution. I've never met a Scotsman yet who wasn't refreshingly direct and scrupulously fair in his dealings. "Let us have no shilly-shallying," exclaims Sandy McKenzie. "All a man must do is keep his chin up, his kilts down—and let the winter gales blow!"

81. SEA STORIES

A moment that makes you suddenly aware of the progress that has been made in conquering dat ol' debil Sea is when you are standing near the prow of the *United States*, wind whipping in your face, as the greatest steamship ever floated knifes through the shimmering blue waters of the Atlantic.

As you will learn from the fact-packed pages of Frank Braynard's *Famous American Ships*, however, and Addie Harding's *America Rides the Liners*, the *United States* is just the latest of a series of vessels launched from American yards that have brought glory to the flag they flew. Our maritime history covers the *Mayflower*, the *Clermont*, the sleek clippers, the ornate river boats, the *Leviathan*, the Grace and Matson liners, and—coming up—the atomic-powered ocean greyhounds now in the blueprint stage.

★ ★ ★

Did you know that a Viking expedition reached what is now the town of Kensington, Minnesota, 130 years before Columbus "discovered" America? That a man named John Fitch had a successful steamboat in operation seventeen years before Fulton's *Clermont* sailed up the Hudson to Albany? That the *United States*, masterpiece of designer William F. Gibbs, and holder of the record for the Ambrose Light–Bishop's Rock run (three days, ten hours, and forty minutes) can also go twenty knots (about twenty-four miles) per hour in *reverse?* Braynard's book tells all this, and a great deal more, and contains his fine drawings to boot.

★ ★ ★

Addie Harding gives the story of the first American sea fight in the War for Independence. Several British sloops sailed into the harbor of Machias, Maine, one day in May, 1775, and announced, "We've come to take some lumber for His Majesty's use." An American skipper named O'Brien (red-headed, and of Scotch-Irish ancestry) was not in the mood to deliver the lumber, however. He sailed his schooner under full canvas straight for the British warships, and his crew picked off the redcoats one by one with musket fire. The British craft, admittedly unprepared for this odd type of naval battle strategy, ran for it—and America's first sea engagement was a complete victory any way you looked at it.

★ ★ ★

America's best-known steamboat race, says Frank Braynard, pitted the *Robert E. Lee* against the *Natchez* in the year 1870. Ten thousand people (including, fortunately, Currier and Ives) lined the levees of New Orleans as the two ships headed up the Mississippi, black smoke billowing from their stacks. The *Lee* won, reaching St. Louis in three days, eighteen hours, and thirteen minutes, as the roustabouts on her freight deck sang:

Shoo fly, don't bodder me!
You k'ain't ketch up wit' de *Robert E. Lee.*

★ ★ ★

Reverting to the *United States*, she has now steamed over half a million miles at sea without once slowing down because of mechanical defect. She can average comfortably thirty-five knots, and can be transformed into an effective unit of the U.S. Navy in short order. "She's a navy ship through and through," says one of her officers, "but no passenger is aware of it." Indeed, so spacious and luxurious she is that one lady aboard summoned a steward and said, "Would you mind directing me to the Atlantic Ocean?"

★ ★ ★

Coming home from Europe, a new movie star was complaining to his wife, "I'll bet I've already handed out five thousand dollars in tips on this tub," when there came a knock on the door. It was a steward, to report, "The captain would be obliged if you and your wife would dine at his table this evening." "How do you like that!" bellowed the star. "All that dough for tips—and now we gotta eat with the crew!"

★ ★ ★

An inexperienced yachtsman, venturing out into Long Island Sound for the first time, decided to run up a few flags as decoration. No sooner were the flags hoisted than every other craft in sight turned tail and fled from the immediate vicinity. Only when he returned to his mooring did the mortified yachtsman discover the meaning of the signal flags he was flying: "SMALL POX ABOARD. AM COMING TO YOUR ASSISTANCE."

★ ★ ★

A rather eccentric member of a country club in Iowa often comes to dinner with a yacht captain's hat on his head, though the only body of water within a radius of a hundred miles is the bird bath in the town plaza. "I come from a seafaring family," he explains. "My father always was hailed as 'the old skipper.'" "That's right," agrees his long-suffering wife grimly, "particularly by landlords and the finance company."

★ ★ ★

"I hate jokes that are made about other people's misfortunes," writes Walter Duryea, "but this fellow Monty I refer to was such a conceited, arrogant waster—a typical rich man's good-for-nothing son—and the yacht he bought was ten times too big and ostentatious. Well, the boiler on it blew up one day and a lady guest, mildly panicked, gurgled, 'Oh, Monty, do you think the boat is going to sink?' 'My dear woman,' huffed Monty indignantly, 'this yacht is completely and absolutely unsinkable . . . glub, glub, glub. . . .'"

82. SECRETARIES

A lovely young lady completed a secretarial course in South Dakota and headed for New York to win fame and fortune. She landed a job in a very big publishing outfit and soon became the top editor's private secretary.

"Give me some idea of what a typical day is like at the office," pleaded her mother back home. So the young lady dutifully drew up the following schedule for her:

9 A.M. Arrive for work. Nothing much to do until boss man and his assistant editors arrive about an hour and a half later.

10:35. Adjust telephone-ringing mechanism for editor with hangover.

10:40. Take elevator down to get sixteen cups of coffee; four with cream and sugar, three with cream but without sugar, four with sugar but without cream, five black. Also get one tea, one black raspberry tonic, and a Hershey bar. Distribute.

10:55. Extract editor from typewriter ribbon which he tried to change himself. He is filthy, but maintains dignity in crisis. Clean his suit and necktie.

11:10. Take fast-typing lady editor up to first-aid station with broken fingernail. She is hysterical; has date to meet famous author that evening. Promised to buy her fake fingernail during my lunch hour and give her manicure. Bucked her up with coffee laced with desk brandy.

11:25. Typed twelve letters for editor doing comparative shopping for refrigerator.

11:40. Sold editor thirty-one 1½-cent stamps, three 17-cent

stamps, found Havana and Miami plane schedules for him, and weighed his empty suitcase.

12:15. Go out to lunch. Very hard to find fake fingernail.

1:10 P.M. Sewed on button for editor. Didn't have needle and thread so used bobby pin and thread torn from old book binding.

1:40. Manufacturing department requests I scotch-tape together one hundred galleys torn into small pieces by mistake between here and printers' plant.

2:30. Boss man and assistant editors drift back from lunch in time to watch something or other on office TV. Jokes heard during luncheon break phoned to several pals. I pretend I do not understand them all.

3:00. Help lady editor who put feet in desk drawer while reading and got stuck in that position.

3:10. Count how many times word "and" is used in our big new novel for research department.

3:20. Water the stock again. Sixteen coffees.

3:40. Nail heel back on editor's shoe.

4:10. Boss man throws lighted match into trash basket, sets it afire, and flees in panic. I extinguish the blaze.

5:00. I miss my train because boss man finally begins dictating answers to morning's mail.

THE HAPPY ENDING. "The boss man called me in to an office party at six, handed me a present (perfume the Stork Club had given him at lunch), and then they read me this poem:

> Mirror, mirror, on the wall
> Who is mother to us all?
> Sewing, feeding, typing, choring,
> Smiling sweetly while we're boring?
> The Joan of Arc from South Dakota.
> To a saint we should promote her.
> Lady fair, our thanks and more.
> Look! Our foreheads touch the floor.

"They should write better poetry, but the sentiment is fine. That's how it is, Mom—and do I love it!"

★ ★ ★

Mr. Sargent was looking over the job-application blank just filled out by Miss Clough. "My dear girl," he said ingratiatingly (she was *very* pretty), "under 'experience' could I persuade you to be just a bit more specific than 'Oh, boy!'?"

★ ★ ★

A bright young Harvard graduate got a job in a downtown bank, and, to his delight, was assigned a secretary who looked like a Hollywood starlet. When he dictated his very first letter to her, he was understandably dazzled. He stopped short in the middle of a sentence, furrowed his brow, and mused, "Do you retire a loan?" The secretary dropped her eyes demurely and murmured, "Not when I can help it."

★ ★ ★

Another enticing secretary was hotly pursued by an ardent sales manager, who promised her, "I'll buy you a sable scarf, a chinchilla coat, a mink cape . . ."

"Thanks," she interrupted. "I think you've gone fur enough."

Later she told a chum, "That manager may be married, but his right eye isn't!"

★ ★ ★

The *Wall Street Journal* tracked down a not-too-bright office girl who, when finally discovered, had thought for eight solid months that the wastepaper chute down to the furnace was a filing cabinet. That's where she had stuffed every letter given her to file.

"That's not the worst of it," mourned the bank V.P. who exposed her. "We figure that we lost three thousand letters as a result of this girl's stupidity—and to this day we haven't needed one of them!"

★ ★ ★

A sweet young thing toyed with the notion of signing up for a shorthand course. "When we get finished with you," promised the enrollment clerk, "you'll be accurate, dependable, and neat." "What about speed?" persisted the applicant. "Our last nine graduates," said the enrollment clerk calmly, "married their bosses inside of five months."

83. SERVANTS

Not so long ago, a Scranton coal tycoon employed a chef named Napoleon whose roasts and sauces were famous for miles around. The president of a nearby university borrowed him one day to cook an important dinner, and Napoleon proudly set forth to fill the engagement, his trusty carving knives wrapped in a piece of old newspaper.

He just did catch his bus, and, breathing heavily, instructed the driver, "Step on the gas, mister. The president is waiting for me." The driver looked warily at the carving knives, nodded, "You're the boss," and drove him straight to a lunatic asylum.

Thinking this must be the university, the cook unwrapped his knives and announced to the guard at the gate, "I'm Napoleon. Where's the party?" Next thing Napoleon knew he was in a padded cell.

University officials—plus his employer—rescued Napoleon some eight hours later.

★ ★ ★

Mr. Collins, entering the kitchen unexpectedly, caught the maid with her face and hands unwashed, and a pile of dishes filling the sink. "Goodness, Jane," he exclaimed, "you're pretty dirty, aren't you?"

"Thank you, Mr. Collins," she smirked. "And I'm even prettier clean!"

★ ★ ★

Prebbles, the new butler at Evergreen Manor, had dubious references, but a certain swagger and glint in his eye that pleased Mrs. Wainwaring.

Passing the vegetables at a formal dinner one evening, Prebbles came to a very deaf old lady. "Peas, ma'am?" he inquired. No answer. "Peas, ma'am?" he repeated more loudly.

The old lady saw him hovering over her and lifted an ear trumpet in his direction.

Prebbles was surprised but undaunted. "Well, if that's the way you want them, lady," he chuckled, "that's the way you'll get them." And down went the peas into the ear trumpet.

★ ★ ★

A new housekeeper, accused of helping herself to the master's liquor when he was not on the premises, waxed properly indignant. "I'll have you know, sir," she declared hotly, "that I come from honest English parents."

"I'm not concerned with your English parents," countered the master. "What's worrying me is your Scotch extraction."

★ ★ ★

In Detroit, Horace Dodge, the automobile builder, had an old gatekeeper on his estate who neglected his duties shamefully, but had been around so long nobody dared criticize him too severely.

One day, however, Dodge's ire was aroused to the point where he hollered, "You're fired," and drove off in high dudgeon to Detroit. When he drove home that evening, however, there was the old gatekeeper big as life. "Confound it," roared Dodge. "Didn't I discharge you this morning?" "You did," agreed the gatekeeper cheerfully, "but I forgive you."

★ ★ ★

There once lived an upstairs maid who had an unfortunate habit of bumping into people. One day she hit the jackpot. She collided first with the head of the house, knocking a freshly made mint julep out of his hands. Next she ran into the wife on the stairs, knocking her down the entire flight. And finally she bumped into Junior, breaking his new chemistry set.

Unable to stand the strain one moment longer, she resigned. "But why?" said her mistress. "We forgive you." "Can't you understand," sobbed the poor maid. "Obviously, I am in the family way."

★ ★ ★

Mrs. Montmorency's new maid, recently imported from Scandinavia, developed a mad crush on the grocery clerk, and felt the impulse to write her first note in the English language. Blushingly, she sought the aid of Mrs. Montmorency.

"How you spell 'wheat'?" she asked, and followed with, "Now how you spell 'loaf'?"

"Making up a list of things we need at the market?" inquired Mrs. M.

"Oh, no," giggled the maid, and showed her letter. It read: "Hey, Mike: I am happy to go dance with you Satday. Wheat all my loaf. Ingrid."

★ ★ ★

Back from a bridge tournament, Mrs. Mayes asked her new maid, "Did you clean out that refrigerator as I asked you to?" "I sure did, ma'am," enthused the maid, "and everything was mighty tasty."

★ ★ ★

A young Irish maid got a job at the home of playwright George Axelrod and couldn't wait to tell her best friend, a cook, about her exciting first week. "You should see the famous people that come to the Axelrods'," she exulted. "In five nights, I waited on Marilyn Monroe, Kitty Carlisle, Lauren Bacall, Arlene Francis, and Frank Sinatra!"

"Glory be," marveled the cook. "And what do they talk about?"

"Us," said the maid.

84. SHAGGY
DOGGEREL

The animal world has its own social register. It is known as "Who's Zoo," and woe betide the unfortunate quadruped whose name has been expunged from its dog-eared pages! Slated for banishment this year, and facing virtual ostrichism, are:

1. A whale who hangs outside the Seaquarium cadging drinks from all his old acquaintances. Obviously, he's a ne'er-do-whale.

2. A rabbit who is constantly reminding her young daughter in public, "At your age, I was already married, and the mother of 218 children."

3. A fly who was swatted as he lit upon an adding machine. His alibi: "I guess my number was up."

4. An ant who wrote a stock market letter advising, "Buy sheep, sell deer."

5. A poor little firefly who became enmeshed in a threshing machine. De-lighted, of course.

6. A red robin who won a blue ribbon for the best nest in the west. "It's really a beautiful nest," said the chairman (a wise old owl), "but why did you leave that big hole in the bottom?" "I always build my nests that way," maintained the robin. "I love to lay eggs—but I *hate* bringing up children."

★ ★ ★

A solitary GI in a distant jungle listening post, avid for company of any sort, finally caught a brilliantly colored parrot, and painstakingly taught it to make what passed for conversation.

One evening the parrot vanished briefly, then came winging back in wild excitement. "A woman!" he screeched. "And what a woman!"

The ecstatic GI seized his trusty rifle and plunged into the underbrush after the parrot. Every time he slowed down, the parrot urged him on with "Oh, boss! What a face! What a figure!" Finally the parrot stopped, pointed, and exulted, "There she is, boss!"

"Blankety, blank blank blank," roared the GI. "*It's another parrot!*"

★ ★ ★

Two lions strolled into a roadside tavern in search of refreshments. "Get a load of that little lady at the end of the bar," whispered one lion appreciatively. "Bah," scoffed the other. "You must be losing your eyesight." "Not at all," persisted lion number one. "In my estimation she's good enough to eat. In fact, I believe I will." And he suited the action to the words.

The next day lion number one turned up with an awful stomach-ache. "Hmpff!" snorted his unsympathetic friend, "I'll bet it's that barbituate."

★ ★ ★

John Fuller envisages what will certainly be the most unusual zoo in the world. It will include a school of whales that has a people of a good time, a clam that mans up, a human-hearted lion, a turtle with an athlete-necked sweater, a hog who speaks man-wash, and a cat who lets gossips out of bags.

★ ★ ★

Shaggy dog fanciers award a blue ribbon to Robert Day's cartoon for *Sports Illustrated*. It depicts a formidable moose nuzzling against a sign in Yellowstone Park. The sign warns "Do not feed the bears." A hand-lettered placard around the moose's neck reminds passers-by "I AM NOT A BEAR."

★ ★ ★

A gent suffering from insomnia resorted to the old remedy of counting sheep as he tossed about in bed one night, but jumped three feet in the air when he distinctly heard one of the sheep bleat to another, "What a night this one's going to be! I've had this character before!"

★ ★ ★

A sickly-looking actor marched into the manager's office of a cinema palace with a gorilla in tow. The manager sighed, "I suppose you're going to tell me this gorilla sings, tells jokes, and does the cha-cha." "Na-a-a," answered the actor. "This animal can't do nuttin'." "Then why did you bring him?" asked the manager. "I had to," said the actor. "He's my agent."

★ ★ ★

According to Billy Gray, the chickens out San Fernando Valley way have perfected a thrilling new game. They line up along the state highway and wait for a car to come tearing along. Then they dart across the road, practically under the wheels of the car.

Any chicken who loses his nerve at the last moment is called high school student.

★ ★ ★

A great violin player stalked into the African jungle armed with nothing more formidable than his fiddle and bow. What's more the music he played was so beautiful that a variety of wild beasts, come to dine on him for dinner, remained to listen in rapt enchantment to his craftsmanship. Thus the circle of his admirers soon included three bloodthirsty lionesses, a wild elephant or two, a leopard, a cougar, and a couple of hooded cobras.

In the middle of "The Moonlight Sonata," however, a panther suddenly leaped out of a tree and, before you could say "Harvey Campbell," ate the poor musician up.

The other animals were simply aghast. "How," demanded one outraged lioness, "could you bear to do away with a man who could produce such exquisite melodies?"

The panther shook his head impatiently, and said, "I'm afraid you'll have to speak a lot louder, my friend. I've grown quite deaf."

FROM A TO ZOO

A is for the alligator who boarded the Super-Chief. "Carry your suitcase?" inquired a redcap. "O.K.," said the alligator, "but watch your step. That's my wife."

B is for the boll weevil who set out with a lifelong pal for the big city. He was a success from the start, but the pal never could get to first base. Needless to say, he became known as the lesser of two weevils.

C is for the clams (steamed) that Steve Allen downed happily on a visit to Cape Cod. After six platters full, he knew he had had enough. A little burp told him.

D is for the dog whose owner sighed, "Poor Rover! We had to shoot him this morning." "Too bad," murmured Mrs. Manges. "Was he mad?" "Well," conceded the owner, "he wasn't exactly pleased."

E is for the elephant who lumbered into a luggage shop and announced, "I'd like to see something new in trunks."

F is for the flea (male) who beseeched another flea (female), "Come up to my place and see my itchings."

G is for the giraffe who escaped from a zoo. "No, sir," reported a bumpkin a hundred miles away to a searcher, "I didn't see no gee-raff, but there *was* a long-necked spotted pony here a while back chewing off the tops of trees."

H is for the hippopotamus who complained to his doctor, "My appetite is failing. I just peck at my food these days—a peck of this and a peck of that."

I is for the incubator chick who was carried into the living room by six-year-old Nancy. She was told sternly, "You take that chick right back to its mommy and daddy." "It hasn't any," maintained Nancy. "All it has is a dirty old lamp."

J is for the jackass who rated an offer of six hundred dollars from a would-be purchaser. "Nope," decided the owner. "That jackass would take it as a personal victory. He's been trying to get rid of me for three years."

K is for the kangaroo who sought out a psychiatrist. "Nothing I do," he complained, "makes me feel jumpy."

L is for the newlywed leopard who leaned back happily in his lair after consuming a gargantuan repast. "Man," he told his bride, "your cooking hits just the right *spots.*"

M is for two moths who performed on TV. No script was necessary. They just flew out and chewed the rag.

N is for the nag who wanted to turn left when his rider wanted to go right. "How did you settle it?" the rider was asked. He answered, "The nag tossed me for it."

O is for the octopuses who strolled Lovers' Lane arm in arm in arm in arm in arm in arm.

P is for the porcupine who walked smack into a cactus bush in the desert and hollered, "Is that you, Ma?"

Q is for the queriman (that's a fish, son) who arrived home near the Navy Yard in a state of obvious intoxication. "Junior," accused his mother, "you've been swimming around a battleship launching again!"

R is for the rabbit who had difficulty hopping. It seems he was keeping one foot in his pocket for good luck.

S is for the schnauzer who was allowed to run free. His leash expired.

T is for the tomcat who was making love to his mate-to-be on the back fence. "I would die for you," proclaimed the tomcat dramatically. She purred coyly, and whispered, "How many times?"

And as for U, V, W, X, Y, and Z, I am omitting them for humanitarian reasons. I feel I've caused literal-minded readers enough shaggravation.

85. SIGNS OF THE TIMES

Just outside a hospital in one of our large cities stand three business establishments side by side, each bent on attracting trade from the many doctors who pass by. On the window of the first, a shoe repair shop, hangs the sign "Physician, heel thyself!" A placard in the second, a liquor store, tersely inquires, "Dry Doc?" The third, a drugstore, has for its motto, "House of Pill Repute."

★ ★ ★

Contributors to my Cerfboard column in *This Week* magazine, who read as they ramble, spotted these laudable efforts of sundry merchants to find new ways of accentuating good buys:

Brooklyn barbershop: "Your hair cut free if we talk first."

Detroit lingerie shop: "We fix flats." Junk yard: "Rust in Peace." Cutlery shop: "Best in Blades. Ask the man who hones one."

Pocono nudist colony: "Come on in! We are never clothed."

On window of a just-completed store in New York's "Little Italy": "In two weeks this will become a Fruit and Vegetable."

Buffalo pawnbroker: "See us at your earliest inconvenience."

Near the exit of a Providence maternity hospital: "Thanks! Call again next year."

Dallas jewelry shop: "Diamond tiaras: $70,000; 3 for $200,000."

Garden supply store in Westchester: "Warning! after planting our seeds, step back quickly!"

Above the cashier's desk of an East Side delicatessen: "You name your favorite newspaper. We'll wrap your herring in it."

★ ★ ★

Some of the signs hung up by proprietors of musty country stores up New England way are a caution. A counter card in one emporium warned: "Please do not play with the cranberries!"; another proclaimed: "The cat is put out every night and it is a lie that she sleeps on the prunes."

A sign on the locked door explained why a store in Vermont opened late one morning: "I will be closed till 9:30 A.M., as I am being married at 9, and don't want to stop beforehand to count eggs or weigh out birdseed."

Another store in Vermont exhibited this warning above the soda-cracker barrel: "Smokers and chewers will please spit on each other, and not on the stove or floor."

Foreign entrepreneurs evidently are getting into the act, too. A lady in Paris with a Left Bank studio to rent advertised: "No bath: suitable for author, artist, or actor." A barber in Coventry, England, boasts: "My ancestors were official hairdressers of Lady Godiva." A sign on a Hong Kong restaurant proclaims: "Best chop suey! American chef!" And Nick Kenny vows he spotted this placard in the window of a Moscow grocery store: "Eat Soviet Brand Breakfast Goodies—or Else!"

If that dedicated look in your eyes means you are dead set on opening a dazzling new hotel or "bar and grille," here are a few signs that may win grudging chuckles from the clientele: (1)

"Don't smoke in bed. The next ashes that hit the floor may be your own." (2) "Don't miss our show every evening. 6 Beautiful Dancing Girls! 5 Beautiful Costumes!" (3) "Try our cafeteria. Courteous and efficient self-service." (4) "We dust our pies daily." (5) "Customers wanted. No experience necessary." (6) In big type: "SIRLOIN STEAK, 25 CENTS." In very small type below: "With meat, $4."

A certain drive-in proprietor in California refused to lose heart when fire gutted the entire premises. He hung a sign outside the wreckage which promised: "CHARCOAL-BROILED EVERYTHING."

★ ★ ★

There's an undertaker in Washington who signs all his letters "Eventually yours." A radio station in Salem, Oregon, has erected a signboard off a main highway informing homeward-bound motorists, "While you were away we spent many pleasant hours with your wife." And at an Alaskan golf club, this sign was posted in the locker room: "Three feet of snow on the greens will make them rather slow this weekend."

★ ★ ★

One man who's going to have to change the proclamation in his window is the owner of a spotless new fish store in San Francisco. "We sell anything that swims," he boasted proudly—till a customer walked in and demanded Esther Williams.

86. SOCIETY

At a high-society costume party in Pasadena, the cutest, most huggable debutante in the room came decked out as a map of California. A well-connected native son studied her appreciatively and nodded. "You do us proud, young lady. I never realized our sunny California had so many beautiful valleys and hills." "Thank you, sir," she purred. "From what part of the state do you hail?"

A moment later, the sound of a hard slap was heard, and the Californian reeled backward. "She never should have done that," he complained bitterly. "All I did was put my finger on San Mateo."

★ ★ ★

An impoverished but elegant young man-about-town in London has just confessed the method by which he acquired a reputation for lavish entertaining without forking out a single penny. He makes it his business to discover exactly when his affluential friends have unbreakable prior engagements, then invites them for those evenings to mythical galas of his own. Thus he gains credit for being a frequent and open-handed host, is invariably invited back—and always accepts.

★ ★ ★

W. Somerset Maugham prefers small parties. "Four is a wonderful number," he decrees. "Six is all right, and eight will do in a pinch. After that it's not a party: it's a rabble."

★ ★ ★

A clumsy guest at Dorothy Rodgers' beautiful country home toppled over a priceless vase which shattered into a hundred pieces on the marble floor. Beside himself with embarrassment and chagrin, the guest (a lifelong friend, by the way) virtually bought out a florist the next day and inundated Mrs. Rodgers with roses and other blooms. Mrs. Rodgers called him up to thank him, her opening remark being, "That you, Bull? This is China Shop!"

★ ★ ★

Tom Sherman, literary editor of the St. Louis *Post Dispatch*, had a phone call recently. A lady urgently requested his presence at a dinner party on the twenty-fourth. "Good," said Tom. "Do you mean the twenty-fourth of this month or the twenty-fourth of next month?" "This month," said the lady. Tom, suddenly remembering, protested, "But the twenty-fourth of this month was yesterday!" "It certainly was," snapped the lady, "and where the hell were you?"

★ ★ ★

An aristocratic lady—Louisburg Square family and all that—took an estate in the Berkshires for the summer and hired a localite to take her driving through the countryside every afternoon. On their first excursion, the well-intentioned driver began telling her all about the region and the characters who inhabited it—until the lady silenced him with a curt, "I hired you to drive for me, sir: not to converse with me."

That was the last time the driver opened his mouth. But when he submitted his bill at the end of the month, there was one item thereon the lady didn't understand. He explained it to her: "That's sass, ten dollars. I don't generally take it, but when I do, I charge for it."

★ ★ ★

A publisher who gives many lavish cocktail parties and dinners for visiting authors and critics gives a valuable tip on how to cut down the costs. "Always serve the champagne in jeroboams," he suggests. "They're so big neither the servants nor guests can sneak off with any unopened bottles."

★ ★ ★

Did you know that there are a dozen or so completely fictitious biographies-in-brief scattered through the pages of Who's Who in America and similar publications of the A. N. Marquis Company?

Who's Who is a trademarked name, with a reputation built over a span of more than fifty years. The "dummy" biographies (the Marquis people refer to them as "burglar alarms") are effective in trapping unscrupulous imitators who use old editions of Who's Who as a basis for compiling their own volume. Invariably they mail an inquiry to one of the "dummies," which puts the Marquis Company on to their trail at once. A secondary purpose of the fictitious inserts is to uncover companies who are using Who's Who as a mailing list, a practice the publishers do their best to discourage.

The actual names of the dummies? That's a deep, dark secret. They're changed for every edition to see that they stay that way!

★ ★ ★

Cholly Knickerbocker reports that the music at a recent society ball was so dreadful that when a waiter fell down with a trayful of crockery, four couples jumped up and started to cha-cha.

★ ★ ★

A scheming young bank clerk, keenly aware of old blue-blooded Mrs. Gottplenty's million-dollar balance, began giving her the red-carpet treatment. He even took her six nasty-tempered, untrained dogs for their constitutional every morning and evening.

As he had hoped, Mrs. Gottplenty remembered the bank clerk in her will.

She left him the dogs.

87. SOUTHLAND

Northern visitors to the charming and historical city of Charleston, South Carolina, have been heard to complain that, while the natives' language is very mellifluent, it's next to impossible to understand what the hell they're talking about. To remedy this deplorable situation, Ashley Cooper, of the Charleston *News and Courier*, has compiled a dictionary of Charlestonese, available from that newspaper's editorial sanctum at the modest price of two bits a throw. Here are a few typical entries:

A BOOT — Approximately.

AIN'T — Sister of one of your parents.

ARGON — A state north of California.

BONE — A blessed event—especially if it occurred in Charleston.

CANE CHEW — Aren't you able to?

FAMINE — Tilling the soil.

HAIL — The abode of integrationists and damyankees.

HARMONY — Cooked grits.

LAYMON — A fruit from which laymon-ade is made.

MINE EYES — Salad dressing.

PASSÉ — Father has spoken.

RAH CHAIR — Where you are at.

SNOW — To breathe heavily while sleeping.

VERSION — The kind of queen Elizabeth was.

WRETCHED — Long name for the nickname Dick.

YAWL — Mode of address used by N'Yawkers when visiting Charleston.

★ ★ ★

One of Walter Davenport's favorite stories concerned a time when a proud citizen of Charleston, attending the University of Wisconsin, was dilating upon the splendors of his home town. A Yankee, thinking to put him in his place, asked, "Where *IS* Charleston?"

Turning slowly toward the enemy, the orator replied with dignity, "Charleston, sir, is that untarnished jewel shining regally at the sacred spot where the Asley and the Cooper join their majestic waters to form the Atlantic Ocean."

★ ★ ★

Suggested bit of dialogue for Tennessee Williams' next romantic play about the magnolia-laden Southland:

"Sugar, ah think mahty highly of yo' new evenin' gown."

"Sho' nuff?"

"It sho does."

★ ★ ★

The All-Southern Turtle Derby was covered by radio recently. The announcer began on a high pitch of excitement, screaming, "They're off and crawling!"

★ ★ ★

The dean of a girls' school in New Orleans could not cure her students of a dangerous habit of crossing an important traffic artery right in front of the school, instead of going to the corner where a policeman was constantly on duty. Warnings, penalties, and statistics of former accidents did no good at all. But then the wise dean had a sign painted and set up in the middle of the block —and immediately every girl walked carefully to the corner before stepping off the sidewalk.

What did the sign say? "Cattle Crossing"!

★ ★ ★

Mims Jemison, of Tuscaloosa, Alabama, sends me this very heartening story:

"Some years ago, a civic-minded merchant in our town named

Dave Rosenau proposed a cup to the 'most useful Tuscaloosian.' Jim Brierton, another wealthy industrialist, promptly proposed Dr. Obediah Dawson for the honor, and his motion was passed unanimously. The most centrally located edifice in town was selected as the site of the ceremony, and Dr. Charles Boyd chosen to preside thereat. Cliff Penick, popular tennis-playing attorney, was named to make the presentation speech, and Mose Coe appointed to ring the church bells summoning folks to the meeting. Now hear this:

"Dave Rosenau happened to be a Jew.

J. L. Brierton happened to be a Catholic.

Dr. Dawson happened to be a Baptist preacher.

The building chosen happened to be the Methodist Church.

Dr. Boyd happened to be a Presbyterian minister.

C. H. Penick happened to be an Episcopalian vestryman.

And Mose Coe happened to be an elder of the First African Baptist Church."

Bravo, Tuscaloosa!

88. SOVIET RUSSIA

A delegate from Moscow was regaling a group of New York newspapermen at one of the town's best—and most expensive—eateries. "You have been deluding your readers about alleged shortages in Russia," he declared, between bites of his *filet mignon.* "We have plenty of everything—luxuries beyond description—and they all belong to the people." "If it's so wonderful there," chuckled one reporter, "what are you doing way off here in New York?" "It just so happens," replied the Moscovite, reaching for the champagne, "that I am absolutely crazy about your lousy capitalist system."

★ ★ ★

An American television executive, visiting Moscow, escaped the eagle eyes of his guide long enough to wander down one of the streets that hadn't been polished up for foreigners' inspection. One multidwelling apartment house looked as though it would collapse any minute. The American snorted, "This structure looks as though nobody ever tried to repair it." The janitor, who understood and spoke English, agreed readily. "You're right," he said with a hearty laugh. "It's just been built!"

★ ★ ★

A pair of Communists from a satellite delegation sneaked off to Miami Beach for a stolen weekend. "What a glorious place this is!" enthused one. "Such gorgeous hotels! Such sun! Such beautiful girls!" "Not so loud, you fool," warned the other. "The miserable capitalists will hear you and start enjoying it, too!"

★ ★ ★

A serious contender for Olympic honors in the next international tests is a swarthy Hungarian whose specialty is throwing the hammer. "It delights me," he told an American reporter, "that I can throw the hammer so far." Then he added in a whisper, "And you ought to see what I could do if they'd let me throw the sickle after it."

★ ★ ★

Stan Freeman is convinced that when *Oklahoma* finally is produced in Moscow, the opening song will go something like this:

> Oh, what a beautiful tractor!
> Oh, what a lovely machine!
> Maybe I shouldn't have backed her
> Into the tomb of Lenin!

★ ★ ★

A distinguished American author had no desire to become a citizen of the Soviet, but he did want the experience of living in Moscow for a spell. Somewhat to his surprise, he wangled a visa for himself and family, and happily set forth. At the border control, however, customs officials eyed his vanload of supplies with open suspicion, and, after searching everything very carefully, made him remove the label from every box and can he was bringing with him.

That may explain a certain difficulty his Ukrainian cook experienced with the canned goods one evening during her first week on the job. Warned not to bother the master with questions, she figured things out for herself—and proudly served for dessert at dinner two cans of championship tennis balls, smothered in sour cream.

★ ★ ★

"Have you heard about poor old Ivan Krumovisch?" whispered a commissar to a friend at a big "do" in the Kremlin. "He's had a fatal accident." "You must be mistaken," countered the friend. "There he is in the flesh laughing at one of Comrade Shepilov's heavy-handed jokes." "Ssh!" cautioned the first Communist. "Poor Krumovisch doesn't even know it himself yet."

★ ★ ★

Three cellmates in a Soviet hoosegow compared notes.
"I was jailed for coming late to work," mourned the first.
"Me, I came too early," recalled the second. "They said this proved I was a capitalist spy."
"And I'm here," nodded the third, "because I arrived exactly on time. They accused me of owning an American watch."

★ ★ ★

Communism, insists John Harold, means doing it the herd way. And Bob Campbell tells about the customer at a Moscow newsstand protesting angrily, "Whaddya mean, ya don't sell the *Daily Capitalist?*"

★ ★ ★

Harry Kurnitz, author of *Once More with Feeling,* has devised a plot for a Soviet comedy which he predicts will have all Moscow in stitches: "A Communist novelist writes a book that wins a big prize, and this time Khrushchev allows him to go to Stockholm to receive it. But then he refuses to come home, so the mortified Soviet officials bump off his wife. Then the novelist happily returns to Russia. Turns out that all he wanted was to get rid of his wife."

★ ★ ★

A couple of top-level Communists, in New York for an economic powwow, were inspecting the Bronx Park Zoo one morning, and came upon a two-humped camel, or dromedary, or whatever you call those darn things. One Commie nudged the other and said, "Look what these filthy capitalists have done to that poor horse!"

89. SPOONERISMS

"A spoonerism," according to the American College Dictionary, "is a slip of the tongue whereby initials or other sounds of words are accidentally transposed." The name is a left-handed tribute to the Reverend W. A. Spooner, a familiar figure in Oxford at the turn of the century, whose numberless bloopers included introducing Victoria as "our queer old dean" and asking a confused lady in his church, "May I sew you to your sheet?" Another time he was heard to ask, "Is this pie occupewed?"

★ ★ ★

A choice spoonerism for late fall telling concerns a star halfback who became so panicky on the eve of a big football game that he broke training and sneaked into a saloon for a couple of drinks to fortify his nerves. Unfortunately, the head coach of the team sought out the same oasis.

The star halfback made a dive for the washroom, praying that the coach hadn't spotted him. He was too late, however. The coach ordered his drink, then added to the waiter, "By the way, see what the back in the boys' room will have."

★ ★ ★

The spotlight now shifts to Torpedo Toplitz, a typical, unimaginative smalltime gangster who had only one consuming passion in life. He loved bread. It was a craving he developed while subsisting on a bread and water diet in some of America's leading hoosegows.

Torpedo often would sit slicing a loaf of bread and consuming same while his mob was planning the details for a bank robbery. Eventually, he acquired a knife big enough to slice two loaves at the same time, and, later still, a veritable snickersnee that sliced *three* loaves simultaneously. Still he was not happy. Still his lust for bread exceeded his supply.

One day, however, Torpedo Toplitz showed up looking positively ecstatic. Exhibiting a fearsome knife three feet long, he swished it playfully and announced, "Boys, dis is my lucky day! I found a four-loaf cleaver!"

★ ★ ★

Frank Lockwood, of Baltimore, is dissatisfied with the quality of paperback books he's been reading of late. He broods, "I must have been making my selection from the trite side of the racks." In nearby Adelphi, meanwhile, Herb Appleton carefully poured a vat of pickle juice down a hillside to prove to himself that dill waters run steep.

★ ★ ★

They tell about a Texas housewife who decided to dye her curtains blue, and set up a big vat in the back yard for the work in hand. In the midst of the operation, a frisky white lamb fell into the vat, and when he was fished out he was a wondrous shade of blue.

A passing motorist fell in love with the little blue lamb at once, and paid the startled housewife about four times what it was worth to cart it off. "Maybe I've got something here," figured the housewife, and promptly threw three more lambkins into the vat. Sure enough, they were sold to motorists in jig time.

So today, ladies and gentlemen, that sweet little housewife is the biggest lamb dyer in Texas.

★ ★ ★

Ruth S. Perot, of Morristown, New Jersey, comes to bat with a story about a couple vacationing at a ski lodge who spent their first evening playing bridge. The wife, no expert, specialized in trumping her partner's aces. The next day she proved she was no better as a skier.

Her husband went down the slope first, leaving a clear trail. The wife followed, but fell at the halfway mark, leaving a track of sit-marks. Chortled the bridge opponent of the previous evening, "There she goes again, rumping her partner's trace!"

★ ★ ★

A couple of big-game hunters, better known for their ingenuity than their stout hearts, devised a new method for bagging a lion. Having observed which waterhole their quarry favored every morning, they poured two cases of Blue Mountain moonshine whiskey therein just before he arrived, then retreated to their jungle perch to await results.

As expected, the king of beasts sampled the doctored water, roared his approval, and promptly drank so much that he passed out cold. The hunters dispatched him at their own convenience, and then invited everybody on safari in those parts to partake of the feast.

"Drop in for dinner Thursday evening," read their invitations, "and dine on the sotted lion."

90. SPORTS

"Let's stop talking about boys," yawned a cuddlesome coed. "Let's talk about bigger things in life." "Such as?" prompted her roommate. "Such as," continued the coed, "football players."

★ ★ ★

Ed McKeever, who once coached the Notre Dame football team, recalled to journalist Max Kase a day when he tried to rouse the Irish for an impending battle with a loaded squad from West Point. His poor father was sick in bed, with an ear glued to the radio, McKeever told the team with a catch in his voice, and a victory over Army would be just the medicine he needed. Unfortunately, Notre Dame was shellacked, 52 to 0. The boys filed disconsolately back to the clubhouse, where the Irish center, Syzmanski, remarked ruefully, "We certainly finished off McKeever's old man, didn't we?"

★ ★ ★

Sidney James, managing editor of *Sports Illustrated*, thinks football coaches of big university teams are about as insecure as it's possible to be, and cites this story to emphasize his point.

After one of Red Sanders' UCLA elevens had enjoyed a spectacularly successful season, a horde of students and happy alumni gathered outside of Sanders' house and hollered until he came out on the porch to greet them. As he opened the door, however, Sanders whispered apprehensively to his wife, "I wonder which one's got the rope!"

★ ★ ★

In a big California college the football coach committed an unpardonable sin. His team lost two important games in succession. The president of the Alumni Association, a compassionate and understanding gentleman, patted him affectionately, and said, "Coach, the Super-Chief pulls out of town in twenty minutes. Be under it."

★ ★ ★

Ernie Kovacs says that a bit of advice ladled out by his old high school football coach has helped guide his destiny. "My boy," advised the coach, "when in doubt, PUNT." "I have no idea what he meant," adds Kovacs, "but, somehow, it's an inspiration."

★ ★ ★

A skinny lad, weighing 150 pounds or less, turned out for the first football practice at one of the Big Ten colleges this fall, but soon thought better of his impulse. "I didn't mind a thing," he reported, "till one bruiser grabbed my left leg, another my right leg, and the first one said to the other, 'Make a wish!'"

★ ★ ★

An awkward moment in international relations popped up one crisp November morning when an English ambassador was escorted through some secret Navy installations in Annapolis. He was suddenly halted by a midshipman on sentry duty.

"Restricted area, sir. You'll have to turn back," said the sentry. "But I'm the British Ambassador," spluttered the visitor. "They've let me see everything up to now. Just what's going on here?"

"Sir," snapped the middy, "it's secret practice for the Army football game."

★ ★ ★

Last year, the great pianist, Artur Rubinstein, was booked for a recital at the University of Kentucky. He arrived in Lexington early in the afternoon, and naturally requested the opportunity to test the piano provided for him. Since the concert was scheduled for the auditorium in which Kentucky's perennial championship basketball team cavorts, this meant that Coach Adolph Rupp's practice session had to be interrupted.

Few people on the Kentucky campus have the temerity to cross Coach Rupp, who now proceeded to deliver an unintended commentary on our entire system of college education. "Interrupt my practice for a piano player!" raged Rupp. "Why, he can play ten notes wrong tonight and nobody will know the difference. But if my team misses a single basket, the whole country will be asking why!"

★ ★ ★

A six-foot-ten beanpole in the Middle West made the all-collegiate basketball honor roll but floundered desperately in the classroom. "My boy won his fourth letter this winter," boasted his coach. "Hmmph," snorted his faculty adviser, "I'll bet you had to read it for him."

★ ★ ★

One of Bradley University's justly famed basketball teams was about to play Yale, and the Bradley coach was particularly anxious to take the Ivy five into camp. All he said to his squad before game time was, "Men, you are about to engage in combat with the sons of your future employers. BUT—they are not your employers YET. So go out there and beat hell out of them!"

They did, too!

★ ★ ★

Clifton Fadiman, the eminent critic, believes in the encouragement of authentic (not publicity-mad) eccentrics who eschew organized sports and take exercise in their own way. He cites as prime cases in point: (1) the French dandy who paraded up and down the Champs Elysées trailing a live lobster at the end of a string, because, he explained, it knew the secrets of the sea; (2) the English "sternutophile" (she spent her days sneezing—on purpose) whose will provided that her coffin be covered with snuff, that her pallbearers carry a box of snuff apiece, and that the minister inhale snuff while delivering the eulogy, and (3) a Mr. Joe Gould, of Greenwich Village, who, upon inheriting a thousand dollars, bought a big radio, took it out on Sixth Avenue, and kicked it to pieces. Mr. Fadiman also recalls an offbeat mathematics professor who always spent his vacations in Brussels so that he could readily organize a mountain-climbing expedition to the highest point in Belgium. Asked how high that point was, the professor replied, "Twelve feet above sea level."

★ ★ ★

At a Canadian winter haven, a fat lady took fourteen indoor ski lessons before she could muster sufficient courage to negotiate a very gentle slope without. She made a good enough getaway, but then lost her balance, and descended the last three-quarters of the slope on her very ample posterior.

"Wonderful," applauded the teacher (anticipating more lucrative lessons). "All you have to do now is eliminate the middle track!"

91. TALL TALES

America's spinners of tall, wildly improbable tales have had to outdo themselves in recent months, goaded by unexpected and formidable competition from official historians of the Soviet.

Unofficial champion is George Pipkin, whose burro suddenly stopped eating flapjacks and stood around moaning. George suspected the burro had a toothache. Sure enough, he had a hole in a front molar big enough to hold a pick and shovel. Then the burro vanished into thin air.

It was a full week before he came back, full of ginger as a burro can get. The toothache obviously was gone. He walked up to George, opened his mouth and let out a terrific bray. And you know what? There was a filling of pure uranium in that hollow tooth. Furthermore, the burro led George to the spot where he had located that uranium, and now George and the burro are each worth fourteen million dollars.

★ ★ ★

Up in the Sierra Nevada mountains, a character known as "Uncle Ben" told a comparable whopper. According to Uncle Ben, he was moseying along the crest of a razorback ridge when he came face to face with the biggest five-point buck he ever had seen. There was no time to reach for his rifle. He just made a flying leap, and locked his arms around the deer's head and his legs under its flanks. Then, by digging his heels into the buck's sides, he steered it straight into camp, bounding from crag to crag at about eighty miles an hour. Zooming by the campfire, he lifted his left leg one inch, and a companion plugged the buck through the heart. The momentum shot Uncle Ben into a pine-needle tree with such force that when they pulled him out, a nearsighted hunter mistook him for a porcupine.

★　★　★

In his book *Texas Tradition*, Ross Phares indicates that gallant swains in pioneer days told the tallest tales of all when boasting of the prowess of their lady loves.

One cowboy vowed that his gal, just to keep fit, walked barefoot five miles every morning on a barbed-wire fence with a wildcat under each arm. Another could tell a bear from a panther in the dark by the "feel of its bite." A third could "sink a steamboat with her bare hands, and scratch furrows a foot deep in the skin of an alligator with her toenails."

Davy Crockett's beloved, of course, had to be the most fabulous of them all. In his diary, Davy solemnly noted that she thought nothing of "milking a wild buffalo, then stealing eggs from an eagle's nest to make her nog."

★　★　★

There was a big discussion around the potbellied stove in Paw Perkins' crossroads grocery a while back. Zeb Smathers declared he didn't expect to plant a single potato this year, seeing as how potato bugs ate up his entire crop last time out in nine days flat.

Wally Harmon sniffed, "You was lucky, Zeb. They et up mine in less than four days!"

Paw Perkins warned the boys that the worst was yet to come. "Couple of potato bugs crawled onto my counter last night," he averred, "and looked over the books to see who had ordered seed for the next planting."

★　★　★

If you have any illusions about the heat in the Midwest in mid-August, harken to the story of three farmers who died on the same day. All left instructions they were to be cremated. The one who had been born in Michigan was cremated first, then the one from Ohio, and their ashes carefully put in copper urns. Now it was the turn of the native from Kansas. At the end of two hours, they opened the furnace, and out he walked, mopping his forehead ever so lightly with a bandanna, and remarking, "Two more days of this hot spell will ruin the corn for sure."

★ ★ ★

There's a softhearted chap in northern Westchester named Homer who can't stand seeing pheasants shot down by hunters. So this year he taught the pheasants how to chew tobacco. As a result not one pheasant has been shot in his county in the past six months. The birds simply hide in thickets, and when a hunter happens by let fly with a mouthful of tobacco juice plumb in his eye.

It was the night Mr. Homer told this story, incidentally, that Mrs. Homer smote her bloomin' liar.

★ ★ ★

There's a tall, tall tale told out Louisville way about a red-headed farmer named Stewart who married a gal whose hair was even redder than his. In time they were blessed with eight red-headed children.

Asked by the county sheriff how he was getting along, Stewart admitted, "I got no cause for complaint. But effen it warn't for the woodpeckers, feedin' the young 'uns might be a problem." "Woodpeckers?" repeated the sheriff. "Yup, woodpeckers," nodded Stewart. "Ye see, them danged woodpeckers think everything that's got a red head is another woodpecker. So we just set the young 'uns out on the rail fence and go in and take a nap. When we get back, them danged woodpeckers have fed 'em all day!"

★ ★ ★

B. A. Botkin, in *A Treasury of American Anecdotes*, tells about a farmer in western Kansas who put a tin roof on his barn. Came

a tornado that blew it right off again, and, when the farmer recovered it, it was twisted and mangled beyond repair.

A friend tipped him off to the fact that a big motorcar manufacturer in Detroit was in the market for scrap tin, so the farmer
crated up what was left of his roof in a big wooden box, with a note
reading, "Please remit."

Just when he despaired of ever hearing from the motorcar company, he received this note: "We can't imagine what hit your car,
mister, but we'll have it fixed for you by the fifteenth of next
month."

★ ★ ★

A comely lass of sixteen was doing her homework for junior
high when a noise at the window caused her to look up from her
book. What she saw froze the marrow in her bones. A huge hideous
werewolf had climbed into the room.

Screaming with terror, the lass backed up toward the door. But
the werewolf, breathing hard, drew ever closer. Suddenly she remembered a legend she had heard as a child: that the sign of the
cross would confound a werewolf and make him dissolve into dust.

Snatching up two pencils she made the necessary sign and
waved it in the monster's face. He stopped in his tracks—then broke
into a raucous laugh.

"Oy," he said, "have you got the wrong werewolf!"

92. TV AND RADIO

With big business zooming to ever dizzier heights, and half the corporations listed on the Stock Exchange getting away with merger, the lives our major magnates are leading are not nearly so joyous and serene as one might imagine.

A steady, twenty-five-hour-a-day pace, for instance, finally caught up with Bill Paley, guiding genius of the Columbia Broadcasting Corporation. He found himself unable to sleep at night, then dozing fitfully in his office in the midst of most important conferences.

His doctor urged moderation, prescribed two kinds of pills to effect a temporary cure. Far from helping Paley, they seemed to work in reverse. The distracted doctor finally located the cause. For a full two weeks, Paley's butler had been faithfully giving him sleeping pills at breakfast, vitamin pills just before he went to bed!

★ ★ ★

The difference between old-time vaudeville and present-day television is graphically highlighted by the veteran comedian, Bert Wheeler. "Years ago," recalls Wheeler, "I could buy a complete vaudeville routine for five hundred bucks and use it without changing a line for five years with no other comic ever thinking of stealing it. Today you pay a thousand for a sketch that lasts one single television program—that is, if some other comic doesn't hear it at rehearsal and beat you to the airwaves with it!"

★ ★ ★

Helpful hint from Jack O'Brian: When a TV emcee introduces anyone as "wonderful," he means just fair. "Great" means pretty good. "Very wonderful" suggests featured billing, and "very very wonderful" means the emcee's equal. "Very very fabulous" indicates that the guest is appearing without pay.

★ ★ ★

Remember when Minerva Pious was playing the role of Pansy Nussbaum on Fred Allen's old—and matchless—radio program? Her husband, Pierre, she used to mourn, was a luckless "schmo" who squandered his entire income at "Epstein Downs" and "Hia-Levy." "Pierre has such bad luck," wailed Mrs. Nussbaum once, "that if it was raining borsch outside, he'd be standing with a fork. He would also miss the potato!"

★ ★ ★

George Axelrod, author of *The Seven-Year Itch* and *Goodbye, Charlie*, worked for radio before he hit pay dirt in the theater. His job was to supply jokes for the leader of a hillbilly band—and the cornier the jokes were, the better the leader liked them. Sophisticated, brand-new gags were promptly consigned to the trash basket, but the leader went into ecstasies over "The dentist told a patient, 'Your teeth are fine but your gums will have to come out,'" and "My girl has such big braces on her teeth that when she smiles she looks like the front of a new sedan. In fact, the other evening, I kissed the car good night and backed *her* into the garage."

Axelrod's peak was reached—in the hillbilly's estimation, at any rate—with "Girdles come in five sizes: small, medium, large, extra large, and whoops! HERE COMES THE SHOWBOAT!"

★ ★ ★

A new comic on a weekly TV variety show failed to wow the sponsor. "That boy," was the verdict, "must be the one who takes the fire out of the chestnuts."

★ ★ ★

A TV rating service phoned a thousand men in Toledo one Sunday evening and asked, "Who are you listening to at this moment?" 934 answered, "My wife."

A pert miss in a TV studio eloped with a hillbilly singer. When she reported back for work, a friend asked, "How did your bridegroom register at the hotel?" "Fine," enthused the bride, "just fine!"

"You've got to be married and a father to really appreciate the wonders of television," declares Carl Hymer. "You can relax in your easy chair and see all your wife and children's favorite shows."

Ernie Kovacs had a very nearsighted singer on his TV program, and took her across the street for a bite when the program was over. In the entrance they brushed against a stalwart gent who greeted her affectionately. Without her glasses she didn't have the faintest idea who he was, so decided to play it safe. She gave him a big fat kiss and pouted, "Why don't you ever call me any more?" When he had left, she asked Ernie, "Who on earth was that?" He answered happily, "That was your first husband—whom you have cut dead for the past ten years."

Kovacs himself had trouble identifying a man who evidently knew him well, and, to cover his embarrassment asked, "Haven't I seen you in Sardi's restaurant recently?" "That's very likely," was the answer. "I've been the headwaiter there since 1945."

Composer Dick Rodgers once considered starring Milton Berle in a TV original, and asked the comedian what the tab would come to. "Dick, I'm so flattered that you want me," Berle assured him earnestly, "that money will be the very last thing I think of—before I get to sleep tonight."

★ ★ ★

Groucho Marx had trouble determining the age of a well-seasoned contestant on a recent TV program. "Are you seventy?"

he hazarded. "Sixty? Fifty?" The old girl simpered at this point, and admitted, "You're getting very warm." "Not if you're fifty, I'm not," vowed Groucho.

★ ★ ★

Jack Benny's daughter Joan proudly exhibited a well-varnished fiddle at a Hollywood musicale recently. Asked how she had come by it, Joan explained blithely, "Father's grandfather passed it down to Father's father, Father's father passed it down to Father, and Father sold it to me."

★ ★ ★

Jack Benny's gravel-voiced associate, Rochester, was recalling his early days in vaudeville. For one date at a carnival he rendered "Swanee River," "Old Man River," "Rising Waters," and "River, Stay 'Way from My Door." When he concluded he clapped the stage manager on the back and said, "Fractured 'em, didn't I?" "Fractured them?" echoed the manager. "You damn near drowned them!"

★ ★ ★

There's one referee who's going to have a hard time getting any more jobs in television. In the last bout he refereed for a TV audience, he was overheard by reporter Mike Connolly admonishing the victor, "You joik: you knocked him out during the commoicial!"

★ ★ ★

Are you a little tired of all those "brief messages from the sponsor" that show how quickly pills can race through your insides? *Printer's Ink* reports a man who tore into the editor's office crying, "I just took one pill each from four different bottles. Watch me closely, boy! *The race is on!*"

★ ★ ★

TV critic Philip Minoff had a soul-satisfying dream the other night. It was a commercial featuring an unctuous, toothy announcer in the foreground, and a burly baseball pitcher winding up in the background. "You see," burbled the announcer as he caressed a supposed unbreakable pane of glass behind him, "if it weren't for this invisible shield . . ." Whereupon the pitcher let loose his fast one, shattered the invisible shield into fragments, and POW! caught the announcer squarely in the jaw . . .

★ ★ ★

Alfred Hitchcock conjured up the most ingenious "lead-in" for a TV commercial I've heard in years. "When I was a lad," recalled Mr. H., "I had an uncle who often stood me to dinner. He always accompanied these dinners with interminable stories about himself. But I listened carefully because he was paying the check. I don't know what reminded me of my dear old uncle, but we are about to have one of our commercials."

★ ★ ★

In TV circles, the names of Mark Goodson and Bill Todman denote top-ranking panel shows. They've got a half-dozen piling up grosses at the same time. "But don't think we haven't got plenty to put up with," Todman told one interviewer. "One day, for instance, we left a washing machine in the studio after 'Winner Take All.' The next morning Arthur Godfrey was in the middle of his show when he spotted it. So he asked a woman sitting in the front row to give her full name. She did and Godfrey said, 'That's absolutely correct. You win that washing machine.' Confound it, Mark and I had to go ahead and pay for it."

★ ★ ★

Our own Goodson-Todman charade, "What's My Line?" has earned its biggest laughs via maladroit questioning of contestants whose occupations we were trying to pin down. Dorothy Kilgallen's "Is yours an inside job?" broke up a circus sword swallower. "Are you famous for your beautiful clothes?" stumped Gypsy Rose Lee. "Can you put anything in it?" was a laugh-provoking query when addressed to a girdlemaker. How could a skunk grower keep a straight face when Ernie Kovacs asked, "Would I give your product to my girl for Christmas?" I couldn't understand why my own question, "Does your work cover a large territory?" convulsed the studio audience till I discovered I had asked it of a diaper service executive.

* * *

Our Arlene Francis did her personal TV show from the poolside of the Beverly Hilton Hotel in California one morning. It was cold and foggy and the pool itself was empty. On the stroke of 6 A.M. the hard-boiled director signaled a young lady who had a heavy blanket wrapped around her and ordered, "Get up on the diving board now and let's see you dive."

She obediently did a dive—but it was a belly-whopper. "That's terrible," groaned the director. "Dive again—and this one better be right!" Again the girl dove. Back on terra firma, Arlene whispered, "I'm sorry you had to dive in this cold weather. Your teeth are chattering. I hope they're paying you well for this."

The young girl said, "Oh, I'm not in the s-s-show, Miss Francis. I'm a guest at the hotel. I j-j-just came d-d-down to watch you do TV!"

* * *

Here are a couple of prize TV "bloopers" spotted by the ever-vigilant Kermit Shafer: From "The Big Pay-Off": "Three of the reindeer who pull Santa's sled are named Prantzer, Dancer, and Blintzes"; from a news report from Maine: "The Bangor police have found a young lady roaming around nude in the woods. She will be held several days for examination"; from a Los Angeles commercial: "Tomorrow's film will star Marilyn Monroe and Jane Russell. Yes, folks, the big ones come from Twentieth Century-Fox!"

★ ★ ★

Several technical terms pop up nowadays in news stories about television, and where would you be if Sam Levenson wasn't on deck to explain them to you? Take the following, for example:

DISSOLVE: The sudden disappearance of a producer right after a poor show.

CREDITS: List of writers who were fired last week.

REMOTE: Possibility of renewal.

PANNING: Review by John Crosby.

ECHO: Production assistant.

MUSIC BRIDGE: Musicians are playing cards in cellar.

★ ★ ★

Bob Hope's reaction was something to behold when the delectable young star, Martha Hyer, told him she would have to talk to him like a Dutch uncle. "Go right ahead," invited Hope, "but I'm afraid you'll never pass your physical."

Hope, incidentally, now identifies himself as that "promising young star of screen, radio, and TV"—adding "some fellows even get me on their electric razors."

★ ★ ★

George Gobel has posted this sign outside his local post office: "Be on the lookout for a tall, handsome man about thirty-two years old, six feet tall. He has dark wavy hair, is intelligent, well dressed, has a wallet stuffed with thousand-dollar bills, and is driving the latest model de luxe convertible. This man is wanted by my sister-in-law, who is single."

★ ★ ★

Jack Paar tells how Zeke Hooper was finally nagged into buying a secondhand TV set by his wife and six children.

The installation man explained, "It won't work till we put this antenna up on the roof."

"Dawgone it," grumbled Zeke. "I told you one of these new-fangled contraptions leads to another. Now we got to put a roof on the house!"

★ ★ ★

Sign spotted at an Atlantic Beach appliance shop: "TV sets sold and rented. Not responsible for summer programs."

★ ★ ★

With all this bestowing of Oscars, Tonys, Emmys, and Peabody Awards that's going on nowadays, Hal Kanter feels the following pioneers can no longer be decently neglected:

1. Pliny the Younger, proprietor of a mammoth drive-in on Long Island. He increased his attendance 360 per cent in one week by simply not showing any movies.

2. An usher at a new smash Broadway musical. She seated 250 patrons in 136 seats with the aid only of one burned-out flashlight and a few crude remarks.

3. A special award for the outstanding technological advance of the year to Miss B. Overpass, candy counter salesgirl at the Acropolis Theater. She can now make 230 gallons of orange juice from a single orange.

★ ★ ★

Supreme Court Justice Bill Douglas says that whenever his colleagues get too cocky, he has only to remind them of the lady contestant on a TV quiz program who admitted she could name only two of the nine current Justices. "Who are they?" asked the M.C. The lady answered, "Charles Evans Hughes and Thomas Jefferson."

★ ★ ★

TV star Mike Wallace cherishes a reply he got from one contestant he encountered on a quiz program. "What would you do," he asked her, "if you found a million dollars in cash lying on the sidewalk?" She pondered momentarily, then answered, "If it was a poor family, I'd return it!"

* * *

A swarthy young contestant on a late lamented giveaway show had progressed all the way to the top rung, and with each correct answer his father in Row A had applauded vociferously and shouted, "Datsa my boy!"

The $64,000 Question was, "Who shot Abraham Lincoln?" After an agonizing silence, the young man confessed, "I don't remember." The audience groaned—all but the father, that is, who hollered "Datsa my boy" louder than ever.

"How can you be so happy?" demanded the man seated next to him. "Don't you realize your son has just lost $64,000?"

"Datsa my boy!" repeated the father ecstatically. "He never squeal on nobody!"

93. TEXAS

First thing any visitor to Texas wants to see—especially a kid who has been goggle-eyed over the exploits of Davy Crockett—is the Alamo, "the Shrine of Texas Liberty." He's prepared to travel miles to see the old fort, and invariably is astonished to find it smack-dab in the middle of San Antonio. No chance of forgetting the Alamo when it stands there, bathed in sunlight, right outside your hotel window!

If you've grown hazy about the details, the Alamo was built about 1756 as the Mission San Antonio de Valero, but was transformed into a fort about 1793. Here, in 1836, Colonel William Travis and 187 Texan stalwarts made an inspired but futile stand against Mexico's Santa Anna and an army of fifteen hundred. The Texans were massacred to a man, but General Sam Houston (who had opposed the stand as futile in the first place) used the cry "Remember the Alamo" as a rallying call to such good purpose that he turned the tables on Santa Anna less than two months later in the decisive Battle of San Jacinto.

For years the wrecked Alamo lay neglected. In one dreary span it was even used to store beer barrels. Now, however, it has been restored to a semblance of its former glory, and is one of America's greatest shrines. John Gunther avers, in fact, that Texas, without consent of Congress, might have split itself into five ordinary-sized states long ago—except that nobody could decide which of the new Texas states would get the Alamo!

★ ★ ★

When I met Maury Maverick, Jr., and Ed Ray, of the San Antonio *News*, in the lobby of the Menger Hotel, I was a bit reluctant to refer to current tall tales about Texas, but I was soon reminded of the fact that nobody enjoys these stories more than Texans themselves. There was one, for instance, about San Antonians being so big and strong they pitch horseshoes with the horse still in them. And another about the zillionaire whose check came back from the bank stamped "Insufficient Funds." He was relieved, however, to find the further notation, "Ours—not yours."

★ ★ ★

Ted Dealey, the Dallas Diogenes, tells of an oil magnate who drove his car to a distributor and said, "I've decided it would be ostentatious to buy a new car again this year. I just want you to do over the inside of this 1960 special model for me. Take out the tennis court and put in a swimming pool."

★ ★ ★

The late and beloved Sam Adams, doing research for a book about General Brock, spent some days at Niagara Falls, in the course of which he made the acquaintance of Mike Halbouty, the Texas oil geologist.

"Look at those falls," marveled Adams. "You'll have to admit you have nothing like that in Texas!"

"No, we haven't," granted Halbouty, "but we've got a plumber in Houston who could stop that leak in fifteen minutes!"

★ ★ ★

A customer walked into a Fifth Avenue shoestore, reports Lon Tinkle, wearing a wide-brimmed Stetson, flowing bow tie, vividly checkered shirt, choke-bore pants, and a pair of beautiful hand-tooled boots. "Got to get me some real shoes," he told a clerk. "The boots pinching you?" asked the clerk. "Heck, no," boomed the customer, "but Cindy Lou and ah aims to visit Europe and I don't want the bloodsuckin' cayutes to know ah'm from Texas."

★ ★ ★

A gal from Tyler and a lad from Amarillo never had liked each other at the state university, and their antagonism deepened when, separately, they both came to New York and made good in a very big way. At a la-de-da social gathering, they met face to face, and the man couldn't resist twitting his old acquaintance to show off for his new friends. "Remember, Sally," he laughed coldly, "when you had just one pair of shoes to your name?" "I sure do, sonny," she replied without a qualm. "You asked me what they were."

★   ★   ★

Two Texans, in a cream-colored convertible with the top down, wheeled up to a motel situated in the heart of the giant redwood forest in California.

One Texan bore down on the proprietor of the motel and demanded anxiously, "Say, pardner, when we gonna drive outa this here pesky underbrush?"

★   ★   ★

The country's most unusual oil tycoon has been uncovered by comic Joey Adams. He sports a ten-gallon hat and hand-painted ties, gives hundred-dollar bills for tips, brags incessantly—and lives in Rhode Island.

★   ★   ★

Robert Q. Lewis boasted that one of his new pals in Dallas was so rich he flew his own plane. "So what," scoffed a Los Angelite. "Lots of people here fly their own planes too." "Inside the house?" asked Robert Q.

★   ★   ★

Where else but in Texas could this happen? A little boy was avidly devouring an ice-cream cone when a lady swathed in mink walked by. The little boy neatly wiped his dripping cone against the back of the lady's ten-thousand-dollar coat. His ten-year-old sister was aghast. "Junior!" she shrilled, "you're getting fur all over your ice cream!"

★   ★   ★

In Texas, the famous story of George Washington and the cherry tree has been subjected to slight variations. There, a sturdy lad from Houston is asked by his pappy, "Who chopped down this here mesquite tree?" "I did," admits the lad. "You admit it?" roars the astounded father. "Son, you just climb into our second Boeing-707 and fly yourself up to Oklahoma. Texas isn't big enough for boys who can't tell a lie."

★ ★ ★

When Stanley Marcus, of Dallas, tells a tale about Texas, one must presume it's authentic. One of his recent reports concerns a rancher who dumped a huge sackful of silver dollars into a bank and said, "I want to deposit this cash. It adds up to sixty-five thousand dollars." "It will take us at least two hours to count this," said the surprised teller. "O.K.," said the rancher, "I'll be back after lunch."

When he returned with his wife, the teller said, "I'm sorry, sir, but we've counted those silver dollars five times, and each time we only get sixty thousand dollars."

"Dawgone, what did I tell you?" grumbled the rancher to his wife. "We brought the wrong sack!"

★ ★ ★

If you can swallow that one, you might also go for the tale of another Texas farmer who was pinched by a motorcycle cop for doing seventy-five miles an hour on the Dallas-Houston highway in his harvesting machine in the middle of a dust storm. "Don't stop me, officer," pleaded the farmer, indicating a solid cloud of dust just behind him. "I planted that alfalfa, and, by golly, I mean to harvest it if I have to follow it clean into the Gulf of Mexico!"

★ ★ ★

Believe it or not, the authoress of this poem, Annie Grey Young, is a TEXAN:

> One day I met a Texan who
> Was talking of his state.

While sitting in the park he said,
"This place is not so great.
A lot of states have cattle
And a lot of states have oil,
And other states grow better crops,
For they have better soil.
Our girls aren't always prettier,
Our men aren't always tall,
And often we say things are big
When they are really small."
I met this man in Austin
And I talked to him all day,
But then two men in white came up
And led the man away.

★ ★ ★

Holiday-minded Texans, asserts native son George Fuermann, in his fine book, *Reluctant Empire,* have countless all-year-round local festivals to choose from. There are Old Maids' Day at Denton, the National Cow-Calling Contest at Miami, the Spinach Festival at Crystal City, Buccaneer Days at Corpus Christi, the State Fair at Dallas, the Rattlesnake Derby at McCamey, the Gabirgsfest in the Hill Country, Mother-in-Law Day at Amarillo, the Shrimp-O-Ree at Aransas Pass, and Splash Day at Galveston.

You've lost me, however. *I* am headed for the East Texas Old Fiddler's Contest in Athens.

94. THE THEATER

Have you ever wondered what plays of modern vintage enjoyed the longest runs on Broadway? *Life with Father,* according to *Variety,* tops the list with a whopping record of 3,224 consecutive performances. Close behind comes *Tobacco Road* with 3,182. *Abie's Irish Rose* is a bad third with 2,327. (Incidentally, both *Tobacco Road* and *Abie* were murdered by the critics, and did practically no business for their first weeks. They were saved by producers who simply would not concede defeat.) Rodgers and Hammerstein nail down fourth and fifth spots with *Oklahoma* (2,248) and *South Pacific* (1,925).

Then come the following: *Harvey:* 1,775; *Born Yesterday:* 1,742; *The Voice of the Turtle:* 1,557; *Arsenic and Old Lace:* 1,444; *Hellzapoppin':* 1,404; *Angel Street:* 1,295; *Lightnin':* 1,291; *The King and I:* 1,246; *Guys and Dolls:* 1,200; *Mister Roberts:* 1,157; *Annie, Get Your Gun:* 1,147; *The Seven-Year Itch:* 1,141; *Pins and Needles:* 1,108; *Kiss Me, Kate:* 1,070; and *The Pajama Game:* 1,052. Where the current *My Fair Lady* will end, know only Herman Levin and Moss Hart and C.B.S!

★ ★ ★

They tell of one man, incidentally, who stood in line so long for tickets to *My Fair Lady* he ended up with three instead of two: two for the show and one for parking.

★ ★ ★

An English star flew to New York for his first visit to America and opened on Broadway that very evening. The critics threw their hats in the air both for him and his play.

The next day a reporter from the society section asked him to tell her his first reactions to America. "It's a wonderful and inspiring country," he enthused, then added, "Of course, all I've seen so far are my reviews."

★ ★ ★

George S. Kaufman admitted to a playwright that the opening night performance of the latter's new drama had bored him to death. "Nevertheless," persisted the playwright, "when the box office opened this morning there was a line down to the corner." "Good for you," enthused Kaufman. "Now all you have to do is stop the word of mouth."

★ ★ ★

The late Alexander Woollcott was not only one of the most merciless and spiteful of critics; he also was one of the fattest. Occasionally he would attempt a well-advertised but short-lived diet, and it was during such a period that one playwright remarked to another, "I hear Woollcott has dropped forty pounds." Playwright Number Two inquired, "On whom?"

★ ★ ★

Paul Nathan tells of the drama editor who set out to interview Alfred Lunt and Lynn Fontanne and posted this sign on his door: "Back at 2:20. Out to Lunts."

★ ★ ★

A play called *I Am a Camera* was a solid hit on Broadway, a few seasons ago, but one critic persisted in sneering at it. He summed up his feelings, in fact, in just two words: "No Leica."

★ ★ ★

Kyle Crichton's concise report on the tryout of a dramatization of *Tom Jones:* "Good Fielding. No hit."

★ ★ ★

An out-of-town lady went to see *West Side Story*—the hit musical about teen-age gangs in New York and pooh-poohed, "What's so original about this one? It's just Booth Tarkington's *Seventeen* with knives!"

★ ★ ★

A lady friend of author Vincent Starrett was attending a play in Chicago one evening when a man seated in the same aisle brushed by her at intermission time. Unfortunately he stamped hard on her foot in so doing, and the woman, in pain, thought angrily to herself, "I hope he breaks his neck."

Coming back to his seat later, the man encountered more trouble with the lady in the end seat, and kept his balance with difficulty. As he passed Starrett's lady friend, he grinned and whispered, "You almost got your wish, didn't you?"

The man was Dunninger, the mind reader.

★ ★ ★

Ed Sullivan decided once that he had a perfect spot for eight brothers who did a spectacular acrobatic act, but he had difficulty getting the head man on the phone. Finally he located the head man's wife. "I'll have to give Joe the message, Mr. Sullivan," she told him. "Joe can't talk to you right now. His seven brothers are standing on him."

★ ★ ★

Josh Logan, of *Mr. Roberts, Picnic,* and *Sayonara* fame, has a passion for buying houses, although he's not always sure what he's going to do with them after he gets them. He bought one old mansion up in Connecticut recently on the spur of the moment, explaining airily to his wife, Nedda, "I picked this one up for a song." "I know," she nodded gently, "a $75,000 song."

★ ★ ★

Nila is the story of a gay and irrepressible Russian emigrée, now Mrs. Robert Magidoff, as told to Willie Snow Ethridge. In the dining room of a Detroit hotel one day, Nila suddenly began acting out a scene of Ophelia's from *Hamlet* for her own amusement, enjoying herself so heartily that she burst into tears. An admiral dripping with gold braid observed her distress and rushed over to offer assistance. When he returned to his table he reported with disgust, "Hell, she isn't suffering. She's reciting Shakespeare!"

★ ★ ★

Fame is a wonderful thing, maintains composer-director Abe Burrows. "When I was a nobody in my home town," he recalls, "they used to yell, 'There goes that bum!' Now that my name is nationally known, they sure have changed their tune. Now they yell, 'There goes that bum Abe Burrows!'"

★ ★ ★

Two brothers made a nice living for years playing the front end and rear end, respectively, of a horse on the stage. Then one day the rear-end impersonator quit—just like that. "I was finally overcome with the unfairness of it all," he explained. "My brother was always whistling at the pretty chorus girls and pinching them—and then they'd kick the heck out of me!"

★ ★ ★

A famous theatrical agent was walking down Broadway when he passed a youngster playing a harmonica. Furthermore, there was a caterpillar on the sidewalk dancing up and down in tune to the music.

"It can't be," cried the agent. "Stop that playing, son." When the music ceased, the caterpillar curled up listlessly on the ground.

"Now start playing again."

The caterpillar was on tiptoe dancing again the moment the boy resumed his tune.

"My fortune's made," exulted the agent. He carefully picked up the caterpillar, linked arms with the boy, and rushed back to his office. "Fellows," he cried, "have I got a novelty act! It'll make 'em forget Sol Hurok!"

The caterpillar was a superb performer. He never missed a cue. Everybody was so delirious about the act that the original notion for a modest presentation gradually expanded into a stupendous spectacle with tons of scenery and acres of beautiful girls. The big star was the caterpillar.

Ten minutes before the curtain was scheduled to go up on opening night, however, the catastrophe occurred. The caterpillar turned into a butterfly.

95. VACATION

Mark Twain once was pinned down on the veranda of the old Mountain View Hotel by a relentless bore whose theme was the decline and fall of the entire modern world. After a particularly gloomy pronouncement, he poked a bony finger into Twain's midriff and croaked, "Has it occurred to you that every time I draw a breath, some helpless soul passes into the great beyond?" "It has," sighed Twain. "Why don't you try cloves?"

★ ★ ★

A couple of zoot-suiters, vacationing in Biloxi, went to see an athlete in a bathing suit climb into a tank to wrestle with an alligator. "My, my," exclaimed one admiringly, "what a crazy way to close a suitcase."

★ ★ ★

"I hear," reported Mrs. A. on the porch of the Tarleton Manor, "that that reckless Mr. M. gave his mother-in-law a Jaguar for her birthday."

"He must want something from his wife," decided Mrs. B., "or else he's suffering from a guilty conscience."

"You don't understand," amplified Mrs. A. "This was a real Jaguar!"

★ ★ ★

VACATION BRIEFS . . .

Maggie O'Flaherty offers this foolproof suggestion for insuring a successful vacation: "Take half the clothes you figured on—and twice the money."

"Summer vacations are no problem to me," boasted one Doubleday salesman. "My boss decides when I'll go and my wife decides where."

Sign at a small ferry slip in east Tennessee: "Passengers must pay in advance as the boat leaks."

A short short short story by Hal Kanter entitled "A Summer Romance": "Beach—peach—reach—ouch."

Warning note near Old Faithful Geyser in Yellowstone Park: "The only time it's really safe to pet a bear is when it is a rug."

A very angry publicity man for a New England winter resort sent out this announcement: "There is no connection whatever between this town's reputation as a popular ski center and the fact that we make 60 per cent of all wooden crutches."

"If you're unable to get away for a vacation," counsels Ray Blackman, "you can get the same feeling by tipping every third person you meet."

Howard Treeger is acquainted with a darling young lady who summers in Newport, winters in Palm Beach, and springs at every man she meets.

At a campsite in the Yosemite, reports Harry Oliver, there's an old outdoor convenience with this notice tacked on the wall: "Please keep the door tightly closed or the porcupines will eat the seat."

Sign at a heated pool at Virginia Beach: "Lady guests are requested not to bother the lifeguard unless drowning."

★ ★ ★

THE LAUGH'S ON ME

Mrs. Horntoot was shifting her headquarters from her Sutton Place apartment to her villa in Newport, but the van hired for the occasion failed to appear. At eleven she phoned the owner and listened to a long and involved explanation.

"All right, all right," she conceded finally. "I am touched by your story—but not moved."

★ ★ ★

At a certain amusement park last summer a college student who had wangled a vacation job on the scenic railway noticed that one sickly, shaking old gent made no effort to get out of his front seat when a ride was completed, but sat huddled down in the seat waiting to go round again. Furthermore, the ticket taker never bothered to ask him for his fare. The student approached him after five rounds and said, "Pardon me, but do you get a particular thrill out of this ride?" "Thrill?" sneered the old man. "I hate it! It makes me acutely sick to my stomach." "Then why do you, like the music, go round and round?" asked the student. "The skinflint who owns this concession," explained the old man, "owes me ten dollars, and I'm going to take it out on him in rides if it kills me!"

96. TERSE VERSE

This is the day of the four-hour motion picture feature and the 1,700-page novel, and, for the poor wretch who is not sufficiently upholstered in the proper place, the devil takes him in the hindmost.

At such a time the poet who can say everything he has to say in two short lines should be doubly blessed.

In fact, clever versifiers, going around with their shorts, may even put poetry back on a paying basis. The last poet before Ogden Nash who could afford to eat *filet mignon* at the Pump Room or Danny's Hideaway was one Dr. Outgo Schmierkase—and he owned a steel mill and seven oil wells on the side.

The shortest poem in the English language undoubtedly is Strickland Gillian's masterpiece entitled "Lines on the Antiquity of Fleas":

Adam
Had 'em.

Equally terse is Bill Benét's "Maid's Day Out":

Thurs.
Hers.

Every oculist in America quaked in his boots the day Dorothy Parker discovered that:

Men seldom make passes
At girls who wear glasses.

Their gloom became even more enveloping when Ogden Nash added:

> A girl who is bespectacled
> Don't even get her nectacled.

At the turn of the century, George Ade coined a popular phrase with this two-liner:

> Last night at twelve I felt immense,
> But now I feel like thirty cents.

Conceivably, Ogden Nash was referring to the same postprandial activity as Mr. Ade when, in a couplet called "Ice Breaking," he observed:

> Candy is dandy,
> But liquor is quicker.

Keith Preston admonishes:

> You must not laugh at your own wheeze:
> A snuffbox has no right to sneeze!

Globe-trotter Irene Keepin reports:

> I've been there. It's no blarney.
> Dublin features Chili con Kearney.

Richard Armour, who obviously patronizes the same restaurants we do, observes:

> Shake and shake the catsup bottle:
> None will come, and then a lot'll.

Mr. Armour also has concluded that:

> Show window mannikins
> Have slender fannikins.

Katherine Balik implores:

> Please diet
> In quiet.

Arthur Guiterman puts it another way:

> Don't tell your friends about your indigestion:
> "How are you!" is a greeting, not a question.

Rash is the motorist who ignores the terse verse Jesse Douglas has posted at the entrance to his place:

> This road isn't passable;
> Not even jackassable!

Samuel Hoffenstein must have been worsted by a fascinating female when he sighed:

> Breathes there a man with soul so tough
> Who says two sexes aren't enough?

A fellow sufferer of Hoffenstein's insists:

> Women do not talk all day:
> It only seems to sound that way.

Suggests Kathy Connell:

> Just think how long a tall giraffe
> Would take to have a belly laugh!

Walter Bemis grumbles:

> She crosses her knees.
> That's the kind of girl she's!

Ida Pardue concludes:

> Life, to the average wife and mother,
> Is one dish-appointment after another.

Mrs. Rose Huber spotted this sign on a Seattle truck:

> Spring has sprung and grass has rizz
> Where last year's reckless driver is.

And Mary Brewster has an optimistic friend who wants her tombstone to read:

> Miss Lovis
> Above is.

Miss Lovis, like the worker in the quarry, seems to be taking a lot for granite!

97. VIP'S

Who are the richest men in America today? In a widely discussed roundup, *Fortune* magazine revealed that the very richest was a J.P. all right, but not, as the general public might have suspected, J. P. Morgan. No, it was a California oil tycoon who simply loathes publicity, and has so many hundred millions he can't even count them. His name is J. P. Getty. ("O.K., I'm worth over a billion," Mr. Getty conceded to an interviewer, "but you must remember that a billion today isn't what it used to be.")

Trailing close behind J. P. Getty, in the order named, come H. L. Hunt of Texas, John D. Rockefeller, Jr., Arthur Vining Davis, and a quartet of Mellons. A couple of million dollars more or less behind the front-runners are Sid Richardson, Howard Hughes, Joe Kennedy, Daniel Ludwig, Alfred Sloan, Jr., Mrs. Frederick Guest, and a slew of Du Ponts. Women, it has been said, are gradually acquiring the wealth of the nation, but in this top echelon, to date at least, there's only one. Better look again a decade hence!

★ ★ ★

One of the affluent parties referred to above is alleged to have thrown his morning mail angrily at his butler, grumbling, "All I ever get these days is stock dividends and checks."

★ ★ ★

Mark Twain once was allowed to buy stock in a publishing house, and boasted to a friend, "This will net me a fortune. They've let me in on the ground floor."

Ten months later the publishing house went bankrupt, and the friend taunted, "I thought you said they let you in on the ground floor." "So they did," maintained Twain, "but there was a son of a gun in the basement!"

Mark Twain explained another time that all true humorists find themselves in the same position: "We have to make people, who would otherwise hang us, believe that we are joking."

★ ★ ★

The late Albert Einstein was not the one to bother his head with the mazes of modern finance. No sooner did he arrive in America than he was persuaded by an unscrupulous broker to put all his savings—some twenty-two thousand dollars—into a list of veritable "cats and dogs." An indignant friend made him sell them at once, and undertook to reinvest the funds in gilt-edged securities.

For twenty years, Dr. Einstein never questioned him once about his holdings. Then the friend informed him that the securities had vaulted to a market value of over $200,000! "Listen," Dr. Einstein interrupted him crossly. "I don't bother you about relativity. Don't you bother me about stocks and bonds!"

★ ★ ★

Beverley Nichols tells about the day a small boy in England was taken to the country home of Sir Winston Churchill. "Keep out of his way," the boy's mother ordered him, "but if he should happen to stumble over you, try to remember he's the Greatest Man in the Whole World—and show the proper respect."

Sure enough, Sir Winston *did* stumble over the boy, who quavered, "Pardon me, sir, but is it true you're the Greatest Man in the Whole World?"

Sir Winston, in no good humor that day, glared at him and answered, "Certainly! Now buzz off!"

★ ★ ★

One of New York's most successful publicists was asked what he did for a living. "I spend my time," he answered, "building great big pedestals for tiny little men."

★ ★ ★

The leading banker of a New England community was guest of honor at an imposing banquet for his eightieth birthday, and five speakers said some mighty flattering things about him. Finally it was the banker's turn.

"Gentlemen," he wheezed cheerfully, *"I must admit I'd rather hear the taffy than the epitaphy."*

★ ★ ★

In an interview aboard his yacht in Miami, the vice-president of a big electronics corporation confided the secret of his sylph-like (238-pound) figure.

"Every morning when I wake up," boasted the magnate, "regardless of the time or how I feel, I touch my shoes twenty-five times. Then, gentlemen, I get up out of bed and put them on."

★ ★ ★

Speaking of vice-presidents, which a lot of Republicans seem to be doing these days, there's a wealth of information on the breed in a new book called *The Executive Life*. Nine hundred top executives, declare the editors, meekly submitted to questioning to make the statistics more than a "guesstimate."

NOW HEAR THIS:

1. More industrial big shots come from the Middle West than from any other section of the country. Fewest come from the Far West. No reasons given—but I can't help wondering about it.

2. Average salary of ranking executives (before taxes): Seventy thousand dollars. Corporation presidents rate approximately thirty thousand dollars more.

3. Best paid are in tobacco, drugs and cosmetics, liquor, music, broadcasting, and—how's that again?—publishing.

4. Of the top 900, 3 are under 40, 100 under 50, and 5 over 80.

5. All but 19 per cent had some college training; 65 per cent had four or more years.

Researchers were astonished at how many V.P.'s expressed a willingness to leave their companies, provided sufficient inducements were offered. Dying for dear old Rutgers, apparently, is one thing; dying for, let us say, a big advertising agency is something else again!

One famous agency has so many vice-presidents (eighty-four, to be exact) that not all of them have even met. A man on the executive floor there who *isn't* a vice-president is automatically treated with great deference. It's figured he must be a client.

Frank Stanton of Columbia Broadcasting says that nineteen C.B.S. V.P.'s in the radio and TV divisions (there are twenty-seven other C.B.S. V.P.'s scattered elsewhere) were appointed partly as a result of "contamination by the ad agencies." "Only a vice-president," he reasons, "can take another vice-president to lunch." There's more protocol observed today on Madison Avenue than there is in the State Department.

The Bank of America has 146 V.P.'s; Hershey Chocolate none. (Maybe there's a bar against them.) One president put a dismissal notice on his head V.P.'s desk while that gentleman was out snatching a three-hour bite, but was outmatched by a brilliant counterattack. The V.P. never let him know he had received the notice. The president was too embarrassed to send another. He dreads the next board meeting, in fact. "Maybe," he worries, "the rascal will have ME fired!"

★ ★ ★

Envy not the country's top business executives! They work, assert researchers, on an average of forty-eight hours a week, plus four nights on the side. Conventions and regional meetings are extra, too. Home is not a sanctuary for these benighted souls; it's a branch office.

"I look forward to the day when my kids are grown up," admits one. "Then I won't have such a guilty conscience about neglecting them."

98. WEATHER

A weather forecaster on Cape Hatteras offers what he calls the definitive reason why hurricanes invariably are named after women. "Figure it out yourself," he urges. "They're hurricanes, not himacanes."

Can you explain the difference between a hurricane, a typhoon, a tornado, and a cyclone? Well, there really isn't any. A severe storm and wind in the West Indies is called a hurricane; in the Far East it's a typhoon; in the Indian Ocean it's called a cyclone, and in the U.S.A. it's usually referred to as a tornado.

The happiest man in Montego Bay is Abercrombie S. Wilkins. A hurricane has just been named after his mother-in-law.

* * *

The worst storm in fifty years didn't bother a potent sultan in Kuwait. He just left a call for eight in the morning.

* * *

In the middle of a terrific storm, Mrs. Weiler tapped nervously on the arm of her husband at the wheel and suggested, "Mightn't it be a good idea to stop and wipe the windshield?" "Wouldn't do a bit of good," snapped Mr. Weiler. "I left my glasses at home."

* * *

A cyclone blew a lonely sheepherder from Wyoming clear into

a nudist camp in Colorado. He took one amazed—and admiring—look at the head lady and inquired, "Who's your tailor?"

★ ★ ★

Who says the boys at the New York weather bureau don't know their stuff? Asked, at the beginning of the summer, to choose their vacation period, they all pulled out the charts—and asked for the same three weeks!

★ ★ ★

One of the forecasters miscalculated. He returned from his furlough complaining that it had rained continuously every day. "You must be exaggerating," commented the bureau chief. "How do you explain your magnificent sunburn?" "Sunburn nothing," grumbled the forecaster, "that's *rust*."

★ ★ ★

A lady in Detroit heard over the radio that a tornado was on its way. Hurriedly, she herded her family into the cellar, and there they huddled for hours, fearfully awaiting the catastrophe.

All this time the radio was going full blast upstairs. It was some five hours later somebody discovered that the station they were tuned in to was in Wichita, Kansas.

★ ★ ★

The Miami *News* included one cheering bit in its coverage of a disastrous hurricane off the Florida Keys. Captain Edney Parker, Mrs. Parker, and their eleven children were clinging precariously to a raft that once had been the roof of their beachside home.

"Edney," gasped Mrs. Parker, "I can't hold on any longer." "Woman," roared Edney, "you can't leave me alone with all these children. You've *got* to hang on." Mrs. Parker did—and the whole family was saved.

99. WELSH RARE BITS

Motorists in Wales are invariably polite, and seldom drive above thirty miles an hour. A partial explanation is the hairpin turns on the mountain roads, another is that their cars simply won't go any faster.

One lady from Croesyceilwg (that's what I said) did ignore the cries of an angry policeman in the town square. "Didn't you hear me yelling for you to stop?" he demanded. "I never dreamed it was you," maintained the little lady innocetly. "I thought it was somebody I had run over."

(Signs around the Croesyceilwg square, incidentally, read, "Please park prettily.")

★ ★ ★

Driving to the Edinburgh Festival last summer, Red Cross director Bob de Lany picked up a couple of English soldiers thumbing frantically at a road sign, "PITY ME." They explained that this was the name of the town, and that it was, of course, the favorite hitchhiker's spot in all the land.

Another time, De Lany was invited by Welsh friends for a weekend in the country. "Our home is very easy to find," they assured him (and when has a suburbanite in any country said otherwise?), but these are the directions they gave him: "You leave Newport in a northeast by east direction and pass through Caerleon, turning left at Ponther, and right at Cumfryd. Thence, tootle through Abersyehan, Ystrad, Llanfyhange, Llantarnam, and Panthrydrun, and there you practically are. If you should miss your way, just ask for the 'Lowlands,' which, for some obscure reason, happens to be on *top* of the bloody mountain. From there you look right down on Bdylwd Voyskod, which, by a happy coincidence, is the roof of our home."

★ ★ ★

Not far from Bdylwd Voyskod nestles the picturesque hamlet of Llanfechpwllgogerych, which is too much for even the native Welsh railroad guards to pronounce. Whenever a through train stops there, the guard simply calls out, "If anybody's getting out here, this is it."

★ ★ ★

The Welsh are a proud and stalwart people, still not completely reconciled to the fact that the English conquered them in 1301. That's when England's King Edward I, in a conciliatory mood, named his son "Prince of Wales." Ever since the title has been borne by the heir apparent to the British throne. At the Coronation, he exchanges it for the title of King—and sometimes later for a suite in the Waldorf Towers.

★ ★ ★

When Helen Hayes was appearing in the role of Queen Victoria, she received a letter from a Welsh lady who claimed to have been a friend of the real Victoria. She was with the Queen, she stated, the day Victoria came upon her oldest son, aged nine, lambasting a playmate. "I just wanted to show him I'm the Prince of Wales," explained the future Edward VII. Victoria yanked him across her knees and gave him a royal tanning, pointing out grimly, "I guess I'd better show you I'm Queen of England!"

★ ★ ★

Red Cross director De Lany spent Christmas last year with a Welsh couple who appeared in a church play called *Halfway to Hell*. The audience loved it, but the local drama critic did not. His review read: "The Pontnewydd Church Players appeared last night in *Halfway to Hell*. They underestimated the distance."

100. WORDS

Americans, sadly remiss when it comes to mastering foreign languages, find this little or no handicap when they venture abroad. Everybody in the world, it seems, not only has learned to speak, or at least understand English, but is intent upon practicing what he has been "teached." Ask a native of any country a question in his own tongue, and it's dollars to doughnuts he'll answer you in English.

It's one thing, however, for a foreigner to learn the rudiments of English in school, and another to master our peculiar and puzzling idioms, spellings, and pronunciations.

One European student, understandably baffled, presented this poetic protest to his professor:

> The wind was rough
> And cold and blough;
> She kept her hands inside her mough.
> It chilled her through,
> Her nose turned blough,
> And still the squall the faster flough.
> And yet although
> There was no snough,
> The weather was a cruel fough.
> It made her cough
> (Please do not scough);
> She coughed until her hat blough ough.

★ ★ ★

A Chinese dignitary, recently arrived in New York, found several pieces of his baggage missing when he arrived at his hotel, and dispatched this angry note to the air line he had patronized: "Mr. Baggage Chief: Gentleman Dear Sir: I doggone seldom where suitcases are. You fly me but not her. You no more fit for baggage chief than for crysake out loud. That all I hope. What the matter of you?"

★ ★ ★

A Tokyo drama critic obviously enjoyed reviewing in English the show at the Nichigeki Music Hall. "A strip show," he pointed out, "is not always indecent and not interesting. Here it is a refreshing and enriched show. Both the stripers and the audience are very enthusiastic which creates a nice atmosphere. Outstanding is prize winner of a beauty contest in Shizuoka Pref., who was forced to make debute by a recommandation of certain producer. She is reportedly very kind especial for gentleman, as she is still single."

★ ★ ★

A funny thing happened in the town of Colchester, Connecticut, the other day. A prominent and law-abiding citizen named Churchill Satterlee got trapped in pages 764 and 765 of an unabridged dictionary.

Mr. Satterlee didn't panic. He penciled a message on a scrap of paper, folded it into a bottle, and set it adrift in the kitchen sink, where it bobbed and pirouetted straight into the Cerfboard office.

The message read: "A FUSCOUS, FUZZLED, GABERLUNZIE FUSTIGATED A FURUNCULAR FUSTILUGS WITH A FUSTY, FUSTIC FUTTOCK." Your editor, after only seven or eight trips to that unabridged dictionary himself, is prepared to tell you that Mr. Satterlee's message means just this: A SOMBER, BEFUDDLED PANHANDLER WHACKED A STOUTISH, BOIL-INFECTED GENTLEMAN WITH A ROTTING TIMBER

FROM THE KEEL OF A VESSEL." It probably hurt, too. See what happens when you increase your word power?

★ ★ ★

The late Samuel Hopkins Adams delighted in reviving salty old words and phrases neglected by current conversationalists.

"How long is it," demanded Adams, "since you've bandied such fine old words as 'gardaloo' (a Bronx cheer), 'chirk as a chitterdale' (cheerful as a katydid), 'hunca munca' (bosh), or 'bonaraba' (a maid no better than she should be)?" Adams particularly remembered the day his grandpa denounced an employee as a "Whimwhamsical hoodle-dasher"—then magnanimously gave him a raise of a dollar fifty a week!

★ ★ ★

The late Will Rogers once heard a talk about author-lexicographer Noah Webster. "Webster," observed the lecturer, "had amazing command of the language. Audiences were spellbound by his mastery of words. His English was just perfect." "Mine would be, too," interrupted Rogers, "if I wrote my own dictionary!"

★ ★ ★

Paul Pride's "Capsule Course in Human Relations":

5 Most Important Words: "I am proud of you."
4 Most Important Words: "What is your opinion?"
3 Most Important Words: "If you please."
2 Most Important Words: "Thank you."
Least Important Word: "I."

★ ★ ★

On what happier note can a book like this end than words of undying love from an innocent and beautiful young maiden? I quote a note received recently by a fortunate young friend of mine at Random House:

"Dear Tony: I have been unable to sleep ever since I broke our engagement. Won't you forget and forgive? Your absence leaves a void nobody else can ever fill. I love you, I love you, I love you. Your adoring Susan.

"P.S. Congratulations on winning the Irish Sweepstakes."

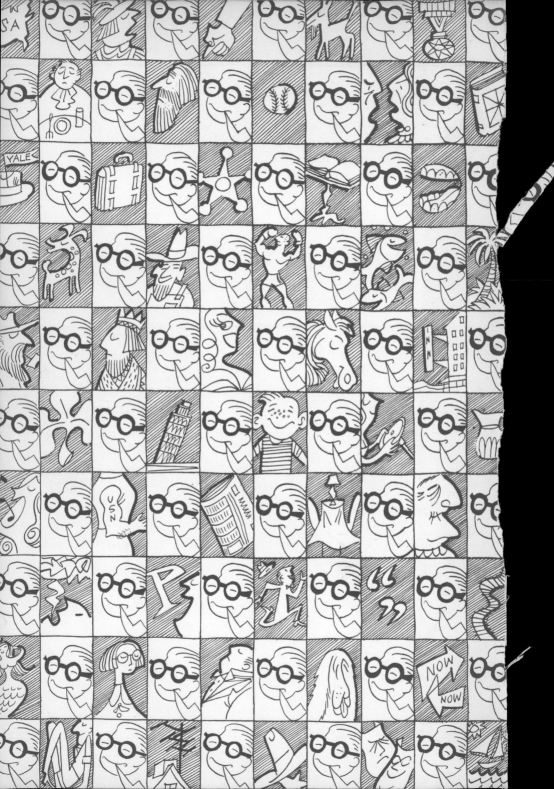